ALMANAC
OF
UNITED STATES SEAPOWER
1989

NAVY LEAGUE OF THE UNITED STATES
Introduction by Trevor Armbrister
Senior Editor, *Reader's Digest*

ARCO
NEW YORK

Cover photo courtesy of U.S. Navy

First ARCO edition published 1989

Copyright © 1989 by the Navy League of the United States

All rights reserved
including the right of reproduction
in whole or in part in any form

 **ARCO**

Simon & Schuster, Inc.
Gulf + Western Building
One Gulf + Western Plaza
New York, NY 10023

DISTRIBUTED BY PRENTICE HALL TRADE SALES

This Arco edition is published by arrangement
with the Navy League of the United States,
Arlington, Virginia

This book was originally published as part
of *The Almanac of Seapower,* 7th Edition, by
the Navy League of the United States

Manufactured in the United States of America

1 2 3 4 5 6 7 8 9 10

Library of Contress Cataloging-in-Publication Data

The Almanac of United States seapower, 1989-1990 / by the Navy League
    of the United States. — 1st Arco ed.
      p. cm.
    "Originally published as part of the Almanac of Seapower, 7th
  ed."—T.p. verso.
    Bibliography: p.
    Includes index.
    ISBN 0-13-023599-7
    1. United States. Navy. 2. United States. Marine Corps.
I. Navy League of the United States.
VA58.4.A44 1989
359'.00973—dc19   89-275
                                                                  CIP

CONTENTS

Introduction by Trevor Armbrister v
About the Navy League vi
Preface vii
Late Word on the FY1990 Defense Budget viii
Congress.. 2
Defense 5
Navy 17
Marines.. 88
Maritime.. 103
Coast Guard 116
Oceanography 127
Reserves 133
Defense and Maritime Leaders 135
Key Personnel Locator 173
Bibliography 178
Index 184

Who are the biggest defense contractors? What states glean the most money from the Pentagon? How much is our military spending on research and development? Finally, what do acronyms such as GWEN (Ground Wave Emergency Network) stand for?

The answers are just a few of the tidbits to be found in the *Almanac of Seapower 1989,* a volume that is indispensable to professional and layman alike. And there is even more: A listing of all submarines and surface ships on active or Reserve duty today, together with analyses of aircraft serving the fleet. There are sections on weapons systems we rely upon, together with detailed accounts of the capabilities of the U.S. Marine Corps and Coast Guard, as well as the faltering state of our Merchant Marine. All in all, this book is a treasure trove.

Trevor Armbrister
Senior Editor
Reader's Digest

ABOUT THE NAVY LEAGUE

"It seems to me that all good Americans interested in the growth of their country and sensitive to its honor, should give hearty support to the policies which the Navy League is founded to further. For the building and maintaining in proper shape of the American Navy, we must rely upon nothing but the broad and farsighted patriotism of our people as a whole."

In December 1902, with these words from President Theodore Roosevelt providing encouragement, the Navy League of the United States was founded. The handful of dedicated Americans who first set forth its mission saw its role as serving as a bridge between the Navy and the public, and as a means of educating their countrymen with regard to the importance of the United States Navy to the growth and security of a young nation. Their farsighted President was fully aware that much more than just the persuasion of the government would be necessary for that patriotism to be stimulated and sustained.

In the 87 years since the Navy League came into being, it has striven ceaselessly to meet the challenge President Roosevelt laid down. It has greatly broadened the scope of its mission in order to provide support for those other vital elements of national sea power—the Marine Corps, the Coast Guard, and the Merchant Marine. It has used its two principal publications, *SEA POWER* magazine and *The Almanac of Seapower,* with increasing effectiveness as its primary means of communicating information about all these elements to our citizenry, and of explicitly elucidating their needs.

From coast to coast it has used forums both general and precise in nature to focus attention on particular aspects of national sea power. It has called upon the diverse talents of its members—now more than 70,000, and all civilians—to assist those who serve us in uniform so magnificently in countless ways—from finding jobs for those leaving the service after having fulfilled their military commitment to providing legal advice and assistance to obtaining affordable housing to helping spouses find work when needed. It has recognized and publicized unique and significant accomplishments by thousands of Navy men and women, Marines, Coast Guardsmen, and civilians by means of a long-standing awards program and honored those individuals for their outstanding achievements.

It has founded, with an assist from a Congressional charter, the Naval Sea Cadet Corps, which provides for thousands of young Americans an education into the maritime history of their country and a disciplined environment in which to learn new skills and improve upon those already present. It also provides for many of these dedicated young people an avenue into the service of their country. This organization and the maritime services have formed a solid partnership from whose activities all participants and the nation have profited greatly.

It has internationalized its educational program by creating and supporting Navy League councils in many overseas locales—in the Pacific, the Atlantic, the Mediterranean, and in the Americas—and at the same time has made excellent use of these outlets to strengthen relations with the peoples of those nations in which they are located. And it has continued to add to the numbers of voices—as exemplified by 334 councils—within our own shores by chartering increasing numbers of new councils each year.

But most importantly, in its 87 years of service to the nation, it has never lost sight of its basic mission of education and of the need to provide support to those who serve us so magnificently in uniform. And it remains dedicated to the improvement of both, with the goal of contributing to keeping the seas free in a peaceful world.

PREFACE

In his book "SEA POWER: A Naval History", one of history's most respected naval leaders, Fleet Admiral Chester B. Nimitz, observed: "When man ceased to look upon streams, rivers, and seas as barriers and learned to use them as highways, he made a giant stride toward civilization. The waterways of the world provided a new mobility—to man himself, later to the products of his toil and skill, and at all times to his ideas."

Later, after tracing the beginnings of the use of sea power, from the Phoenicians of 2,500 B.C. onward, he defined sea power: "It is clearly more inclusive than naval power. It comprises not only combat craft and weapons but also auxiliary craft, commercial shipping, bases, and trained personnel. It is measured in terms of ability to use the sea in defiance of rivals and competitors. The phrase is also applied to a nation possessing a high degree of such ability: a sea power is a nation capable of exercising sea power. The capacity of a nation to use the sea is based upon the character and numbers of its population, the character of its government, the soundness of its economy, the quality and numbers of its harbors, the extent of its coastline, its colonies, and the location of homeland, bases, and colonies with respect to sea traffic."

Our nation became a true sea power during World War II. At war's end it was, unquestionably, the paramount sea power in the world in all respects. But in the years since then, the means of exercising sea power have changed markedly. Maintaining it has become far more difficult because of tremendous increases in the complexity of the instruments of sea power, and in turn the far higher costs of creating them. Maintaining supremacy on the seas also has become exceedingly more challenging, because of remarkable, and in some instances unexpected, surges in maritime strength and capability by nations who seek to make greater use of the seas as a means of extending their own influence.

It has been our view that far too little generally is known and understood about the elements that enter into creating, maintaining, and using sea power. Therefore, we have sought to provide in this special edition of the *The Almanac of Seapower*, principally by a combination of statistical data and brief descriptive commentary, a means of becoming more familiar with the most important elements of U.S. seapower:

- Those in our Congress principally responsible for carrying out the mandate of our Constitution "to provide for and maintain a Navy."
- Details of our complex defense budget.
- The Navy's base structure, and descriptions of the ships, aircraft, and weapons which enable it to carry out its mission in support of national security.
- The Marines and the Coast Guard, and their roles and tools of their trade.
- The nation's merchant marine, what it once was, what it has declined to, and how it compares with other nations' merchant marines.
- The oceans, and what we put into and take from them.
- The leaders, those in uniform and out, who are charged with ensuring that U.S. sea power can be and is used to maintain our national security.
- And summations of writings about sea power and those people, forces, and weapons which are a part of its past, present, and possible future use.

We have no illusions that this edition will answer all questions about sea power which readers may have. Indeed, we hope that what they read and digest herein will stimulate questions galore. For the presence of sea power in its broadest sense may well determine the future of our nation and its people, and it is our goal for this volume to serve as a stepping stone to a realization of this truth.

JACK H. MORSE, *National President*
Navy League of the United States

Late Word on the FY 1990 Defense Budget

As deliberations over the FY 1990 budget for national defense began in Washington late in winter, there were signs that increasingly rough seas lay ahead for the nation's maritime services. Not that the Navy, Marine Corps, and to a somewhat lesser extent the Coast Guard, were not ready and able to meet worldwide commitments imposed upon them, for they now are better able to do so than perhaps has been the case at any time since the end of World War II. Despite contentions to the contrary, the sizeable expenditures during the Reagan years to bring ALL the military services—but NOT the merchant marine—up from the depths in which they found themselves at the end of the decade of the 1970s have paid remarkable dividends.

But as the maritime services seek to cope with budget limitations of zero growth imposed by President Bush, there are warning signals across a broad spectrum of problems that very likely will become more difficult to cope with in the years ahead. Here are some of them:

- This year the Navy will be short 1,500 midgrade pilots, a shortage that has increased 400 since last year. Further, commercial airlines anticipate three times as many requirements for new pilots as military separations would fill.
- The Navy also has a shortage of 500 senior-grade nuclear-trained officers, those who man strategic ballistic missile and attack submarine and many surface combatants.
- Navy re-enlistment rates are the lowest in five years. In addition, there has been a decline in the percentage of high school graduates coming into the Navy, while the numbers of personnel of the lowest mental grade being accepted have increased.
- Retention rates of outstanding sailors, those who must operate and maintain tomorrow's ever more sophisticated ships, aircraft, and weapons, are declining.
- Proposed pay increases over the next five years for military personnel are 3.6%, 3.1%, 3.0%, 3.0%, 3.0%. But, according to the Navy's uniformed leader, the Chief of Naval Operations, the gap between military and civilian pay NOW is 10.1%. Further, the rate of inflation the past two years has been 4.4%, and there are indications it will rise. Even if it remained at that same 4.4% level, military pay would fall another 6.3% behind civilian pay over that five-year period.
- Every service has an increasing backlog of maintenance—ships, aircraft, vehicles, and shore installations. In time, lessened maintenance can only result in lessened readiness, and in reduced ability to provide proper support for fighting forces at sea.
- In certain vital areas, proposed procurement levels are sharply down. For example, when the Navy presented to Congress in 1986 its proposed five-year procurement plan for fiscal years 1987–1991, it indicated it would be seeking funding for 403 aircraft in FY 1990 and 422 in FY 1991. However, in the FY 1990–1991 Reagan budget, BEFORE President Bush stated that he would not ask for the 2% growth that budget contained, the Navy sought only 192 aircraft in FY 1990 and 236 in FY 1991, a combined total of only 52.4% of the earlier forecast of aircraft requirements over that two-year period.

The cumulative effect of these and many other problems facing the maritime services may not be felt immediately. But, as has been acknowledged by Navy leaders, the potential is there for a return to the devastation of readiness that characterized the performance of the services in the late 1970s. In his first statement before Congress in 1989, the Chief of Naval Operations observed that overall readiness of some aircraft squadrons had improved over 250% since the early 1980s. For that to happen, the readiness of those units would have to have sunk to 28% or below, a level that would hardly characterize them as effective fighting forces. It is unlikely that Congress again would permit a degradation of readiness of that magnitude. But in the battle to reduce the budget deficit, sizeable cuts in defense spending could without question bring about marked reductions in overall effectiveness.

Given the initiatives announced and proposed by Secretary General Mikhail Gorbachev to reduce Soviet military capabilities and expenditures, should these problems greatly concern Americans? Do not the Gorbachev actions and proposals reflect an overall reduction in the threat posed by Soviet military might against the United States? From a maritime point of view, the answer is, definitely, "no".

There has been no reduction in the rates of construction of either Soviet submarines or surface combatants, and the effectiveness of the newer ships entering the Navy far exceeds those of older Soviet ships. In 1988, the Soviets launched one each of four different new classes of nuclear submarines and a second large-deck aircraft carrier, while a new nuclear cruiser and two conventionally powered destroyers became operational.

Similar growth patterns have characterized aircraft and weapons programs for the Soviet Navy. Research and development also remains a high Soviet priority, and outstanding successes give credence to Soviet abilities in R&D. A dramatic example is the quietness of the AKULA-class attack submarines, something the United States had not projected the Soviets to attain until the 1990s.

In short, although the overall size of the Soviet Navy may decrease marginally, its capability across the board continues to increase, and no diminution of quality in any area of endeavour is anticipated.

Further, the Soviets continue to provide a tremendous amount of military assistance to allies and Third World countries throughout the world. In 1987, the Soviets delivered $21 billion of military material to over 30 nations. Sales to other nations remained at a high level in 1988, which also saw the lease of a Soviet guided-missile submarine to India, the first instance of one country providing a nuclear submarine to another. In our own hemisphere, 1988 saw only a modest decrease in Soviet military tonnage delivered to Nicaragua from the record high in 1987. And there were more Soviet military advisors in Latin America (including Cuba) and Africa than there were United States military advisors throughout the world.

Because of Soviet military assistance, and because of actions taken on their own, more and more nations allied with or customers of the Soviet Union are steadily increasing their military capabilities with increasingly capable and more sophisticated ships, submarines, aircraft, and weapons. As a result, the potential challenge to U.S. maritime services becomes greater than ever.

On U.S. shores, the Coast Guard has encountered unique budgetary problems in recent years because it must compete for funding with a number of programs of high political and public interest, such as AMTRAK and urban mass transit. In a number of instances in the recent past, it has come off second best, although there now appears to be greater recognition that Coast Guard needs must be met if it is to be able to meet its normal requirements which are so important to so many Americans AND be an effective player in the war against drugs, a war that unquestionably will increase in tempo in the months ahead. Proposed funding in the FY 1990 budget appears to reflect that realization. The Coast Guard budget also contains a long-overdue request for funding for an icebreaker, a class of ship of which the United States is desperately short; it has but two oceangoing icebreakers left in its inventory.

The merchant marine remains the forgotten child of the maritime services. It has declined steadily in size and capability since the end of World War II, when it was without question the predominant merchant marine in the world. In the years since then, the United States merchant fleet dropped from 1st to 10th in world ranking, while the Soviet Union's rose from 22nd to 2nd, behind only Liberia. But despite annual recommendations over the last two decades by various groups and interests for action by both the Executive and Legislative branches of Congress to rectify the situation, almost nothing of substance has taken place. In 1986, a prestigious Commission on Merchant Marine and Defense was constituted to address the issue of merchant marine ineptitude in depth, and to make both interim and final recommendations that would enable it to begin to regain its stature and be better able to serve the nation both in peace and in war. Regrettably, almost none of the Commission's initial recommendations were adopted, and it appears unlikely that those made in its final report, published in January, will enjoy any greater success. As a result, it is likely that for years to come the United States will fail to compete effectively on the high seas in peacetime with its merchant marine, and will be desperately short of sealift in time of conflict.

SEA POWER: *CONGRESS*

Retirements, death, an election defeat, and a resignation took an unusual toll among senior members of the six committees of Congress that are primarily concerned with national security and the capabilities of the sea services. As a consequence, missing from the 101st Congress were two of the three most senior senators in the 100th Congress, four Democratic members of the House Armed Services Committee with over 115 years of collective service among them, the second most senior members of both the House Appropriations and Merchant Marine and Fisheries Committees, and a 10-term member of the House who had chaired the Defense Subcommittee of the Appropriations Committee.

The two senior senators not returning were John C. Stennis (D-MS), who was elected to the Senate in 1947, and William Proxmire (D-WI) who became a senator in 1957. Both retired, leaving Strom Thurmond (R-SC), 86, as the most senior senator. Stennis, former chairman of the Armed Services Committee and its ranking member after its present chairman, Sam Nunn (D-GA), was chairman of the Appropriations Committee. Proxmire was a member of the latter committee.

At the end of his 41st year in the Senate, Stennis, whose leadership and wisdom in defense matters will be sorely missed, was advised by the Navy that a nuclear aircraft carrier will bear his name. CVN 74, one of two carriers funded by Congress in FY 1988, will be named the JOHN C. STENNIS; it will become the second modern carrier to bear the name of a political leader whose outstanding leadership contributed immensely to national security. The other is the CARL VINSON (CVN 70), named for the Georgia Democrat who chaired first the Naval Affairs Committee in the House and later the Armed Services Committee.

Two other senators, Lawton Chiles (D-FL), a member of the Appropriations Committee, and Paul Trible (R-VA), a member of the Commerce, Science, and Transportation Committee, also retired, and Lowell Weicker (R-CT), a member of the Appropriations Committee who was seeking his fourth term, was defeated in a close race. A much more junior senator, Dan Quayle (R-IN), departed the Senate for a unique reason. He moved from the Legislative to the Executive Branch to become Vice President.

In the House, the former chairman of the Armed Services Committee, Melvin Price (D-IL), died while serving in his 22nd term, Dan Daniel, (D-VA), died while serving in his 10th, and Bill Nichols (D-AL), was elected to his 12th term but died before the 101st Congress convened. The fourth senior Democrat on that committee not to return was Sam Stratton (D-NY), who retired after serving 15 years. The loss of all that knowledge and experience to a single committee of Congress at one time is a grievous one indeed.

Also retiring from the House was Edward Boland (D-MA), the ranking member of the Appropriations Committee after its chairman, Jamie L. Whitten, (D-MS). Boland served 18 terms.

UNITED STATES SENATE

COMMITTEE ON APPROPRIATIONS
ROBERT C. BYRD, West Virginia, Chairman

Democrats	Republicans
DANIEL K. INOUYE, Hawaii	MARK O. HATFIELD, Oregon
ERNEST F. HOLLINGS, South Carolina	TED STEVENS, Alaska
J. BENNETT JOHNSTON, Louisiana	JAMES A. McCLURE, Idaho
QUENTIN N. BURDICK, North Dakota	JAKE GARN, Utah
PATRICK J. LEAHY, Vermont	THAD COCHRAN, Mississippi
JIM SASSER, Tennessee	BOB KASTEN, Wisconsin
DENNIS DeCONCINI, Arizona	ALFONSE M, D'AMATO, New York
DALE BUMPERS, Arkansas	WARREN B. RUDMAN, New Hampshire
FRANK R. LAUTENBERG, New Jersey	ARLEN SPECTER, Pennsylvania
TOM HARKIN, Iowa	PETE V. DOMENICI, New Mexico
BARBARA A. MIKULSKI, Maryland	CHARLES E. GRASSLEY, Iowa
HARRY REID, Nevada	DON NICKLES, Oklahoma
BROCK ADAMS, Washington	*PHIL GRAMM, Texas*
WYCHE FOWLER JR., Georgia	
ROBERT KERREY, Nebraska	

COMMITTEE ON ARMED SERVICES
SAM NUNN, Georgia, Chairman

Democrats	Republicans
J. JAMES EXON, Nebraska	JOHN W. WARNER, Virginia
CARL LEVIN, Michigan	STROM THURMOND, South Carolina
EDWARD M. KENNEDY, Massachusetts	WILLIAN S. COHEN, Maine
JEFF BINGAMAN, New Mexico	PETE WILSON, California
ALAN J. DIXON, Illinois	JOHN McCAIN, Arizona
JOHN GLENN, Ohio	*MALCOLM WALLOP, Wyoming*
ALBERT GORE JR., Tennessee	*SLADE GORTON, Washington*
TIMOTHY E. WIRTH, Colorado	*TRENT LOTT, Mississippi*
RICHARD C. SHELBY, Alabama	*DAN COATS, Indiana*
ROBERT C. BYRD, West Virginia	

COMMITTEE ON COMMERCE, SCIENCE, AND TRANSPORTATION
ERNEST F. HOLLINGS, South Carolina, Chairman

Democrats	REPUBLICANS
DANIEL K. INOUYE, Hawaii	JOHN C. DANFORTH, Missouri
WENDELL H. FORD, Kentucky	BOB PACKWOOD, Oregon
J. JAMES EXON, Nebraska	LARRY PRESSLER, South Dakota
ALBERT GORE JR., Tennessee	TED STEVENS, Alaska
JOHN D. ROCKEFELLER IV, West Virginia	BOB KASTEN, Wisconsin
LLOYD BENTSEN, Texas	JOHN McCAIN, Arizona
JOHN KERRY, Massachusetts	*CONRAD BURNS, Montana*
JOHN B. BREAUX, Louisiana	*SLADE GORTON, Washington*
RICHARD BRYAN, Nevada	*TRENT LOTT, Mississippi*
CHARLES ROBB, Virginia	

(Names appearing in italics reflect newly appointed members of committees.)

Losing his seat after 10 terms was a colleague of Boland's on that committee, Bill Chappell (D-FL), chairman of the Defense Subcommittee, who was defeated in a hotly contested election whose results were challenged by Chappell, but subsequently upheld. Resigning from the Merchant Marine and Fisheries Committee while in his 10th term was Mario Biaggi (D-NY), the ranking member of that committee after its chairman, Walter B. Jones (D-NC). Biaggi, a strong supporter of the Coast Guard and merchant marine, subsequently was convicted of federal racketeering, conspiracy, and extortion in connection with the highly publicized Wedtech case.

Two Republican House members, Mac Sweeney (TX) and Jack Davis (IL), both members of the Armed Services Committee, lost their bids to return to Congress. Sweeney also was a member of the Merchant Marine and Fisheries Committee. Two other Republicans, Jack Kemp (NY), a member of the Appropriations Committee, and Robert Badham (CA), the third ranking Republican on the Armed Services Committee, chose not to seek re-election. Kemp, a nine-term House member, sought the Presidency, but withdrew as a candidate after faring poorly in the primaries. Subsequently he was named by President Bush as Secretary of Housing and Urban Development. Two Washington Democrats, Don Bonker and Mike Lowry, both members of the Merchant Marine and Fisheries Committee, sought election to the Senate seat being vacated by Republican Daniel J. Evans; however, each failed in his quest, Bonker losing to Lowry in the primary election, and Lowry in turn to Slade Gorton in the national election.

Despite the absence in the 101st Congress of so many elder statesmen of both Houses, only one chairmanship among the six committees changed hands, Robert C. Byrd (D-WVA) succeeding Stennis as chairman of the Appropriations Committee. Byrd, who had stepped down as Senate Majority Leader, also was named a member of the Armed Services Committee. All other chairmen, all Democrats—Senate Chairmen Nunn and Ernest Hollings (SC) of the Commerce, Science, and Transportation Committee, and House Chairmen Les Aspin (D-WI), of the Armed Services Committee, Whitten, now in his 25th term, and Jones—were solidly entrenched and unchallenged.

Daniel Inouye (D-HI), now in his fifth term, was named to head the Defense Subcommittee of the Senate Appropriations Committee. John P. Murtha (D-PA), became the successor to Chappell as chairman of the Defense Subcommittee of the House Appropriations Committee.

Two Senate veterans, Phil Gramm (R-TX) and Brock Adams (D-WA), were named to the Appropriations Committee, along with newly elected Democrats Wyche Fowler, Jr., (GA) and Robert Kerrey (NB). Kerrey was awarded the Congressional Medal of Honor for heroism in combat in Vietnam.

Coming to the Armed Services Committee, in addition to Byrd, were Republicans Malcolm Wallop (WY), just elected to his third term, and newly elected Senators Gorton, Trent Lott (MI), and Dan Coats (IN), who was named to fill the vacancy left by Vice President Quayle. Although new to the

U.S. HOUSE OF REPRESENTATIVES
COMMITTEE ON APPROPRIATIONS
JAMIE L. WHITTEN, Mississippi, Chairman

Democrats
WILLIAM H. NATCHER, Kentucky
NEAL SMITH, Iowa
SIDNEY R. YATES, Illinois
DAVID R. OBEY, Wisconsin
EDWARD R. ROYBAL, California
LOUIS STOKES, Ohio
TOM BEVILL, Alabama
BILL ALEXANDER, Arkansas
JOHN P. MURTHA, Pennsylvania
BOB TRAXLER, Michigan
JOSEPH D. EARLY, Massachusetts
CHARLES WILSON, Texas
LINDY (MRS. HALE) BOGGS, Louisiana
NORMAN D. DICKS, Washington
MATTHEW F. McHUGH, New York
WILLIAM LEHMAN, Florida
MARTIN OLAV SABO, Minnesota
JULIAN C. DIXON, California
VIC FAZIO, California
W.G. "BILL" HEFNER, North Carolina
LES AuCOIN, Oregon
DANIEL K. AKAKA, Hawaii
WES WATKINS, Oklahoma
WILLIAM H. GRAY III, Pennsylvania
BERNARD J. DWYER, New Jersey
STENY H. HOYER, Maryland
BOB CARR, Michigan
ROBERT J. MRAZEK, New York
RICHARD J. DURBIN, Illinois
RONALD D. COLEMAN, Texas
ALAN B. MOLLOHAN, West Virginia
ROBERT LINDSAY THOMAS, Georgia
CHESTER G. ATKINS, Massachusetts
JIM CHAPMAN, Texas

Republicans
SILVIO O. CONTE, Massachusetts
JOSEPH M. McDADE, Pennsylvania
JOHN T. MYERS, Indianna
CLARENCE E. MILLER, Ohio
LAWRENCE COUGHLIN, Pennsylvania
C. W. BILL YOUNG, Florida
RALPH REGULA, Ohio
VIRGINIA SMITH, Nebraska
CARL D. PURSELL, Michigan
MICKEY EDWARDS, Oklahoma
BOB LIVINGSTON, Louisiana
BILL GREEN, New York
JERRY LEWIS, California
JOHN EDWARD PORTER, Illinois
HAROLD ROGERS, Kentucky
JOE SKEEN, New Mexico
FRANK R. WOLF, Virginia
BILL LOWERY, California
VIN WEBER, Minnesota
THOMAS D. DeLAY, Texas
JIM KOLBE, Arizona
DEAN A. GALLO, New Jersey

COMMITTEE ON ARMED SERVICES
LES ASPIN, Wisconsin, Chairman

Democrats
CHARLES E. BENNETT, Florida
G.V. "SONNY" MONTGOMERY, Mississippi
RONALD V. DELLUMS, California
PATRICIA SCHROEDER, Colorado
BEVERLY B. BYRON, Maryland
NICHOLAS MAVROULES, Massachusetts
EARL HUTTO, Florida
IKE SKELTON, Missouri
MARVIN LEATH, Texas
DAVE McCURDY, Oklahoma
THOMAS M. FOGLIETTA, Pennsylvania
ROY DYSON, Maryland
DENNIS M. HERTEL, Michigan
MARILYN LLOYD, Tennessee
NORMAN SISISKY, Virginia
RICHARD RAY, Georgia
JOHN M. SPRATT JR., South Carolina
FRANK McCLOSKEY, Indiana
SOLOMON, P. ORTIZ, Texas
GEORGE "BUDDY" DARDEN, Georgia
TOMMY F. ROBINSON, Arkansas
ALBERT G. BUSTAMANTE, Texas
GEORGE J. HOCHBRUECKNER, New York
JOSEPH E. BRENNAN, Maine
OWEN B. PICKETT, Virginia
H. MARTIN LANCASTER, North Carolina
LANE EVANS, Illinois
JAMES BILBRAY, Nevada
JOHN TANNER, Tennessee
MICHAEL R. McNULLY, New York

Republicans
WILLIAM L. DICKINSON Alabama
FLOYD SPENCE, South Carolina
BOB STUMP, Arizona
JIM COURTER, New Jersey
LARRY J. HOPKINS, Kentucky
ROBERT W. DAVIS, Michigan
DUNCAN L. HUNTER, California
DAVID O'B. MARTIN, New York
JOHN R. KASICH, Ohio
HERBERT H. BATEMAN, Virginia
BEN BLAZ, Guam
ANDY IRELAND, Florida
JAMES V. HANSEN, Utah
JOHN G. ROWLAND, Connecticut
CURT WELDON, Pennsylvania
JON KYL, Arizona
ARTHUR RAVENEL JR., South Carolina
BOB DORNAN, California
JOEL HEFLEY, Colorado
JIM McCRERY, Louisiana
RONALD K. MACHTLEY, Rhode Island

(Names appearing in italics reflect newly appointment members of the committee.)

Senate, Lott is no stranger to Washington, having served eight terms in the House.

Five new senators were named to the Commerce, Science, and Transportation Committee—Republicans Lott, Gorton, and Conrad Burns (MT), and Democrats Richard Bryan (NV) and Charles Robb (VA). Robb, immediate past governor of Virginia, is former President Lyndon Johnson's son-in-law.

In the House, a number of Representatives elected in 1986 or earlier were newly named to the Armed Services, Appropriations, or Merchant Marine and Fisheries Committees. Republicans Bob Dornan (CA), a five-term veteran, and Joel Hefley (CO), in his second term, were named to the Armed Services Committee, as was second-termer Democrat James Bilbray (TX). Two Democrats, Chester Atkins (MA) and Jim Chapman (TX), and a Republican, Dean Gallo (NJ), all now in their third term, became members of the Appropriations Committee. James Inhofe (R-OK) was named to the Merchant Marine and Fisheries Committee in his second term. Nine newly elected Congressmen also were named to those three committees.

COMMITTEE ON MARINE AND FISHERIES
WALTER B. JONES, North Carolina, Chairman

Democrats
GERRY E. STUDDS, Massachusetts
CARROLL HUBBARD JR., Kentucky
WILLIAM J. HUGHES, New Jersey
EARL HUTTO, Florida
W. J. "BILLY" TAUZIN, Louisiana
THOMAS M. FOGLIETTA, Pennsylvania
DENNIS M. HERTEL, Michigan
ROY DYSON, Maryland
WILLIAM O. LIPINSKI, Illinois
ROBERT A. BORSKI, Pennsylvania
THOMAS R. CARPER, Delaware
DOUGLAS H. BOSCO, California
ROBIN TALLON, South Carolina
SOLOMON P. ORTIZ, Texas
CHARLES E. BENNETT, Florida
THOMAS J. MANTON, New York
OWEN B. PICKETT, Virginia
JOSEPH E. BRENNAN, Maine
GEORGE J. HOCHBRUECKNER, New York
BOB CLEMENT, Tennessee
STEPHEN J. SOLARZ, New York
FRANK PALLONE JR., New Jersey
GREG H. LAUGHLIN, Texas
NITA M. LOWEY, New York
JOLENE UNSOELD, Washington

Republicans
ROBERT W. DAVIS, Michigan
DON YOUNG, Alaska
NORMAN F. LENT, New York
NORMAN D. SHUMWAY, California
JACK FIELDS, Texas
CLAUDINE SCHNEIDER, Rhode Island
HERBERT H. BATEMAN, Virginia
H. JAMES SAXTON, New Jersey
JOHN R. MILLER, Washington
HELEN DELICH BENTLEY, Maryland
HOWARD COBLE, North Carolina
CURT WELDON, Pennsylvania
PATRICIA F. SAIKI, Hawaii
WALLY HERGER, California
JIM BUNNING, Kentucky
JAMES M. INHOFE, Oklahoma
PORTER GOSS, Florida

KEY CONGRESSIONAL PHONE NUMBERS*

House Committees
Appropriations Subcommittee on Defense.....225-2847
Armed Services Committee...................225-4151
Merchant Marine and Fisheries Committee....225-4047
Coast Guard and Navigation Subcommittee ...225-8204

Senate Committees
Appropriations Subcommittee on Defense.....224-7258
Armed Services Committee...................224-3871
Commerce, Science, and Transportation
Subcommittee on Merchant Marine
(also Coast Guard) 224-4766

Members of Congress 224-3121

Cloakroom Announcements
(For running accounts of proceedings on House and Senate floors)

House: Democratic.........................225-7400
       Republican........................225-7430
Senate: Democratic........................224-8541
       Republican........................224-8601

Documents
(For information/copies of bills and reports)
House 225-3456
Senate 224-4321

Government Printing Office
(For copies of committee reports, etc.) 783-3238

Legislative Information
(For information on status of legislation,
either House or Senate, name of
committee to which bill was referred,
number of committee report, etc.)...........225-1772

Military Liaison
Navy/Marines: House 225-7124
       or 225-4395
       Senate 224-4681
Coast Guard: House 225-4775
       Senate 224-2913

*Area code for all numbers: 202

When writing to a member of Congress, use the following addresses:

SENATOR:

The Honorable_____
U.S. Senate, Washington, D.C. 20510

REPRESENTATIVE:

The Honorable_____
U.S. House of Representatives
Washington, D.C. 20515

SEA POWER: *DEFENSE*

In the short message to Congress that preceded the lengthy discussion of the FY 1989 amended defense budget, Secretary of Defense Frank C. Carlucci made a number of observations that provided much food for thought:

"While our forces are now stronger, we continue to face a host of threats. Foremost among them is Soviet military power, the single most significant factor we consider in determining the force required to guarantee our national security. Neither glasnost nor the stirrings of economic reform within the Soviet Union have resulted in any redirection of resources away from the Soviet military machine. Deterring Soviet, or Soviet-inspired aggression will remain the prime aim of our national security strategy, and the benchmark against which we must measure our strength.

"Our struggle to safeguard our security is made even more difficult by the current fiscal climate. The FY 1989 amended budget is $33 billion less than our proposed spending level sent to the Congress only last year. In order to make such significant reductions, entire programs have been eliminated and force levels reduced.

"At the same time there has been no parallel reduction in our nation's global responsibilities. On the contrary, there is reason to believe that as we enter the 1990s our responsibilities may well increase. Western Europe, the Middle East, the Pacific rim, Soviet adventurism in our own hemisphere, the need to assure uninterrupted transit through vital sea lanes—the Persian Gulf is one case in point—require constant attention if U.S. interests are to be safeguarded. Reducing the resources we require to meet our global responsibilities—without any reduction in those responsibilities themselves—increases the risks to our interests and those of our friends and allies.

"The plan outlined in the following pages meets the target for defense spending set by the President and Congress at their November 1987 Budget Summit. To meet that target we have had to accept another real decline compared to the FY 1988 budget. The plan therefore represents a continuation of one of the least noticed facts about the defense budgets of the 1980s: the real decline in defense spending. Indeed, the erosion of our defense effort in real terms is entering its fourth year. Beginning in FY 1986, defense spending has decreased by nearly 11 percent in real terms. The FY 1989 amended budget continues that decline.

"We can all recognize that defense spending may be affected by domestic considerations. But changing domestic considerations do not alter the external threats we face. . . ."

Congress and the Department of Defense honored the November 1987 Budget Summit agreement between Congress and the administration which fixed total FY 1989 allocations for national defense at $299.5 billion in budget authority, and $294.0 billion in total obligation authority. By passing the budget before 1 October, the 100th Congress became the first Congress since 1976 to complete action on all appropriation bills before the start of the fiscal year.

The Department of the Navy was authorized 100 percent of its total request of $96.6 billion in budget authority but had $97.7 billion appropriated, 101.1 percent of its request. However, there were a number of sharp discrepancies between Navy requests for authorization and funding on individual programs and Congressional action

Table D-1
FEDERAL BUDGET TRENDS
(Dollars in Millions)

Fiscal Year	Federal Outlays as a % of GMP	DoD Outlays as a % of Federal Outlays	DoD Outlays as a % of GNP	Non-DoD Outlays as a % of Federal Outlays	Non-DoD Outlays as a % of GNP	DoD Outlays as a % of Net Public Spending*
1950	16.0	27.5	4.4	72.5	11.6	18.5
1955	17.6	51.5	9.1	48.5	8.6	35.6
1960	18.2	45.0	8.2	55.0	10.0	30.3
1965	17.5	38.8	6.8	61.2	10.7	25.2
1970	19.8	39.4	7.8	60.6	12.0	25.5
1971	19.9	35.4	7.0	64.6	12.8	22.4
1972	20.0	32.6	6.5	67.4	13.5	20.6
1973	19.1	29.8	5.7	70.2	13.4	19.0
1974	19.0	28.8	5.5	71.2	13.5	18.3
1975	21.8	25.5	5.6	74.5	16.2	16.5
1976	21.9	23.6	5.2	76.4	16.7	15.4
1977	21.1	23.4	4.9	76.6	16.2	15.5
1978	21.1	22.5	4.7	77.5	16.4	15.2
1979	20.5	22.8	4.7	77.2	15.8	15.4
1980	22.2	22.5	5.0	77.5	17.2	15.3
1981	22.7	23.0	5.2	77.0	17.5	15.8
1982	23.7	24.5	5.8	75.5	17.9	16.7
1983	24.3	25.4	6.2	74.6	18.2	17.3
1984	23.1	25.9	6.0	74.1	17.1	17.5
1985	24.0	25.9	6.2	74.1	17.8	17.7
1986	23.6	26.8	6.3	73.2	17.3	18.1
1987	22.8	27.3	6.2	72.7	16.6	18.0
1988	22.4	26.2	5.9	73.8	16.5	17.5
1989	21.7	26.1	5.7	73.9	16.0	17.0

*Federal, State, and Local net spending excluding government enterprises (such as the postal service and public utilities) except for any support these activities receive from tax funds.

Source: Secretary of Defense Annual Report to the Congress, FY 1989

DEFENSE

Table D-2
100 BIGGEST DEFENSE CONTRACTORS

(The 100 companies [including their subsidiaries] receiving the largest dollar volume of prime contract awards from the Department of Defense during fiscal 1987.)

(in thousands of dollars)

#	Company	Amount
1.	McDonnell Douglas Corp.	7,715,243
2.	General Dynamics Corp.	7,040,956
3.	General Electric Co.	5,801,795
4.	Lockheed Corp.	5,573,547
5.	General Motors Corp.	4,081,723
6.	Raytheon Co.	3,819,984
7.	Martin Marietta Corp.	3,726,483
8.	United Technologies Corp.	3,587,022
9.	The Boeing Co.	3,547,343
10.	Grumman Corp.	3,392,714
11.	Unisys Corp.	2,267,911
12.	Rockwell International Corp.	2,237,847
13.	Tenneco Inc.	2,052,941
14.	Litton Industries Inc.	2,035,397
15.	Honeywell Inc.	2,007,993
16.	International Business Machines	1,821,625
17.	Westinghouse Electric Corp.	1,684,123
18.	Textron Inc.	1,546,349
19.	GTE Corp.	1,475,075
20.	The LTV Corp.	1,307,673
21.	TRW Inc.	1,135,038
22.	Texas Instruments Inc.	1,109,377
23.	Northrop Corp.	1,068,222
24.	ITT Corp.	995,127
25.	Allied-Signal Inc.	943,001
26.	Gencorp Inc.	873,783
27.	The Singer Co.	814,348
28.	FMC Corp.	743,691
29.	Gibbons Green Van Amerongen	721,027
30.	Morton Thiokol Inc.	705,841
31.	Hercules Inc.	693,593
32.	Loral Corp.	691,656
33.	American Telephone & Telegraph Co.	640,636
34.	Morrison Knudsen Corp.	637,274
35.	Philips Gloeilampenfabrieken	603,142
36.	Motorola Inc.	564,741
37.	Ford Motor Co.	508,578
38.	Eaton Corp.	499,605
39.	CFM International Inc.	434,979
40.	Royal Dutch Petroleum Co.	420,358
41.	Massachusetts Institute of Technology	411,483
42.	Computer Sciences Corp.	389,089
43.	Emerson Electric Co.	375,296
44.	Bell Boeing JV	375,273
45.	Chevron Corp.	365,418
46.	Teledyne Inc.	359,364
47.	Johns Hopkins University	356,007
48.	The Mitre Corp.	353,360
49.	Oshkosh Truck Corp.	352,728
50.	Olin Corp.	352,057
51.	The Aerospace Corp.	338,926
52.	Exxon Corp.	336,990
53.	Zenith Electronics Corp.	336,909
54.	Pan Am Corp.	318,332
55.	The Penn Central Corp.	316,725
56.	Dyncorp Inc.	312,184
57.	Harris Corp.	302,624
58.	Harsco Corp.	299,125
59.	Science Applications International Corp.	295,420
60.	E Systems Inc.	279,881
61.	Atlantic Richfield Co.	272,015
62.	Avondale Industries Inc.	269,748
63.	Chrysler Corp.	268,081
64.	Rolls Royce Inc.	260,613
65.	Tracor Inc.	253,248
66.	Control Data Corp.	229,617
67.	Kaman Corp.	221,488
68.	Forstmann Little & Co.	218,462
69.	Hewlett Packard Co.	208,234
70.	Digital Equipment Corp.	199,395
71.	Draper Charles Stark Lab.	198,249
72.	United Industrial Corp.	196,999
73.	Eastman Kodak Co.	188,262
74.	BDM International Inc.	185,254
75.	MIP Instandsetzungsbetric	178,211
76.	Cubic Corp.	175,897
77.	Gould Inc.	175,350
78.	Duchossois Enterprises Inc.	173,866
79.	The Coastal Corp.	163,109
80.	Figgie International Holdings	161,162
81.	Arvin Industries Inc.	156,768
82.	Day & Zimmerman Inc.	155,245
83.	Mtr Oils Hellas Corinth Ref	152,975
84.	Tiger International Inc.	150,668
85.	Amoco Inc.	146,899
86.	Cray Research Inc.	146,471
87.	The Mason Co.	*144,085
88.	Sequa Corp.	142,749
89.	Xerox Corp.	142,298
90.	Contel Corp.	140,625
91.	Logicon Inc.	139,827
92.	Colt Industries Inc.	139,009
93.	Clabir Corp.	138,704
94.	General Electric Co. P.L.C.	138,078
95.	Mobil Corp.	136,563
96.	Todd Shipyards Corp.	130,924
97.	Bollinger Machine Shop & Shipyard	130,898
98.	Capital Marine Corp.	124,056
99.	AEL Industries Inc.	122,953
100.	Sundstrand Corp.	122,390

*Based on information received after the close of FY 1987, this amount is understated by $101,073 (thousands).

on those programs.

Just before Navy and Marine Corps representatives began last spring their annual pilgrimages to Capitol Hill in support of the Navy budget, the then Secretary of the Navy, James H. Webb, Jr., who had succeeded John F. Lehman in that post, submitted his resignation after clashing with Secretary Carlucci over DOD budget philosophy in general and in particular the decision to decommission 16 frigates in FY 1988 and FY 1989. Secretary Webb was vigorously opposed to reducing the size of the fleet, particularly since it has not yet reached the 600-ship level, and wished to make cuts elsewhere in the Navy budget. However, Secretary Carlucci apparently believed one means of demonstrating to Congress that DOD truly meant business in reducing its expenditures was to reduce the numbers of ships in the fleet. Secretary Webb's protest was not heeded, so he resigned. He was succeeded by William Ball, who would finish out the second Reagan term as the third Secretary of the Navy in that short time span.

The prospects for any increases in the defense budget in the immediate future, absent any real or perceived significant threat to the security of the country, were bleak. During the presidential campaign, neither candidate indicated that he would seek budget increases, although Vice President Bush pledged to ensure the nation remained strong militarily. But even had both candidates pledged they would seek increases in spending for defense if they were elected, it was unlikely that the Democratic Congress would have concurred in such increases. Accordingly, modernizing and maintaining the readiness of the forces that are in being may prove to be a most difficult task in the years immediately ahead.

The Navy's ship construction program was given a boost by Congress when it authorized building five DDG-51s rather than the three that were included in the Navy budget. The Navy long had been on record that an annual construction rate of five or more DDG-51s was needed to enable turn-of-the-century force-level requirements to be met and also to provide a viable, two-shipbuilder industrial base. However, its request for five had been reduced by two before the DOD budget went to Congress, but then Congress added funds for a fourth ship and authorized the expenditure of unobligated prior-year funds from a number of different programs, including some Army and Air Force projects, for a fifth. The Secretary of the Navy also was authorized to limit competition among shipbuilders to build these ships to two yards; that decision would in all likelihood leave Bath Iron Works, which currently is building the *Arleigh Burke* (DDG-51) and *John Paul Jones* (DDG-53), and Ingalls Shipbuilding, which is constructing *John Barry* (DDG-52), as the only yards constructing this class of ship.

Congress also took an unusual action with regard to authorizing and funding construction of fleet oilers of the *Henry J. Kaiser* (TAO-187) class. It authorized construction of two, the number requested by the Navy, but then provided funds to build five. Building five would complete the construction program for these ships, and also help reduce construction costs for each ship.

Also authorized and funded was construction of the first of a new class of attack submarine, the *Seawolf* (SSN-21). This program still has many critics, many of whom argue that the Navy should continue building improved versions of the SSN-688 class rather than investing so much now in a submarine that, they contend, will be outperformed by Soviet submarines. However, the Navy claims the SSN-21 class will be markedly superior to the improved SSN-688s and will be able to more than hold its own against its Soviet counterparts. Construction of *Seawolf* is scheduled to begin in November 1989; it will be built by either Newport News Shipbuilding or the

Table D-3

WHERE MILITARY DOLLARS ARE SPENT
(FY 1987 Estimated)
($ in thousands)

State	PERSONNEL COMPENSATION					PRIME CONTRACT AWARDS		
	Civilian Pay	Military Active Duty Pay	Reserve & National Guard Pay	Retired Military Pay	Total Compensation	Civil Functions Contracts	Military Functions Contracts	Total Contracts
Alabama	733,880	566,681	211,426	443,502	1,955,489	51,962	1,608,895	1,660,857
Alaska	187,543	416,704	27,583	58,636	690,466	28,037	527,037	555,074
Arizona	288,609	504,376	62,776	475,029	1,330,790	26,646	3,184,190	3,210,836
Arkansas	126,654	195,037	66,605	235,391	623,687	41,348	696,504	737,852
California	3,771,612	5,796,140	438,903	2,717,643	12,724,298	84,851	24,429,660	24,514,511
Colorado	296,463	793,655	81,135	493,353	1,664,606	1,754	2,714,461	2,716,215
Connecticut	143,984	275,314	42,393	122,810	584,501	983	5,029,522	5,030,505
Delaware	46,750	85,650	23,349	54,173	209,922	9,253	188,692	197,945
District of Columbia	535,441	388,437	64,701	47,701	1,035,650	10,694	1,261,185	1,271,879
Florida	884,550	2,738,207	132,848	1,879,264	5,634,869	64,842	5,732,656	5,797,498
Georgia	1,006,421	1,238,798	288,021	682,457	3,215,697	54,686	3,457,797	3,512,483
Hawaii	528,727	1,228,713	48,485	164,746	1,970,671	7,188	454,261	461,449
Idaho	33,097	107,248	26,132	84,122	250,599	9,839	64,318	74,157
Illinois	585,265	755,143	157,980	286,171	1,784,559	100,881	1,823,474	1,924,355
Indiana	411,875	153,054	172,447	172,102	909,478	3,023	2,227,744	2,230,767
Iowa	40,830	13,182	55,538	76,099	185,649	5,465	594,629	600,094
Kansas	176,112	514,441	143,238	173,284	1,007,075	5,000	1,239,903	1,244,903
Kentucky	353,653	729,101	107,754	197,533	1,388,041	36,794	425,273	462,067
Louisiana	224,114	506,362	106,819	290,347	1,127,642	216,576	1,468,815	1,685,391
Maine	277,164	155,812	27,382	103,138	563,496	3,376	827,028	830,458
Maryland	1,270,944	832,467	132,220	501,349	2,736,980	40,009	4,712,445	4,752,454
Massachusetts	313,612	227,692	140,368	229,014	910,686	9,818	8,675,284	8,685,102
Michigan	355,614	194,036	105,299	198,911	853,860	22,233	1,843,748	1,865,981
Minnesota	74,393	27,936	96,080	117,918	316,327	25,513	2,400,681	2,426,194
Mississippi	298,376	392,063	85,115	214,874	990,428	98,694	1,375,028	1,473,722
Missouri	566,269	295,332	195,697	293,589	1,350,887	48,692	5,947,845	5,996,537
Montana	33,504	71,070	24,358	53,461	182,393	719	92,770	93,489
Nebraska	104,028	307,339	36,163	111,717	559,247	9,013	247,689	256,702
Nevada	59,208	185,188	15,316	173,813	433,525	95	232,024	232,119
New Hampshire	40,139	92,866	21,179	102,061	256,245	624	468,316	468,940
New Jersey	822,907	361,965	153,129	268,763	1,606,764	61,815	3,220,703	3,282,518
New Mexico	286,162	348,447	31,200	206,326	872,135	5,919	577,750	583,669
New York	496,951	495,775	205,522	316,852	1,515,100	33,618	9,591,185	9,624,803
North Carolina	397,813	1,912,695	112,644	605,335	3,028,487	32,328	1,210,335	1,242,663
North Dakota	47,540	198,600	22,554	23,395	292,089	4,025	154,304	158,329
Ohio	976,581	315,418	141,762	335,581	1,769,342	33,216	4,516,486	4,549,702
Oklahoma	700,152	604,478	124,509	318,399	1,747,538	19,450	588,416	607,866
Oregon	92,807	25,202	51,360	190,044	359,413	58,849	229,733	286,582
Pennsylvania	1,359,001	334,707	292,313	424,467	2,410,488	70,704	3,773,961	3,844,665
Rhode Island	129,820	138,685	27,446	69,593	365,544	960	476,974	477,934
South Carolina	532,968	1,156,622	149,856	472,887	2,312,333	9,862	561,207	571,069
South Dakota	38,995	124,601	22,563	36,219	222,378	7,645	49,914	57,559
Tennessee	188,153	200,822	102,938	362,631	854,544	28,702	957,219	985,921
Texas	1,723,214	2,657,470	302,081	1,883,370	6,566,135	109,337	8,544,786	8,654,123
Utah	593,487	127,922	56,852	98,743	877,004	363	1,182,706	1,183,069
Vermont	16,613	2,688	19,345	29,620	68,266	323	112,933	113,256
Virginia	3,175,271	4,041,168	171,096	1,375,415	8,762,950	50,264	7,757,218	7,807,482
Washington	827,353	1,052,505	122,954	655,578	2,658,390	51,558	3,060,467	3,112,025
West Virginia	46,777	11,575	32,427	82,432	173,211	25,902	124,166	150,068
Wisconsin	78,670	28,820	175,892	116,164	399,546	13,753	937,393	951,146
Wyoming	28,387	74,119	12,021	33,042	147,569	1,103	46,275	47,378
Total United States	26,328,423	34,002,328	5,467,774	18,658,434	84,456,989	1,636,304	131,626,059	133,262,363
Guam	107,524	207,804	5,950	11,765	333,043	1,075	101,801	102,876
Puerto Rico	63,049	69,903	55,205	58,330	246,487	54,863	268,237	323,100
Other U.S. Possessions	21,263	5,590	4,358	4,866	36,077	292	210,667	210,959
Total United States & Selected Areas	26,520,289	34,285,625	5,533,287	18,733,395	85,072,596	1,692,534	132,206,764	133,899,298

Table D-4

DOD'S BUDGET FOR RESEARCH, DEVELOPMENT, TEST, AND EVALUATION

($ in millions)

	TOTAL OBLIGATIONAL AUTHORITY		
	FY 1987	FY 1988 (Estimate)	FY 1989 (Estimate)
BY COMPONENT			
Army	4,699.0	4,670.7	5,030.7
Navy	9,292.4	9,512.9	9,216.2
Air Force	15,050.5	15,165.4	14,932.1
Defense Agencies	6,768.1	7,661.8	8,667.8
Defense Test and Evaluation	119.9	182.1	166.9
Defense Oper. Test and Evaluation	11.3	70.2	143.4
Total	35,941.3	37,263.1	38,157.1
BY RESEARCH CATEGORY			
Research	893.6	901.4	916.5
Exploratory Development	2,343.2	2,392.3	2,360.9
Advanced Development	10,426.3	12,445.5	11,174.1
Engineering Development	9,340.6	9,640.5	11,587.5
Management and Support	2,942.7	2,513.8	2,559.8
Operational Systems Development	9,994.9	9,369.6	9,558.4
Total	35,941.3	37,263.1	38,157.1
BY BUDGET ACTIVITY			
Technology Base	3,236.8	3,293.7	3,277.4
Advanced Technology Development	5,031.8	5,433.7	6,507.3
Strategic Programs	7,703.3	7,390.7	6,524.6
Tactical Programs	11,031.6	12,211.7	13,092.7
Intelligence & Communications	4,702.3	4,882.2	4,469.8
Defensewide Mission Support	4,235.5	4,051.2	4,285.4
Total	35,941.3	37,263.1	38,157.1
BY FYDP* PROGRAM			
Strategic Forces	1,147.2	831.8	696.8
General Purpose Forces	2,192.0	1,762.9	2,011.9
Intelligence and Communications	6,361.8	6,244.6	6,204.9
Airlift/Sealift	97.0	26.9	12.9
Guard and Reserve	37.3	60.0	83.3
Research and Development (FYDP* Program 6)	25,946.4	27,893.5	28,598.7
Central Supply and Maintenance	150.7	177.2	217.5
Training Medical and Other	4.4	—	—
Support of Other Nations	4.3	3.6	4.2
Special Operations Forces	0.2	262.4	326.9
Total	35,941.3	37,263.1	38,157.1

*Five-year defense program
Source: '88 Defense Almanac

Electric Boat Division of General Dynamics, both of which are involved in the design process. A construction-contract award is expected to be made early in FY 1989.

The remainder of the Navy ship-construction program was authorized and funded as requested, with the exception of one oceanographic ship whose design was not considered to be advanced to the point that it should be included in the FY 1989 budget. It includes one Trident ballistic-missile submarine, two improved SSN-688 attack submarines, one LSD-41 amphibious assault ship, one AOE-6 class fast combat support ship, two MHC-51 coastal minehunters, and three SWATH TA-GOS 19 class ocean surveillance ships. Also approved and funded was the jumboization of two AO-177 oilers.

The Navy had requested authorization and funding for nine LCACs for the Marine Corps; however, Congress provided funds to build 15, with a goal of making possible a lower unit cost.

A year ago, a major problem for the Navy was getting an agreement on how to modernize and refurbish its aging and trouble-plagued fleet of attack aircraft. It had hoped to obtain authorization and funding to build an upgraded version of the A-6E, the A-6F; however, that program was quashed by Congress, which approved continuing development of the Advanced Tactical Aircraft and also the construction of 11 improved A-6Es; that number later was reduced to 10. In FY 1989, Congress did not concur in the Navy's request for funding of A-6 modernization, although it did indicate that KA-6Bs and EA-6As should be considered for conversions to A-6Gs, if and when approval for that particular modernization program finally is given. Meanwhile, new A-6Es and many older ones now in the fleet await new wings which, unfortunately, are neither available nor likely to be forthcoming soon because the Boeing Corporation, which was awarded a contract to construct new wings composed of epoxy to replace metal wings which had developed cracks because of fatigue, has encountered extreme difficulty in meeting specifications and has yet to complete a single approved wing. Development of the ATA continues, although the Navy and the Air Force differ on whether it should be subsonic (Navy preference) or supersonic.

The Navy had requested funding for 72 F/A-18s; however, in another departure from the budget request, Congress added funding for an additional 12 in order to make possible a lower unit cost. Congress also added funds to the sum requested by the Navy for construction of nine EA-6Bs and directed the Navy not to build less than 12.

The somewhat embattled program to develop and produce the tilt-rotor V-22 Osprey was given a sizable boost when Congress approved the Navy's request for $335.3 million for advance procurement. At one point in 1988 consideration apparently was given by the Navy, much against Marine Corps desires, to delaying production of the aircraft for a year because of budget constraints. However, the Marines prevailed, although Congress did order DOD to submit with the FY 1990 budget a new five-year procurement plan and by 31 December 1988 a re-evaluation of procurement strategy because the numbers of V-22s planned for procurement had dropped sharply from original estimates, since the Army had dropped out of the program and the Navy was re-evaluating its V-22 needs.

Multi-year procurement was authorized for Marine AV-8Bs, with the requested 24 being funded. That program, too, was threatened by budgetary constraints, but Congress sided solidly with the Marines. Congress also provided $55 million that had not been requested to complete the buy-out of the AH-1W helicopter program.

The Navy fared reasonably well in the procurement of missiles, although several programs had extra funds appropriated for missile buys even though the expenditures of those funds was not authorized by Congress. The usual annual buy of 66 Trident D-5 missiles was funded, as were 475 Tomahawks, down from the 610 requested but the same number funded in FY 1988. Because of continuing problems with the development and production of AMRAAM, $40 million was authorized and $57.5 million appropriated for

Table D-5

MAJOR WEAPON SYSTEMS AND COMBAT FORCES
(Highlights)

	FY 1984	FY 1986	FY 1987	FY 1988 (Estimate)	FY 1989 (Estimate)
STRATEGIC					
Strategic Offense					
Land-Based ICBMs*					
Titan	32	7	—	—	—
Minuteman	1,000	998	973	954	950
Peacekeeper	—	2	27	46	50
Strategic Bombers**					
B-52G/H	241	241	234	234	234
B-1B	—	18	58	90	90
FB-111A***	56	56	52	48	48
Fleet Ballistic Launchers (SLBMs)*					
Poseidon (C-3 and C-4)	384	320	336	368	400
Trident	72	144	192	192	192
Strategic Defense Interceptors					
(PAA**/Squadrons)					
Active	90/5	76/4	54/3	36/2	36/2
Air National Guard	162/10	198/11	195/11	216/12	216/12

*Number on-line
**Primary Aircraft Authorized
***Begin transfer to the tactical air forces in the early 1990s as F-111G

	FY 1984	FY 1986	FY 1987	FY 1988 (Estimate)	FY 1989 (Estimate)
GENERAL PURPOSE					
Land Forces					
Army Divisions					
Active	16	18	18	18	18
Reserve	8	10	10	10	10
Marine Corps Divisions					
Active	3	3	3	3	3
Reserve	1	1	1	1	1
Tactical Air Forces (Primary Aircraft Authorized/Squadrons)					
Air Force Attack/fighter					
Active	1,734/77	1,764/78	1,812/81	1,762/79	1,746/79
Reserve	852/43	876/43	900/44	894/43	876/43
Navy Attack/Fighter					
Active	616/63	758/65	752/67	758/67	792/70
Reserve	75/9	107/10	101/10	120/10	118/10
Marine Corps Attack/Fighter					
Active	256/24	333/25	331/25	346/25	341/25
Reserve	90/8	94/8	96/8	96/8	96/8
Naval Forces					
Strategic Forces Ships	41	45	43	42	42
Battle Forces Ships	425	437	445	439	443
Support Forces Ships	46	55	58	61	65
Reserve Forces Ships	12	18	22	28	30
Total Deployable Battle Forces	**524**	**555**	**568**	**570**	**580**
Other Reserve Forces Ships	24	21	21	20	18
Other Auxiliaries	9	7	5	5	5
Total Other Forces	**33**	**28**	**26**	**25**	**23**
AIRLIFT AND SEALIFT					
Intertheater Airlift*					
C-5A	70	66	66	66	66
C-5B	—	5	14	32	44
C-141	234	234	234	234	234
KC-10A	25	48	57	57	57
Intratheater Airlift*					
Air Force					
C-130	520	504	559	521	513
Navy and Marine Corps					
Tactical Support	85	88	88	92	92
Sealift Ships					
Active					
Tankers	21	24	20	20	20
Cargo	30	40	41	41	41
Reserve**	106	122	135	144	151

*Primary Aircraft Authorized
**Includes useful National Defense Reserve Fleet ships and the Ready Reserve Force
Source: SECDEF Annual Report to Congress

Table D-6
MILITARY INSTALLATIONS AND PROPERTIES
(FY 1987)
(Does not include Reserve centers and minor properties)

UNITED STATES	Army	Navy	Marine Corps	Air Force	Defense Agencies	Total DoD
Alabama	18	8	—	9	—	35
Alaska	11	3	—	33	—	47
Arizona	5	1	1	13	—	20
Arkansas	2	—	—	4	—	6
California	13	49	8	34	1	105
Colorado	4	—	—	9	—	13
Connecticut	1	2	—	2	—	5
Delaware	—	—	—	3	—	3
Dist. of Columbia	2	5	1	2	—	10
Florida	—	32	—	20	1	53
Georgia	8	3	1	9	—	21
Hawaii	15	19	2	10	1	47
Idaho	—	—	—	4	—	4
Illinois	6	4	—	5	—	15
Indiana	5	3	—	3	—	11
Iowa	2	—	—	3	—	5
Kansas	4	—	—	3	1	8
Kentucky	4	1	—	2	—	7
Louisiana	2	2	—	7	—	11
Maine	—	4	—	4	1	9
Maryland	8	13	—	5	1	27
Massachusetts	5	3	—	14	—	22
Michigan	4	—	—	7	—	11
Minnesota	1	1	—	3	—	5
Mississippi	2	5	—	6	—	13
Missouri	4	—	—	7	1	12
Montana	2	—	—	3	—	5
Nebraska	2	—	—	5	—	7
Nevada	2	2	—	8	—	12
New Hampshire	1	1	—	2	—	4
New Jersey	8	3	—	4	—	15
New Mexico	3	1	—	5	—	9
New York	8	7	—	21	—	36
North Carolina	2	2	7	7	—	18
North Dakota	—	—	—	8	—	8
Ohio	3	2	—	12	2	19
Oklahoma	3	—	—	10	—	13
Oregon	1	2	—	2	—	5
Pennsylvania	7	7	—	7	1	22
Rhode Island	—	5	—	3	—	8
South Carolina	1	8	2	7	1	19
South Dakota	—	—	—	2	—	2
Tennessee	3	3	—	6	1	13
Texas	10	11	—	24	—	45
Utah	4	1	—	7	1	13
Vermont	2	—	—	1	—	3
Virginia	13	18	3	2	1	37
Washington	3	11	—	8	—	22
West Virginia	—	—	—	2	—	2
Wisconsin	2	—	—	4	—	6
Wyoming	—	—	—	3	—	3
Total United States	**206**	**242**	**25**	**384**	**14**	**871**

Source: '88 Defense Almanac

continued procurement of Sparrow missiles, which AMRAAM ultimately is to succeed. No Sparrows had been requested by the Navy.

The request for 660 Phoenix missiles was reduced to 450, but those for 138 Harpoon missiles and 1,307 Harm were funded in their entirety. 200 Hellfire missiles were sought, but Congress provided funding for 1,000 in order to allow for effective competition between two suppliers. However, the Navy's request for 64 Penguin missiles, which is a joint NATO venture, was not funded because of contracting delays and anticipated delays in operational and technical evaluation.

250 RAM, 1,310 Standard, and 731 Maverick missiles also were funded. Procurement of 261 MK 48 ADCAP torpedoes was authorized, but Appropriations Committees tacked on enough dollars for 320, and also admonished DOD to ensure that future budget requests contain quantities that support a dual-sourcing MK 48 ADCAP procurement strategy, which would be at least 320. Funding also was provided for 140 advanced lightweight MK 50 torpedoes.

$17.5 million had been authorized for procurement of Vertical Launch Asroc missiles, and another $30 million for R&D. Subsequently, the Appropriations Committees, concerned lest ships find their launchers empty of these weapons before the ASW stand-off weapon Sea Lance was ready for deployment, appropriated $105 million for procurement of 300 missiles.

Of particular note in procurement for the Marine Corps was the increase from 14 to 66 in the numbers of M-1 A1 battle tanks authorized and funded. The Marines also received authority to procure Hawk missiles on a multi-year basis; 467 of those missiles were funded in FY 1989. So also were 3,115 Dragon missiles, 6,950 Stingers, and 2,585 TOWs.

Congress authorized and appropriated $27.9 billion for Operations and Maintenance for the Navy and Marine Corps; that sum represented 99.7 percent of the original request. However, in order to get down to markedly reduced budget levels *before* the DOD budget was sent to Congress, a sizable number of overhaul and repair projects were deferred, including many ship overhauls. If defense spending continues at anticipated low levels in the immediate future, such delays in overhaul and repair could in time impact sharply on the Navy's ability to sustain operations at sea. Congress did provide $60 million to help pay the bill for the

Table D-7

DEPARTMENT OF DEFENSE
AIRLIFT AND SEALIFT FORCES HIGHLIGHTS

	FY 1980	FY 1984	FY 1986	FY 1987	FY 1988	FY 1989
Intertheater Airlift (PAA)[a]						
C-5A	70	70	66	66	66	66
C-5B	—	—	5	14	32	44
C-141	234	234	234	234	234	234
KC-10A	—	25	48	57	57	57
C-17	—	—	—	—	—	—
Intratheater Airlift (PAA)[a]						
Air Force						
C-130	482	520	504	559	521	513
C-123	64	—	—	—	—	—
C-7A	48	—	—	—	—	—
Navy and Marine Corps						
Tactical Support	97	85	88	88	92	92
Sealift Ships, Active						
Tankers	21	21	24	20	20	20
Cargo	23	30	40	41	41	41
Reserve[b]	26	106	122	135	144	151

[a] PAA—Primary Aircraft Authorized.
[b] Includes useful National Defense Reserve Fleet ships and the Ready Reserve Force.
Source: Secretary of Defense Annual Report to the Congress, FY 1989

Table D-8

DEPARTMENT OF DEFENSE
GENERAL PURPOSE FORCES HIGHLIGHTS

	FY 1980	FY 1984	FY 1986	FY 1987	FY 1988	FY 1989
Land Forces						
Army Divisions:						
Active	16	16	18	18	18	18
Reserve	8	8	10	10	10	10
Marine Corps Divisions:						
Active	3	3	3	3	3	3
Reserve	1	1	1	1	1	1
Tactical Air Forces (PAA Squadrons)[a]						
Air Force Attack/Fighter						
Active	1,608/74	1,734/77	1,764/78	1,812/81	1,762/79	1,746/79
Reserve	758/36	852/43	876/43	900/44	894/43	876/43
Navy Attack/Fighter						
Active	696/60	616/63	758/65	752/67	758/67	792/70
Reserve	120/10	75/9	107/10	101/10	120/10	118/10
Marine Corps Attack/Fighter						
Active	329/25	256/24	333/25	331/25	334/25	341/25
Reserve	84/7	90/8	94/8	96/8	94/8	96/8
Naval Forces						
Strategic Forces Ships	48	41	45	43	42	42
Battle Forces Ships	384	425	437	445	439	443
Support Forces Ships	41	46	55	58	61	65
Reserve Forces Ships	6	12	18	22	28	30
Total Deployable Battle Forces	479	524	555	568	570	580
Other Reserve Forces Ships	44	24	21	21	20	18
Other Auxiliaries	8	9	7	5	5	5
Total Other Forces	52	33	28	26	25	23

[a] PAA—Primary Aircraft Authorized
Source: Secretary of Defense Annual Report to the Congress, FY 1989

Table D-9
DEPARTMENT OF DEFENSE—B/A BY APPROPRIATION[a]
(Dollars in Millions)

	FY 1983	FY 1984	FY 1985	FY 1986[b]	FY 1987	FY 1988	FY 1989
Current Dollars							
Military Personnel	45,688	48,363	67,773	67,867	74,010	76,145	78,399
Retired Pay	16,155	16,503	*	*	*	*	*
Operation & Maintenance	66,540	70,950	77,803	74,888	79,607	80,684	85,649
Procurement	80,355	86,161	96,842	92,506	80,234	81,027	80,037
Research, Development, Test and Evaluation	22,798	26,867	31,327	33,609	35,644	36,695	38,157
Special Foreign Currency Program	4	3	9	2	4	—	—
Military Construction	4,512	4,510	5,517	5,281	5,093	5,354	5,743
Family Housing & Homeowners Assistance Program	2,712	2,669	2,890	2,803	3,075	3,149	3,272
Revolving & Management Funds	1,075	2,774	5,088	5,235	2,612	830	764
Trust Funds, Receipts & Deductions	−365	−650	−447	−1,055	−809	−726	−1,237
Total—Direct Program (B/A)	**239,474**	**258,150**	**286,802**	**281,136**	**279,469**	**283,159**	**290,784**
Constant FY 1989 Dollars							
Military Personnel	56,874	57,481	75,277	73,178	78,760	78,543	78,399
Retired Pay	19,721	19,484	*	*	*	*	*
Operation & Maintenance	78,763	82,790	88,720	85,185	87,841	83,605	85,649
Procurement	97,881	101,552	110,736	102,444	85,815	83,669	80,037
Research, Development, Test and Evaluation	27,863	31,679	35,836	37,438	38,426	38,035	38,157
Special Foreign Currency Program	5	4	10	2	4	—	—
Military Construction	5,523	5,345	6,337	5,888	5,478	5,535	5,743
Family Housing & Homeowners Assistance Program	3,256	3,113	3,276	3,108	3,312	3,263	3,272
Revolving & Management Funds	1,311	3,260	5,782	5,787	2,811	862	764
Trust Funds, Receipts & Deductions	−445	−764	−508	−1,165	−871	−754	−1,237
Total—Direct Program (B/A)	**290,752**	**303,942**	**325,467**	**311,864**	**301,575**	**292,758**	**290,784**

[a]Numbers may not add to totals due to rounding.
[b]Lower Budget Authority in the Military Personnel Accounts in FY 1986 reflects the congressional direction to finance $4.5 billion for the military pay raise and retirement accrual costs by transfers from prior year unobligated balances.
*Retired Pay accrual included in Military Personnel Appropriation.
Source: Secretary of Defense Annual Report to the Congress, FY 1989

Table D-10
DEPARTMENT OF DEFENSE—B/A BY COMPONENT[a]
(Dollars in Millions)

	FY 1983	FY 1984	FY 1985	FY 1986[b]	FY 1987	FY 1988	FY 1989
Current Dollars							
Department of the Army	57,529	62,181	74,270*	73,149*	73,994*	75,790*	77,806*
Department of the Navy	81,854	82,088	99,015*	96,131*	93,500*	100,141*	96,437*
Department of the Air Force	74,074	86,108	99,420*	94,903*	91,624*	88,150*	97,224*
Defense Agencies/OSD/JCS	9,256	10,746	13,126	15,520	19,185	17,015	18,611
Defense-wide	16,761	17,027	970	1,433	1,168	2,064	706
Total—Direct Program (B/A)	**239,474**	**258,150**	**286,802**	**281,136**	**279,469**	**283,159**	**290,784**
Constant FY 1989 Dollars							
Department of the Army	70,991	73,924	84,570*	81,105*	79,797*	78,345*	77,806*
Department of the Navy	99,176	96,526	112,313*	106,571*	100,812*	103,471*	96,437*
Department of the Air Force	88,607	100,515	112,264*	105,108*	98,883*	91,177*	97,224*
Defense Agencies/OSD/JCS	11,517	12,876	15,215	17,489	20,829	17,626	18,611
Defense-wide	20,461	20,101	1,106	1,590	1,254	2,138*	706
Total—Direct Program (B/A)	**290,752**	**303,942**	**325,467**	**311,864**	**301,575**	**292,758**	**290,784**

[a]Numbers may not add to totals due to rounding.
[b]Lower Budget Authority in the Military Personnel Accounts in FY 1986 reflects the congressional direction to finance $4.5 billion for the military pay raise and retirement accrual costs by transfers from prior year unobligated balances.
*Includes Retired Pay accrual.
Source: Secretary of Defense Annual Report to the Congress, FY 1989

Table D-11

WHERE THEY SERVE
(As of 31 March 1988)

(Countries/regional areas where 100 or more United States military members are assigned.
Area totals include countries with less than 100 assigned United States military members.)

REGIONAL AREA/COUNTRY	TOTAL	ARMY	NAVY	MARINE CORPS	AIR FORCE
United States, United States Territories, Special Locations					
Continental United States	1,305,475	464,801	268,511	144,706	427,457
Alaska	22,703	9,147	2,105	177	11,274
Hawaii	46,804	18,452	12,621	9,717	6,014
Guam	8,778	37	4,353	366	4,022
Johnston Atoll	132	122	2	—	8
Puerto Rico	3,507	396	2,803	173	135
Transients	46,534	15,183	14,786	5,692	10,873
Afloat	189,214	—	188,148	1,066	—
Total	1,623,284	508,214	493,369	161,897	459,804
Western & Southern Europe					
Belgium	3,633	1,551	128	38	1,916
Germany (Fed. Republic & West Berlin)	247,255	205,435	337	95	41,388
Greece	3,385	466	529	14	2,376
Greenland	211	—	—	—	211
Iceland	3,267	3	1,772	81	1,411
Italy	14,869	4,085	4,675	271	5,838
Netherlands	3,451	828	17	11	2,595
Norway	221	33	42	23	123
Portugal	1,686	56	377	13	1,240
Spain	9,132	25	3,730	198	5,179
Turkey	4,902	1,206	109	20	3,567
United Kingdom	29,580	266	2,359	380	26,575
Afloat	18,347	—	16,331	2,016	—
Total	340,243	214,019	30,444	3,307	92,473
East Asia & Pacific					
Australia	750	9	438	8	295
Japan (including Okinawa)	48,940	2,152	7,168	22,216	17,404
Philippines	16,746	476	5,718	965	9,587
Republic of Korea	47,992	32,473	403	3,473	11,643
Thailand	111	51	10	17	33
Afloat	22,319	—	19,420	2,899	—
Total	137,081	35,200	33,243	29,643	38,995
Africa, Near East & South Asia					
Bahrain	140	7	117	7	9
British Indian Ocean Territory (includes Diego Garcia)	1,365	4	1,260	86	15
Egypt	1,490	1,359	29	41	61
Saudi Arabia	428	148	43	19	218
Afloat	12,012	—	11,555	457	—
Total	16,258	1,778	13,054	1,016	410
Other Western Hemisphere					
Bermuda	1,454	—	1,379	75	—
Canada	535	8	390	11	126
Cuba (Guantanamo)	2,511	—	1,867	642	2
Honduras*	1,423	1,393	5	13	12
Panama	10,617	7,209	487	176	2,745
Afloat	7,116	—	7,116	—	—
Total	24,376	8,871	11,391	1,154	2,960

*Includes military personnel on TDY for planning and conduct of exercises

Antarctica					
Total	134	35	99	—	—
Eastern Europe					
Total	205	73	4	110	18
Worldwide					
Ashore	1,892,749	768,211	339,189	190,689	594,660
Afloat	249,008	—	242,570	6,438	—
Total	2,141,757	768,211	581,759	197,127	594,660

Source: Defense '88 Almanac

Table D-12

DEPARTMENT OF DEFENSE STRATEGIC FORCES HIGHLIGHTS

	FY 1980	FY 1984	FY 1986	FY 1987	FY 1988	FY 1989
Strategic Offense Land-Base ICBMs[a]						
Titan	52	32	7	—	—	—
Minuteman	1,000	1,000	998	973	954	950
Peace Keeper	—	—	2	27	46	50
Strategic Bombers (PAA)[b]						
B-52D	75	—	—	—	—	—
B-52G/H	241	241	241	234	234	234
B-1B	—	—	18	58	90	90
FB-111A[c]	56	56	56	52	48	48
Fleet Ballistic Launchers (SLBMs)[a]						
Polaris	80	—	—	—	—	—
Poseidon (C-3 and C-4)	336	384	320	336	368	400
Trident	—	72	144	192	192	192
Strategic Defense Interceptors (PAA/Squadrons)[b]						
Active	127/7	90/5	76/4	54/3	36/2	36/2
Air National Guard	165/10	162/10	198/1	195/11	216/12	216/12

[a]Number on-line.
[b]Primary Aircraft Authorized.
[c]Begin Transfer to the TAF in the early 1990s as F-111G.

Source: Secretary of Defense Annual Report to the Congress, FY 1989

Navy's extended operations in the Persian Gulf and also $87.5 million toward improving the Navy's ability to respond to the medical needs of active duty personnel, dependents, and retirees.

Navy personnel end strength was established at 593,200, the number requested. The Marines were authorized 197,200, also the number requested, but down 2,900 from their authorized end strength at the end of FY 1987. Both the Air Force and the Army were reduced by 500 personnel.

The Navy and Marines were granted substantial relief from the joint-duty officer management requirements that had been set forth in the JCS Reorganization Act in 1987. In addition, the 2 percent cuts in officer end strength that had been mandated for each of FY 1989 and FY 1990 were repealed by Congress. This was most welcome to the Navy in particular, which still was building toward the numbers of personnel required to operate and sustain a 600-ship Navy and could ill afford having its officer strength reduced.

A 4.1 percent increase in pay was voted by Congress, almost double the 2.2 percent increase funded in FY 1988. Although certainly welcomed by the nation's men and women in uniform, it did nothing to narrow the gap between civilian and military pay that has been widening for the past several years. Congress also approved a new bonus program for aviators to, as an incentive, keep more of them in uniform and counter ever-growing losses to commercial airlines. Also approved was

Table D-13

COMPARING PRODUCTIVITY GROWTH
(Index: 1977 = 100.0)

Year	United States	France	West Germany	Japan	United Kingdom
1960	62.2	36.4	40.3	23.2	55.5
1961	64.0	38.5	42.2	26.3	55.5
1962	66.7	40.9	45.1	27.4	56.8
1963	71.2	42.8	47.0	29.6	59.7
1964	74.6	46.0	50.9	33.6	63.7
1965	76.6	49.2	54.0	35.0	65.7
1966	77.4	53.1	56.3	38.5	67.8
1967	77.4	56.3	60.1	44.2	71.0
1968	79.8	62.3	64.9	49.8	76.2
1969	80.8	65.8	69.1	57.5	78.0
1970	80.8	69.6	71.2	64.8	79.7
1971	85.3	73.3	74.0	68.6	83.5
1972	89.0	77.7	78.9	75.3	89.1
1973	93.4	82.2	84.0	83.1	95.6
1974	90.6	85.2	87.4	86.5	97.4
1975	92.9	88.5	90.1	87.7	95.2
1976	97.1	95.0	96.5	94.3	99.5
1977	100.0	100.0	100.0	100.0	100.0
1978	101.5	105.7	103.1	108.0	101.5
1979	101.4	110.3	108.2	114.8	102.4
1980	101.4	112.0	108.6	122.7	101.7
1981	103.6	116.4	111.0	127.2	107.0
1982	105.9	123.5	112.6	135.0	113.6
1983	112.0	128.8	119.1	142.3	123.0
1984	116.6	133.8	123.5	152.5	129.5
1985	121.7	138.3	128.9	163.7	134.2
1986	126.0	140.9	168.2	168.2	138.2

Productivity in manufacturing sectors of selected countries, growth measured by output per worker-hour. Data for 1986 are estimates.

Source: Department of Labor, Bureau of Labor Statistics, Office of Productivity and Technology, June 1987

Table D-14

CIVILIAN PERSONNEL
(As of March 31, 1988)

Most civilian employees of the Department of Defense are hired directly by the military departments, the Defense agencies, or the Office of the Secretary of Defense and the Organization of the Joint Chiefs of Staff and are designated as "direct hire" civilians. In general, salaried personnel are described as "white collar" and wage board personnel "blue collar."

In a few foreign countries, substantial numbers of foreign nationals, who are technically employees of the host country (or an agency of that government), are assigned to work with U.S. forces under contracts or agreements with the host government. These foreign nationals are designated "indirect hire" civilians.

	ARMY	NAVY/ MARINE CORPS	AIR FORCE	OTHER	TOTAL DoD
Direct Hire	382,277	348,297	247,844	95,457	1,073,875
Salaried	279,797	220,386	163,392	83,004	746,479
Wage Board	102,480	127,911	84,552	12,453	327,396
Indirect Hire	58,383	10,464	12,331	1,613	82,791
Total	440,660	358,761	260,175	97,070	1,156,666

Source: '88 Defense Almanac

Table D-15

U.S. MILITARY PERSONNEL IN FOREIGN AREAS[a]
(End-Year—In Thousands)

	FY 1976[b]	FY 1979	FY 1980	FY 1981	FY 1982	FY 1983	FY 1984	FY 1985	FY 1986	FY 1987
Germany	213	239	244	248	256	254	254	247	250	250
Other Europe	61	61	65	64	67	70	73	75	75	73
Europe, Afloat	41	25	22	25	33	18	25	36	32	31
South Korea	39	39	39	38	39	39	41	42	43	45
Japan	45	46	46	46	51	49	46	47	48	50
Other Pacific	27	15	15	15	15	15	16	16	17	18
Pacific, Afloat (including Southeast Asia)	24	22	15	25	33	34	18	20	20	17
Miscellaneous Foreign	8	11	42	39	34	41	38	32	38	40
Total	460	458	489	502	528	520	511	515	523	524

[a] Numbers may not add to totals due to rounding.
[b] September 30 data used for consistency.
Source: Secretary of Defense Annual Report to the Congress, FY 1989

Table D-16

MINORITIES IN UNIFORM
(As of December 1987)

	BLACK AMERICANS		HISPANIC AMERICANS		OTHER*		TOTAL	
	Number	Percent	Number	Percent	Number	Percent	Number	Percent
OFFICERS								
Army	11,080	10.2	1,595	1.5	2,973	2.7	15,648	14.5
Navy	2,508	3.5	1,324	1.8	1,890	2.6	5,722	7.9
Marines	939	4.7	364	1.8	302	1.5	1,605	8.1
Air Force	5,749	5.4	2,160	2.0	2,668	2.5	10,577	9.9
Total DoD	20,276	6.6	5,443	1.8	7,833	2.5	33,552	10.9
ENLISTED								
Army	199,200	27.2	27,131	4.1	26,862	4.0	253,193	38.1
Navy	77,580	15.2	23,932	4.7	28,850	5.6	130,362	25.5
Marines	37,031	20.7	10,140	5.7	5,856	3.3	53,027	29.7
Air Force	85,102	17.2	18,435	3.7	16,705	3.4	120,242	24.3
Total DoD	398,913	21.6	79,638	4.3	78,273	4.2	556,824	30.1

*Includes Native Americans, Alaskan Natives and Pacific Islanders

Source: '88 Defense Almanac

a special medical-pay program designed to enhance retention of medical officers. Congress did repeal an amendment that would have required 25 percent of officer accessions in FY 1989 be medical.

Congress authorized $9.38 billion for Navy and Marine Corps research and development, an increase of $166 million over the $9.22 billion requested, but still $129 million below the FY 1988 authorization. The single largest increase in the R&D budget was $85 million for the Advanced Tactical Fighter; no funds had been requested for this line item in the Navy budget.

Table D-17

EDUCATION
(As of Dec. 31, 1987)

OFFICERS
Below baccalaureate	15,001
Baccalaureate only degree	169,005
Advanced degree	105,353
Unknown	17,976
Total	307,335

ENLISTED
No high school diploma or GED	50,119
High school graduate or GED	1,660,216
Alternate Education Credential	19,292
1-4 years college (no degree)	61,701
Baccalaureate degree	41,660
Advanced degree	3,001
Unknown	12,936
Total	1,848,925

Source: Defense '88 Almanac

Table D-18

MILITARY AND CIVILIAN PERSONNEL STRENGTH[a]
(End Fiscal Years—In Thousands)

	Actuals FY 1976	FY 1980	FY 1981	FY 1982	FY 1983	FY 1984	FY 1985	FY 1986	FY 1987	Programmed FY 1988	FY 1989
Active Component Military											
Army	779	777	781	780	780	780	781	781	781	772	772
Navy	524	517	529	542	558	565	571	581	587	593	593
Marine Corps	192	188	191	192	194	196	198	199	200	197	197
Air Force	585	558	570	583	592	597	602	608	607	576	576
Total	2,081	2,040	2,071	2,097	2,123	2,138	2,151	2,169	2,174	2,138	2,138
Reserve Component Military (Selected Reserve)											
ARNG	362	367	389	408	417	434	440	446	453	457	465
Army Reserve	195	213	232	257	266	275	292	310	319	324	339
Naval Reserve[b]	97	97	98	105	109	121	130	142	149	153	162
MC Reserve	30	36	37	40	43	41	42	42	43	44	45
ANG	91	96	98	101	102	105	109	113	113	116	118
Air Force Reserve	48	60	62	64	67	70	75	79	80	82	86
Total	823	869	917	975	1,005	1,046	1,088	1,130	1,157	1,176	1,213
Direct Hire Civilian											
Army[c]	329	312	318	321	332	344	359	354	357	340	340
Navy	311	298	310	308	328	332	342	332	343	337	329
Air Force[c]	248	231	233	235	238	240	250	250	252	252	250
Defense Agencies	71	75	79	80	81	85	91	92	96	97	97
Total	959	916	940	945	980	1,000	1,043	1,027	1,049	1,027	1,016

[a]Numbers may not add to totals due to rounding.
[b]Navy Training and Administration of Reserves (TARS) personnel are counted in the Selected Reserve from FY 1980 on. Prior to FY 1980, TAR personnel are included in the Active Military.
[c]These totals include Army and Air National Guard technicians, who were converted from State to Federal employees in FY 1979.

Source: Secretary of Defense Annual Report to the Congress, FY 1989

SEA POWER: *NAVY*

The mission of the Navy, as set forth in the U.S. code, is "to be prepared to conduct operations at sea in support of U.S. national interests."

To do this, the Navy, with the strength of 614,336 (as of Sepember 30, 1988), maintains a sea force of 603 ships and a tactical air force of some 1,460 planes, in conjunction with a Marine Corps with a strength of 197,127.

There's much more. The Navy also:
• Directs and maintains the Military Sealift Command, consisting of 120 strategic sealift, fleet auxiliary and special mission ships.
• Administers 47 naval air stations/naval air facilities and 27 naval stations/naval bases throughout the United States.
• Manages through its naval supply system $35 billion worth of equipment and acquires over $11 billion of material and services each year. It also stocks some 2.7 million line items of repair parts and components and fills more than 7.9 million demands from the fleet annually.
• Operates a world-wide "Resale System" consisting of five programs: Navy Exchanges, Commissary Stores, Uniform Shops, Navy Lodges, and Ships' Stores Afloat. The system has about 26,000 employees, most of whom are paid with non-appropriated funds.
• Operates 37 hospitals with over 7,656 beds. Fifty thousand military and civilian medical personnel annually treat over 12 million outpatients and admit more than 250,000 to inpatient care.
• Designs missiles, ships, boats, and aircraft.
• Operates banks, homes, apartments, schools, radio and television stations, shipping ports, and motor pools.
• Builds bridges, hospitals, roads, and airfields.
• Conducts research in mathematics, physics, materials, fluid and solid mechanics, biology, psychology, lasers, chemistry, electronics, ocean sciences and technology, arctic environment, acoustics, geology and geophysics, superconductivity, and atmospheric sciences. The Office of Naval Research manages two laboratories, an ocean research and development activity, an environmental prediction facility, the Naval Institute for Oceanography and one overseas office, as well as numerous research-related field activities.
• Finances and operates eight shipyards, 50 printing plants, two ordnance stations, nine public works centers, 17 research and experimental and test stations and laboratories; and six Poseidon/Trident activities.
• Operates a four-year, degree granting institution, graduating about 1,000 naval officers annually.
• Administers Naval Reserve Officer Training Corps programs at 65 colleges and universities throughout the country. About 1,400 officers are commissioned annually in these programs.
• Operates a postgraduate school conferring a master's and doctoral degrees upon Navy, other service, civilian, and international military students annually.
• Participates in graduate programs in major colleges and universities throughout the United States. These programs lead to the award of additional advanced degrees to Navy officers.
• Operates a professional war college and medical school.
• Sponsors a two-year, associate degree granting program for eligible enlisted personnel in fields related to specific Navy ratings; also, an Enlisted Commissioning Program, which is an undergraduate program that provides enlisted personnel in the Navy or Naval Reserve an opportunity to earn a regular commission in a participating Naval Reserve Officers Training Corps upon completion of degree requirements for a non-technical degree in not more than 30 calendar months, or technical degree in not more than 36 calendar months.
• Administers approximately 4,500 recruiters in the field, six Navy recruiting areas, 41 recruiting districts and approximately 17,000 recruiting facilities located in the 50 states, Puerto Rico, the Virgin Islands, the Republic of the Philippines, Guam, Panama Canal Zone, and Europe.

U.S. Naval Academy

U.S. NAVAL ACADEMY

The U.S. Naval Academy is the undergraduate professional college of the Navy. Founded in 1845, the academy today features beautiful and modern facilities on 322 acres along the Severn River in Annapolis, Md. About 1,200 men and 120 women enter USNA each year; nearly 80 percent of them complete the rigorous four-year program of moral, mental, and physical development, and graduate with commissions in the Navy or Marine Corps.

Degrees and Majors: Midshipmen select one of 18 majors—eight in engineering, six in science and mathematics, and four in the humanities and social science. All must complete a core curriculum designed to give future naval officers a solid foundation in technical areas, the humanities, naval science, physical education, and leadership. Graduates are awarded Bachelor of Science degrees.

Costs: Tuition, room and board costs are borne by the government in return for at least five years' commissioned service by graduates. Midshipmen also are paid $500 a month to cover uniforms, books, equipment and personal needs.

Admission: Candidates must qualify scholastically, medically, and physically; meet general eligibility requirements as to citizenship, age, character and marital status; and obtain a nomination from a member of Congress or other source.

For detailed information, call:
1-800-638-9156 toll-free,
or write
Director of Candidate Guidance
U.S. Naval Academy
Annapolis, Md. 21402

Table N-1
WHERE TO GO FOR NAVY INFORMATION

To get in touch with someone in the Navy	Naval Military Personnel Command (NMPC-05) Department of the Navy Washington, D.C. 20370-5005 (202) 694-5011, 694-3155, 694-9221, 694-7720	
To get in touch in an emergency	Contact closest Red Cross office and give rank and ship or unit address	
Casualty assistance hot line Marine Corps hot line	(703) 694-1787	
For list of naval hospital and dispensaries worldwide	Special Assistant for Public Affairs Naval Medical Command (MEDCOM 00D4) Department of the Navy 2300 E St. N.W. Washington, D.C. 20372-5120 (202) 653-1315	
For assistance from the Navy Relief Society	The local chapter of the Navy Relief Society or The local chapter of the American Red Cross or Headquarters, Navy Relief Society Room 1228 801 N. Randolph St. Arlington, Va. 22203 (202) 696-4904	
For list of all Navy Family Centers worldwide For Navy policy on drugs For Navy physical fitness standards	Naval Military Personnel Command (NMPC-014) Department of the Navy Washington, D.C. 20370-5000 (202) 694-1006	
For information on Navy nutritional standards	Navy Food Service Systems Office Code FS1 Department of the Navy Washington, D.C. 20374-1662 (202) 433-3093	
For addresses and phone numbers of Navy bands	Head, Music and Arts Branch Community Relations Division Office of Information Department of the Navy Washington, D.C. 20350-1200 (202) 697-9344	
To obtain a Navy speaker	Navy Speakers Bureau Office of Information Department of the Navy Washington, D.C. 20350-1200 (202) 697-0333	
For information on the Blue Angels	Community Relations Division Office of Information Department of the Navy Washington, D.C. 20350-1200 (202) 697-7291 or Navy Flight Demonstration Squadron (Blue Angels) Naval Air Station Pensacola, Fla. 32508-7801 (904) 452-2583	
For verification and issuance of medals or unit awards	National Personnel Records Center Navy Reference Branch 9700 Page Blvd. St. Louis, Mo. 63132 (314) 263-7141	
For information on Uniformed Services Health Benefits Program (USHBP) or the Civilian Health and Medical Program of the Uniformed Services (CHAMPUS)	The health benefits counselor at the nearest Navy or Marine Corps command or Commander Naval Medical Command Department of the Navy Washington, D.C. 20372-5120 (202) 653-1127	
For information on Servicemen's Group Life Insurance	Office of Servicemen's Group Life Insurance 213 Washington St. Newark, N.J. 07102 (201) 877-7676	
For change of next of kin or beneficiary if you hold National Service Life Insurance or U.S. Government Life Insurance	The Veterans Administration office that maintains your insurance records	
For miscellaneous Navy retirement assistance	Retired Personnel Support Section Naval Military Personnel Command (NMPC-N643) Department of the Navy Washington, D.C. 20370-5643 (202) 694-3197	
Admission to the U.S. Naval Home	Governor U.S. Naval Home Gulfport, Miss. 39507 (601) 896-3110	
For information on retired pay and allowances, SBP annuities, or arrears of pay Survivors of deceased retirees: whom to notify	Navy Finance Center Retired Pay Department (Code 301) Anthony J. Celebrezze Federal Building Cleveland, Ohio 44199 Toll Free: 1-800-321-1080	
For assistance to survivors of deceased retirees	Casualty Assistance Branch Naval Military Personnel Command (NMPC-642) Department of the Navy Washington, D.C. 20370-5000 (202) 694-2926	
For application for headstone or grave marker	Director Monument Service (#2) Veterans Administration 1425 K St. N.W. Room 617 Washington, D.C. 20420 (202) 275-1480	
Phone numbers of Navy information offices outside Washington, D.C.	Atlanta . . . . (404) 347-2101 Boston . . . . (617) 951-2690 Chicago . . . . (312) 606-0360 Dallas . . . . (214) 767-2553 Los Angeles . . . . (213) 209-7481 New York . . . . (212) 826-4653 San Francisco . . . . (415) 765-9111 Norfolk . . . . (804) 444-4297 San Diego . . . . (619) 235-1984	

Source: Department of the Navy, Office of Information

NAVY AND MARINE BASES IN THE UNITED STATES WITH 500 OR MORE PERMANENT PERSONNEL

ALASKA
NAS ADAK, FPO Seattle 98791-1200

ARIZONA
Commanding Officer, MCAS Yuma 85369

CALIFORNIA
Naval Air Rework Facility, NAS Alameda 94501-5201
NAS Alameda 94501
Marine Corps Logistics Base, Barstow 92311
MCB Camp Pendleton 92055
NH Camp Pendleton 92055-5008
NWC China Lake 93555-6001
NWS Concord 94520-5000
NAS Lemoore 93246-5001
NSY Long Beach 90822-5099
NH, 7500 E. Carson Street, Long Beach 90822
NS Long Beach 90822-5000
NAS Miramar, San Diego 92145-5000
NAS Moffett Field 94035-5000
Naval Postgraduate School, Monterey 93943
NSC Oakland 94625-5000
NH Oakland 94627-5000
NPWC, Box 24003, Oakland 94623
NAS Point Mugu 93042
Pacific Missile Test Center, Point Mugu 93042-5000
Naval Ship Weapon Systems Engineering Station, Port Hueneme 93043-5007
Naval Construction Battalion Center, Port Hueneme 93043
Western Division, Naval Facilities Engineering Command, Box 727, San Bruno 94066-0720
NH San Diego 92134-5000
Fleet Combat Training Center, Pacific, San Diego 92147
Fleet ASW Training Center, Pacific, San Diego 92147
NS San Diego 92136-5000
Recruit Training Command, NTC San Diego 92133-2000
NAS, North Island, San Diego 92135-5112
Naval Air Rework Facility, NAS, North Island, San Diego 92135
Naval Electronic Systems Engineering Center, Box 80337, San Diego 92138
NPWC, NB San Diego 92136-5113
NSC, 937 N. Harbor Drive, San Diego 92132-5044
NTC San Diego 92133-5000
Fleet Training Center, NS San Diego 92136-5035
Naval Ocean Systems Center, San Diego 92152-5000
Service School Command, San Diego 92133-3000
Naval Amphibious Base, Coronado, San Diego 92155
NS, Treasure Island, San Francisco 94130
MCAS, El Toro, Santa Ana 92709
Marine Corps Recruit Depot, San Diego 92140
NWS Seal Beach 90740-5000
MCAS (Helicopter), Tustin 92710-5001
Marine Corps Air-Ground Combat Center, Twentynine Palms 92270
Mare Island NSY, Vallejo 94592
Combat Systems Technical Schools Command, Mare Island, Vallejo 94592-5018

CONNECTICUT
NSB, New London, Box 00, Groton 06349-5000
New London Lab, Naval Underwater Systems Center Detachment, New London 06320
NH Groton 06349-5600
Naval Submarine School, Box 700, Groton 06349-5700
Naval Submarine Support Facility, New London, Groton 06349

DISTRICT OF COLUMBIA
Naval Facilities Engineering Command, Chesapeake Division, Bldg. 212, Washington Navy Yard 20374-2121
Naval Air Systems Command Headquarters 20361-0001
Space and Naval Warfare Systems Command 20363-5100
Naval Sea Systems Command Headquarters 20362-5101
Naval Supply Systems Command Headquarters 20376-5000
Naval Military Personnel Command 20370-5000
OPNAV Support Activity 20350
Naval Research Lab 20375
Naval District Washington, D.C., Washington Navy Yard 20374-2002
Navy Regional Data Automation Center, Washington Navy Yard 20374-1662
Naval Intelligence Support Center, 4301 Suitland Road 20390-5140
Marine Barracks 20390

FLORIDA
NAS Cecil Field 32215-5000
Naval Air Rework Facility, NAS Jacksonville 32212
NH Jacksonville 32214
NAS Jacksonville 32212-5000
NSC Jacksonville 32512
NAS Key West 33040-5000
NS Mayport 32228
NAS, Whiting Field, Milton 32570-5000
NH Orlando 32813-5200
Naval Training Systems Center, Orlando 32813-7100
NTC Orlando 32813-5005
Recruit Training Command, Orlando 32813-6100
Naval Coastal Systems Center, Panama City 32407-5000
Naval Air Rework Facility, Bldg. 604, NAS Pensacola 32508-5300
NH Pensacola 32512
Naval Technical Training Center, Corry Station, Pensacola 32511-5000
Naval Education and Training Program Management Support Activity, Pensacola 32509-5000
NPWC, NAS Pensacola 32508-6500
NAS Pensacola 32508-5000

GEORGIA
Marine Corps Logistics Base, Albany 31704
NSB Kings Bay 31547-5000

HAWAII
Communication Area Master Station, Eastern Pacific, Wahiawa, Oahu 96786
NAS Barbers Point 96862
MCAS Kaneohe Bay 96863
NS Pearl Harbor 96860
Pearl Harbor NSY, Box 400, Pearl Harbor 96860
NSB Pearl Harbor 96860
NPWC Pearl Harbor 96860
NSC, Box 300, Pearl Harbor 96860-5300

IDAHO
Nuclear Power Training Unit, Box 2751, Idaho Falls 83403

ILLINOIS
Service School Command, Bldg. 520, Great Lakes 60088-5400
NAS Glenview 60026-5000
NTC Great Lakes 60088-5000
NPWC, Bldg. 1A, Great Lakes 60088-5600
Recruit Training Command, NTC Great Lakes 60088-5300
NH Great Lakes 60088-5230

INDIANA
Naval Weapons Support Center, Crane 47522-5000
Naval Avionics Center, 6000 East 21st St., Indianapolis 46219-2189

KENTUCKY
Naval Ordnance Station, Louisville 40214

MAINE
NAS Brunswick 04011

MARYLAND
Annapolis Lab, David W. Taylor Ship Research & Development Center Detachment, Annapolis 21402-1198
United States Naval Academy, Annapolis 21402-5000
Naval Medical Command, National Capital Region, Bethesda 20814
David W. Taylor Naval Ship Research & Development Center, Bethesda 20084-5000
Naval Ordnance Station, Indian Head 20640-5000
Naval Air Test Center, Patuxent River 20670-5304
Naval Surface Weapons Center Detachment, White Oak, 10901 New Hampshire Ave., Silver Spring 20903-5000

20 NAVY

MISSISSIPPI
Naval Oceanographic Office, National Space Technology Station Laboratory, Bay St. Louis 39522-5001
Naval Construction Battalion Center, Gulfport 39501-5000
NAS Meridian 39309-5000

MISSOURI
Marine Corps Finance Center, Kansas City 64197

NEVADA
NAS Fallon 89406

NEW HAMPSHIRE
Portsmouth NSY, Portsmouth 03804-5000

NEW JERSEY
NWS, Earle, Colts Neck 07722-5000
Naval Air Engineering Center, Lakehurst 08733-5000
Naval Air Propulsion Center, Box 7176, Trenton 08628-0176

NEW YORK
Nuclear Power Training Unit, Box 300, Ballston Spa 12020

NORTH CAROLINA
NH Camp Lejeune 28542
MCB Camp Lejeune 28542
MCAS Cherry Point 28533
Naval Air Rework Facility, MCAS Cherry Point 28533-5030

OHIO
Navy Finance Center, Anthony J. Celebrezze Federal Building, Cleveland 44199-2055

PENNSYLVANIA
Navy Fleet Material Support Office, Box 2010, Mechanicsburg 17055-0787
Navy Ships Parts Control Center, Box 2020, Mechanicsburg 17055-0788
Naval Ship Systems Engineering Station, NB Philadelphia 19112-5083
NH, 17th & Pattison Ave., Philadelphia 19145
Naval Facilities Engineering Command, Northern Division, Philadelphia 19112
Navy Aviation Supply Office, 700 Robbins Avenue, Philadelphia 19111-5098
NSY Philadelphia 19112
Naval Air Development Center, Warminster 18974-5000

RHODE ISLAND
Naval Education and Training Center, Newport 02841-5000
Naval Underwater Systems Center, Newport 02841-5047
NH Newport 02841

SOUTH CAROLINA
MCAS Beaufort 29902
NH Beaufort 29902
NH Charleston 29408-6900
NWS Charleston 29408
NS Charleston 29408-5000
NSC Charleston 29408-6300
NSY Charleston 29408
Polaris Missile Facility, Atlantic, Charleston 29408-5700
Naval Facilities Engineering Command, Southern Division, Box 10068, Charleston 29411-0068
Marine Corps Recruit Depot, Parris Island 29905

TENNESSEE
Naval Air Technical Training Center, NAS Memphis, Millington 38054-5059
NAS Memphis, Millington 38054-5000
NH Millington 38054

TEXAS
NAS Chase Field, Beeville 78103-5000
NAS Corpus Christi 78419-5000
NAS Kingsville 78363-5000

VIRGINIA
NAS, Oceana, Virginia Beach 23460-5120
Headquarters Battalion, Headquarters US MC, Henderson Hall, Arlington 22214
Naval Facilities Engineering Command Headquarters, 200 Stovall St., Alexandria 22332-2300
Naval Surface Weapons Center, Dahlgren 22448-5000
FTC Norfolk 23511-6285
Naval Amphibious Base, Little Creek, Norfolk 23521
Naval Air Rework Facility, NAS Norfolk 23511-5899
NAS Norfolk 23511
Naval Communication Area Master Station, Atlantic, Norfolk 23511-6898
Naval Facilities Engineering Command, Atlantic Division, Norfolk 23511-6287
NPWC Norfolk 23511-6098
NS Norfolk 23511-6000
NSC Norfolk 23512-5000
NH Portsmouth 23708-5000
Norfolk NSY, Portsmouth 23709-5000
Marine Corps Development and Education Command, Quantico 22134
Marine Corps Air Facility, Quantico 22134
Fleet Combat Training Center, Atlantic, Dam Neck, Virginia Beach 23461-5200
Naval Guided Missiles School, Dam Neck, Virginia Beach 23461-5250
NWS Yorktown 23691-5000

WASHINGTON
Puget Sound NSY, Bremerton 98314-5000
NSC Puget Sound, Bremerton 98314-5100
Naval Undersea Warfare Engineering Station, Keyport 98345-0580
NAS Whidbey Island, Oak Harbor 98278-5000
NSB Bangor, Bremerton 98315-5000
NH Bremerton 98314-5315
Strategic Weapons Facility, Pacific, Bremerton, Silverdale 98315-5500
Trident Refit Facility, Bangor, Bremerton 98315-5300

NAVY AND MARINE OVERSEAS WITH 500 OR MORE PERMANENT PERSONNEL

BERMUDA
U.S. NAS FPO New York 09560

CUBA (Guantanamo Bay)
U.S. NAS, FPO New York 09593
U.S. NS, FPO New York 09593

ICELAND (Keflavik)
U.S. NAS, FPO New York 09571

JAPAN (Iwakuni)
U.S. MCAS, FPO Seattle 98764

MARIANA ISLANDS (Agana, Guam)
U.S. NAS, FPO San Francisco 96637-1200
U.S. NPWC, FPO San Francisco 96630-2937
U.S. Naval Ship Repair Facility, FPO San Francisco 96630-1400
U.S. Naval Communication Area Master Station, WESTPAC, FPO San Francisco 96630-1800

OKINAWA (Kawasaki)
U.S. MCB Camp Smedley D. Butler, FPO Seattle 98773

PUERTO RICO (Roosevelt Roads)
U.S. NS, FPO Miami 34051

REPUBLIC OF THE PHILIPPINES (Subic Bay)
U.S. NAS, FPO San Francisco 96654-1200

SICILY (Sigonella)
U.S. NAS, FPO New York 09523

SPAIN (Rota)
U.S. NS, FPO New York 09540-1000

DIEGO GARCIA
U.S. Navy Support Facility, FPO San Francisco 96685-2000

CHANGES IN SHIP FORCES OF THE U.S. NAVY INVENTORY
1 OCTOBER 1987 THROUGH 30 SEPTEMBER 1988

EFFECTIVE DATE	FLEET	SHIP TYPE	HULL NO.	SHIP NAME	FROM STATUS	TO STATUS
100987		TAOT	1012	MISSION BUENAVENTURA	NOSTAT	RRF
102287	PAC	TAO	0190	ANDREW J HIGGINS	NEWCN	MSC NFAF
102387		TAKR	5077	CAPE LAMBERT	NOSTAT	RRF
102787		TACS	0004	GOPHER STATE	CONV	RRF
113087	LANT	FFG	0021	FLATLEY	ACTIVE	NRF
120187	LANT	TAH	0020	COMFORT	CONV	MSC ROS
120787		TAK	1014	CAPE NOME	NOSTAT	RRF
012388	LANT	CG	0056	SAN JACINTO	NEWCN	ACTIVE
012888	PAC	CV	0063	KITTY HAWK	ACTIVE	ACT/SLEP
013188	PAC	FFG	0027	MAHLON S TISDALE	ACTIVE	NRF
020888		TACS	0005	FLICKERTAIL STATE	CONV	RRF
022688	PAC	SSN	0583	SARGO	ACTIVE	ISNAC
022988		TAK	2033	BUYER	NOSTAT	RRF
022988		TAK	5075	CAPE JOHNSON	NOSTAT	RRF
022988		TAOT	5005	MISSION CAPISTRANO	NOSTAT	RRF
031588		TAK	2039	CAPE GIRARDEAU	NOSTAT	RRF
031588		TAK	5051	CAPE GIBSON	NOSTAT	RRF
033188		TAK	1809	AMERICAN VICTORY	RRF	NOSTAT
033188		TAKR	5078	CAPE LOBOS	NOSTAT	RRF
041288		TACS	0006	CORNHUSKER STATE	CONV	RRF
041588		TAK	5030	SANTA BARBARA	RRF	NOSTAT
042888	LANT	SSN	0588	SCAMP	ACTIVE	ISNAC
042988		TAK	5031	SANTA CLARA	RRF	NOSTAT
051388		TAK	5032	SANTA CRUZ	RRF	NOSTAT
051688	LANT	CV	0062	INDEPENDENCE	ACT/SLEP	ACTIVE
053188		TAK	5033	SANTA ELENA	RRF	NOSTAT
061588		TAK	5034	SANTA ISABEL	RRF	NOSTAT
061888	LANT	SSN	0597	TULLIBEE	ACTIVE	ISNAC
063088		TAK	5035	SANTA LUCIA	RRF	NOSTAT
070988	LANT	SSN	0723	OKLAHOMA CITY	NEWCN	ACTIVE
071388		TAK	5077	CAPE JUBY	NOSTAT	RRF
071588		TAK	1808	HATTIESBURG VICTORY	RRF	NOSTAT
080688	LANT	SSN	0751	SAN JUAN	NEWCN	ACTIVE
081288	PAC	CG	0057	LAKE CHAMPLAIN	NEWCN	ACTIVE
081988	PAC	TAGOS	0013	ADVENTUROUS	NEWCN	MSC NFAF
091288	PAC	TAO	0193	WALTER S DIEHL	NEWCN	MSC NFAF
093088	PAC	TAK	5076	NOBLE STAR	NOSTAT	MSC NFME
093088	PAC	TAKR	0010	MERCURY	MSC NFSL	MSC NFME
093088	LANT	ATF	0159	PAIUTE	ISNAC	ACTIVE
093088	LANT	ATF	0160	PAPAGO	ISNAC	ACTIVE
093088	PAC	FF	1041	BRADLEY	ACTIVE	ISNAC
093088	LANT	FF	1043	EDWARD MCDONNEL	ACTIVE	ISNAC
093088	PAC	FF	1048	SAMPLE	ACTIVE	ISNAC
093088	PAC	FFG	0001	BROOKE	ACTIVE	ISNAC
093088	PAC	FFG	0002	RAMSEY	ACTIVE	ISNAC
093088	PAC	FFG	0003	SCHOFIELD	ACTIVE	ISNAC
093088	LANT	FFG	0004	TALBOT	ACTIVE	ISNAC
093088	LANT	FFG	0005	RICHARD L PAGE	ACTIVE	ISNAC
093088	LANT	FFG	0022	FAHRION	ACTIVE	NRF
093088	LANT	SS	0582	BONEFISH	ACTIVE	ISNAC
093088	PAC	SSN	0579	SWORDFISH	ACTIVE	ISNAC

DEFINITIONS OF THE STATUS ABBREVIATIONS FOLLOW:

ACTIVE	ACTIVE FLEET
CONV	IN CONVERSION
ISNAC	INACTIVE SHIP IN NAVY CUSTODY
LEASE	LEASE
LOAN	LOAN
MSC NFAF	NAVAL FLEET AUXILIARY FORCE
MSC NFME	NAVAL FLEET MOBILITY ENHANCEMENT
MSC NFSL	MSC NUCLEUS FLEET—SEALIFT
MSC NFSS	MSC NUCLEUS FLEET—SCIENTIFIC SUPPORT
MSC ROS	REDUCED OPERATING STATUS
MSC CHLT	MSC CHARTER—LONG TERM
NDRF	RESERVED FOR NAVY—NATIONAL DEFENSE RESERVE FLEET
NEWCN	NEW CONSTRUCTION
NRF	NAVAL RESERVE FORCE
SCRAFT	SERVICE CRAFT
STRIKE	STRIKE FROM NAVAL VESSEL REGISTER
TNDRF	RESERVED FOR MSC—NATIONAL DEFENSE RESERVE FLEET
SLEP	SERVICE LIFE EXTENSION PROGRAM

GLOSSARY

AAW: Antiair Warfare
AAWS: Airborne Adverse Weather Weapons System
ABM: Antiballistic Missile
AC: Active Component
ACCS: Army Command and Control System
ACM: Advanced Cruise Missile
ACMR: Air Combat Maneuvering Range
ACIP: Aviation Career Incentive Pay
Ada: DoD Computer Programming Language
ADATS: Air Defense/Antitank System
ADCAP: Advanced Capability (torpedo)
ADDS: Army Data Distribution System
ADI: Air Defense Initiative
ADP: Automated Data Processing
AE: Assault Echelon
AFV: Armored Family of Vehicles
AGR: Active Guard and Reserve
AID: Agency for International Development
AIDS: Acquired Immuno-Deficiency Syndrome
AIM: Air-Intercept Missile
AIS: Automated Information System
ACLM: Air-Launched Cruise Missile
ALMV: Air-Launched Miniature Vehicle
ALS: Advanced Launch System
AMRAAM: Advanced Medium-Range Air-to-Air Missile
ANG: Air National Guard
ANZUS: Australia-New Zealand-United States (Treaty)
AOCP: Aviation Officer Continuation Pay
AOE: Multipurpose Stores Ship
ASAT: Antisatellite
ASDS: Advanced SCM Delivery System
ASW: Antisubmarine Warfare
ATA: Advanced Tactical Aircraft
ATACMS: Army Tactical Missile System
ATAS: Air-to-Air Stinger
ATARS: Advanced Tactical Air Reconnaissance System
ATB: Advanced Technology Bomber
ATF: Advanced Tactical Fighter
ATM: Antitactical Missile
ATSD (IO): Assistant to the Secretary of Defense (Intelligence Oversight)
AUTOVON: Automatic Voice Network
AWACS: Airborne Warning and Control System

BA: Budget Authority
BAMC: Brooke Army Medical Center
BFV: Bradley Fighting Vehicle
BM/C^3: Battle Management/Command, Control, and Communications
BMEWS: Ballistic Missile Early Warning System
BSTS: Boost Surveillance and Tracking System
BTI: Balanced Technology Initiative

C^3: Command, Control, and Communications
C^{3}CM: Command, Control, and Communications Countermeasures
C^{3}I: Command, Control, Communications, and Intelligence
CBR: Chemical, Biological, Radiological
CDI: Conventional Defense Improvements
CHAMPUS: Civilian Health and Medical Program of the Uniformed Services
CINC: Commander in Chief
COCOM: Coordinating Committee for Multilateral Export Controls
COMSEC: Communications Security
CONUS: Continental United States
CRAF: Civil Reserve Air Fleet
CS: Competitive Strategies
CSI: Competitive Strategies Initiative
CSOC: Consolidated Space Operations Center

CV: Aircraft Carrier
CVN: Aircraft Carrier, Nuclear Powered
CY: Calendar Year or Current Year
DAB: Defense Acquisition Board
DARE: Drug Abuse Resistance Education
DARPA: Defense Advanced Research Projects Agency
DCAA: Defense Contract Audit Agency
DCIMI: Defense Council on Integrity and Management Improvement
DDDR&E(T&E): Deputy Director, Defense Research, Engineering, Test, and Evaluation
DDG: Guided Missile Destroyer
DDN: Defense Data Network
DDS: Dry Deck Shelters
DDT&E: Director, Defense Test and Evaluation
DEPMEDS: Deployable Medical Systems
DEW: Directed-Energy Weapons, Distant Early Warning
DIA: Defense Intelligence Agency
DINET: Defense Industrial Network
DLA: Defense Logistics Agency
DMA: Defense Mapping Agency
DNA: Defense Nuclear Agency
DoD: Department of Defense
DoE: Department of Energy
DOT&E: Director, Operational Test and Evaluation
DPC: Defense Planning Committee
DRB: Defense Resources Board
DRG: Diagnosis Related Group
DSB: Defense Science Board
DSCS: Defense Satellite Communications System
DSN: Defense Switched Network
DST: Defense and Space Talks
DTSA: Defense Technology Security Administration

EC: Electronic Combat
ECI: Employment Cost Index
ECM: Electronic Countermeasures
ELF: Extremely Low Frequency
ELV: Expendable Launch Vehicles
EMP: Electromagnetic Pulse
ENSCE: Enemy Situation Correlation Element
ERIS: Exoatmospheric Reentry Vehicle Interceptor System
ESF: Economic Support Fund
ESM: Electronic Support Measures
EW: Electronic Warfare

FAADS: Forward-Area Air Defense System
FFG: Guided Missile Frigate
FLOT: Forward Line of Troops
FMS: Foreign Military Sales
FMSCR: Foreign Military Sales Credit (Financing)
FOFA: Follow-On Forces Attack
FORSCOM: Forces Command
FY: Fiscal Year
FYDP: Five-Year Defense Program

GAO: General Accounting Office
GLCM: Ground-Launched Cruise Missile
GNP: Gross National Product
GOCO: Government-Owned Contractor Operated
GPS: Global Positioning System
G-R-H: Gramm-Rudman-Hollings
GS: General Schedule
GSTS: Ground-Based Surveillance and Tracking System
GWEN: Ground Wave Emergency Network

HARM: High-Speed Antiradiation Missile
HCS: Helicopter Combat Support Special Squadron
HEDI: High Endo-Atmospheric Defense
HHG: Household Goods

HIV: Human Immuno-deficiency Virus
HNS: Host Nation Support

ICBM: Intercontinental Ballistic Missile
IFF: Identification Friend or Foe
IG: Inspector General
IHPTET: Integrated High Performance Turbine Engine Technology
IIR: Imaging Infrared
IMA: Individual Mobilization Augmentees
IMET: International Military Education and Training
IMC: Internal Management Control
IMIP: Industrial Modernization Incentives Program
INDCONS: Industrial Alert Conditions
INF: Intermediate-Range Nuclear Forces
INFOSEC: Information Security
ING: Inactive National Guard
IR: Infrared
IRR: Individual Ready Reserve
IRS: Internal Revenue Service
IUSS: Integrated Undersea Surveillance System

JCS: Joint Chiefs of Staff
JMMC: Joint Military Medical Command
JSTARS: Joint Surveillance/Target Attack Radar System
JRMB: Joint Requirements and Management Board
JROC: Joint Requirements Oversight Council
JT&E: Joint Test and Evaluation
JTFME: Joint Task Force Middle East
JTIDS: Joint Tactical Information Distribution System

KEW: Kinetic Energy Weapons

LAMP: Land-Air Maritime Patrol
LANTIRN: Low-Altitude Navigation and Targeting Infrared System for Night
LCAC: Landing Craft, Air Cushion
LDCs: Lesser Developed Countries
LEDET: Law Enforcement Detachment
LF: Low Frequency
LHX: Light Helicopter Experimental
LIC: Low-Intensity Conflict
LOS-F-H Line-of-Sight Forward-Heavy
LOS-R: Line-of-Sight Rear
LRAACA: Long-Range Air ASW Capability Aircraft
LRINF: Longer Range Intermediate-Range Nuclear Forces
LVT: Assault Amphibian Vehicle

MAB: Marine Amphibious Brigade
MAD: Mutual Assured Destruction
MAF: Marine Amphibious Force
MAP: Military Assistance Program
MAW: Marine Aircraft Wing
MIDEASTFOR: Middle East Force
MiG: Mikoyan-Gurevich (Soviet aircraft)
MILCON: Military Construction
Milstar: Military Strategic and Tactical Relay System
MIMIC: Microwave/Millimeter Wave Integrated Circuit
MIP: Model Installation Program, Management Improvement Plan
MIRV: Multiple Independently-Targetable Reentry Vehicle
MLRS: Multiple-Launch Rocket System
MMP: Master Mobilization Plan
MOA: Memorandum of Agreement
MOU: Memorandum of Understanding
MPS: Maritime Prepositioning Ship
MPTS: Manpower, Personnel, Training, and Safety
MRT: Miniature Receive Terminal
MRTFB: Major Range Test Facility Base
MSE: Mobile Subscriber Equipment
MYP: Multiyear Procurement
MWR: Morale, Welfare, and Recreation

NASP: National Aerospace Plane
NATO: North Atlantic Treaty Organization
Navstar: Navigation Satellite Timing and Ranging
NCA: National Command Authorities
NCMS: National Center for Manufacturing Sciences
NEACP: National Emergency Airborne Command Post
NFIP: National Foreign Intelligence Program
NLOS: Non-Line-of-Sight System
NMCC: National Military Command Center
NORAD: North American Aerospace Defense Command
NPG: Nuclear Planning Group
NRRCs: Nuclear Risk Reduction Centers
NSA: National Security Agency
NSDD: National Security Decision Directive
NSNF: Nonstrategic Nuclear Forces
NWS: North Warning System

OCONUS: Outside of the Continental United States
O&M: Operation and Maintenance
OJCS: Organization of the Joint Chiefs of Staff
OMB: Office of Management and Budget
OPTEMPO: Operating Tempo
OSD: Office of the Secretary of Defense
OT&E: Operational Test and Evaluation
OTH: Over-the-Horizon
OTH-B Over-the-Horizon Backscatter (radar)

PAVE PAWS: Phased-Array Radars
PBA: Production Base Analyses
PCS: Permanent Change of Station
PECI: Productivity Enhancing Capital Investment
PGM: Precision Guided Munitions
PIF: Productivity Investment Fund
PIOB: President's Intelligence Oversight Board
PKO: Peacekeeping Operations
PLRS: Position, Location, and Reporting System
POL: Petroleum, Oil, and Lubricants
POMCUS: Prepositioning of Materiel Configured to Unit Sets
P&Q: Productivity and Quality Team
PPBS: Planning, Programming, and Budgeting System
PPI: Planned Product Improvements
PRC: People's Republic of China

R&D: Research and Development
RC: Reserve Component
RDT&E: Research, Development, Test, and Evaluation
REFORGER: Return of Forces to Germany
ROK: Republic of Korea
RO/RO: Roll-on/Roll-off
ROTHR: Relocatable Over-the-Horizon Radar
RPV: Remotely Piloted Vehicle
RRF: Ready Reserve Force
RV: Reentry Vehicles

S&T: Science and Technology
SAC: Strategic Air Command
SADARM: Science and Destroy Armor
SALT: Strategic Arms Limitation Treaty, Strategic Arms Limitations Talks
SAM: Surface-to-Air-Missile, Sea Air Mariner
SASC: Senate Armed Services Committee
SATKA: Surveillance, Acquisition, Tracking, and Kill Assessment
SBI: Space-Based Interceptor
SDI: Strategic Defense Initiative
SDIO: Strategic Defense Initiative Organization
SDS: Strategic Defense System
SEAL: Sea-Air-Land
SEMATECH: Semiconductor Manufacturing Technology Institute

SFS: Surface Effect Fast Sealift
SHORAD C²: Short-Range Air Defense Command and Control
SICBM: Small ICBM
SINCGARS: Single-Channel Ground and Airborne System
SINCGARS-V: Single-Channel Ground and Airborne System, VHF
SLBM: Submarine-Launched Ballistic Missile
SLCM: Submarine-Launched Cruise Missile
SLEP: Service Life Extension Program
SLKT: Survivability, Lethality, and Key Technologies
SM: Standard Missile
SLOC: Sea Line of Communications
SNA: Soviet Naval Aviation
SNF: Short-Range Nuclear Forces
SOF: Special Operations Forces
SRAM: Short-Range Attack Missile
SSBM: Ballistic Missile Submarine, Nuclear-Powered
SSGN: Cruise Missile Attack Submarine, Nuclear-Powered
SSN: Attack Submarine, Nuclear-Powered
SSTC: Space Systems Test Capabilities
SSTS: Space-Based Surveillance and Tracking System
START: Strategic Arms Reduction Talks
Su: Sukhoy (aircraft)
SWA: Southwest Asia
SWCM: Special Warfare Craft, Medium
SWS: Special Warfare Systems

T&E: Test and Evaluation
TEC: Test and Evaluation Committee
TACS: Auxiliary Crane Ship
TASM: Tactical Air-to-Surface Missile
TEC: Test and Evaluation Committee
TFW: Tactical Fighter Wing
TGSM: Terminally Guided Submunitions
TIARA: Tactical Intelligence and Related Activities
TLAM: Tomahawk Land Attack Missile
TOA: Total Obligational Authority
TOW: Tube-Launched, Optically Tracked, Wire-Guided (antitank missile)
TRI-TAC Joint Tactical Communications Program
TRSS: Tactical Remote Sensor System

UHF: Ultrahigh Frequency
URI: University Research Initiative
USCENTCOM: United States Central Command
USCINCCENT: United States Commander in Chief, Central Command
USCINCEUR: United States Commander in Chief, Europe
USCINCLANT: United States Commander in Chief, Atlantic Command
USCINCNORAD: United States Commander in Chief, North American Aerospace Defense Command
USCINCPAC: United States Commander in Chief, Pacific Command
USCINCSO: United States Commander in Chief, Southern Command
USCINCSPACE: United States Commander in Chief, Space
USCINCSOC: United States Commander in Chief, Operations Command
USCINCSOUTH: United States Commander in Chief, Southern Command
USCINCTRANS: United States Commander in Chief, Transportation Command
USD (A): Under Secretary of Defense (Acquisition)
USD (P): Under Secretary of Defense (Policy)
USSOCOM: United States Special Operations Command
USSR: Union of Soviet Socialist Republics
USSOUTHCOM: United States Southern Command
USTRANSCOM: United States Transportation Command

VA: Veterans Administration
VE: Value Engineering
VHA: Variable Housing Allowance
VHF: Very High Frequency
VHSIC: Very High Speed Integrated Circuit
VLF: Very Low Frequency
VLS: Vertical Launch System
VLSI: Very Large Scale Integration
V/STOL: Vertical/Short Take-Off and Landing

WARMAPS: Wartime Manpower Planning System
WHNS: Wartime Host Nation Support
WIMS: Worldwide Intratheater Mobility Study
WIS: WWMCCS Information Systems
WWMCCS: Worldwide Military Command and Control System
WTVD: Western Theater of Military Operations (Soviet Term)

NAVY MUSEUMS

CEC/SEABEE Museum
Port Hueneme, CA 93043

Navy/Marine Corps and
Coast Guard Museum of the Pacific
Treasure island, CA 94130

Submarine Force Library and Museum
Groton, CT 06349

Navy Memorial Museum
Washington, D.C. 20374

Naval Aviation Museum
Pensacola, FL 32508

Naval Supply Corps Museum
Athens, GA 30601

Pacific Submarine Museum
Pearl Harbor, HI 96860

Naval Air and Test Evaluation Museum
Patuxent River, MD 20670

Navy Academy Museum
Annapolis, MD 21402

Naval War College Museum
Newport, RI 02840

Hampton Roads Naval Museum
Norfolk, VA 23511

Amphibious Museum
Norfolk, VA 23521

Naval Undersea Warfare Museum
Keyport, WA 98345-0580

MARINE CORPS MUSEUMS

Navy/Marine Corps Museum
Treasure Island, CA 94130

Ranch House Museum
Camp Pendleton, CA 92055

SHIPS/NAVY

The figures listed as the complement for each class of ship represent the average manpower requirements for those ships. However, actual manning may differ from the average requirement, depending on availability of personnel, specific mission requirements, etc.

STRATEGIC FORCES

BALLISTIC MISSILE SUBMARINES (SSBN)

Ohio Class

DISPLACEMENT: 18,700 tons dived.
LENGTH: 560 feet.
BEAM: 42 feet.
SPEED: 20-plus knots.
POWER PLANT: one nuclear reactor, two geared turbines, one shaft, 60,000 shaft horsepower.
ARMAMENT: 24 tubes for Trident missiles, four torpedo tubes.
COMPLEMENT: 155.
BUILDER: General Dynamics' Electric Boat Division.

Benjamin Franklin, Lafayette, and James Madison Classes

DISPLACEMENT: 8,250 tons dived.
LENGTH: 425 feet.
BEAM: 33 feet.
SPEED: 20 knots surfaced; approximately 30 dived.
POWER PLANT: one nuclear reactor, two geared turbines, one shaft, 15,000 shaft horsepower.
ARMAMENT: 16 tubes for Poseidon or Trident missiles, four torpedo tubes.
COMPLEMENT: 143.
BUILDERS: SSBNs 616, 617, 623, 626, 628, 631, 633, 640, 643, 645, 655, 657, 659, General Dynamics' Electric Boat Division; 624, 629, 634, 642, 658, Mare Island Naval Shipyard; 620, 636, Portsmouth Naval Shipyard; 622, 625, 627, 630, 632, 635, 641, 644, 654, 656, Newport News Shipbuilding.

BRIEFING: The Navy's SSBN program represents at one end of the spectrum perhaps the finest example in naval history of industry and government cooperation in the building of a ship, the creation of a weapons system, and the marriage of the two. The original 41-ship fleet, headed by George Washington (SSBN-598), came into being with a minimum of difficulty and has been a most credible deterrent force in the almost 30 years since the first SSBN was commissioned. Only eight years elapsed between the commissioning of George Washington and the last ship in the program, Will Rogers (SSBN-659). At the other end of the spectrum, the early days of the Ohio-class Trident SSBN program were marred by cost overruns, construction delays, protests by opponents of nuclear weapons, and questions about the capabilities of both the submarine and the missile system. However, over the years shipyard performance improved markedly, ship and missile performances were exemplary, and the Navy now regards these ships as "the most effective warships of their kind in the world." Tennessee (SSBN-734) in January became the ninth ship of the class to be commissioned and the first to receive the advanced D-5 Trident missile. Six others are under construction, and it is anticipated that one ship will be funded each year until the current tentative goal of 20 is reached. The original Polaris missiles in the non-Trident submarines were replaced by the more advanced Poseidon missiles, and in 12 of the remaining 27 Poseidon submarines these missiles were in turn replaced by Trident C-3 missiles, the forerunner of the D-5; the latter ultimately will be refitted in the first eight Ohio-class ships. Fourteen of the original Polaris SSBNs have either been withdrawn from service or converted to attack submarines. During 1987 the SSBN force completed 91 deterrent patrols, including 27 by Trident SSBNs.

MICHIGAN (SSBN-727) Ohio Class

ULYSSES S. GRANT (SSBN-631) *James Madison Class*

BENJAMIN FRANKLIN (SSBN-640) *Benjamin Franklin Class*

Ohio Class

SSBN-726 Ohio; Bangor, WA (SE 98799-2093)
SSBN-727 Michigan; Bangor, WA (SE 98799-2096)
SSBN-728 Florida; Bangor, WA (SE 98799-2099)
SSBN-729 Georgia; Bangor, WA (SE 98799-2102)
SSBN-730 Henry M. Jackson; Bangor, WA (SE 98799-2105)
SSBN-731 Alabama; Bangor, WA (SE 98799-2108)
SSBN-732 Alaska; Bangor, WA (SE 98799-2111)
SSBN-733 Nevada; Bangor, WA (SE 98799-2114)

Benjamin Franklin Class

SSBN-640 Benjamin Franklin; Charleston, SC (MI 34091-2057)
SSBN-641 Simon Bolivar; Charleston, SC (MI 34090-2060)
SSBN-642 Kamehameha; Groton, CT (NY 09576-2063)
SSBN-643 George Bancroft; Charleston, SC (MI 34090-2066)
SSBN-644 Lewis and Clark; Charleston, SC (MI 34091-2069)
SSBN-645 James K. Polk; Portsmouth, NH (NY 09582-2072)
SSBN-654 George C. Marshall; Groton, CT (NY 09587-2075)
SSBN-655 Henry L. Stimson; Charleston, SC (MI 34093-2078)
SSBN-656 George Washington Carver; Groton, CT (NY 09566-2081)
SSBN-657 Francis Scott Key; Charleston, SC (MI 34091-2084)
SSBN-658 Mariano G. Vallejo; Charleston, SC (MI 34093-2087)
SSBN-659 Will Rogers; Groton, CT (NY 09586-2090)

Lafayette Class

SSBN-616 Lafayette; Groton, CT (NY 09577-2000)
SSBN-617 Alexander Hamilton; Bremerton, WA (NY 09573-2003)
SSBN-620 John Adams; Charleston, SC (MI 34093-2009)
SSBN-622 James Monroe; Charleston, SC (MI 34092-2012)
SSBN-624 Woodrow Wilson; Charleston, SC (MI 34093-2018)
SSBN-625 Henry Clay; Charleston, SC (MI 34090-2021)
SSBN-626 Daniel Webster; Groton, CT (NY 09591-2024)

ALEXANDER HAMILTON (SSBN-617) *Lafayette Class*

James Madison Class

SSBN-627 James Madison; Charleston, SC (MI 34092-2027)
SSBN-628 Tecumseh; Charleston, SC (MI 34093-2030)
SSBN-629 Daniel Boone; Charleston, SC (MI 34090-2033)
SSBN-630 John C. Calhoun; Charleston, SC (MI 34090-2036)
SSBN-631 Ulysses S. Grant; Groton, CT (NY 09570-2039)
SSBN-632 Von Steuben; Charleston, SC (MI 34093-2042)
SSBN-633 Casimir Pulaski; Charleston, SC (MI 34092-2045)
SSBN-634 Stonewall Jackson; Charleston, SC (MI 34091-2048)
SSBN-635 Sam Rayburn; Charleston, SC (MI 34092-2051)

SURFACE COMBATANTS

NIMITZ (CVN-68) *Nimitz Class*

AIRCRAFT CARRIERS (CVN, CV)

Nimitz Class
DISPLACEMENT: 91,487 tons full load (CVN-71, 96, 358).
LENGTH: 1,040 feet.
BEAM: 134 feet.
FLIGHT DECK WIDTH: 252 feet.
SPEED: 30-plus knots.
POWER PLANT: two nuclear reactors, four geared steam turbines, four shafts, 260,000 shaft horsepower.
AIRCRAFT: 90-plus.
ARMAMENT: Sea Sparrow missiles, Phalanx CIWSs—three on *Nimitz* and *Eisenhower*, four on *Vinson*, four to be installed on later ships of class.
COMPLEMENT: 3,150+ ship's company; 2,480 in air wing.
BUILDER: Newport News Shipbuilding.

Enterprise Class
DISPLACEMENT: 89,600 tons full load.
LENGTH: 1,040 feet.
BEAM: 133 feet.
FLIGHT DECK WIDTH: 252 feet.
SPEED: approximately 35 knots.
POWER PLANT: eight nuclear reactors, four geared steam turbines, four shafts, 280,000 shaft horsepower.
AIRCRAFT: approximately 90.
ARMAMENT: Sea Sparrow missiles, three Phalanx CIWSs.
COMPLEMENT: 3,319 ship's company; 2,480 in air wing.
BUILDER: Newport News Shipbuilding.

John F. Kennedy Class
DISPLACEMENT: 82,000 tons full load.
LENGTH: 1,052 feet.
BEAM: 130 feet.
FLIGHT DECK WIDTH: 252 feet.
SPEED: 30-plus knots.
POWER PLANT: eight boilers, four geared steam turbines, four shafts, 280,000 shaft horsepower.
AIRCRAFT: approximately 85.
ARMAMENT: Sea Sparrow missiles, three Phalanx CIWSs.
COMPLEMENT: 3,045 ship's company; 2,480 in air wing.
BUILDER: Newport News Shipbuilding.

Kitty Hawk Class
DISPLACEMENT: 80,800 tons full load.
LENGTH: 1,046 feet.
BEAM: 130 feet.
FLIGHT DECK WIDTH: 252 feet.
SPEED: 30-plus knots.
POWER PLANT: eight boilers, four geared steam turbines, four shafts, 280,000 shaft horsepower.
AIRCRAFT: approximately 85.
ARMAMENT: Terrier missiles in *Constellation* to be replaced by Sea Sparrow missiles; Sea Sparrow missiles in *Kitty Hawk* and *America*. Three Phalanx CIWSs.
COMPLEMENT: 2,970+ ship's company; 2,480 in air wing.
BUILDERS: CV-63, New York Shipbuilding; 64, New York Naval Shipyard; 66, Newport News Shipbuilding.

ENTERPRISE (CVN-65) *Enterprise Class*

CORAL SEA (CV-43) *Midway Class*

CONSTELLATION (CV-64) *Kitty Hawk Class*

Forrestal Class

DISPLACEMENT: 75,900 to 79,300 tons full load.
LENGTH: 1,063 to 1,086 feet.
BEAM: 129 feet.
FLIGHT DECK WIDTH: 252 feet.
SPEED: 33 knots.
POWER PLANT: eight boilers, with *Forrestal's* plant approximately 50 percent lower in psi (pounds per square inch) than those of other ships in class; four geared steam turbines; four shafts; 260,000 shaft horsepower for *Forrestal*, 280,000 for others.
AIRCRAFT: approximately 90.
ARMAMENT: Sea Sparrow missiles. Three Phalanx CIWSs being installed in each during SLEP overhauls.
COMPLEMENT: 3,019 ship's company; 2,480 in air wing.
BUILDERS: CVs 59, 61, Newport News Shipbuilding; 60, 62, New York Naval Shipyard.

Midway Class

DISPLACEMENT: 62,000 tons full load.
LENGTH: 979 feet.
BEAM: 121 feet.
FLIGHT DECK WIDTH: 238 feet.
SPEED: 30-plus knots.
POWER PLANT: 12 boilers, four geared steam turbines, four shafts, 212,000 shaft horsepower.
AIRCRAFT: approximately 75.
ARMAMENT: Sea Sparrow missiles, three Phalanx CIWSs.
COMPLEMENT: 2,890+ ship's company; 2,239 in air wing.
BUILDER: Newport News Shipbuilding.

BRIEFING: USS Ranger, delivered in 1934, was the first ship designed as an aircraft carrier. However, carriers did not come into their own until World War II, when they became the most important ships in the fleet, particularly in the Pacific. Despite the fact that carrier task forces have been called upon hundreds of times since World War II to serve as the principal manifestation of U.S. strength and response in times of crisis, and acquitted themselves exceptionally well in Korea and Vietnam—although admittedly without the opposition encountered in World War II—carriers still are highly controversial because of their high cost and alleged vulnerability to modern long-range, high-speed, low-altitude missiles. The Navy considers 15 carrier battle groups (CBGs) the mininum it needs to meet the three-ocean defense requirement imposed by the numerous bilateral and multilateral treaties to which the United States is a party. Forrestal was the first carrier designed to operate jet aircraft; Enterprise the first with nuclear propulsion. Although Enterprise clearly demonstrated the inestimable value of nuclear propulsion in ships of this size and kind, two carriers laid down later were built with turbines driven by fossil fuel because the cost of nuclear reactors was deemed too high for the unquestioned operational advantages to compensate. However, all carriers constructed since 1964 have been nuclear powered. Funding for two Nimitz-class ships was approved in the FY 1983 budget; this unusual funding of two carriers in the same budget has permitted more rapid construction and will enable them to join the fleet almost two years earlier than if they had been funded singly. Theodore Roosevelt (CVN-71) commissioned in late 1987, became the 14th deployable carrier. Abraham Lincoln (CVN-72) becomes the 15th deployable carrier this year. George Washington (CVN-73) will replace one of the older carriers in 1991. In 1987 funding was requested—and approved—in the FY 1988 budget for two additional Nimitz-class carriers, and in the debate over the FY 1989 defense budget a proposal by Senator Edward Kennedy (D-Mass.) to require the Navy to retire Coral Sea (CV-43) and Midway (CV-41) before the newly funded carriers were completed was defeated. Initial contracts for construction of these ships were awarded to Newport News Shipbuilding early last year. Meanwhile, carrier battle groups continued to be called upon whenever U.S. interests were threatened in areas where CBGs could respond. When Samuel B. Roberts (FFG-58) struck a mine in a newly laid mine field in the Persian Gulf last spring, the first question asked by newly appointed Secretary of Defense Frank Carlucci was: "Where are the carriers?" Carriers would remain on scene in that troubled area throughout 1988. Carrier aircraft loading will vary according to their sizes and missions, but might well include two fighter squadrons of F-14s, two attack squadrons of F/A-18s or A-7s (until these aircraft are phased out), and one of A-6s; one ASW squadron of SH-3 or SH-60F helicopters, EA-6B electronic-warfare aircraft; KA-6 tankers, and E-2C early-warning and control aircraft.

SARATOGA (CV-60) *Forrestal Class*

Nimitz Class

CVN-68 Nimitz; Bremerton, WA (SF 98780-2820)
CVN-69 Dwight D. Eisenhower; Norfolk, VA (NY 09532-2830)
CVN-70 Carl Vinson; Alameda, CA (SF 96629-2840)
CVN-71 Theodore Roosevelt; Norfolk, VA (NY 09599-2871)

Enterprise Class

CVN-65 Enterprise; Alameda, CA (SF 96636-2810)

John F. Kennedy Class

CV-67 John F. Kennedy; Norfolk, VA (NY 09538-2800)

Kitty Hawk Class

CV-63 Kitty Hawk; Philadelphia, PA (NY 09535-2770) (SLEP)
CV-64 Constellation; San Diego, CA (SF 96635-2780)
CV-66 America; Norfolk, VA (NY 09531-2790)

Forrestal Class

CV-59 Forrestal; Mayport, FL (MI 34080-2730)
CV-60 Saratoga; Portsmouth VA (NY 09543-2740)
CV-61 Ranger; San Diego, CA (SF 96633-2750)
CV-62 Independence; San Diego, CA (SF 96618-2760)

Midway Class

CV-41 Midway; Yokosuka, Japan (SF 96631-2710)
CV-43 Coral Sea; Norfolk, VA (NY 09550-2720)

30 NAVY

BATTLESHIPS (BB)

Iowa Class

DISPLACEMENT: 58,000 tons full load.
LENGTH: 887 feet.
BEAM: 108 feet.
SPEED: 35 knots.
POWER PLANT: eight boilers, four geared turbines, four shafts, 212,000 shaft horsepower.
AIRCRAFT: one LAMPS MkIII helicopter.
ARMAMENT: nine 16-inch guns; 12 five-inch/.38-caliber guns; four Phalanx CIWSs, 20 40mm (in BB-63 only); Tomahawk and Harpoon missiles.
COMPLEMENT: 1,518.
BUILDERS: BBs 61, 63, New York Navy Yard; 62, 64 Philadelphia Navy Yard.

BRIEFING: The four Iowa-class battleships, the second largest battleships ever built (two Japanese BBs were larger) all saw action in World War II and Korea, then were "mothballed." New Jersey was activated for service in Vietnam, but again was decommissioned after less than 18 months in the fleet. All four ships have been completely modernized and provided with Tomahawk, Harpoon, and Phalanx weapons systems, the latest electronics and communications equipment, and accommodations for three helicopters. New Jersey, commissioned 28 December 1982, first was deployed to the Pacific, thence to the Mediterranean, where on 14 December 1983 she fired her 16" guns at other than practice targets for the first time since rejoining the fleet. Targets were gun emplacements in Beirut, Lebanon. Iowa's modernization was expedited so she could be deployed to the Mediterranean as the relief for New Jersey; she was recommissioned 8 April 1964. Missouri was modernized in Long Beach Naval Shipyard and was recommissioned 10 May 1986 in San Francisco, where the Navy hopes ultimately to homeport her. However, there is considerable opposition to that plan, and funding for dredging and pier construction has been blocked. Wisconsin's activation was completed by Ingalls Shipbuilding last fall; she was recommissioned 22 October 1988. Ultimately she will be homeported in Corpus Christi and Iowa in New York when new facilities in those ports are completed. These behemoths can serve as integrated parts of carrier battle groups, spearhead assault forces, or lead their own surface-action groups. Missouri and Iowa SAGs have deployed to the Persian Gulf area since the United States commenced escorting U.S.-flagged Kuwaiti tankers through the Gulf in 1987. The Navy has taken steps to improve upon the quality of projectiles, powder, primer, and powder bags for these ships' 16" guns with the goal of improving upon accuracy and reliability of ammunition. It also has utilized RPVs (remotely piloted vehicles) from their decks; these operations, after early failures during recovery operations, have proven quite successful.

NEW JERSEY (BB-62) *Iowa Class*

Iowa Class

BB-61 Iowa; Norfolk, VA (NY 09546-1100)
BB-62 New Jersey; Long Beach, CA (SF 96688-1110)
BB-63 Missouri; Long Beach, CA (SF 96689-1120)
BB-64 Wisconsin; Norfolk, VA (NY 09552-1130)

IOWA (BB-61) *Iowa Class*

TICONDEROGA (CG-47) *Ticonderoga Class*

CRUISERS (CG, CGN)

Ticonderoga Class

DISPLACEMENT: 9,600 tons full load.
LENGTH: 563 feet.
BEAM: 55 feet.
SPEED: 30-plus knots.
POWER PLANT: four gas turbines, two shafts, 80,000 shaft-horsepower.
AIRCRAFT: two LAMPS MkI helicopters (47, 48), LAMPS MkIII in 49 and later ships.
ARMAMENT: Tomahawk, Harpoon, and Standard missiles, anti-submarine rockets, two five-inch/54-caliber guns, two Phalanx CIWSs.
COMPLEMENT: 358.
BUILDERS: CG 47-50, 52-57, Ingalls Shipbuilding; 51, Bath Iron Works.

Virginia Class

DISPLACEMENT: 11,000 tons full load.
LENGTH: 585 feet.
BEAM: 63 feet.
SPEED: 30-plus knots.
POWER PLANT: two nuclear reactors, two geared turbines, two shafts, 100,000 shaft horsepower.
AIRCRAFT: one helicopter.
ARMAMENT: Tomahawk, Harpoon, and Standard missiles, anti-submarine rockets, two five-inch/54-caliber guns, two triple torpedo tubes two Phalanx CIWSs.
COMPLEMENT: 562.
BUILDER: Newport News Shipbuilding.

California Class

DISPLACEMENT: 10,450 tons full load.
LENGTH: 596 feet.
BEAM: 61 feet.
SPEED: 30-plus knots.
POWER PLANT: two nuclear reactors, two geared turbines, two shafts, 60,000 shaft horsepower.
AIRCRAFT: none.
ARMAMENT: Harpoon and Standard missiles, anti-submarine rockets, two five-inch/54-caliber guns, six triple torpedo tubes, two Phalanx CIWSs.
COMPLEMENT: 595.
BUILDER: Newport News Shipbuilding.

Truxtun Class

DISPLACEMENT: 9,127 tons full load.
LENGTH: 564 feet.
BEAM: 58 feet.
SPEED: 30 knots.
POWER PLANT: two nuclear reactors, two geared turbines, two shafts, 60,000 shaft horsepower.
AIRCRAFT: one helicopter.
ARMAMENT: Harpoon and Standard missiles, anti-submarine rockets, one five-inch/54-caliber gun, four fixed torpedo tubes, two Phalanx CIWSs.
COMPLEMENT: 591.
BUILDER: New York Shipbuilding.

Bainbridge Class

DISPLACEMENT: 8,592 tons full load.
LENGTH: 565 feet.
BEAM: 58 feet.
SPEED: 30 knots.
POWER PLANT: two nuclear reactors, two geared turbines, two shafts, 60,000 shaft horsepower.
AIRCRAFT: none.
ARMAMENT: Harpoon and Standard missiles, anti-submarine rockets, two 20mm guns, two triple torpedo tubes, two Phalanx CIWSs.
COMPLEMENT: 558.
BUILDER: Bethlehem Steel.

Long Beach Class

DISPLACEMENT: 17,525 tons full load.
LENGTH: 721 feet.
BEAM: 73 feet.
SPEED: 30-plus knots.
POWER PLANT: two nuclear reactors, two geared turbines, two shafts, 80,000 shaft horsepower.
AIRCRAFT: deck for utility helicopter.
ARMAMENT: Harpoon and Standard missiles, anti-submarine rockets, two five-inch/38-caliber guns, two triple torpedo tubes, two CIWSs.
COMPLEMENT: 958.
BUILDER: Bethlehem Steel.

SOUTH CAROLINA (CGN-37) *California Class*

Belknap Class

DISPLACEMENT: 7,930 tons full load.
LENGTH: 547 feet.
BEAM: 55 feet.
SPEED: 32.5 knots.
POWER PLANT: two geared turbines, two shafts, 85,000 shaft horsepower.
AIRCRAFT: one LAMPS MkI helicopter.
ARMAMENT: Harpoon and Standard missiles, anti-submarine rockets, two Phalanx CIWSs, one five-inch/54-caliber gun, two triple torpedo tubes.
COMPLEMENT: 479.
BUILDERS: CGs 26-28, 32, 34, Bath Iron Works; 29, 31, Puget Sound Naval Shipyard; 30, San Francisco Naval Shipyard; 33, Todd Shipyards.

Leahy Class

DISPLACEMENT: 7,800 tons full load.
LENGTH: 533 feet.
BEAM: 55 feet.
SPEED: 32.7 knots.
POWER PLANT: four boilers, two geared turbines, two shafts, 85,000 shaft horsepower.
AIRCRAFT: none.
ARMAMENT: Harpoon and Standard missiles, anti-submarine rockets, two Phalanx CIWSs, two triple torpedo tubes.
COMPLEMENT: 423.
BUILDERS: CGs 16-18, Bath Iron Works; 19, 20, New York Shipbuilding; 21, 24, Puget Sound Naval Shipyard; 22, Todd Shipyards; 23, San Francisco Naval Shipyard.

BRIEFING: The Navy's goal of 27 Aegis-equipped cruisers was brought closer to fruition in 1987 by the surprising action of Congress to authorize and fund construction of the last five ships in the current program, while at the same time deleting the Navy's request for funding for three Burke-class destroyers. Congress' action culminated a remarkable reversal of opinion toward these ships, which just six years ago were being derided as top-heavy, gold-plated, and possessed of an ineffective air-defense system. However the superlative performances of Ticonderoga (CG-47) and Yorktown (CG-48) in meeting unusually demanding requirements in the Mediterranean during 1983-86 effectively muted these criticisms. The tragic shootdown of an Iranian commercial aircraft in the Persian Gulf on 3 July 1988 by Vincennes (CG-49) did not negate the fact that the Aegis air-defense system has proven to be remarkably capable; it gives ships of the class and other ships with which they might be operating an unprecedented defensive capability against high-performance aircraft and surface-, air-, and submarine-launched missiles. Its radar enables it to control all friendly aircraft in its operating area and still have the capability for surveillance, detection, and tracking of enemy aircraft and missiles. The Chairman of the Joint Chiefs of Staff observed in his endorsement of the report of the Navy's investigation into the shootdown of the Iranian aircraft that the Aegis system ". . . performed as designed and subsequent analysis indicated that the sensor data collected was accurate." However, he and others recommended the display system of Aegis be improved, and the Navy immediately set forth to carry out those recommendations. The vertical launch system, successfully tested in Bunker Hill (CG-52) in 1986, allowed the Tomahawk cruise missile to be added to its arsenal and those of later ships. Other improvements in capability are planned for ships of this class, including a new SPY-1 radar, which will be installed first aboard Princeton (CG-59), and new computers and displays, which will be installed first aboard Chosin (CG-65). Certain improvements will be backfitted into existing ships of the class. Tomahawk also will be installed in the four ships of the Virginia class, but not in ships of the Belknap and California classes because of weight constraints, nor in the Leahy class, Long Beach, Bainbridge, or Truxtun. All cruisers not receiving Tomahawk will receive extensive radar and missile improvements under the New Threat Upgrade program.

Ticonderoga Class

CG-47 Ticonderoga; Norfolk, VA (NY 09588-1158)
CG-48 Yorktown; Norfolk, VA (NY 09594-1159)
CG-49 Vincennes; San Diego, CA (SF 96682-1169)
CG-50 Valley Forge; San Diego, CA (SF 96682-1170)
CG-51 Thomas S. Gates; Norfolk, VA (NY 09570-1171)
CG-52 Bunker Hill; Yokosuka, Japan (SF 96661-1172)
CG-53 Mobile Bay; Mayport, FL (MI 34092-1173)
CG-54 Antietam; Long Beach, CA (SF 96660-1174)
CG-55 Leyte Gulf; Mayport, FL (MI 35091-1175)
CG-56 San Jacinto; Norfolk, VA (NY 09587-1176)
CG-57 Lake Champlain; San Diego, CA (SF 96671-1177)

Virginia Class

CGN-38 Virginia; Norfolk, VA (NY 09590-1165)
CGN-39 Texas; Alameda, CA (SF 98799-1166)
CGN-40 Mississippi; Norfolk, VA (NY 09578-1167)
CGN-41 Arkansas; Bremerton, WA (SF 96660-1168)

California Class

CGN-36 California; Alameda, CA (SF 96662-1163)
CGN-37 South Carolina; Norfolk, VA (NY 09587-1164)

Truxtun Class

CGN-35 Truxtun; San Diego, CA (SF 96679-1162)

LONG BEACH (CGN-9) *Long Beach Class*

TRUXTUN (CGN-35) *Truxtun Class*

BAINBRIDGE (CGN-25) *Bainbridge Class*

MISSISSIPPI (CGN-40) *Virginia Class*

34 NAVY

BIDDLE (CG-34) *Belknap Class*

Bainbridge Class

CGN-25 Bainbridge; Norfolk, VA (NY 09565-1161)

Long Beach Class

CGN-9 Long Beach; Bremerton, WA (SF 96671-1160)

Belknap Class

CG-26 Belknap; Gaeta, Italy (NY 09565-1149)
CG-27 Josephus Daniels; Norfolk, VA (NY 09567-1150)
CG-28 Wainwright; Charleston SC (MI 34093-1151)
CG-29 Jouett; San Diego, CA (SF 96669-1152)
CG-30 Horne; San Diego, CA (SF 96667-1153)
CG-31 Sterett; Subic Bay, RP (SF 96678-1154)
CG-32 William H. Standley; San Diego, CA (SF 96678-1155)
CG-33 Fox; San Diego, CA (SF 96665-1156)
CG-34 Biddle; Norfolk, VA (NY 09565-1157)

Leahy Class

CG-16 Leahy; Long Beach, CA (SF 96671-1140)
CG-17 Harry E. Yarnell; Norfolk, VA (NY 09594-1141)
CG-18 Worden; Pearl Harbor, HI (SF 96683-1142)
CG-19 Dale; Philadelphia, PA (MI 34090-1143)
CG-20 Richmond K. Turner; Charleston, SC (MI 34093-1144)
CG-21 Gridley; San Diego, CA (SF 96666-1145)
CG-22 England; San Diego, CA (SF 96664-1146)
CG-23 Halsey; San Diego, CA (SF 96667-1147)
CG-24 Reeves; Yokosuka, Japan (SF 96677-1148)

REEVES (CG-24) *Leahy Class*

DESTROYERS (DD, DDG)

Burke Class

DISPLACEMENT: 8,300 tons full load.
LENGTH: 466 feet.
BEAM: 59 feet.
SPEED: 30-plus knots.
POWER PLANT: four gas turbines, two shafts, 50,000 shaft horsepower.
AIRCRAFT: landing platform and handling facilities only.
ARMAMENT: Harpoon, Tomahawk, and Standard missiles, vertical launch ASROC, two vertical launch systems, anti-submarine rockets, two Phalanx CIWS, one 5-inch/54-caliber gun, two triple torpedo tubes.
COMPLEMENT: 303.
BUILDERS: Bath Iron Works, 51, 53; Ingalls Shipbuilding, 52.

Spruance Class

DISPLACEMENT: 7,810 tons full load.
LENGTH: 563 feet.
BEAM: 55 feet.
SPEED: 33 knots.
POWER PLANT: four gas turbines, two shafts, 80,000 shaft horsepower.
AIRCRAFT: one Sea King or two LAMPS MkI helicopters. (LAMPS III helicopters planned.)
ARMAMENT: Harpoon and NATO Sea Sparrow missiles, anti-submarine rockets, two Phalanx CIWS (on almost all ships), two 5-inch/54-caliber guns, two triple torpedo tubes.
COMPLEMENT: 324.
BUILDER: Ingalls Shipbuilding.

Kidd Class

DISPLACEMENT: 8,300 tons full load.
LENGTH: 563 feet.
BEAM: 55 feet.
SPEED: 33 knots.
POWER PLANT: four gas turbines, two shafts, 80,000 shaft horsepower.
AIRCRAFT: two LAMPS I helicopters. (LAMPS III planned.).
ARMAMENT: Harpoon and Standard missiles, anti-submarine rockets, two Phalanx CIWS, two 5-inch/54-caliber guns, two triple torpedo tubes.
COMPLEMENT: 346.
BUILDER: Ingalls Shipbuilding.

Charles F. Adams Class

DISPLACEMENT: 4,500 tons full load.
LENGTH: 437 feet.
BEAM: 47 feet.
SPEED: 30 knots.
POWER PLANT: four boilers, two geared turbines, two shafts, 70,000 shaft horsepower.
AIRCRAFT: none.
ARMAMENT: Harpoon and Standard missiles, anti-submarine rockets, two 5-inch/54-caliber guns, two triple torpedo tubes.
COMPLEMENT: 360.
BUILDERS: DDGs 2, 3, 10, 11, Bath Iron Works; 4-6, 15-17, New York Shipbuilding; 7, 8, 12, 13, Defoe Shipbuilding; 9, 14, 23, 24, Todd Shipyards; 18, 19, Avondale Shipyards; 20-22, Puget Sound Bridge and Dry Dock.

Farragut Class

DISPLACEMENT: approximately 5,800 tons full load.
LENGTH: 512 feet.
BEAM: 52 feet.
SPEED: 33 knots.
POWER PLANT: four boilers, two geared turbines, two shafts, 85,000 shaft horsepower.
AIRCRAFT: none.
ARMAMENT: Harpoon and Standard missiles, anti-submarine rockets, one 5-inch/54 caliber gun, two triple torpedo tubes.
COMPLEMENT: 401.
BUILDERS: DDGs 37-39, Bethlehem Steel; 40, 41, Puget Sound Naval Shipyard; 42, San Francisco Naval Shipyard; 43, 44, Philadelphia Naval Shipyard; 45, 46, Bath Iron Works.

BRIEFING: The Arleigh Burke (DDG-51), first of a new and long-awaited class of guided-missile destroyers, is being built by Bath Iron Works, which in 1985 was awarded the contract for her construction after unusually keen competition for that contract among three shipyards. She is scheduled for completion in February 1991. Two other ships of the class also are under construction, John Paul Jones (DDG-53) by Bath and Barry (DDG-52) by Ingalls Shipbuilding, which was awarded the contract to build that ship after Congress specified that one of the two ships funded in FY 1987 must be built by a second shipyard. The Navy had requested funding for three ships in FY 1988; however, that request was ignored by Congress, which instead funded the last five ships of the Aegis-cruiser program. To meet turn-of-the-century force-level requirements, and to maintain a viable two-shipbuilder industrial base as well as a true competitive environment, the Navy needs authorization and fund-

BURKE (DDG-51) *Burke Class* (Artist Concept)

KIDD (DDG-993) *Kidd Class*

ing for at least five DDG-51s annually. In FY 1989, although DOD held the Navy's initial request to three, Congress provided funding for four in FY 1989 funds and authorized the expenditure of unexpended prior-year funds for a fifth. Meanwhile, Spruance-class destroyers, the first to employ gas turbines as their main propulsion systems, are undergoing modernization in a long-range program, during which they will receive, among other warfighting assets, Lamps III helicopters, Tomahawk missiles, and (for the handful of ships which do not yet have them on board) Phalanx CIWS. In addition, 24 ships of the class will receive the Vertical Launch System (VLS) and Vertical Launch Asroc (VLA). The modernization program, which got underway in 1985, will give the 31 ships of the class the capability of serving as effective ASW platforms well into the 21st century.

Spruance Class

DD-963 Spruance; Mayport, FL (NY 09587-1201)
DD-964 Paul F. Foster; Long Beach, CA (SF 96665-1202)
DD-965 Kinkaid; San Diego, CA (SF 96670-1203)
DD-966 Hewitt; San Diego, CA (SF 96667-1204)
DD-967 Elliot; San Diego, CA (SF 96664-1205)
DD-968 Arthur W. Radford; New Orleans, LA (NY 09586-1206)
DD-969 Peterson; Norfolk, VA (NY 09582-1207)
DD-970 Caron; Norfolk, VA (NY 09566-1208)
DD-971 David R. Ray; Long Beach, CA (SF 96677-1209)
DD-972 Oldendorf; Yokosuka, Japan (SF 96674-1210)
DD-973 John Young; San Diego, CA (SF 96686-1211)
DD-974 Comte de Grasse; Norfolk, VA (NY 09566-1212)
DD-975 O'Brien; San Diego, CA (SF 96674-1213)
DD-976 Merrill; San Diego, CA (SF 96672-1214)
DD-977 Briscoe; Norfolk, VA (NY 09565-1215)
DD-978 Stump; Norfolk, VA (NY 09587-1216)
DD-979 Conolly; Norfolk, VA (NY 09566-1217)
DD-980 Moosbrugger; Charleston, SC (MI 34092-1218)
DD-981 John Hancock; Mayport, FL (MI 34091-1219)

CONYNGHAM (DDG-17) *Charles F. Adams Class*

FARRAGUT (DDG-37) *Farragut Class*

ELLIOT (DD-967) *Spruance Class*

DD-982 Nicholson; Charleston, SC (MI 34092-1220)
DD-983 John Rodgers; Charleston, SC (MI 34092-1221)
DD-984 Leftwich; Pearl Harbor, HI (SF 96671-1222)
DD-985 Cushing; San Diego, CA (SF 96662-1223)
DD-986 Harry W. Hill; San Diego, CA (SF 96667-1224)
DD-987 O'Bannon; Charleston, SC (MI 34092-1225)
DD-988 Thorn; Charleston, SC (MI 34093-1226)
DD-989 Deyo; Charleston, SC (MI 34090-1227)
DD-990 Ingersoll; Pearl Harbor, HI; (SF 96668-1228)
DD-991 Fife; San Diego, CA (SF 96665-1229)
DD-992 Fletcher; San Diego, CA (SF 96665-1230)
DD-997 Hayler; Norfolk, VA (NY 09573-1231)

Kidd Class

DDG-993 Kidd; Norfolk, VA (NY 09576-1265)
DDG-994 Callaghan; San Diego, CA (SF 96662-1266)
DDG-995 Scott; Norfolk, VA (NY 09587-1267)
DDG-996 Chandler; San Diego, CA (SF 96662-1268)

BUCHANAN (DDG-14) *Charles F. Adams Class*

Charles F. Adams

DDG-2 Charles F. Adams; Mayport, FL (MI 34090-1232)
DDG-3 John King; Norfolk, VA (NY 09595-1233)
DDG-4 Lawrence; Norfolk, VA (NY 09577-1234)
DDG-5 Claude V. Ricketts; Norfolk, VA (NY 09586-1235)
DDG-6 Barney; Norfolk, VA (NY 09565-1236)
DDG-7 Henry B. Wilson; San Diego, CA (SF 96683-1237)
DDG-8 Lynde McCormick; San Diego, CA (SF 96672-1238)
DDG-9 Towers; Yokosuka, Japan (SF 96679-1239)
DDG-10 Sampson; Mayport, FL (MI 34093-1240)
DDG-11 Sellers; Charleston, SC (MI 34093-1241)
DDG-12 Robison; San Diego, CA (SF 96677-1242)
DDG-13 Hoel; San Diego, CA (SF 96667-1243)
DDG-14 Buchanan; San Diego, CA (SF 96661-1244)
DDG-15 Berkeley; San Diego, CA (SF 96661-1245)
DDG-16 Joseph Strauss; Pearl Harbor, HI (SF 96678-1246)
DDG-17 Conyngham; Norfolk, VA (NY 09566-1247)
DDG-18 Semmes; Charleston, SC (MI 34093-1248)
DDG-19 Tattnall; Mayport, FL (MI 34093-1249)
DDG-20 Goldsborough; Pearl Harbor, HI (SF 96666-1250)
DDG-21 Cockrane; Yokosuka, Japan (SF 96662-1251)
DDG-22 Benjamin Stoddert; Pearl Harbor, HI (SF 96678-1252)
DDG-23 Richard E. Byrd; Norfolk, VA (NY 09565-1253)
DDG-24 Waddell; San Diego, CA (SF 96683-1254)

Farragut Class

DDG-37 Farragut; Norfolk, VA (NY 09569-1255)
DDG-38 Luce; Mayport, FL (MI 34091-1256)
DDG-39 MacDonough; Charleston, SC (MI 34092-1257)
DDG-40 Coontz; Norfolk, VA (NY 09566-1258)
DDG-41 King; Norfolk, VA (NY 09576-1259)
DDG-42 Mahan; Charleston, SC (MI 34092-1260)
DDG-43 Dahlgren; Norfolk, VA (NY 09567-1261)
DDG-44 William V. Pratt; Charleston, SC (MI 34092-1262)
DDG-45 Dewey; Charleston, SC (MI 34090-1263)
DDG-46 Preble; Norfolk, VA (NY 09582-1264)

FRIGATES (FFG, FF)

Oliver Hazard Perry Class
DISPLACEMENT: 3,585 tons full load.
LENGTH: 445 feet.
BEAM: 45 feet.
SPEED: 29 knots.
POWER PLANT: two gas turbines, one shaft, 41,000 shaft horsepower.
AIRCRAFT: two LAMPS MkI helicopters (33 ships will have MkIII capability).
ARMAMENT: Harpoon and Standard missiles, one 76mm/62-caliber gun, one Phalanx CIWS.
COMPLEMENT: 206.
BUILDERS: FFGs 7, 8, 11, 13, 15, 16, 21, 24, 26, 29, 32, 34, 36, 39, 42, 45, 47, 49, 50, 53, 55, 56, 58, 59, Bath Iron Works; 10, 20, 22, 28, 31, 37, 40, 48, 52, Todd Shipyards, Seattle; 9, 12, 14, 19, 23, 25, 27, 30, 33, 38, 41, 43, 46, 51, 54, 57, 60, 61, Todd Shipyards, San Pedro.

Brooke Class
DISPLACEMENT: 3,426 tons full load.
LENGTH: 414 feet.
BEAM: 44 feet.
SPEED: 27.2 knots.
POWER PLANT: two boilers, two geared turbines, one shaft, 35,000 shaft horsepower.
AIRCRAFT: one LAMPS Mk1 helicopter.
ARMAMENT: Tartar and Standard missiles, anti-submarine rockets, one 5-inch/38-caliber gun, two triple torpedo tubes.
COMPLEMENT: 277.
BUILDER: FFG 6, Bath Iron Works.

Glover Class
DISPLACEMENT: 3,426 tons full load.
LENGTH: 414 feet.
BEAM: 44 feet.
SPEED: 27 knots.
POWER PLANT: two boilers, two geared turbines, one shaft, 35,000 shaft horsepower.
AIRCRAFT: one LAMPS MkI helicopter to be installed.
ARMAMENT: anti-submarine rockets, one 5-inch/38-caliber gun, two triple torpedo tubes.
COMPLEMENT: 280.
BUILDER: Bath Iron Works.

Knox Class
DISPLACEMENT: 3,877 tons full load FFs 1052-1077, 4,200 tons full load, remainder of class.
LENGTH: 438 feet.
BEAM: 47 feet.
SPEED: 27 knots.
POWER PLANT: two boilers, two geared turbines, one shaft, 35,000 horsepower.
AIRCRAFT: one LAMPS MkI helicopter.
ARMAMENT: Harpoon missiles, Sea Sparrow missiles, anti-submarine rockets, one 5-inch/54-caliber gun, four fixed torpedo tubes, one Phalanx CIWS being installed on all ships of the class.
COMPLEMENT: 288.
BUILDERS: FF 1052-1054, 1062, 1064, 1066, 1070, Todd, Seattle; 1055, 1058, 1060, 1067, 1071, 1074, 1076, Todd, San Pedro; 1057, 1063, 1065, 1069, 1073, Lockheed, Seattle; 1056, 1059, 1061, 1068, 1072, 1075, 1077-1097, Avondale Shipyards.

Garcia Class
DISPLACEMENT: 3,403 tons full load.
LENGTH: 414 feet.
BEAM: 44 feet.
SPEED: 27.5 knots.
POWER PLANT: two boilers, two geared turbines, one shaft, 35,000 shaft horsepower.
AIRCRAFT: one LAMPS MkI helicopter.
ARMAMENT: anti-submarine rockets, two five-inch/38-caliber guns, two triple torpedo tubes.
COMPLEMENT: 270.
BUILDERS: 1040, Bethlehem Steel, San Francisco; 1044, Avondale Shipyards; 1047, 1049, Defoe Shipbuilding; 1050, Lockheed Shipbuilding.

Bronstein Class
DISPLACEMENT: 2,650 tons full load.
LENGTH: 371 feet.
BEAM: 40 feet.
SPEED: 26 knots.
POWER PLANT: two boilers, two geared turbines, one shaft, 20,000 shaft horsepower.
AIRCRAFT: none.
ARMAMENT: anti-submarine rockets, two 3-inch/50-caliber guns, two triple torpedo tubes.
COMPLEMENT: 286.
BUILDER: Avondale Shipyards.

RENTZ (FFG-46) *Oliver Hazard Perry Class*

BRIEFING: The number of Navy frigates topped 100 before fiscal constraints necessitated the decommissioning of 16 ships of the Brooke and Garcia classes; ten of these ships were decommissioned in 1988, and the remainder will follow this year. Two other frigates sustained severe damage in the Persian Gulf in 1987 and 1988, Stark *(FFG-31) having been hit and set afire by two Exocet missiles fired by an Iraqi aircraft in May 1987 and* Samuel B. Roberts *(FFG-58) striking an Iranian mine in April 1988. The Navy's investigation into the extent of damage suffered by* Stark *pointed to many of the limitations resulting from building this class of ship on a "design to cost" basis. Although* Stark *did survive, the absence of certain materials and equipment that would have helped prevent the rapid spread of fire, and the presence of others of lesser quality, made it more difficult to cope with the blaze that cost the lives of 37 and decimated portions of the ship. The failure to install these materials and equipment during construction or during subsequent overhauls resulted from initial financial constraints and the high cost of extensive refitting after construction.* Samuel B. Roberts, *which was almost broken in half by the force of the explosion of the mine which she hit, was prevented from going to the bottom only by a magnificent application of damage-measures by an exceptionally well trained crew inspired by a commanding officer who refused to give up his ship even though it appeared she could sink at any time. Astonishingly, no lives were lost as the result of the explosion. Repairs to* Stark *were completed last August;* Samuel B. Roberts *still is under repair. Both ships will fight again. Congress has directed the Navy to modernize frigates of the Knox class, but the extent of the modernization measures is not known precisely. As of now, there are no plans for construction of another class of frigate.*

KOELSCH (FF-1049) *Garcia Class*

BRONSTEIN (FF-1037) *Bronstein Class*

Oliver Hazard Perry Class

FFG-8 McInerney; Mayport, FL (MI 34092-1466)
FFG-24 Jack Williams; Mayport, FL (MI 34093-1480)
FFG-25 Copeland; San Diego, CA (SF 96662-1481)
FFG-26 Gallery; Mayport, FL (MI 34091-1482)
FFG-28 Boone; New Orleans, LA (MI 34093-1484)
FFG-29 Stephen W. Groves; Mayport, FL (MI 34091-1485)
FFG-30 Reid; San Diego, CA (SF 96677-1486)
FFG-31 Stark; Mayport, FL (MI 34093-1487)
FFG-32 John L. Hall; Mayport, FL (MI 34091-1488)
FFG-33 Jarrett; Long Beach, CA (SF 96669-1489)
FFG-34 Aubrey Fitch; Mayport, FL (MI 34091-1490)
FFG-36 Underwood; Mayport, FL (MI 34093-1491)
FFG-37 Crommelin; Long Beach, CA (SF 96662-1492)
FFG-38 Curts; Long Beach, CA (SF 96662-1493)
FFG-39 Doyle; Mayport, FL (MI 34090-1494)
FFG-40 Halyburton; Charleston, SC (MI 34091-1495)
FFG-41 McClusky; San Diego, CA (SF 96672-1496)
FFG-42 Klakring; Charleston, SC (MI 34091-1497)
FFG-43 Thach; San Diego, CA (SF 96679-1498)
FFG-45 Dewert; Charleston, SC (MI 34090-1499)
FFG-46 Rentz; San Diego, CA (SF 96677-1500)
FFG-47 Nicholas; Charleston, SC (MI 34092-1501)
FFG-48 Vandergrift; Long Beach, CA (SF 96682-1502)
FFG-49 Robert G. Bradley; Charleston, SC (MI 34090-1503)
FFG-50 Taylor; Charleston, SC (MI 34093-1504)
FFG-51 Gary; Long Beach, CA (SF 96666-1505)
FFG-52 Carr; Charleston, SC (MI 34090-1506)
FFG-53 Hawes; Charleston, SC (MI 34091-1507)
FFG-54 Ford; Long Beach, CA (SF 96665-1508)
FFG-55 Elrod; Charleston, SC (MI 34091-1509)
FFG-56 Simpson; Newport, RI (NY 09587-1570)
FFG-57 Reuben James; Long Beach, CA (SF 96669-1511)
FFG-58 Samuel B. Roberts; Newport RI (NY 09586-1512)
FFG-59 Kauffman; Newport, RI (NY 09569-1513)
FFG-60 Rodney M. Davis; Long Beach, CA (SF 96663-1514)

Brooke Class

FFG-6 Julius A. Furer; Philadelphia, PA (MI 34091-1464)

STEIN (FF-1065) *Knox Class*

Glover

FF-1098 Glover; Norfolk, VA (NY 09570-1458)

Knox Class

FF-1052 Knox; Long Beach, CA (96670-1412)
FF-1055 Hepburn; San Diego, CA (SF 96667-1415)
FF-1056 Connole; Newport, RI (NY 09566-1416)
FF-1057 Rathburne; Pearl Harbor, HI (SF 96677-1417)
FF-1058 Meyerkord; San Diego, CA (SF 96672-1418)
FF-1059 W.S. Sims; Mayport, FL (MI 34093-1419)
FF-1062 Whipple; Pearl Harbor, HI (SF 96683-1422)
FF-1063 Reasoner; San Diego, CA (SF 96677-1423)
FF-1064 Lockwood; Long Beach, CA (SF 96671-1424)

FF-1065 Stein; San Diego, CA (SF 96678-1425)
FF-1066 Marvin Shields; San Diego, CA (SF 96678-1426)
FF-1067 Francis Hammond; Yokosuka, Japan (SF 96667-1427)
FF-1068 Vreeland; Mayport, FL (MI 34093-1428)
FF-1069 Bagley; San Diego, CA (SF 96661-1429)
FF-1070 Downes; San Diego, CA (SF 96663-1430)
FF-1071 Badger; Pearl Harbor, HI (SF 96661-1431)
FF-1073 Robert E. Peary; Pearl Harbor, HI (SF 96675-1433)
FF-1074 Harold E. Holt; Pearl Harbor, HI (SF 96667-1434)
FF-1075 Trippe; Boston, MA (MI 34093-1435)
FF-1076 Fanning; San Diego, CA (SF 96665-1436)
FF-1077 Oullet; Pearl Harbor, HI (SF 96674-1437)
FF-1078 Joseph Hewes; Charleston, SC (MI 34091-1438)
FF-1079 Bowen; Charleston, SC (MI 34090-1439)
FF-1080 Paul; Mayport, FL (MI 34092-1440)
FF-1081 Aylwin; Charleston, SC (MI 34090-1441)
FF-1082 Elmer Montgomery; Mayport, FL (MI 34092-1442)
FF-1083 Cook; San Diego, CA (SF 96662-1443)
FF-1084 McCandless; Norfolk, VA (NY 09578-1444)
FF-1085 Donald B. Beary; Norfolk, VA (NY 09565-1445)
FF-1086 Brewton; Pearl Harbor, HI (SF 96661-1446)
FF-1087 Kirk; Long Beach, CA (SF 96670-1447
FF-1088 Barbey; San Diego, CA (SF 96661-1448)
FF-1089 Jesse L. Brown; Charleston, SC (MI 34090-1449)
FF-1090 Ainsworth; Norfolk, VA (NY 09564-1450)
FF-1092 Thomas C. Hart; Norfolk, VA (NY 09573-1452)
FF-1093 Capodanno; Newport, RI (NY 09566-1453)
FF-1094 Pharris; Norfolk, VA (NY 09582-1454)
FF-1095 Truett; Norfolk, VA (NY 09588-1455)
FF-1097 Moinester; Norfolk, VA (NY 09578-1457)

Garcia Class

FF-1040 Garcia; Philadelphia, PA (MI 34091-1402)
FF-1044 Brumby; Portland, ME (MI 34090-1405)
FF-1047 Voge; Mayport, FL (MI 34093-1407)
FF-1049 Koelsch; Mayport, FL (MI 34091-1409)
FF-1050 Albert David; San Diego, CA (SF 96663-1410)

Bronstein Class

FF-1037 Bronstein; San Diego, CA (SF 96661-1400)
FF-1038 McCloy; Norfolk, VA (NY 09578-1401)

FORD (FFG-54) *Oliver Hazard Perry Class*

SALT LAKE CITY (SSN-716) *Los Angeles Class*

ATTACK SUBMARINES (SSN, SS)

Los Angeles Class

DISPLACEMENT: 6,900 tons dived.
LENGTH: 360 feet.
BEAM: 33 feet.
SPEED: 30-plus knots dived.
POWER PLANT: one nuclear reactor, two geared turbines, one shaft, approximately 35,000 shaft horsepower.
ARMAMENT: Harpoon and Tomahawk missiles, SUBROC (688-699), Mk48 torpedoes, four torpedo tubes, VLS.
COMPLEMENT: 143.
BUILDERS: SSNs 688, 689, 691, 693, 695, 711-718, 721-723, 750, Newport News Shipbuilding; 690, 692, 694, 696-710, 719-720, 724, 725, 751-752, General Dynamics' Electric Boat Division.

Narwhal Class

DISPLACEMENT: 5,350 tons dived.
LENGTH: 314 feet.
BEAM: 38 feet.
SPEED: 30-plus knots dived.
POWER PLANT: one nuclear reactor, two steam turbines, one shaft, 17,000 shaft horsepower.
ARMAMENT: Torpedoes, four torpedo tubes; Harpoon; Tomahawk missiles to be fitted.
COMPLEMENT: 129.
BUILDER: General Dynamics' Electric Boat Division.

Glenard P. Lipscomb Class

DISPLACEMENT: 6,480 tons dived.
LENGTH: 365 feet.
BEAM: 32 feet.
SPEED: 25-plus knots dived.
POWER PLANT: one nuclear reactor, turbine-electric drive, one shaft.
ARMAMENT: SUBROC, torpedoes, four torpedo tubes; Harpoon; Tomahawk missiles to be fitted.
COMPLEMENT: 129.
BUILDER: General Dynamics' Electric Boat Division.

Ethan Allen Class

DISPLACEMENT: 7,880 tons dived.
LENGTH: 410 feet.
BEAM: 33 feet.
SPEED: 30 knots dived.
POWER PLANT: one nuclear reactor, two geared turbines, one shaft, 15,000 shaft horsepower.
ARMAMENT: torpedoes, four torpedo tubes (16 missile tubes used in earlier SSBN role now plugged).
COMPLEMENT: 132.
BUILDER: Newport News Shipbuilding.

Sturgeon Class

DISPLACEMENT: 4,640 tons dived.
LENGTH: 292 feet.
BEAM: 32 feet.
SPEED: 30-plus knots dived.
POWER PLANT: one nuclear reactor, two steam turbines, one shaft, 15,000 shaft horsepower.
ARMAMENT: Harpoon, SUBROC, torpedoes, four torpedo tubes; Tomahawk missiles to be fitted.
COMPLEMENT: 129.
BUILDERS: SSNs 637, 650, 667, 669, 673-676, 678, 679, 681, 684, General Dynamics' Electric Boat Division; 638, 649, General Dynamics' Quincy Shipbuilding Division; 639, 647, 648, 652, 680, 682, 683, Ingalls Shipbuilding; 646, 660, Portsmouth Naval Shipyard; 662, 665, 666, 672, 677, San Francisco Naval Shipyard; 651, 653, 661, 663, 664, 668, 670, 686, 687, Newport News Shipbuilding.

Skate Class

DISPLACEMENT: approximately 2,500 tons full load.
LENGTH: 268 feet.
BEAM: 25 feet.
SPEED: 25-plus knots dived.
POWER PLANT: one nuclear reactor, two steam turbines, two shafts, 6,600 shaft horsepower.
ARMAMENT: torpedoes, eight torpedo tubes.
COMPLEMENT: 122.
BUILDERS: SSN-578, General Dynamics' Electric Boat Division; 579, 584, Portsmouth Naval Shipyard.

Skipjack Class

DISPLACEMENT: 3,513 tons dived.
LENGTH: 252 feet.
BEAM: 31 feet.
SPEED: 30-plus knots dived.
POWER PLANT: one nuclear reactor, two steam turbines, one shaft, 15,000 shaft horsepower.
ARMAMENT: torpedoes, six torpedo tubes.
COMPLEMENT: 118.
BUILDERS: SSN-585, General Dynamics' Electric Boat Division; 590, 592, Ingalls Shipbuilding; 591, Newport News Shipbuilding.

Permit Class

DISPLACEMENT: approximately 4,200 tons dived.
LENGTH: SSN-605, 297 feet; 613-615, 292 feet; others, 278 feet.
BEAM: 32 feet.
SPEED: 30-plus knots dived.
POWER PLANT: one nuclear reactor, two steam turbines, one shaft, 15,000 shaft horsepower.
ARMAMENT: SUBROC, torpedoes, four torpedo tubes; Harpoon missiles being fitted.
COMPLEMENT: 127.
BUILDERS: SSNs 594, 595, Mare Island Naval Shipyard; 596, 607, 621, Ingalls Shipbuilding; 603, 604, 612, New York Shipbuilding; 605, 606, Portsmouth Naval Shipyard; 613-615, General Dynamics' Electric Boat Division.

BRIEFING: Submarine warfare was revolutionized by the marriage of nuclear power and the submarine; it created what was viewed by most naval experts as the true submersible. That spectacular step forward in ship construction and propulsion was embodied first in Nautilus (SSN-571), the world's first nuclear-powered vessel. Her message on 17 January 1955, "Underway on nuclear power," was a milestone in naval history. The Navy initially experimented with two types of nuclear reactors—one cooled by liquid sodium, the other by pressurized water—before scuttling that cooled by liquid sodium. It also experimented with different sizes and shapes of hulls and with varying kinds of weapons and electronics systems. Permit-class SSNs, laid down in the early 1960s, were the first to be built in sizeable numbers; 13 remain in commission. The Sturgeon and Los Angeles classes, the latter still building, also were authorized and funded in large numbers. Even so, the U.S. Navy's undersea fleet is far smaller than that of the Soviet Union, which not only has a much greater capability for building nuclear-powered submarines, but has made maximum use of it. Nautilus predated the first Soviet SSN by five years, but the United States failed to maintain that early lead. Still, U.S. nuclear-powered submarines are considered the world's most advanced technologically, although the Soviets have made tremendous strides in this respect, particularly in the areas of hull strength, speed, and, most importantly, quieting. The Navy is seeking a total force of 66 Los Angeles-class submarines, of which 41 have been delivered. The improved SSN-688 class is, the Navy claims, twice as capable as early ships of the class. These ships have vertical launch systems, increased firepower, and major improvements in quieting and in combat systems. A new class of SSN, the first of which will be named Seawolf, will replace the Los Angeles class. The first funding for development was contained in the FY 1985 budget; initial funding for construction is contained in the FY 1989 budget. Despite problems with the development of its sophisticated combat system, SSN 21 development now appears to be on schedule with regard to design and construction objectives. In the 18 years between the commissioning of Los Angeles in 1976 and the anticipated completion of Seawolf, the Soviet Union will have put to sea at least 14 different classes of nuclear-powered submarines. The Navy also has three diesel-powered submarines in commission, all of which are more than 25 years old.

FINBACK (SSN-670) *Sturgeon Class*

SKIPJACK (SSN-585) *Skipjack Class*

Los Angeles Class

SSN-688 Los Angeles; Pearl Harbor, HI (SF 96671-2368)
SSN-689 Baton Rouge; Norfolk, VA (NY 09565-2369)
SSN-690 Philadelphia; Groton, CT (NY 09582-2370)
SSN-691 Memphis; Norfolk, VA (NY 09578-2371)
SSN-692 Omaha; Pearl Harbor, HI (SF 96674-2372)
SSN-693 Cincinnati; Norfolk, VA (NY 09566-2373)
SSN-694 Groton; Groton, CT (NY 09570-2374)
SSN-695 Birmingham; Pearl Harbor, HI (SF 96661-2375)
SSN-696 New York City; Pearl Harbor, HI (SF 96673-2376)
SSN-697 Indianapolis; Pearl Harbor, HI (SF 96668-2377)
SSN-698 Bremerton; Pearl Harbor, HI (SF 96661-2378)
SSN-699 Jacksonville; Norfolk, VA (NY 09575-2379)
SSN-700 Dallas; Groton, CT (NY 09567-2380)
SSN-701 La Jolla; San Diego, CA (SF 96671-2381)
SSN-702 Phoenix; Norfolk, VA (NY 09582-2382)
SSN-703 Boston; Groton, CT (NY 09565-2383)
SSN-704 Baltimore; Norfolk, VA (NY 09565-2384)
SSN-705 City of Corpus Christi; Groton, CT (NY 09566-2385)
SSN-706 Albuquerque; Groton, CT (NY 09564-2386)
SSN-707 Portsmouth; San Diego, CA (SF 96675-2387)
SSN-708 Minneapolis-Saint Paul; Norfolk, VA (NY 09578-2388)
SSN-709 Hyman G. Rickover; Norfolk, VA (NY 09586-2389)
SSN-710 Augusta; Groton, CT (NY 09564-2390)
SSN-711 San Francisco; Pearl Harbor, HI (SF 96678-2391)
SSN-712 Atlanta; Norfolk, VA (NY 09564-2392)
SSN-713 Houston; San Diego, CA (SF 96667-2393)
SSN-714 Norfolk; ; Norfolk, VA (NY 09579-2394)
SSN-715 Buffalo; Pearl Harbor, HI (SF 96661-2395)
SSN-716 Salt Lake City; San Diego, CA (SF 96678-2396)
SSN-717 Olympia; Pearl Harbor, HI (SF 96674-2397)
SSN-718 Honolulu; Pearl Harbor, HI (SF 96667-2398)
SSN-719 Providence; Groton, CT (NY 09582-2399)
SSN-720 Pittsburgh; Groton, CT (NY 09582-2400)
SSN-721 Chicago; Norfolk, VA (NY 09566-2401)
SSN-722 Key West; Norfolk, VA (NY 09576-2402)
SSN-723 Oklahoma City; Norfolk, VA (09581-2403)
SSN-724 Louisville; San Diego, CA (SF 96671-2404)
SSN-724 Helena; Pearl Harbor, HI (SF 95667-2405)
SSN-751 San Juan; Groton, CT (NY 09587-2407)

Ethan Allen Class

SSN-609 Sam Houston; Pearl Harbor, HI (SF 96667-2321)
SSN-611 John Marshall; Norfolk, VA (NY 09578-2322)

Sturgeon Class

SSN-637 Sturgeon; Charleston, SC (MI 34093-2329)
SSN-638 Whale; Groton, CT (NY 09501-2330)
SSN-639 Tautog; Bremerton, WA (SF 96679-2331)
SSN-646 Grayling; Vallejo, CA (MI 34091-2332)
SSN-647 Pogy; San Diego, CA (SF 96675-2333)
SSN-648 Aspro; Vallejo, CA (SF 96660-2334)
SSN-649 Sunfish; Norfolk, VA (MI 34093-2335)
SSN-650 Pargo; New London, CT (NY 09582-2336)
SSN-651 Queenfish; Pearl Harbor, HI (SF 96676-2337)
SSN-652 Puffer; Pearl Harbor, HI (SE 98799-2338)
SSN-653 Ray; Charleston, SC (MI 34092-2339)
SSN-660 Sand Lance; Charleston, SC (MI 34093-2340)
SSN-661 Lapon; Norfolk, VA (NY 09577-2341)
SSN-662 Gurnard; San Diego, CA (SF 96666-2342)
SSN-663 Hammerhead; Norfolk, VA (NY 09501-2343)
SSN-664 Sea Devil; Charleston, SC (MI 34093-2344)
SSN-665 Guitarro; San Diego, CA (SF 96666-2345)
SSN-666 Hawkbill; Pearl Harbor, HI (SF 96667-2346)
SSN-667 Bergall; Norfolk, VA (SF 96661-2347)
SSN-668 Spadefish; Norfolk, VA (NY 09587-2348)
SSN-669 Seahorse; Bremerton, WA (SE 98799-2349)
SSN-670 Finback; Norfolk, VA (NY 09569-2350)
SSN-672 Pintado; San Diego, CA (SF 96675-2352)

SWORDFISH (SSN-579) *Skate Class*

44 NAVY

GUARDFISH (SSN-612) *Permit Class*

SSN-673 Flying Fish; Bremerton, WA (SE 98799-2353)
SSN-674 Trepang; New London, CT (NY 09588-2354)
SSN-675 Bluefish; Portsmouth, NH (NY 09565-2355)
SSN-676 Billfish; New London, CT (NY 09565-2356)
SSN-677 Drum; San Diego, CA (SF 96663-2357)
SSN-678 Archerfish; Groton, CT (NY 09564-2358)
SSN-679 Silversides; Norfolk, VA (NY 09587-2359)
SSN-680 William H. Bates; San Diego, CA (SF 96661-2360)
SSN-681 Batfish; Charleston, SC (MI 34090-2361)
SSN-682 Tunny; Bremerton, WA (SF 98799-2362)
SSN-683 Parche; Vallejo, CA (SF 96675-2363)
SSN-684 Cavalla; Pearl Harbor, HI (SF 96662-2364)
SSN-686 L. Mendel Rivers; Charleston, SC (MI 34092-2366)
SSN-687 Richard B. Russell; Vallejo, CA (SF 96677-2367)

Narwhal Class

SSN-671 Narwhal; Charleston, SC (MI 34092-2351)

Glenard P. Lipscomb Class

SSN-685 Glenard P. Lipscomb; Norfolk, VA (NY 09577-2365)

Skipjack Class

SSN-585 Skipjack; Groton, CT (NY 09587-2305)
SSN-590 Sculpin; Groton, CT (NY 09587-2307)
SSN-591 Shark; Groton, CT (NY 09587-2308)

Permit Class

SSN-594 Permit; San Diego, CA (SF 96675-2310)
SSN-595 Plunger; San Diego, CA (SF 96675-2311)
SSN-596 Barb; San Diego, CA (SF 96661-2312)
SSN-603 Pollack; Vallejo, CA (SF 96675-2316)
SSN-604 Haddo; San Diego, CA (SF 96667-2317)
SSN-605 Jack; New London, CT (NY 09575-2318)
SSN-606 Tinosa; New London, CT (NY 09588-2319)
SSN-607 Dace; Bremerton, WA (SE 98799-2320)
SSN-612 Guardfish; San Diego, CA (SF 96666-2323)
SSN-613 Flasher; San Diego, CA (SF 96665-2324)
SSN-614 Greenling; New London, CT (NY 09570-2325)
SSN-615 Gato; Portsmouth, NH (NY 09570-2326)
SSN-621 Haddock; San Diego, CA (SF 96667-2328)

Darter Class

SS-576 Darter; Sasebo, Japan (SF 96663-3401)

Barbel Class

SS-580 Barbel; Sasebo, Japan (SF 96661-3402)
SS-581 Blueback; San Diego, CA (SF 96661-3403)

BARB (SSN-596) *Permit Class*

TAURUS (PHM-3) *Pegasus Class*

TARAWA (LHA-1) *Tarawa Class*

PATROL COMBATANTS MISSILESHIPS (HYDROFOIL) (PHM)

Pegasus Class

DISPLACEMENT: 240 tons full load.
LENGTH: foils extended, 133 feet; foils retracted, 145 feet.
BEAM: 28 feet.
SPEED: foilborne, 48 knots; hullborne, 12 knots.
POWER PLANT: foilborne, one gas turbine, 18,000 shaft horsepower, waterjet propulsion units; hullborne, two diesels, 1,600 brake horsepower, waterjet propulsion units.
AIRCRAFT: none.
ARMAMENT: eight Harpoon missiles, one 76mm gun.
COMPLEMENT: 23.
BUILDER: Boeing Marine Systems.

BRIEFING: This class of ship was conceived originally as a NATO ship to be built jointly by Germany, Italy, and the United States; however, when the European countries withdrew from the project, only one six-ship squadron was authorized, funded, and, despite an attempt by the Department of Defense to have those funds rescinded, ultimately built. Those six ships now form a single squadron operating out of Key West. They are the Navy's fastest ships, with good range on their diesels, excellent seakeeping qualities, amazingly fast response to requirements for speed, and a potent punch. In the more than four years they have operated as a unit, they have encountered very few problems and have established an unusually high availability rate while participating in a variety of missions, including extensive involvement in the national drug-interdiction program. Their electronic-countermeasures suite and command-and-launch control system are being upgraded to improve both their offense and defense. However, there are no plans in the near term for major upgrades in their weapons capabilities.

Pegasus Class

PHM-1 Pegasus; Key West, FL (MI 34092-3408)
PHM-2 Hercules; Key West, FL (MI 34091-3409)
PHM-3 Taurus; Key West, FL (MI 34093-3410)
PHM-4 Aquila; Key West, FL (MI 34090-3411)
PHM-5 Aries; Key West, FL (MI 34090-3412)
PHM-6 Gemini; Key West, FL (MI 34091-3413)

AMPHIBIOUS ASSAULT SHIPS (LHA, LHD, LPH)

Wasp Class (LHD)

DISPLACEMENT: 40,500 tons full load.
LENGTH: 844 feet.
BEAM: 106 feet.
SPEED: 20-plus knots.
POWER PLANT: two boilers, two geared turbines, two shafts, 70,000 shaft horsepower.
AIRCRAFT: mix of 30 helicopters and 6-8 AV-8B Harriers.
ARMAMENT: Sea Sparrow missiles, three Phalanx CIWSs.
COMPLEMENT: 1,080 ship's company; 1,873 troops.
BUILDER: Ingalls Shipbuilding.

Tarawa Class (LHA)

DISPLACEMENT: 39,300 tons full load.
LENGTH: 820 feet.
BEAM: 106 feet.
FLIGHT DECK WIDTH: 118 feet.
SPEED: 24 knots.
POWER PLANT: two boilers, two geared turbines, two shafts, 70,000 shaft horsepower.
AIRCRAFT: flight deck can operate a maximum of nine CH-53 Sea Stallion or 12 CH-46 Sea Knight helicopters. Mix of these and AV-8A V/STOL Harriers can be accommodated in LHA-2-5 but not in LHA-1.
ARMAMENT: three five-inch/54-caliber guns, two Phalanx CIWSs.
COMPLEMENT: 843 ship's company; 1,703 troops.
BUILDER: Ingalls Shipbuilding.

Iwo Jima Class (LPH)

DISPLACEMENT: approximately 18,000 tons full load.
LENGTH: 602 feet.
BEAM: 84 feet.
FLIGHT DECK WIDTH: 104 feet.
SPEED: 23 knots.
POWER PLANT: two boilers, one geared turbine, one shaft, 22,000 shaft horsepower.
AIRCRAFT: hangar deck can accommodate 20 CH-46 Sea Knight or 11 CH-53 Sea Stallion helicopters, or combination of both. Seven Sea Knights or four Sea Stallions can take off simultaneously.
ARMAMENT: Sea Sparrow missiles, four three-inch/50-caliber guns.
COMPLEMENT: 684.
BUILDERS: LPH-2, Puget Sound Naval Shipyard; 3, 7, 9, 11, Philadelphia Naval Shipyard; 10, 12, Ingalls Shipbuilding.

BRIEFING: Iwo Jima (LPH-2) was the first ship designed and contructed specifically to operate helicopters. Each ship of the class can carry a Marine battalion landing team, its weapons and equipment, a reinforced squadron of transport helicopters, and support personnel. In addition to serving as platforms for V/STOL aircraft, ships of the class also have served as sea-control ships and have demonstrated further versatility in providing platforms for minesweeping helicopters. There originally were to be nine LHAs of the Tarawa class, but the number was reduced to five after extensive cost overruns during an unusually long construction period. Those ships provide the Marine Corps with a superb means of ship-to-shore movement by helicopter in augmentation of movement of other troops and equipment by landing craft. They have extensive storage capacity for vehicles, palletized stores, and aviation and vehicle fuel. They also can accommodate four landing craft utility (LCUs). The new Wasp-class LHDs are scheduled to replace the Iwo Jima-class ships in the 1990s. With modifications to the basic LHA hull to permit accommodation of three LCACs (air-cushion landing craft) and the latest model Harrier V/STOL aircraft, as well as helicopters, the LHD can serve in the dual role of amphibious assault ship and small aircraft carrier. Wasp, first of the class and being built by Ingalls Shipbuilding, is scheduled for delivery in March 1989. Construction of Essex (LHD-2) is scheduled to commence in July 1988 and of Kearsage (LHD-3) in July 1989. Funding for LHD-4 was included in the FY 1989 budget. Ingalls will build all three of these ships. Funding for LHD-5 will be sought in FY 1991. The Navy now hopes to build nine of these ships.

WASP (LHD-1) (Artist Concept) *Wasp Class*

Tarawa Class

LHA-1 Tarawa; San Diego, CA (SF 96661-1172)
LHA-2 Saipan; Norfolk, VA (NY 09549-1605)
LHA-3 Belleau Wood; San Diego, CA (SF 96623-1610)
LHA-4 Nassau; Norfolk, VA (NY 09557-1615)
LHA-5 Peleliu; Long Beach, CA (SF 96624-1620)

Iwo Jima Class

LPH-2 Iwo Jima; Norfolk, VA (NY 09561-1625)
LPH-3 Okinawa; San Diego, CA (SF 96625-1630)
LPH-7 Guadalcanal; Norfolk, VA (NY 09562-1635)
LPH-9 Guam; Norfolk, VA (NY 09563-1640)
LPH-10 Tripoli; San Diego, CA (SF 96626-1645)
LPH-11 New Orleans; San Diego, CA (SF 96627-1650)
LPH-12 Inchon; Norfolk, VA (NY 09529-1655)

INCHON (LPH-12) *Iwo Jima Class*

AMPHIBIOUS TRANSPORT DOCKS (LPD)

Austin Class
DISPLACEMENT: approximately 17,000 tons full load.
LENGTH: 570 feet.
BEAM: 84 feet.
SPEED: 21 knots.
POWER PLANT: two boilers, two steam turbines, two shafts, 24,000 shaft horsepower.
AIRCRAFT: up to six CH-46 Sea Knight helicopters.
ARMAMENT: four three-inch/50-caliber guns; two Phalanx CIWSs being fitted.
COMPLEMENT: 425 ship's company; approximately 900 troops.
BUILDERS: LPDs 4-6, New York Naval Shipyard; 7, 8, Ingalls Shipbuilding; 9, 10, 12-15, Lockheed Shipbuilding.

Raleigh Class
DISPLACEMENT: 13,600 tons full load.
LENGTH: 522 feet.
BEAM: 84 feet.
SPEED: 21 knots.
POWER PLANT: two boilers, two steam turbines, two shafts, 24,000 shaft horsepower.
AIRCRAFT: landing only.
ARMAMENT: six three-inch/50-caliber guns.
COMPLEMENT: 429 ship's company; 930 troops.
BUILDER: New York Naval Shipyard.

BRIEFING: These versatile ships replace amphibious transports (APA), amphibious cargo ships (AKA), and the older LSDs. Although their capabilities are less than those of the new Whidbey Island class of LSD, the 11 ships of the Austin class, built between 1965-1971, were considered sufficiently modern to have their service lives extended by a SLEP program commencing in 1988 that would have extended their service lives to 2005. However, Congress balked at funding the program, and as a result the ships will receive less extensive modernization during overhaul periods.

Austin Class
LPD-4 Austin; Norfolk, VA (NY 09564-1707)
LPD-5 Ogden; Long Beach, CA (SF 96674-1708)
LPD-6 Duluth; San Diego, CA (SF 96663-1709)
LPD-7 Cleveland; San Diego, CA (SF 96662-1710)
LPD-8 Dubuque; Sasebo, Japan (SF 96663-1711)
LPD-9 Denver; San Diego, CA (SF 96663-1712)
LPD-10 Juneau; San Diego, CA (SF 96669-1713)
LPD-12 Shreveport; Norfolk, VA (NY 09587-1714)
LPD-13 Nashville; ; Norfolk, VA (NY 09579-1715)
LPD-14 Trenton; Norfolk, VA (NY 09588-1716)
LPD-15 Ponce; Norfolk, VA (NY 09582-1717)

Raleigh Class
LPD-1 Raleigh; Norfolk, VA (NY 09586-1705)
LPD-2 Vancouver; San Francisco, CA (SF 96682-1706)

AMPHIBIOUS CARGO SHIPS (LKA)

Charleston Class
DISPLACEMENT: 20,700 tons full load.
LENGTH: 575 feet.
BEAM: 82 feet.
SPEED: 20 knots.
POWER PLANT: two boilers, one steam turbine, one shaft, 22,000 shaft horsepower.
ARMAMENT: six three-inch/50-caliber guns; two Phalanx CIWSs being fitted.
COMPLEMENT: 356 ship's company; 226 troops.
BUILDER: Newport News Shipbuilding.

BRIEFING: These ships, which carry heavy equipment and supplies for amphibious assaults, are the first class of ship designed specifically for this role. Four of the five ships in the class had been transferred to the reserve fleet in the late 1970s and early 1980s, even

DULUTH (LPD-6) *Austin Class*

SAINT LOUIS (LKA-116) *Charleston Class*

though they were just a decade old. However, the obvious need for additional sealift resulting from the 1979 upheaval in the Middle East and the possibility of U.S. involvement in that remote area resulted in all four being returned to the active fleet in 1982-83. They are among the first Navy ships to have a fully automated main propulsion plant.

Charleston Class

LKA-113 Charleston; Norfolk, VA (NY 09566-1700)
LKA-114 Durham; San Diego, CA (SF 96663-1701)
LKA-115 Mobile; Long Beach, CA (SF 96672-1702)
LKA-116 Saint Louis; Sasebo, Japan (SF 96678-1703)
LKA-117 El Paso; Norfolk, VA (NY 09568-1704)

DOCK LANDING SHIPS (LSD)

Whidbey Island Class

DISPLACEMENT: 15,726 tons full load.
LENGTH: 609 feet.
BEAM: 84 feet.
SPEED: 20-plus knots.
POWER PLANT: four medium-speed diesels, two shafts, 34,000 brake horsepower.
AIRCRAFT: helicopter and V/STOL-capable.
ARMAMENT: two Phalanx CIWS guns, two 20mm AA guns.
COMPLEMENT: 340 ship's company; 338 troops.
BUILDERS: LSD 41-43 Lockheed Shipbuilding; 44-49, Avondale Shipyards.

WHIDBEY ISLAND (LSD-41) *Whidbey Island Class*

MOUNT VERNON (LSD-39) *Anchorage Class*

Anchorage Class

DISPLACEMENT: 13,600 tons full load.
LENGTH: 553 feet.
BEAM: 84 feet.
SPEED: 22 knots.
POWER PLANT: two boilers, steam turbines, two shafts, 24,000 shaft horsepower.
AIRCRAFT: helicopter-capable.
ARMAMENT: six three-inch/50-caliber guns (two Phalanx CIWS guns being fitted).
COMPLEMENT: 355 ship's company; 376 troops.
BUILDERS: LSD-36, Ingalls Shipbuilding; 37-40, General Dynamics' Quincy Shipbuilding Division.

Thomaston Class

DISPLACEMENT: 12,000 tons full load.
LENGTH: 510 feet.
BEAM: 84 feet.
SPEED: 22.5 knots.
POWER PLANT: two boilers, steam turbines, two shafts, 24,000 shaft horsepower.
AIRCRAFT: helicopter-capable.
ARMAMENT: six three-inch/50-caliber guns.
COMPLEMENT: 330 ship's company; 340 troops.
BUILDER: Ingalls Shipbuilding.

ALAMO (LSD-33) *Thomaston Class*

BRIEFING: Whidbey Island (LSD-41), commissioned in 1985, was the long-awaited first of a new class of the versatile, durable dock landing ships which first saw service during World War II but which really came into their own during the Korean War. Their ability to ballast down to flood a well deck makes possible loading at sea and transporting virtually any type of cargo that can be carried by utility landing craft (LCU) and small amphibious craft. LSDs can accommodate a sizeable number of troops. The Marine Corps long had sought replacement of the aging Thomaston class, only three of which remain in commission, but a decade passed before funding of Whidbey Island was approved. Three of that eight-ship class have been delivered, three others are scheduled for delivery later this year, and the remaining two are under construction. The Navy had sought funding in FY 1988 for the first two of a variant of the LSD-41 which will have greater cargo-carrying capability, but budget constraints necessitated halving that planned request. Funding for the second of what the Navy hopes will be at least a 10-ship class will be sought in FY 1990. The LSD-41 class has far greater storage space than its predecessors, much improved facilities for embarked troops, greater operating range, and room for four of the Marines' new LCACs (air-cushion landing craft). Also notable is the ship's medium-speed-diesel propulsion system, considerably more economical than steam or gas turbines.

Whidbey Island Class

LSD-41 Whidbey Island; Little Creek, Norfolk, VA (NY 09591-1729)
LSD-42 Germantown; San Diego, CA (SF 96666-1730)
LSD-43 Fort McHenry; San Diego, CA (SF 96665-1731)

Anchorage Class

LSD-36 Anchorage; Long Beach, CA (SF 96660-1724)
LSD-37 Portland; Little Creek, Norfolk, VA (NY 09582-1725)
LSD-38 Pensacola; Little Creek, Norfolk, VA (NY 09582-1726)
LSD-39 Mount Vernon; Long Beach, CA (SF 96672-1727)
LSD-40 Fort Fisher; San Diego, CA (SF 96665-1728)

Thomaston Class

LSD-32 Spiegel Grove; Little Creek, Norfold, VA (NY 09587-1720)
LSD-33 Alamo; San Diego, CA (SF 96660-1721)
LSD-34 Hermitage; Little Creek, Norfolk, VA (NY 09573-1722)

HARLAN COUNTY (LST-1196) *Newport Class*

TANK LANDING SHIPS (LST)

Newport Class

DISPLACEMENT: 8,450 tons full load.
LENGTH: 522 feet.
BEAM: 69 feet.
SPEED: 20 knots.
POWER PLANT: six diesels, two shafts, 16,000 brake horsepower.
ARMAMENT: four three-inch/50-caliber guns; Phalanx CIWS to be fitted.
COMPLEMENT: 290 ship's company; 400 troops.
BUILDERS: LSTs 1179-1181, Philadelphia Naval Shipyard; 1182-1198, National Steel and Shipbuilding.

BRIEFING: Ships of this class are larger and faster than earlier LSTs and are the first to depart from the bow-door design that characterized the workhorses of World War II. The hull form necessary for the attainment of the 20-knot speeds of contemporary amphibious squadrons would not permit bow doors. Accordingly, ships of this class offload cargo and vehicles by means of a 112-foot ramp over their bow. A stern gate also makes possible offloading amphibious vehicles directly into the water. The 20 ships of this class, all commissioned between June 1969 and August 1972, are the only LSTs remaining in the fleet.

Newport Class

LST-1179 Newport; Little Creek, Norfolk, VA (NY 09579-1800)
LST-1180 Manitowoc; Little Creek, Norfolk, VA (NY 09578-1801)
LST-1181 Sumter; Little Creek, Norfolk, VA (NY 09587-1802)
LST-1182 Fresno; Long Beach, CA (SF 96665-1803)
LST-1183 Peoria; San Diego, CA (SF 96675-1804)
LST-1184 Frederick; San Diego, CA (SF 96665-1805)
LST-1185 Schenectady; San Diego, CA (SF 96678-1806)
LST-1186 Cayuga; San Diego, CA (SF 96662-1807)
LST-1187 Tuscaloosa; San Diego, CA (SF 96679-1808)
LST-1188 Saginaw; Little Creek, VA (NY 09587-1809)
LST-1189 San Bernardino; Sasebo, Japan (SF 96678-1810)
LST-1192 Spartanburg County; Little Creek, Norfolk, VA (NY 09587-1813)
LST-1193 Fairfax County; Little Creek, Norfolk, VA (NY 09569-1814)
LST-1194 La Moure County; Little Creek, Norfolk, VA (NY 09577-1815)
LST-1195 Barbour County; San Diego, CA (SF 96661-1816)
LST-1196 Harlan County; Little Creek, Norfolk, VA (NY 09573-1817)
LST-1197 Barnstable County; Little Creek, Norfolk, VA (NY 09565-1818)
LST-1198 Bristol County; San Diego, CA (SF 96661-1819)

SAGINAW (LST-1188) *Newport Class*

BLUE RIDGE (LCC-19) *Blue Ridge Class*

AMPHIBIOUS COMMAND SHIPS (LCC)

Blue Ridge Class

DISPLACEMENT: 19,290 tons full load.
LENGTH: 596 feet.
BEAM: 82 feet.
SPEED: 23 knots.
POWER PLANT: steam turbine, two boilers, one shaft, 22,000 shaft horsepower.
ARMAMENT: Sea Sparrow missiles, four three-inch/50-caliber anti-aircraft weapons, two Phalanx CIWS.
AIRCRAFT: none, although each ship has a helicopter landing area.
COMPLEMENT: crew, LCC-19, 799; LCC-20, 821; Flag, LCC-19, 241; LCC-20, 188.
BUILDER: LCC-19, Philadelphia Naval Shipyard; LCC-20, Newport News.

BRIEFING: These are the only ships to be designed initially for an amphibious command ship role. Earlier amphibious command ships lacked sufficient speed to operate with a 20-knot amphibious force. Subsequently, both ships became fleet flagships. Blue Ridge became the Seventh Fleet flagship in 1979 and is homeported in Yokosuka, Japan; Mount Whitney became the Second Fleet flagship in 1981.

Blue Ridge Class

LCC-19 Blue Ridge; Yokosuka, Japan (SF 96628-3300)
LCC-20 Mount Whitney; Norfolk, VA (NY 09517-3310)

LANDING CRAFT (AIR CUSHION) (LCAC)

DISPLACEMENT: 200 tons full load.
LENGTH: 88 feet.
BEAM: 47 feet.
SPEED: 40 knots with payload; 50 knots maximum.
CARGO CAPACITY: 60 tons.
POWER PLANT: four Avco-Lycoming gas turbines; 12,280 brake horsepower; two shrouded reversible-pitch propellers; four double-entry fans for lifts.
ARMAMENT: none.
RANGE: 200 miles at 50 knots with payload.
COMPLEMENT: 5.
BUILDER: Textron Marine Systems, Lockheed Shipbuilding.

BRIEFING: These speedy air-cushion vehicles, working with modern helicopters, are expected to literally revolutionize amphibious landing tactics. With LCACs in the fleet, an amphibious task force could be nearly 500 miles away from its objective at H-Hour minus 24 and still make a pre-dawn attack launched from beyond an enemy's horizon. The LCAC's air-cushion capability also allows it to proceed inland to discharge its cargo on dry, trafficable terrain, thus helping to avoid a significant build-up of troops, equipment, and material at the surf zone. With its speed, and because it is not restricted by tides, beach gradients, and surf conditions, the LCAC makes possi-

LCAC

ble a four-fold increase in accessible beach areas. The first LCAC was delivered by Textron Marine Systems in 1984, and the first operational LCAC unit was activated in 1987 at Camp Pendleton, CA, where its LCACs underwent extensive testing. A number of changes and improvements were required in those first LCACs and those to follow, and the delay in incorporating them resulted in a delay in contract awards for construction of the last three LCACs funded in FY 1985 and the 12 funded in 1986. The Navy did not seek procurement funds for LCACs in FY 1987 or FY 1988, but did seek funds for nine in FY 1989. Congress subsequently funded 15 in order to take advantage of lower costs resulting from dual-source procurement. Lockheed Shipbuilding Corporation, which was selected as the second builder and built a new yard at Gulfport in which to construct LCACs, subsequently sold that yard to Avondale, which will continue to build them.

MINE WARFARE SHIPS (MSO, MCM, MHC)

Avenger Class

DISPLACEMENT: 1,040 tons full load.
LENGTH: 224 feet.
BEAM: 39 feet.
SPEED: 14 knots.
POWER PLANT: four diesels, two shafts, 2,400 brake horsepower.
AIRCRAFT: none.
ARMAMENT: two .50-caliber machine guns.
COMPLEMENT: 72.
BUILDERS: MCM-1, -3, -5, -6, -8, Peterson Builders; -2, -4, -7, Marinette Marine Corporation.

Agressive Class

DISPLACEMENT: 720 tons full load.
LENGTH: 172 feet.
BEAM: 36 feet.
SPEED: 14 knots.
POWER PLANT: two diesels, two shafts, 2,280 brake horsepower.
AIRCRAFT: none.
ARMAMENT: one 40mm or one 20mm.
COMPLEMENT: 76.
BUILDERS: MSO-443, Higgins; 448, Martinolich Shipbuilding; 490, J.M. Martinac Shipbuilding.

BRIEFING: For many years, the Navy paid scant attention to its mine-countermeasures program. The last MSO built by the Navy was included in the 1954 shipbuilding program and commissioned in 1958. Not until December 1982, when the keel was laid for Avenger (MCM-1), was construction commenced on another MCM ship. Because of a number of serious problems encountered during construction, Avenger was not delivered until the late summer of 1987. However, initial reports of her performance during testing after she transited to the Atlantic were outstanding. Defender (MCM-2) will not be delivered until early 1989, more than five years after the start of her construction, and Sentry (MCM-3) will be completed in 1988 but not before ice forms on the Great Lakes and precludes passage to the sea until the spring of 1989. Three other MCMs are scheduled for delivery in 1989, and two others are under construction. Contracts for construction of MCMs 9-11 will be awarded early in 1989, but funds for the last three in the 14-ship program were not included in the FY 1989 shipbuilding program. Seventeen minesweeper hunters (MSH) also were in the Navy's plans, and the contract for the first of these was awarded to Textron Marine Systems in FY 1984. This class of ship was to have a surface-effect-ship hull and be built of glass-reinforced plastic (GRP) foam composite material; GRP technology is used by several European navies for their minewarfare ships. The first MSH was scheduled for delivery in 1987; however, a test section undergoing shock tests failed to meet Navy expectations. Subsequently, in 1986, it was decided not to proceed further with the MSH program, but to adopt a design perfected by Intermarine SPA, an Italian shipyard. Its Lerici-class minesweepers, monohull GRP ships, now are being used by three navies. A design contract for a coastal minehunter (MHC) was awarded to Intermarine SPA in August 1986, and a construction contract for the lead ship of a 17-ship MHC class was awarded to Intermarine USA in May 1987. Construction of that ship at Intermarine USA's Savannah, GA, shipyard commenced in May 1988; it is to be completed in 1991. A second U.S. construction source also will be developed. Until the building programs for the MCM and MHC produce sizeable numbers of new ships for the fleet, the Navy must rely principally on three active MSOs in the fleet and the 18 assigned to the Naval Reserve, which in time also will operate the new minewarfare ships. Several of the MSOs were deployed to the Persian Gulf in the late summer of 1987 to sweep mines planted by Iran. The absence from the scene of any U.S. minesweeping capability when mines first were encountered resulted in widespread criticism of the Navy's overall lack of capability and of its failure to move more rapidly in the inauguration and prosecution of construction of modern mine-countermeasures ships.

FIDELITY (MSO-443) *Aggressive Class*

Avenger Class

MCM-1 Avenger; Charleston, SC (MI 34090-1921)

Aggressive Class

MSO-443 Fidelity; Panama City, FL (MI 34091-1908)
MSO-448 Illusive; Charleston, SC (MI 34091-1910)
MSO-490 Leader; Charleston, SC (MI 34091-1917)

AVENGER (MCM-1) *Avenger Class*

SACRAMENTO (AOE-1) *Sacramento Class*

FAST COMBAT SUPPORT SHIPS (AOE)

Sacramento Class

DISPLACEMENT: approximately 53,000 tons full load.
LENGTH: 793 feet.
BEAM: 107 feet.
SPEED: 26 knots.
POWER PLANT: four boilers, geared turbines, two shafts, 100,000 shaft horsepower.
AIRCRAFT: two CH-46 Sea Knight helicopters.
ARMAMENT: four three-inch/50-caliber guns; rockets and two Phalanx CIWSs to be fitted.
COMPLEMENT: 594-621.
BUILDERS: AOEs 1, 3, 4, Puget Sound Naval Shipyard; 2, New York Shipbuilding; AOE 6, National Steel and Shipbuilding.

BRIEFING: These ships, the largest underway replenishment ships in the world, with capacities of more than 190,000 barrels of oil, 2,150 tons of ammunition, 500 tons of dry stores, and 250 tons of refrigerated stores, provide rapid replenishment of all these cargoes to Navy task forces. Ultimately, the Navy hopes to have 15 AOE/AOR ship types in the fleet and plans to seek funding for four AOEs in the FY 1987-1991 period. One was authorized in FY 1987, and is under construction; the second was funded in FY 1989, and the last two will be sought in FY 1991.

Sacramento Class

AOE-1 Sacramento; San Diego, CA (SF 96678-3012)
AOE-2 Camden; Bremerton, WA (SE 98799-3013)
AOE-3 Seattle; Norfolk, VA (NY 09587-3014)
AOE-4 Detroit; Norfolk, VA (NY 09567-3015)

REPLENISHMENT OILERS (AOR)

Wichita Class

DISPLACEMENT: 38,100 tons full load.
LENGTH: 659 feet.
BEAM: 96 feet.
SPEED: 20 knots.
POWER PLANT: three boilers, steam turbines, two shafts, 32,000 shaft horsepower.
AIRCRAFT: two CH-46 Sea Knight helicopters.
ARMAMENT: two Phalanx CIWSs, 20mm or 40mm gun, Sea Sparrow missiles.
COMPLEMENT: 115.
BUILDERS: 1-6, General Dynamics, Quincy; 7, National Steel and Shipbuilding.

BRIEFING: These large combination petroleum-munitions underway replenishment ships are smaller than AOEs but larger than almost all foreign ships with similar capability. They can carry 160,000 barrels of petroleum, 600 tons of munitions, 200 tons of dry stores, and 100 tons of refrigerated stores. They also have highly automated cargo-handling equipment. Although there are plans to build new AOEs, there are none at the moment to construct new AORs.

Wichita Class

AOR-1 Wichita; Oakland, CA (SF 96683-3023)
AOR-2 Milwaukee; Norfolk, VA (NY 09578-3024)
AOR-3 Kansas City; Oakland, CA (SF 96670-3025)
AOR-4 Savannah; Norfolk, VA (NY 09587-3026)
AOR-5 Wabash; Long Beach, CA (SF 96683-3027)
AOR-6 Kalamazoo; Norfolk, VA (NY 09576-3028)
AOR-7 Roanoke; Long Beach, CA (SF 96677-3029)

ROANOKE (AOR-7) *Wichita Class*

AMMUNITION SHIPS (AE)

Kilauea Class

DISPLACEMENT: approximately 20,000 tons full load.
LENGTH: 564 feet.
BEAM: 81 feet.
SPEED: 20 knots.
POWER PLANT: three boilers, geared turbines, one shaft, 22,000 shaft horsepower.
AIRCRAFT: two CH-46 Sea Knight helicopters.
ARMAMENT: four three-inch/50-caliber guns; two Phalanx CIWSs being fitted.
COMPLEMENT: 380.
BUILDERS: AE-26, 27, General Dynamics' Quincy Shipbuilding Division; 28, 29, Bethlehem Steel, Sparrows Point, MD; 32-35, Ingalls Shipbuilding.

Suribachi and Nitro Class

DISPLACEMENT: 17,000 tons full load.
LENGTH: 512 feet.
BEAM: 72 feet.
SPEED: approximately 20 knots.
POWER PLANT: two boilers, geared turbines, one shaft, 16,000 shaft horsepower.
AIRCRAFT: none.
ARMAMENT: four three-inch/50-caliber guns.
COMPLEMENT: 349.
BUILDER: Bethlehem Steel, Sparrows Point, MD.

BRIEFING: Ammunition ships, like all of the other types of the Navy's major fleet-support ships, were in markedly increased demand after the upheaval in Iran and Soviet invasion of Afghanistan. As a consequence, two Nitro-class ships which had been transferred to the reserve fleet were returned to the active fleet in 1982. A new class of AE is included in the Navy's long-range building plans, and the first was to have been sought in FY 1986. Now, however, funds for it will be requested in FY 1991. Kilauea (T-AE-26) is operated by the Military Sealift Command and is unarmed.

Kilauea Class

AE-27 Butte; Earle, NJ (NY 09565-3005)
AE-28 Santa Barbara; Wpnsta, Charleston, SC (MI 34093-3006)
AE-29 Mount Hood; Concord, CA (SF 96672-3007)
AE-32 Flint; Concord, CA (SF 96665-3008)
AE-33 Shasta; Concord, CA (SF 96678-3009)
AE-34 Mount Baker; Wpnsta, Charleston, SC (MI 34092-3010)
AE-35 Kiska; Concord, CA (SF 96670-3011)

Nitro Class

AE-23 Nitro; Earle, NJ (NY 09579-3002)
AE-24 Pyro; Concord, CA (SF 96675-3003)
AE-25 Haleakala; Guam, MI (SF 96667-3004)

Suribachi Class

AE-21 Suribachi; Earle, NJ (NY 09587-3000)
AE-22 Mauna Kea; Concord, CA (SF 96672-3001)

FLEET OILERS (AO)

Cimarron Class (AO-177)

DISPLACEMENT: 27,500 tons full load.
LENGTH: 592 feet.
BEAM: 88 feet.
SPEED: 20 knots.
POWER PLANT: two boilers, one steam turbine, one shaft, 24,000 shaft horsepower.
AIRCRAFT: none.
ARMAMENT: two 20mm Phalanx CIWSs being fitted.
COMPLEMENT: 212.
CARGO CAPACITY: 120,000 barrels.
BUILDER: Avondale Shipyards.

Ashtabula Class

DISPLACEMENT: 34,750 tons full load.
LENGTH: 644 feet.
BEAM: 75 feet.
SPEED: 18 knots.
POWER PLANT: steam turbine, four boilers, two shafts, 13,500 shaft horsepower.
AIRCRAFT: none. A small area for vertical replenishment is provided.
ARMAMENT: two 3-inch/50-caliber AA weapons.
COMPLEMENT: 374.
BUILDER: Bethlehem Steel, Sparrows Point, MD.

BRIEFING: The number of Navy-manned fleet oilers has diminished steadily as more and more Military Sealift Command ships, all civilian manned and unarmed, have assumed responsibilities for supplying ships of the fleet. However, the Navy does plan to "jumboize" the five ships of the Cimarron class, all of which were commissioned between 1981-83. The first two conversions of ships of this class soon will be under way, and funds to convert two more were included in the FY 1989 budget.

BUTTE (AE-27) *Kilauea Class*

PLATTE (AO-186) *Cimarron Class*

Cimarron Class

AO-177 Cimarron; Pearl Harbor, HI (SF 96662-3018)
AO-178 Monongahela; Norfolk, VA (NY 09578-3019)
AO-179 Merrimack; Norfolk, VA (NY 09578-3020)
AO-180 Willamette; Pearl Harbor, HI (SF 96683-3021)
AO-186 Platte; Norfolk, VA (NY 09582-3022)

Ashtabula Class

AO-98 Caloosahatchee; Norfolk, VA (NY 09566-3016)
AO-99 Canisteo; Norfolk, VA (NY 09566-3017)

FLEET OCEAN TUGS

Abnaki Class

DISPLACEMENT: 1,640 tons full load.
LENGTH: 205 feet.
BEAM: 38.5 feet.
SPEED: 16.5 knots.
POWER PLANT: diesel electric, four diesels, one shaft, 3,000 brake horsepower.
COMPLEMENT: 99.
BUILDER: Charleston Shipbuilding and Drydock Company.

BRIEFING: Paiute *(ATF-159)* and Papago *(ATF-160)*, *both over 40 years old, were recommissioned in late 1987. Three other ships of the class still are in the Reserve Fleet, five now are Coast Guard ships, and a sizeable number sail in foreign navies.*

ATF-159 Paiute; Little Creek, Norfolk, VA (MI 34092-3215)
ATF-169 Papago; Little Creek, Norfolk, VA (NY 09582-3216)

COMBAT STORES SHIPS (AFS)

Mars Class

DISPLACEMENT: approximately 16,000 tons full load.
LENGTH: 581 feet.
BEAM: 79 feet.
SPEED: 20 knots.
POWER PLANT: three boilers, steam turbines, one shaft, 22,000 shaft horsepower.
AIRCRAFT: two UH-46 Sea Knight helicopters.
ARMAMENT: four three-inch/50-caliber guns; two Phalanx CIWSs to be fitted.
COMPLEMENT: 436.
BUILDER: National Steel and Shipbuilding.

BRIEFING: Although five of the seven ships of the Mars class are over 20 years old, they are in excellent condition to respond to the additional requirements placed on the Navy's auxiliary forces by the steady build-up toward a 600-ship Navy and the continued deployment of task forces to the Indian Ocean. However, no further acquisition of ships of this type is contemplated at this time.

Mars Class

AFS-1 Mars; Oakland, CA (SF 96672-3030)
AFS-2 Sylvania; Norfolk, VA (NY 09587-3031)
AFS-3 Niagara Falls; Guam, MI (SF 96673-3032)
AFS-4 White Plains; Guam, MI (SF 96683-3033)
AFS-5 Concord; Norfolk, VA (NY 09566-3034)
AFS-6 San Diego; Norfolk, VA (NY 09587-3035)
AFS-7 San Jose; Guam, MI (SF 96678-3036)

MARS (AFS-1) *Mars Class*

MATERIAL SUPPORT SHIPS

HUNLEY (AS-31) *Hunley Class*

SUBMARINE TENDERS (AS)

L.Y. Spear and Emory S. Land Classes

DISPLACEMENT: approximately 23,000 tons.
LENGTH: 644 feet.
BEAM: 85 feet.
SPEED: 20 knots.
POWER PLANT: two boilers, steam turbines, one shaft, 20,000 shaft horsepower.
AIRCRAFT: none.
ARMAMENT: two 40mm guns, four 20mm guns.
COMPLEMENT: ASs 36 and 37, 625; 39-41, 617.
BUILDERS: ASs 36, 37 General Dynamics' Quincy Shipbuilding Division; 39-41, Lockheed Shipbuilding.

Simon Lake Class

DISPLACEMENT: AS-33, 19,934 tons; 34, 21,089 tons.
LENGTH: 644 feet.
BEAM: 85 feet.
SPEED: 20 knots.
POWER PLANT: two boilers, steam turbines, one shaft, 20,000 shaft horsepower.
AIRCRAFT: none.
ARMAMENT: four 20mm guns.
COMPLEMENT: AS-33, 915; AS-34, 660.
BUILDERS: AS-33, Puget Sound Naval Shipyard; 34, Ingalls Shipbuilding.

Hunley Class

DISPLACEMENT: 19,000 tons full load.
LENGTH: 599 feet.
BEAM: 83 feet.
SPEED: 19 knots.
POWER PLANT: diesel-electric, one shaft, 15,000 brake horsepower.
AIRCRAFT: none.
ARMAMENT: four 20mm guns.
COMPLEMENT: AS-31, 612; AS-32, 659.
BUILDERS: AS-31, Newport News Shipbuilding; 32, Ingalls Shipbuilding.

Fulton and Proteus Classes

DISPLACEMENT: ASs 11 and 18, 16,230 tons full load; 19, 19,200 tons full load.
LENGTH: ASs 11 and 18, 530.5 feet; 19, 575 feet.
BEAM: 73 feet.
SPEED: 15.4 knots.
AIRCRAFT: none.
ARMAMENT: four 20mm guns.
COMPLEMENT: approximately 573-706.
BUILDERS: AS-11, Mare Island, CA, Navy Yard; 18, 19, Moore Shipbuilding and Drydock.

BRIEFING: These four classes of ships reflect the difficulties encountered by the Navy over the years in acquiring enough modern, responsive support ships and in upgrading the capabilities of older

EMORY S. LAND (AS-39) *Emory S. Land Class*

ones to permit keeping pace with ever-changing fleet requirements. Proteus (AS-19), for example, joined the fleet in 1944 and then had to be modernized extensively 15 years later to give her the capability to service the first strategic nuclear missiles, the Polaris. Only four ASs were built between 1944 and 1970 when Spear (AS-36) was commissioned, and another eight years passed between the commissionings of the second ship of that class, Dixon (AS-37), and the Emory S. Land (AS-39). Meanwhile, capabilities of ships already operational were being improved upon constantly to cope with advances in missilery and nuclear propulsion. The Hunley, Simon Lake, and Proteus classes are configured especially to service ballistic-missile submarines. The Land and Spear classes were designed and fitted to accommodate SSNs, and can service simultaneously four submarines moored alongside.

Spear Class

AS-36 L.Y. Spear; Norfolk, VA (NY 09547-2600)
AS-37 Dixon; San Diego, CA (SF 96648-2605)

Emory S. Land Class

AS-39 Emory S. Land; Norfolk, VA (NY 09545-2610)
AS-40 Frank Cable; Charleston, SC (MI 34086-2615)
AS-41 McKee; San Diego, CA (SF 96621-2620)

Simon Lake Class

AS-33 Simon Lake; Holy Loch, Scotland (MI 34085-2590)
AS-34 Canopus; Kings Bay, GA (MI 34087-2595)

Hunley Class

AS-31 Hunley; Norfolk, VA (NY 09559-2580)
AS-32 Holland; Charleston, SC (MI 34079-2585)

Fulton Class

AS-11 Fulton; New London, CT (NY 09534-2565)
AS-18 Orion; La Maddalena, Italy (NY 09513-2570)

Proteus Class

AS-19 Proteus; Guam, MI (SF 96646-2575)

DESTROYER TENDERS (AD)

Yellowstone and Samual Gompers Class

DISPLACEMENT: approximately 22,500 tons full load.
LENGTH: 644 feet.
BEAM: 85 feet.
SPEED: 20 knots.
POWER PLANT: two boilers, steam turbines, one shaft, 20,000 shaft horsepower.
AIRCRAFT: none.
ARMAMENT: ADs 37 and 38, four 20mm guns; 41-43, two 40mm and two 20mm guns.
COMPLEMENT: approximately 1,300-1,500.
BUILDERS: ADs 37, 38, Puget Sound Naval Shipyard; 41-43, National Steel and Shipbuilding.

Dixie Class

DISPLACEMENT: 18,000 tons full load.
LENGTH: 530 feet.
BEAM: 73 feet.
SPEED: 18.2 knots.
POWER PLANT: four boilers, geared turbines, two shafts, 12,000 shaft horsepower.
AIRCRAFT: none.
ARMAMENT: four 20mm guns.
COMPLEMENT: approximately 870.
BUILDERS: AD-15, New York Shipbuilding; 18, 19, Tampa Shipbuilding.

BRIEFING: These ships so vital to the fleet range in age from the venerable Dixie-class ship Prairie (AD-15), commissioned in 1940 and now the oldest active ship in commission in the Navy, to the new Shenandoah (AD-44), commissioned in late 1983. Because of the advent of nuclear power and the phenomenal advances in electronics and weaponry, AD capabilities have had to be vastly increased. The Gompers and Yellowstone classes are the first of post-World War II design; however, more than 15 years elapsed between the launching of the second of the Gompers class, Puget Sound (AD-38), and Yellowstone (AD-41). These classes, which have a helicopter platform and hangar and are equipped with two 30-ton and two 6½-ton

SHENANDOAH (AD-44) *Yellowstone Class*

58 NAVY

PRAIRIE (AD-15) *Dixie Class*

cranes, can provide services simultaneously to as many as six destroyers moored alongside. Although earlier plans had called for additional ADs in the FY 1987 and 1988 budgets, none is included in the current five-year shipbuilding plan.

Yellowstone Class

AD-41 Yellowstone; Norfolk, VA (NY 09512-2525)
AD-42 Acadia; San Diego, CA (SF 96647-2530)
AD-43 Cape Cod; San Diego, CA (SF 96649-2535)
AD-44 Shenandoah; Norfolk, VA (NY 09551-2540)

Samuel Gompers Class

AD-37 Samuel Gompers; Alameda CA (SF 96641-2915)
AD-38 Puget Sound; Norfolk, VA (NY 09544-2520)

Dixie Class

AD-15 Prairie; Long Beach, CA (SF 96639-2500)
AD-18 Sierra; Charleston, SC (MI 34084-2505)
AD-19 Yosemite; Mayport, FL (MI 34083-2510)

REPAIR SHIPS (AR)

Vulcan Class

DISPLACEMENT: approximately 16,270 tons full load.
LENGTH: 529 feet.
BEAM: 73 feet.
SPEED: 19.2 knots.
POWER PLANT: four boilers, steam turbines, two shafts, 11,000 shaft horsepower.
AIRCRAFT: none.
ARMAMENT: four 20mm guns.
COMPLEMENT: 841.
BUILDERS: AR-5, New York Shipbuilding; 6-8, Los Angeles Shipbuilding and Drydock.

BRIEFING: These relatively ancient ships, all of World War II vintage and funded under 1939 and 1940 shipbuilding programs spearheaded by the farsighted Georgia congressman, Carl Vinson, still serve a useful purpose. The ships can simultaneously repair a large number of ship systems and subsystems and would be invaluable in time of conflict.

Vulcan Class

AR-5 Vulcan; Norfolk, VA (NY 09548-2545)
AR-8 Jason; San Diego, CA (SF 96644-2560)

JASON (AR-8) *Vulcan Class*

SAFEGUARD (ARS-50) *Safeguard Class*

SALVAGE SHIPS (ARS, ATS)

Safeguard Class

DISPLACEMENT: 2,880 tons full load.
LENGTH: 255 feet.
BEAM: 50 feet.
SPEED: 14 knots.
POWER PLANT: diesels, two shafts, 4,200 shaft horsepower.
AIRCRAFT: none.
ARMAMENT: two 20mm guns.
COMPLEMENT: 90.
BUILDER: Peterson Builders.

Edenton Class

DISPLACEMENT: 2,929 tons full load.
LENGTH: 282 feet.
BEAM: 50 feet.
SPEED: 16 knots.
POWER PLANT: four diesels, two shafts, 6,000 brake horsepower.
AIRCRAFT: none.
ARMAMENT: two 20mm guns.
COMPLEMENT: 115.
BUILDER: Brooke Marine, Lowestoft, England.

Bolster Class

DISPLACEMENT: 2,045 tons full load.
LENGTH: 213 feet.
BEAM: 44 feet.
SPEED: 14.8 knots.
POWER PLANT: diesel-electric, two shafts, 3,060 shaft horsepower.
AIRCRAFT: none.
ARMAMENT: two 20mm guns.
COMPLEMENT: ARS-41, 69; ARS-43, 103.
BUILDER: Basalt Rock Co.

BRIEFING: Following the commissioning of Recovery (ARS-43), the last of the Bolster class, in 1946, a quarter of a century passed before the Navy sought to modernize its salvage-ship capability with the three Edenton-class ships, one of two classes of ships built for the Navy in Great Britain in the last two decades. Then another decade passed before the keel laying of Safeguard (ARS-50). That ship and three sister ships, the last of which was delivered to the fleet in 1986, with the Edenton-class ships fulfill fleet salvage-ship requirements for the immediate future, although one ARS is scheduled to be funded in FY 1990. The latter ships also have a rescue capability, can support diver operations to a depth of 850 feet, and can lift submerged objects weighing up to 300 tons from a depth of 120 feet.

Safeguard Class

ARS-50 Safeguard; Pearl Harbor, HI (SF 96678-3221)
ARS-51 Grasp; Little Creek, Norfolk, VA (NY 09570-3220)
ARS-52 Salvor; Pearl Harbor, HI (SF 96678-3222)
ARS-53 Grapple, Little Creek, Norfolk, VA (NY 09570-3223)

Edenton Class

ATS-1 Edenton; Little Creek, Norfolk, VA (NY 09568-3217)
ATS-2 Beaufort; Sasebo, Japan (SF 96661-3218)
ATS-3 Brunswick; Sasebo, Japan (SF 96661-3219)

Bolster Class

ARS-39 Conserver; Pearl Harbor, HI (SF 96662-3202)
ARS-41 Opportune, Little Creek, Norfolk, VA (NY 09581-3204)
ARS-43 Recovery; Little Creek, Norfolk, VA (NY 09586-3206)

EDENTON (ATS-1) *Edenton Class*

SUBMARINE RESCUE SHIPS (ASR)

Pigeon Class

DISPLACEMENT: 4,200 tons full load.
LENGTH: 251 feet.
BEAM: 86 feet.
SPEED: 15 knots.
POWER PLANT: four diesels, two shafts, 6,000 brake horsepower.
AIRCRAFT: none.
ARMAMENT: two 20mm guns.
COMPLEMENT: 197 ship's company; 24 submersible operators.
BUILDER: Alabama Drydock and Shipbuilding.

Chanticleer Class

DISPLACEMENT: 2,320 tons full load.
LENGTH: 251 feet.
BEAM: 44 feet.
SPEED: 15 knots.
POWER PLANT: diesel electric, one shaft, 3,000 brake horsepower.
AIRCRAFT: none.
ARMAMENT: two 20mm guns.
COMPLEMENT: 103.
BUILDERS: ASR-9, Moore Shipbuilding and Drydock; 13-15, Savannah Machine and Foundry.

BRIEFING: No submarine rescue ships were commissioned for more than a quarter of a century after Sunbird (ASR-15) joined the fleet in 1947. The two Pigeon-class ships are the first in the world to be built specifically for the submarine-rescue mission and, except for one Military Sealift Command Ship, are the first catamaran-hull ships to be built for the Navy since Robert Fulton's Demologos in 1812. They are capable of transporting, servicing, lowering, and raising two Deep Submergence Rescue Vessels (DSRV) and supporting saturation or conventional diving operations to depths of 850 feet. They can support divers indefinitely, lowering them to the ocean floor in pressurized transfer chambers for open-sea work periods. ASRs also serve as operation control ships for salvage operations. No new ASRs are included in the Navy's long-range shipbuilding plans.

Pigeon Class

ASR-21 Pigeon; San Diego, CA (SF 96675-3211)
ASR-22 Ortolan; Charleston, SC (MI 34092-3212)

Chanticleer Class

ASR-9 Florikan; Pearl Harbor, HI (SF 96665-3207)
ASR-13 Kittiwake; Norfolk, VA (NY 09576-3208)
ASR-14 Petrel; Charleston, SC (MI 34092-3209)
ASR-15 Sunbird; Groton, CT (NY 09587-3210)

MISCELLANEOUS AUXILIARY SHIPS

BRIEFING: Coronado (AGF-11) and La Salle (AGF-31) are converted LPDs which have been modified to serve as flagships. La Salle is a veteran of Middle East duty, having served as flagship of the Middle East force for more than a decade. She became the focus of unusual media attention following the attack on Stark (FFG-31) by an Iraqi aircraft in the Persian Gulf in 1987. Coronado also has seen Middle East duty as the relief of La Salle, when the latter was undergoing overhaul. She now is the flagship of Commander, Third Fleet, and is homeported in Hawaii. Dolphin (AGSS-555) is an experimental, deep-diving research submarine which reportedly has reached greater depths than any other operational submarine. She provides support to the Naval Ocean Systems Center and several other Navy research facilities. Lexington (AVT-16), commissioned in February 1943, is the only active ship of the 23 Essex-class carriers built from 1942-1946. She has been training pilots since 1962. She is scheduled for replacement by Coral Sea (CV-43) in 1991, 50 years after she was laid down. Sphinx (ARL-24) is the last of a number of LSTs that were converted into repair ships during World War II, and which, although limited in size and capability, performed yeoman service to the amphibious fleet in particular.

Miscellaneous Auxiliary Ships

Coronado (AGF-11); Pearl Harbor, HI (SF 96662-3330)
La Salle (AGF-31); Philadelphia, PA (NY 09577-3320)
Dolphin (AGSS-555); San Diego, CA (SF 96663-3400)
Lexington (AVT-16); Pensacola, FL (MI 34088-2700)
Sphinx (ARL-24); Key West, FL (NY 09587-2625)

PIGEON (ASR-21) *Pigeon Class*

NAVAL RESERVE FORCES

DESTROYER

Hull Class

DD-946 Edson; Newport, RI (NY 09568-1200)

FRIGATES

Knox Class

FF-1053 Roark; San Francisco, CA (SF 96677-1413)
FF-1054 Gray; San Francisco, CA (SF 96666-1414)
FF-1060 Lang; San Francisco, CA (SF 96671-1420)
FF-1061 Patterson; Philadelphia, PA (NY 09582-1421)
FF-1072 Blakely; Charleston, SC (MI 34090-1432)
FF-1091 Miller; Newport, RI (NY 09578-1451)
FF-1096 Valdez; Newport, RI (NY 09590-1456)

Oliver Hazard Perry Class

FFG-7 Oliver Hazard Perry; Philadelphia, PA (NY 09582-1465)
FFG-9 Wadsworth; Long Beach, CA (SF 96683-1467)
FFG-10 Duncan; Long Beach, CA (SF 96663-1468)
FFG-11 Clark; Philadelphia, PA (NY 09566-1469)
FFG-12 George Philip; San Diego, CA (SF 96675-1470)
FFG-13 Samuel Eliot Morison; Charleston, SC (MI 34092-1471)
FFG-14 Sides; Long Beach, CA (SF 96678-1472)
FFG-15 Estocin; Philadelphia, PA (NY 09569-1473)
FFG-16 Clifton Sprague; Philadelphia, PA (NY 09578-1474)
FFG-19 John A. Moore; Long Beach, CA (SF 96672-1475)
FFG-20 Antrim; Mayport, FL (MI 34090-1476)
FFG-21 Flatley; Mayport, FL (MI 34091-1477)
FFG-22 Fahrion; Charleston, SC (MI 34091-1478)
FFG-23 Lewis B. Puller; Long Beach, CA (SF 96675-1470)
FFG-27 Tisdale; San Diego, CA (SF 96679-1479)

LANDING CRAFT CARRIERS

Newport Class

LST-1190 Boulder; Little Creek, Norfolk, VA (NY 09565-1811)
LST-1191 Racine; Long Beach, CA (SF 96677-1812)

MINESWEEPERS

Aggressive Class

MSO-427 Constant; San Diego, CA (SF 96662-1900)
MSO-433 Engage; Mayport, FL (MI 34091-1901)
MSO-437 Enhance; Tacoma, WA (SE 98799-1902)
MSO-438 Esteem; Seattle, WA (SE 98799-1903)
MSO-439 Excel; San Francisco, CA (SF 96664-1904)
MSO-440 Exploit; Newport, RI (NY 09568-1905)
MSO-441 Exultant; Charleston, SC (MI 34091-1906)
MSO-442 Fearless; Charleston, SC (MI 34091-1907)
MSO-446 Fortify; Little Creek, Norfolk, VA (NY 09569-1909)
MSO-449 Impervious; Mayport, FL (MI 34091-1911)
MSO-455 Implicit; Tacoma, WA (SE 98799-1912)
MSO-456 Inflict; Little Creek, Norfolk, VA (NY 09574-1913)
MSO-464 Pluck; San Diego, CA (SF 96675-1914)
MSO-488 Conquest; Seattle, WA (SE 98799-1915)
MSO-489 Gallant; San Francisco, CA (SF 96666-1916)
MSO-492 Pledge; Seattle, WA (SE 98799-1918)

Acme Class

MSO-509 Adroit; Little Creek, Norfolk, VA (NY 09564-1919)
MSO-511 Affray; Newport, RI (NY 09564-1920)

FLEET SUPPORT SHIPS

Bolster Class

ARS-38 Bolster; Long Beach, CA (SF 96661-3201)
ARS-40 Hoist; Little Creek, Norfolk, VA (NY 09583-3203)
ARS-42 Reclaimer; Pearl Harbor, HI (SF 96677-3255)

GRAY (FF-1054) *Knox Class*

GALLANT (MSO-489) *Aggressive Class*

NAVAL FLEET AUXILIARY FORCE

The Military Sealift Command long has been assigned the responsibility for supporting all components of the Department of Defense, and occasionally those of other elements of the government as well, in both peacetime and wartime. However, it required the upheaval in Iran and the Soviet invasion of Afghanistan in the late 1970s to focus national attention on the inadequacies of the forces available for strategic sealift, and particularly in terms of supporting U.S. forces in the Indian Ocean area. The resulting close scrutiny of sealift forces and their capabilities also spotlighted the meager means available for handling cargo in areas where modern port facilities were almost nonexistent. The dismal overall sealift situation was worsened by two other factors: (1) The U.S. merchant marine had been, and still was, in a state of decline; (2) A large percentage of modern merchant ships potentially available for sealift in time of emergency were containerships which were not configured to effectively handle military cargo. Since these deficiencies were faced up to, a number of actions have been taken both to add to the numbers of ships readily available for sealift and to greatly enhance the ability to both move and handle military cargo. Further emphasis was given to the importance of strategic sealift by its formal establishment by the Navy as one of the Navy's three primary functions; it joins sea control and power projection. As of 1 January 1989, the Military Sealift Command controlled a force comprising more than 120 ships, including approximately 70 strategic sealift ships, in addition to the steadily increasing numbers of ships in the Ready Reserve Force. In 1988, the Military Sealift Command became part of the newly formed unified command, the U.S. Transportation Command, which also has Air Force and Army elements.

JOSHUA HUMPHREYS (TAO-188) *Henry J. Kaiser Class*

OILERS (TAO)

Henry J. Kaiser Class (TAO-187)

DISPLACEMENT: 40,000 tons full load.
LENGTH: 677.5 feet.
BEAM: 97.5 feet.
SPEED: 20 knots.
POWER PLANT: two fully automatic diesel engines, twin shafts, 32,540 shaft horsepower.
AIRCRAFT: none (landing platform for vertical replenishment provided).
CARGO CAPACITY: 180,000 barrels of gas-turbine and diesel fuel.
COMPLEMENT: 96 civilian, 21 Navy.
BUILDERS: 187-190, 193, 195, 197-198, Avondale Shipyards; 191-192, 194, 196, Pennsylvania Shipbuilding.

Mispillion Class (Jumboized) (TAO-105)

DISPLACEMENT: approximately 34,000 tons full load.
LENGTH: 644 feet.
BEAM: 75 feet.
SPEED: 16 knots.
POWER PLANT: geared turbines, four boilers, two shafts, 13,500 shaft horsepower.
AIRCRAFT: none (landing platform for vertical replenishment provided).
CARGO CAPACITY: 150,000 barrels.
COMPLEMENT: 111 civilian, 21 Navy.
BUILDER: Sun Shipbuilding, Chester.

Neosho Class (TAO-143)

DISPLACEMENT: 38,000 tons full load.
LENGTH: 655 feet.
BEAM: 86 feet.
SPEED: 20 knots.
POWER PLANT: geared turbines, two boilers, two shafts, 28,000 shaft horsepower.
AIRCRAFT: none (landing platform for vertical replenishment provided).
CARGO CAPACITY: 180,000 barrels.
COMPLEMENT: 107 civilians, 21 Navy.
BUILDERS: 143, Bethlehem Steel, Quincy; 144-148, New York Shipbuilding, Camden.

BRIEFING: The Henry J. Kaiser (TAO-187), the first of what will be an 18-ship class of oilers, was delivered in 1986. Four others have been delivered since then, two others are scheduled for completion this year, and five others are under construction. The Navy sought funds for two in FY 1989, but Congress appropriated funds for five to permit completing procurement of the entire class. These ships will have a capacity for small quantities of fresh and frozen provisions, stores, and other materials which will permit full replenishment of some of their customers. As they join the fleet, they will permit retirement of some of the oilers of the 1940s (Mispillion class) and 1950s (Neosho class).

Henry J. Kaiser Class

TAO-187 Henry J. Kaiser; No home port assigned. (NY 09576-4086)
TAO-188 Joshua Humphreys; No home port assigned. (NY 09573-4087)
TAO-189 John Lenthall; No home port assigned. (NY 09577-4091)
TAO-190 Andrew J. Higgins; No home port assigned. (SF 96667-4001)
TAO-193 Walter S. Diehl; No home port assigned. (SF 96663-4020)

Mispillion Class (Jumboized)

TAO-105 Mispillion; Oakland, CA (SF 96672-4030)
TAO-106 Navasota; Oakland, CA (SF 96673-4037)
TAO-107 Passumpsic; Oakland, CA (SF 96675-4044)
TAO-108 Pawcatuck; Bayonne, NJ (NY 09582-4045)
TAO-109 Waccamaw; Bayonne, NJ (MI 34093-4072)

Neosho Class

TAO-143 Neosho; Bayonne, NJ (NY 09579-4039)
TAO-144 Mississinewa; Bayonne, NJ (MI 34092-4031)
TAO-145 Hassayampa; Oakland, CA (SF 96667-4016)
TAO-146 Kawashiwi; San Diego, CA (SF 96670-4022)
TAO-147 Truckee; Bayonne, NJ (NY 09588-4068)
TAO-148 Ponchatoula; Oakland, CA (SF 96675-4046)

SURVEILLANCE SHIPS (TAGOS)

Stalwart Class

DISPLACEMENT: 2,285 tons full load.
LENGTH: 224 feet.
BEAM: 43 feet.
SPEED: 11 knots.
POWER PLANT: four diesel generators, two shafts, 3,200 brake horsepower.
AIRCRAFT: none.
COMPLEMENT: 25 civilians.
BUILDERS: 1-12, Tacoma Boatbuilding Company; 13-18, Halter Marine.

TAGOS-19 Class

DISPLACEMENT: 4,200 tons full load.
LENGTH: 231 feet.
BEAM: 93 feet.
SPEED: 10.7 knots.
POWER PLANT: two Caterpillar diesel-General Electric generator combinations, one in each side of the hull, twin shafts, 1,600 shaft horsepower.
AIRCRAFT: none.
COMPLEMENT: 21 civilian, 13 Navy technicians.
BUILDER: McDermott Marine, Morgan City, LA

BRIEFING: These small, unarmed, civilian-manned auxiliary ships are destined to play a prominent role in augmenting overall ASW capability. They will tow sophisticated sonar gear (SURTASS) which will make possible a much broader area of coverage against forays by enemy submarines and more rapid transformation of information

PAWCATUCK (TAO-108) *Mispillion Class*

PREVAIL (TAGOS-8) *Stalwart Class*

for analysis. Operational results from the deployment of the first group of the monohulled Stalwart (TAGOS-1) class were excellent; however, their seakeeping qualities in the higher latitudes left something to be desired. Accordingly, in order to make possible more effective operation in these latitudes, the Navy elected to cease construction of the monohulled ships with the 18th ship, and to embark upon a program of construction of SWATH (small waterplane area twin hull) ships. A contract was awarded in October 1986 to McDermott Marine for construction of TAGOS-19, the first of the class, with an option for construction of three others, which were funded in FY 1989. The Navy plans to seek three more in FY 1990 and two in FY 1991, bringing the total number of TAGOS ships to 27. TAGOS-19 is scheduled for delivery in February 1990, and the last of the monohulled ships in March 1990.

TAGOS-1 Stalwart; Little Creek, Norfolk, VA (NY 09587-4077)
TAGOS-2 Contender; Pearl Harbor, HI (SF 96682-4082)
TAGOS-3 Vindicator; Little Creek, Norfolk, VA (NY 09590-4083)
TAGOS-4 Triumph; Pearl Harbor, HI (SF 96679-4084)
TAGOS-5 Assurance; Pearl Harbor, HI (SF 96660-4085)
TAGOS-6 Persistent; Little Creek, Norfolk, VA (NY 09582-4047)
TAGOS-7 Indomitable; Pearl Harbor, HI (SF 96668-4067)
TAGOS-8 Prevail; Little Creek, Norfolk, VA (NY 09582-4002)
TAGOS-9 Assertive; Oakland, CA (SF 96660-4011)
TAGOS-10 Invincible; Little Creek, Norfolk, VA (NY 09574-4041)
TAGOS-13 Adventurous; Pearl Harbor, HI (SF 96670-4084)

COMBAT STORES SHIPS (TAFS)

Ex-British Lyness Class

DISPLACEMENT: 16,792 tons full load.
LENGTH: 524 feet.
BEAM: 72 feet.
SPEED: 18 knots.
POWER PLANT: one diesel, 11,520 brake horsepower.
AIRCRAFT: two UH-46 Sea Knight helicopters.
ARMAMENT: none.
COMPLEMENT: 25 civilian, 44 Navy.
BUILDER: Swan Hunter & Wigham Richardson Ltd., Wallsend-On-Tyne.

BRIEFING: These ships formerly were Royal Navy replenishment ships; they were purchased from Great Britain in 1982-83 because of the increased logistics requirements resulting from the decision to maintain two carrier battle groups in the Indian Ocean during, and for a considerable time after, the Iranian hostage crisis. They are slightly more than 20 years old and have been extensively modernized with improved communications and underway-replenishment facilities. They have proven to be welcome additions to the fleet, and became even more valuable when it was decided after the attack on the Stark to sharply increase the U.S. naval presence in and adjacent to the Persian Gulf.

TAFS-8 Sirius; Norfolk, VA (NY 09587-4064)
TAFS-9 Spica; Oakland, CA (SF 96678-4066)
TAFS-10 Saturn; Norfolk, VA (NY 09587-4052)

SIRIUS (TAFS-8) *Lyness Class*

FLEET OCEAN TUGS (TATF)

Powhatan Class

DISPLACEMENT: 2,260 tons full load.
LENGTH: 226 feet.
BEAM: 42 feet.
SPEED: 15 knots.
POWER PLANT: two diesels, two shafts, controllable pitch propellers.
COMPLEMENT: 17 civilian, four Navy.
BUILDER: Marinette Marine Corporation, Wisconsin.

BRIEFING: The seven ships in this class, the oldest of which was placed in service in July 1979, are the first fleet ocean tugs to be built by the Navy since the Papago (ATF-160) in 1945. They have a 300-brake-horsepower bow thruster, a 10-ton-capacity crane, and a 53.6 ton bollard pull. Space is provided for light armament in time of war. No other ships of this type are included in the five-year shipbuilding plan.

TATF-166 Powhatan; No home port assigned. (NY 09582-4048)
TATF-167 Narragansett; No home port assigned. (SF 96673-4035)
TATF-168 Catawba; No home port assigned. (SF 96662-4047)
TATF-169 Navajo; No home port assigned. (SF 96673-4036)
TATF-170 Mohawk; No home port assigned. (NY 09578-4033)
TATF-171 Sioux; No home port assigned. (SF 96678-4063)
TATF-172 Apache; No home port assigned. (NY 09564-4003)

FLEET BALLISTIC MISSILE SHIPS (TAK)

Marshfield

DISPLACEMENT: 11,500 tons full load.
LENGTH: 455 feet.
BEAM: 28.5 feet.
SPEED: 17 knots.
POWER PLANT: steam turbine, two boilers, one shaft, 8,500 shaft horsepower.
CREW: 69 civilians, Navy security personnel.
BUILDER: Oregon Shipbuilding, Portland.

POWHATAN (TATF-166) *Powhatan Class*

Vega

DISPLACEMENT: 18,365 tons full load.
LENGTH: 483 feet.
BEAM: 68 feet.
SPEED: 21 knots.
POWER PLANT: steam turbine, two boilers, one shaft, 12,500 shaft horsepower.
CREW: 67 civilians, seven Navy.
BUILDER: Sun Shipbuilding and Drydock, Chester, Pa.

BRIEFING: Marshfield *and* Vega *both are former merchant ships which have been converted to support SSBN tenders and have been fitted to carry 16 ballistic missiles.*

TAK-282 Marshfield; No home port assigned. (FL 34092-4026)
TAK-286 Vega; No home port assigned. (FL 34093-4070)

VEGA (TAK-286) *Vega Class*

NAVAL FLEET MOBILITY ENHANCEMENT

MARITIME PREPOSITIONED SHIPS (MPS) (TAK)

MAERSK CONVERSIONS

DISPLACEMENT: 46,552 long tons full load.
LENGTH: 755 feet.
BEAM: 90 feet.
SPEED: 17.5 knots.
POWER PLANT: one diesel, one screw, 16,800 shaft horsepower.
ENDURANCE: 10,800 nautical miles.
AIRCRAFT: none.
ARMAMENT: none.
CAPACITY: bulk POL, 1.3 million gallons; water, 85,000 gallons; equipment and vehicles, 1/5 of Marine Amphibious Brigade (MAB).
COMPLEMENT: 27 civilians and 6 maintenance personnel.
CONVERTING SHIPYARD: Bethlehem Steel, Sparrows Point, MD (3); Beaumont, TX (2).

WATERMAN CONVERSIONS

DISPLACEMENT: 48,754 long tons full load.
LENGTH: 821 feet.
BEAM: 105.5 feet.
SPEED: 20 knots.
POWER PLANT: two geared turbines, two boilers, one screw, 30,000 shaft horsepower.
ENDURANCE: 13,000 nautical miles.
AIRCRAFT: none.
ARMAMENT: none.
CAPACITY: bulk POL, 1.5 million gallons; water, 91,938 gallons; equipment and vehicles, 1/4 of MAB.
COMPLEMENT: 29 civilians and 6 maintenance personnel.
CONVERTING SHIPYARD: National Steel and Shipbuilding.

AMSEA NEW CONSTRUCTION

DISPLACEMENT: 40,846 long tons full load.
LENGTH: 654.6 feet.
BEAM: 105.5 feet.
SPEED: 18 knots.
POWER PLANT: two diesels, one screw, 26,000 shaft horsepower.
ENDURANCE: 12,840 nautical miles.
AIRCRAFT: none.
ARMAMENT: none.
CAPACITY: bulk POL, 1.6 million gallons; water, 98,994 gallons; equipment and vehicles, 1/4 of MAB.
COMPLEMENT: 30 civilians and 6 maintenance personnel.
BUILDER: General Dynamics, Quincy.

BRIEFING: These 13 ships provide additional lift for Marine amphibious forces. Eight relatively new merchant ships were purchased for the purpose of conversion; the remaining five are new construction. They form three squadrons. The first, which was completed and loaded in 1984, operates in eastern and northern Atlantic waters. The second, which was completed and loaded in 1985, replaced five prepositioned ships in the Indian Ocean and operates in that area. The third, which was completed and loaded in 1986, operates in the western Pacific. Each squadron contains the equipment and 30 days of supplies for a Marine Expeditionary Brigade and is capable of off-loading at piers or from offshore with special equipment with which they have been fitted. However, the ships themselves have no amphibious capability. The prepositioning concept and the unique combined capabilities of these ships have been enthusiastically welcomed and supported by the Marine Corps.

CPL LOUIS J. HAUGE, JR. (TAK-3000)

TAK-3000 Cpl Louis J. Hauge, Jr.; No home port assigned. (SF 96667-7247)
TAK-3001 Pfc William B. Baugh; No home port assigned. (SF 96667-7250)
TAK-3002 Pfc James Anderson, Jr.; No home port assigned. (SF 96660-7258)
TAK-3003 1st Lt Alex Bonnyman, Jr.; No home port assigned. (SF 96661-7260)
TAK-3004 Pvt Harry Fisher; No home port assigned. (SF 96665-7259)
TAK-3005 Sgt Matej Kocak; No home port assigned. (NY 09505-7248)
TAK-3006 Pfc Eugene A. Obregon; No home port assigned. (NY 09505-7253)
TAK-3007 Maj Stephen W. Pless; No home port assigned. (NY 09505-7209)
TAK-3008 Lt John P. Bobo; No home port assigned. (NY 09505-7255)
TAK-3009 Pfc DeWayne T. Williams; No home port assigned. (NY 09505-7210)
TAK-3010 1st Lt Baldomero Lopez; No home port assigned. (SF 96666-7223)
TAK-3011 1st Lt Jack Lummus; No home port assigned. (NY 09505-7232)
TAK-3012 Sgt William R. Button; No home port assigned. (NY 09505-7262)

LT JOHN P. BOBO (TAK-3008)

SPECIAL MISSION SUPPORT SHIPS

WILKES (TAGS-33) *Silas Bent Class*

OCEANOGRAPHIC SHIPS

Silas Bent Class

DISPLACEMENT: 2,620 tons full load.
LENGTH: 287 feet.
BEAM: 48 feet.
SPEED: 14.5 knots cruising.
RANGE: 7,000 nautical miles at cruising speed.
POWER PLANT: diesel electric, one shaft, 3,600 shaft horsepower.
CREW: 47 civilians, 28 scientific personnel.
BUILDERS: TAGS-26, American Shipbuilding, Lorain, Ohio; 27, Christy Corporation, Sturgeon Bay, WI; 33-34, Defoe Shipbuilding, Bay City, MI.

Conrad Class

DISPLACEMENT: 1,300 tons full load.
LENGTH: 208-plus feet.
BEAM: 39 feet.
SPEED: 12 knots, cruising.
RANGE: TAGOR-7, 12,000 nautical miles; 12-13, 9,000 nautical miles.
POWER PLANT: diesel electric, one shaft, 1,200 shaft horsepower.
CREW: 26 civilian, 15 scientific personnel.
BUILDERS: 7, Marietta Manufacturing, Point Pleasant, WV; 12-13, Northwest Marine Iron Works, Portland, OR.

Chauvenet Class

DISPLACEMENT: 4,000 tons full load.
LENGTH: 393 feet.
BEAM: 54 feet.
SPEED: 13 knots, cruising.
RANGE: 12,000 miles at cruising speed.
POWER PLANT: geared diesel, one shaft, 3,600 shaft horsepower.
CREW: 69 civilian, 67 scientific personnel, 22 Coastal Survey Team personnel, 19 helicopter detachment.
BUILDER: Upper Clyde Shipbuilders, Glasgow, Scotland.

Bowditch Class

DISPLACEMENT: 13,050 tons full load.
LENGTH: 455 feet.
BEAM: 62 feet.
SPEED: 16.5 knots, cruising.
RANGE: 30,000 nautical miles at 14 knots.
POWER PLANT: steam turbine, one shaft, 8,500 shaft horsepower.
CREW: 60 civilians, 38 scientific personnel.
BUILDER: Oregon Shipbuilding, Portland.

H.H. Hess

DISPLACEMENT: 17,874 tons full load.
LENGTH: 564 feet.
BEAM: 76 feet.
SPEED: 20 knots.
POWER PLANT: steam turbine, two boilers, one shaft, 19,250 shaft horsepower.
CREW: 69 civilians, 14 scientific personnel, 27 Navy technicians.
BUILDER: National Steel and Shipbuilding.

BRIEFING: Ships of the Conrad class were the first ships built for the purpose of Naval Oceanography. Because they were completed over a seven-year period, and were subject to changes before and during construction, they vary in detail, with different bridge, side structure, mast, and laboratory arrangements. Three of the nine ships in the class were transferred to foreign governments, and three others are operated by U.S. academic institutions. Of the nine AGSs, Dutton is by far the oldest, having originally been a 1945 vintage Liberty ship which was converted to a deep ocean survey ship in 1958. Two new construction AGSs, Maury and Tanner, are replacing Dutton and Bowditch, which was scrapped in 1987. The four Silas Bent-class ships were designed specifically for oceanographic survey operations; they were completed between 1965-1971. Chauvenet and Harkness are the largest survey ships to be built specifically for that role. H.H. Hess is a converted merchant ship completed in 1964 and converted during 1975-1977. Hayes is being converted to an acoustic research vessel, with delivery planned for March 1990. Construction-contract awards for two coastal hydrographic survey ships (TAGS-51/52) were made in 1988; they also are scheduled for delivery in 1990. However, the inclusion of an oceanographic research ship, this one to be built on a SWATH-type hull, in the FY 1989 budget was delayed a year because the design was considered to be immature.

Silas Bent Class

TAGS-26 Silas Bent; No home port assigned. (SF 96661-4005)
TAGS-27 Kane; No home port assigned. (NY 09576-4021)
TAGS-33 Wilkes; No home port assigned. (NY 09591-4073)
TAGS-34 Wyman; No home port assigned. (SF 96683-4074)

Conrad Class

TAGOR-7 Lynch; No home port assigned. (NY 09577-4025)
TAGOR-12 De Steiguer; No home port assigned. (SF 96663-4012)
TAGOR-13 Bartlett; No home port assigned. (NY 09565-4004)

68 NAVY

Chauvenet Class

TAGS-29 Chauvenet; No home port assigned. (SF 96662-4009)
TAGS-32 Harkness; No home port assigned. (NY 09573-4015)

Bowditch Class

TAGS-22 Dutton; No home port assigned. (NY 09567-4013)
TAGS-38 H.H. Hess; No home port assigned. (NY 09573-4018)

CABLE REPAIR SHIPS (TARC)

Neptune Class

DISPLACEMENT: 7,400 tons full load.
LENGTH: 369 feet.
BEAM: 47 feet.
SPEED: 14 knots.
POWER PLANT: turbo-electric, two boilers, two shafts, 4,000 shaft horsepower.
CREW: 71 civilian, 6 Navy, 25 technicians.
BUILDER: Pusey and Jones, Wilmington, DE.

Zeus

DISPLACEMENT: 14,225 tons full load.
LENGTH: 511.5 feet.
BEAM: 73 feet.
SPEED: 15 knots.
POWER PLANT: diesel-electric, two shafts, 10,200 brake horsepower.
CREW: 88 civilian, 6 Navy, 30 technicians.
BUILDER: National Steel and Shipbuilding.

BRIEFING: The two ships of the Neptune class were built as Army cable ships; they were completed in 1946, laid up until the early 1950s, and then transferred to the Navy. They were transferred to the Military Sealift Command in 1973 and extensively modernized 1979-1982. Until their re-engining during this period, they were the last ships in the Navy with reciprocating engines. Zeus was the first cable ship built specifically for the Navy. She can lay up to 1,000 miles of cable in depths up to 9,000 feet. All three ARCs support the Navy's SOSUS system.

TARC-2 Neptune; No home port assigned. (SF 96673-4040)
TARC-6 Albert J. Myer; No home port assigned. (SF 96672-4034)
TARC-7 Zeus; No home port assigned. (SF 96687-4076)

UNDERSEA SURVEILLANCE SHIP (TAGOR)

Mizar

DISPLACEMENT: 4,942 tons full load.
LENGTH: 262 feet.
BEAM: 51.5 feet.
SPEED: 12 knots.
POWER PLANT: diesel-electric, two shafts, 3,200 brake horsepower.
CREW: 46 civilians, 15 technicians, 5 Navy.
BUILDER: Avondale Shipyards.

BRIEFING: Mizar and a sister ship originally were built to carry cargo for Army projects in the Arctic. In 1964-1965 she received an extensive conversion to an AGOR. She was a key participant in the search for the sunken submarine Thresher (SSN-593) in 1964 and later helped to locate the sunken Scorpion (SSN-589) in the Atlantic and the Soviet Golf-class diesel submarine in the mid-Pacific. She also participated in the search for the hydrogen bomb lost at sea off Palomares, Spain, in 1966. She is operated by the Military Sealift Command for the Navy's Space and Naval Warfare Systems Command.

TAGOR-13 Mizar; No home port assigned. (SF 96672-4032)

NAVIGATION TEST SUPPORT SHIP (TAG)

Vanguard

This ship, more than 40 years old, served initially as a Navy oiler, and since has been converted twice, first to a missile-range instrumentation ship and then to a navigation research ship. She is operated by the Military Sealift Command for the Navy's Strategic System Project Office.

TAG-194 Vanguard; No home port assigned. (MI 34093-4069)

ZEUS (TARC-7) *Zeus Class*

READY RESERVE FORCE

BRIEFING: Over the years this force was permitted to decline to fewer than 25 ships. However, increased emphasis on sealift resulted in decisions to increase it markedly. Its planned ultimate size has climbed each year for the past several years; the current goal is 120 ships by 1992. More than half the ships in the RRF are break bulk cargo ships, but it also includes tankers, auxiliary crane ships, containerships, aviation support ships, and a troopship. Most RRF ships will be maintained at the three National Defense Reserve Fleet sites: James River, VA, Beaumont, TX, and Suisun Bay, CA. More than 60 of the 92 ships in the RRF at the end of 1988 were being maintained in a five-day readiness status. Each RRF ship is designated to be crewed and operated by a particular shipping firm. Periodically ships are broken out to participate in readiness exercises or to carry out special missions. $35.4 million was provided in FY 1989 for continued support of the program. In FY 1990, funding for the RRF will become the responsibility of the Department of Transportation.

KEYSTONE STATE (TACS-1)

AUXILIARY CRANE SHIPS (TACS)

DISPLACEMENT: 25,660 long tons full load.
LENGTH: 668.5 feet.
BEAM: 76 feet.
SPEED: 20 knots.
POWER PLANT: geared steam turbine, one shaft, 19,250 shaft horsepower.
AIRCRAFT: none.
COMPLEMENT: 65 civilians (including crane operators).
CONVERTING YARDS: 1-2, DeFoe Shipbuilding Company, Bay City, MI; 3, Dillingham Ship Repair, Portland, OR; 4-6, NORSHIPCO, Norfolk, VA; 7-8, Tampa Shipyards, Tampa, FL.

BRIEFING: These ships incorporate a unique capability stemming from the need to be able to offload containers and other heavy equipment from non-self-sustaining containerships in areas where port facilities range from meager to none. Because of different hull configurations of the ships being converted to crane ships, some will have three pedestals with two cranes each, and others but two pedestals with two cranes each. Each single crane can lift 30 long tons, twin cranes 60 long tons, and two sets of twin cranes in tandem 105 long tons. The cranes can handle loads in 3-5 foot seas. Six ships have been converted and two others were to complete conversion in December 1988 and February 1989. All will be maintained in a 5-day readiness state in the Ready Reserve Force.

AVIATION LOGISTICS SUPPORT SHIPS (TAVB)

DISPLACEMENT: 23,800 long tons full load.
LENGTH: 602 feet.
BEAM: 90 feet.
POWER PLANT: two boilers, geared steam turbine, one shaft, 30,000 shaft horsepower.
SPEED: 23 knots at 80 percent power.
AIRCRAFT: none.
COMPLEMENT: 41 civilians plus 300 Marines (when fully manned).
CONVERTING YARD: Todd-Galveston.

BRIEFING: These converted ships provide the capability to load the vans and equipment of a Marine Corps aviation intermediate maintenance activity and transport them to the desired theater of operation. They have both a roll-on/roll-off and self-sustaining containership configuration which will permit them to offload both alongside and offshore. After the aviation equipment is offloaded, they can revert to a standard sealift role to carry 600 containers if required. The only two ships of this type completed conversion in 1987 and are being maintained in a reduced operating status.

HOSPITAL SHIPS (TAH)

DISPLACEMENT: 69,360 long tons full load.
LENGTH: 894 feet.
BEAM: 106 feet.
SPEED: 17.5 knots.
POWER PLANT: geared steam turbine, two boilers, one shaft, 24,500 shaft horsepower.
ENDURANCE: 13,420 nautical miles.
CAPACITY: 1,000 beds, 12 operating rooms.
COMPLEMENT: 1,207 (including 73 civilian crew, 387 Navy support and communications personnel, and 820 Naval medical personnel).
CONVERSION: National Steel and Shipbuilding Company.

BRIEFING: When the conversion of the first of these two San Clemente-class tankers was completed in the fall of 1986, the Navy had a hospital ship in its inventory for the first time in more than a decade. She is the Mercy (TAH-19). The last hospital ship to serve fleet personnel had been the Sanctuary (TAH-17), commissioned in 1946, subsequently mothballed, then recalled from the Reserve Fleet for duty during the Vietnam War, and once again mothballed. Her overall poor condition ruled out modernization. The second conversion, completed in late 1987, became the Comfort (TAH-20), which will be based on the east coast. Mercy will be based on the west coast. Both ships will have skeleton crews and medical staffs aboard. They will be able to get underway in five days from notification of need. Mercy departed in February 1987, even before she had completed her final contract trials, for the Philippines, where she provided medical care to civilians throughout many areas of the islands. She returned to the United States in July 1987.

TAH-19 Mercy; Oakland, CA (SF 96672-4090)
TAH-20 Comfort; Baltimore, MD (NY 09566-4008)

MERCY (TAH-19)

(Ships in the Ready Reserve Force often are activated for special missions, overhauls and repair work, training, and participation in exercises. During those periods they would normally operate from areas other than the sites where they normally are maintained. However, in the listing that follows, RRF ships are placed in the areas to which they are assigned when inactive. None of the ships in the RRF have home ports assigned.)

EAST REGION

FREIGHTERS

TAK-285 Southern Cross
TAK-1001 Admiral Wm. M. Callaghan
TAK-1014 Cape Nome
TAK-5005 Adventurer
TAK-5006 Aide
TAK-5007 Ambassador
TAK-5008 Banner
TAK-5009 Cape Ann
TAK-5010 Cape Alexander
TAK-5011 Cape Archway
TAK-5012 Cape Alava
TAK-5013 Cape Avinof
TAK-5015 Agent
TAK-5016 Lake
TAK-5017 Pride
TAK-5018 Scan
TAK-5019 Courier
TAK-5037 Cape Canso
TAK-5040 Cape Canaveral
TAK-5042 Cape Carthage
TAK-5043 Cape Catoche
TAK-5075 Cape Johnson
TAK-5077 Cape Juby
TAKR-5052 Cape Douglas
TAKR 5053 Cape Domingo
TAKR-5054 Cape Decision
TAKR-5055 Cape Diamond
TAKR-5066 Cape Hudson
TAKR-5076 Cape Henry
TAKR-5077 Cape Lambert
TAKR-5078 Cape Lobos

AUXILIARY CRANE SHIPS

TACS-1 Keystone State
TACS-4 Gopher State
TACS-5 Flickertail State
TACS-6 Cornhusker State

TROOP SHIP

TAP-1000 Patriot State

GULF REGION

SEATRAIN SHIPS

TAK-5020 Washington
TAK-5021 Maine

TANKERS

TAOT-165 American Explorer
TAOT-181 Potomac
TAOT-1012 Mission Buenaventura
TAOT-5005 Mission Capistrano

FREIGHTERS

TAK-2016 Pioneer Commander
TAK-2018 Pioneer Contractor
TAK-2019 Pioneer Crusader
TAK-2033 Buyer
TAK-2035 Gulf Shipper
TAK-2036 Gulf Trader
TAK-5022 Santa Ana
TAK-5026 Del Viento
TAK-5036 Cape Chalmers
TAK-5038 Cape Charles
TAK-5039 Cape Clear
TAK-5041 Cape Cod
TAK-5044 Gulf Banker
TAK-5045 Gulf Farmer
TAK-5046 Gulf Merchant
TAK-5049 Del Monte
TAK-5050 Del Valle
TAKR-5063 Cape May
TAKR-5064 Cape Mendocino
TAKR-5065 Cape Mohican
TAKR-5070 Cape Flattery
TAKR-5071 Cape Florida
TAKR-5073 Cape Farewell
TAKR-5074 Cape Catawba
TAKR-5075 American Osprey
TAKR-5076 Cape Inscription

WEST REGION

TANKERS

TAOT-151 Shoshone

GASOLINE TANKERS

TAOG-78 Nodaway
TAOG-81 Alatna
TAOG-82 Chattahoochee

FREIGHTERS

TAK-184 Northern Light
TAK-2039 Cape Girardeau
TAK-5029 California
TAK-5051 Cape Gibson
TAK-5056 Cape Breton
TAK-5057 Cape Bover
TAK-5058 Cape Borda
TAK-5059 Cape Bon
TAK-5060 Cape Blanco
TAK-5061 Austral Lightning
TAKR-7 Comet
TAKR-9 Meteor
TAKR-11 Jupiter
TAKR-5062 Cape Isabel
TAKR-5068 Cape Horn
TAKR-5069 Cape Edmont

AUXILIARY CRANE SHIPS

TACS-2 Gem State
TACS-3 Grand Canyon State

The following ships are being readied for service in the Ready Reserve Force. Some will replace older ships already in the RRF; others such as merchantmen being converted to auxiliary crane ships (TACS) will increase the size of the force. Almost all of the ships acquired for the RRF are given new names upon their entry into it.

Ship Name	Type	RRF Entry Date
Diamond State	TACS-7	15 December 1988
Equality State	TACS-8	21 February 1989
American Altair	TACS-9	Date to be decided
American Draco	TACS-10	Date to be decided
Edward Rutledge	LASH	Date to be decided
Benjamin Harrison	LASH	Date to be decided
American Banker	TACS-11	Date to be decided

QUAPAW (ATF-110)

SWATH (Artist Concept)

POINT LOMA (AGDS-2)

COMMENT: Many other kinds of ships and craft contribute immensely to the overall capability of the fleet. Prominent among them are submersibles, which are operated in support of search, rescue, research, and deep-ocean recovery activities. Two are nuclear powered. Two deep-submergence rescue vessels were developed and constructed after the loss of the submarine Thresher in 1963 to provide a capability for rescuing survivors from submarines disabled on the ocean floor above their hull collapse depth. The research submersible Alvin, which has made over 1,000 dives and made headlines during the mission to photograph the sunken liner Titanic, is operated by the Woods Hole Oceanographic Institute for the Office of Naval Research.

Also of great importance are large and medium harbor tugs, available in relatively large numbers and vital to harbor operations. Several converted WWII ships and craft still support weapons testing, research, and recovery operations. Patrol craft (YP) are used extensively to train future officers at the Naval Academy and at Officer Candidate School at Newport, RI, and also are being given an inshore minesweeping capability. Utility landing craft (LCU) have served as real workhorses in the amphibious forces; several new classes have been built in the last three decades. A unique craft is the LWT, a warping tug designed to handle pontoon causeways and thus to make easier the offloading of ships in areas where port facilities are lacking.

Also contributing significantly to fleet operations are floating drydocks, which supplement fixed drydock facilities at major naval installations, support fleet ballistic submarines at forward bases, and provide repair capabilities in forward areas. The largest of those currently active, with a capacity of 40,000 tons, is at the Naval Base at Subic Bay in the Philippines.

The Navy has experimented in recent years with a few kinds of ships and craft representative of advanced technologies. Foremost among these have been ships and craft operating on the surface-effect principle. SES technology has been successfully incorporated in the new Marine Corps landing craft, air cushion (LCAC). The SWATH (Small Waterplane Area Twin Hull) principle is considered by many in the Navy to offer high potential for fleet operations and is being incorporated into surveillance ships (TAGOS); the first of this class of ship is scheduled for completion in early 1990. The Marines are seeking a new class of amphibious ship to replace LKAs, LSTs, and LPDs; its design is under development. The Navy is pursuing "high leverage technologies" that hold promise for improved hull-propulsion-plant and combat-system effectiveness. Superconducting electric motors, composite materials and hull coatings, high-energy weapons, and advanced electronics and photonics are among the technologies being pursued for application in new surface ships in the 21st century.

AIRCRAFT/NAVY

HORNET

F/A-18 HORNET

WING SPAN: 37.5 feet.
LENGTH: 56 feet.
HEIGHT: 15 feet, 3½ inches.
WEIGHT: fighter mission takeoff, 36,710 pounds; attack mission takeoff, 49,224 pounds.
SPEED: more than 1,360 mph.
CEILING: approximately 50,000 feet.
RANGE: fighter mission, 400 nautical-mile radius; attack mission, 575 nautical-mile radius; ferry range, more than 2,000 nautical miles.
POWER PLANT: two General Electric F404-GE-400 low-bypass turbofan engines; 16,000 pounds static thrust.
CREW: F/A-18A and C, one; F/A-18B and D, two.
CONTRACTOR: prime, McDonnell Douglas; airframe, Northrop.

BRIEFING: The multimission Hornet was designed and developed as both a fighter and an attack aircraft. It is replacing Navy and Marine Corps F-4s and A-7s. It can carry up to 17,000 pounds of armament, including Sparrow, Sidewinder, and Harm missiles on nine stations. Its radar and forward-looking infrared (FLIR) display sensors have both air-to-air and air-to-ground capabilities. The head-up display (HUD) allows the pilot to be kept fully informed of his instruments without taking his eyes off the target. Reliability and ease of maintenance were emphasized in the F/A-18 design. Over 700 Hornets have been delivered and are flying three times the hours without failure flown by other Navy tactical aircraft, while requiring half the maintenance time. As a consequence, F/A-18 squadrons are manned with far fewer personnel than other Navy squadrons. The first major upgrade of the F/A-18, the single seat F/A-18C and dual-seat F/A-18D, began delivery in 1987. The F/A-18C/D features survivability enhancements, improved maintenance monitoring hardware, and provisions for the new AMRAAM AIM-120 and Maverick AGM-65F missiles when they reach the fleet. The F/A-18 will receive an improved night-attack capability beginning this year, and a reconnaissance version is under development, but behind its original schedule for delivery in 1990. 84 aircraft were funded in both FY 1988 and FY 1989, with Congress adding 12 to the Navy's request for 72 in FY 1989. The F/A-18 is flown by Australia, Canada, and Spain, and Kuwait will begin buying the aircraft in 1989.

F-14 TOMCAT

WING SPAN: 64 feet unswept; 38 feet swept.
LENGTH: 62.7 feet.
HEIGHT: 16 feet.
WEIGHT: empty, 40,469 pounds; maximum take-off, 74,349 pounds.
SPEED: maximum, 1,544 mph; cruise, 576 mph.
CEILING: more than 56,000 feet.
RANGE: combat, 500 nautical miles; ferry range, 2,000 nautical miles.
POWER PLANT: two Pratt and Whitney TF-30-P412A turbofan engines with afterburners; 20,900 pounds static thrust; on remainder of F-14A+ aircraft and on F-14Ds, F-110-GE-400 augmented turbofan engines with afterburner and 27,000-29,000 pounds static thrust.
CREW: two.
CONTRACTOR: Grumman Aerospace.

BRIEFING: In 1969 Grumman was selected as the winner of a design competition to build the F-14 as a replacement for the F-4; after a somewhat stormy beginning it has emerged as a versatile and capable combat aircraft. The aircraft's sophisticated radar-missile combination enables it to simultaneously track 24 targets and attack six with Phoenix missiles while continuing to scan the airspace. It can select and destroy targets up to 100 miles away. Its original TF-30 engine's performance was deemed by the Navy to be far below desired standards, and in 1984 the Navy announced that the General Electric F-110 turbofan engine had been selected to equip all future F-14A aircraft and the upgraded F-14D version. As of January 1989, F-110 engines had been installed in 36 F-14 aircraft. The

TOMCAT

F-14D, which will have markedly improved avionics, radar, communications, and weaponry, is expected to have significant avionics commonality with the F/A-18 and the improved A-6. Five prototype F-14Ds are testing various kinds of new equipment, and development is on schedule with first production deliveries to commence in March 1990. The Navy's ultimate goal is an F-14D fleet by the year 2000.

A-6E INTRUDER

WING SPAN: 53 feet.
LENGTH: 55 feet.
HEIGHT: 16 feet.
WEIGHT: empty, 26,746 pounds; maximum catapult takeoff, 58,600 pounds.
SPEED: maximum at sea level, 647 mph; cruise at optimum altitude, 476 mph.
CEILING: 42,400 feet.
RANGE: 2,380 nautical miles ferry range; 878 nautical miles with maximum military load.
POWER PLANT: two Pratt and Whitney J52-P-8B turbojet engines; 9,300 pounds static thrust each. (For A-6F, two F-404-GE-400D augmented turbofan engines with 18,000 pounds static thrust.)
CREW: two.
CONTRACTOR: Grumman Aerospace.

BRIEFING: The several versions of the A-6 medium-attack, all-weather, day-night, carrier-based aircraft have been a mainstay of the Navy and Marine Corps air arms for more than two decades. Constantly being improved upon over this time span, it is used for close-air-support, interdiction, and deep-strike missions. Seven versions of the basic design have been built, with the EA-6B and the A-6E still being in production. The A-6E has an advanced electronics package, and can carry external weapons loads of 18,000 pounds; it is configured for both Harm and Harpoon missiles. At one time, the A-6E production line was a target for elimination by Congress; however, the aircraft's performance in recent years, and particularly during the 1986 attacks on Libyan targets, buttressed its reputation as an outstanding attack aircraft. The wings of the A-6E, however, are being replaced because of the discovery of cracks resulting from accelerated fatigue; the new aluminum composite wings were developed and are being produced by Boeing. In FY 1988, the Navy had sought authorization and funding for an improved version of the A-6E, the A-6F. Although Congress did appropriate funds for the construction program, it subsequently refused to authorize expenditure of those funds by the Navy, and the A-6 program remained at a standstill throughout early FY 1988. Congress subsequently approved the use of a portion of FY 1988 appropriations to construct 10 improved A-6Es. It also directed the Navy to tell Congress specifically what kind of improved A-6 aircraft, other than an A-6F, it wished to procure in future years. It is anticipated that the Navy will seek a digitalized version of the A-6E. Ultimately A-6 aircraft will be replaced by the Advanced Tactical Aircraft (ATA), which currently is under development with the Navy being the sponsoring service.

INTRUDER

CORSAIR

A-7 CORSAIR

WING SPAN: 39 feet.
LENGTH: 46 feet.
HEIGHT: 16 feet.
WEIGHT: empty, 19,111 pounds; maximum takeoff, 42,000 pounds.
SPEED: maximum at 5,000 feet, with 12 Mk82 bombs, 646 mph; after dropping bombs, 684 mph.
CEILING: 35,500 feet.
RANGE: maximum ferry range with internal fuel, 1,981 nautical miles; with internal and external fuel, 2,485 nautical miles.
POWER PLANT: one Allison TF-41-A-2 non-after-burning turbofan engine.
CONTRACTOR: Vought.

BRIEFING: After two decades of service in the fleet, and also with the Air Force, the A-7 is being replaced with the F/A-18. Originally built on the F-8U Crusader airframe in order to keep costs down, the A-7 has gone through several modifications since the A-7A first was flown in 1965. The A-7E now carries varying payloads of bombs and missiles as well as a 20mm gatling gun; its maximum payload of armament is more than 15,000 pounds. Eight stations are available for ordnance. More than 1,500 A-7s have been built for the Navy, Air Force, and foreign air forces. No further Navy purchases of the A-7 are contemplated, and the Navy does not plan to try to upgrade it. The last two A-7E squadrons will complete transition to F/A 18s during FY 1993.

EA-6B PROWLER

WING SPAN: 53 feet.
LENGTH: 60 feet.
HEIGHT: 16 feet.
WEIGHT: empty, 32,162 pounds; maximum takeoff, 65,000 pounds.
SPEED: maximum at sea level, 651 mph; cruise, 481 mph.
CEILING: 38,000 feet, with five ECM pods.
COMBAT RANGE: 2,083 nautical miles with maximum external fuel.
POWER PLANT: two Pratt and Whitney J52-P-408 turbojet engines; 11,200 pounds static thrust.
CREW: four (including three electronic warfare officers).
CONTRACTOR: Grumman Aerospace.

BRIEFING: This slightly longer version of the A-6, the extra length having been added to accommodate electronic-warfare personnel and equipment, is the Navy's first aircraft designed and built specifically for tactical electronic warfare. Its primary missions are active and passive defense of a task force and degradation and suppression of enemy defense systems by jamming. Avionics equipment has progressed through four generations of modernization; the latest modernization makes it possible for the aircraft to jam two different frequency bands simultaneously from each of its five wing- and fuselage-mounted pods. A fifth-generation modernization involves a major upgrade of the EA-6Bs receiver processors, computer system, navigation/instruments equipment, and radar/communications jamming capability. The upgrade allows the crew to more rapidly evaluate and prosecute a larger number of threats. The Navy, after having its requested FY 1988 buy of six EA-6Bs doubled by Congress because the proposed buy was deemed insufficient to meet Navy and Marine Corps needs, saw its requested FY 1989 buy of six increased to 12 for the same reason.

PROWLER

E6-A TACAMO

WING SPAN: 145 feet, 9 inches.
LENGTH: 153 feet.
HEIGHT: 42 feet, 5 inches.
WEIGHT: gross take-off, 342,000 pounds.
SPEED: 512 knots.
CEILING: 42,000 feet; patrol altitude, 25,000-30,000 feet.
RANGE: unrefueled, 6,700 nautical miles with 16 hours on-station endurance.
POWER PLANT: CFM International F-108-CF-100 (CFM 56-24-2) turbofan engines.
CREW: four flight crew, five mission crew.
CONTRACTOR: Boeing.

BRIEFING: A highly important but little-known Navy aircraft role is that of serving as the means of relaying VLF signals to strategic missile submarines. Currently, modified C-130 aircraft, EC-130Qs, are serving as the TACAMO (Take Charge and Move Out) platforms. The Navy plans to replace them with aircraft of the modified 707/C-137/E-3 design, two of which were funded in FY 1986. Three were funded in each of FY 1987 and FY 1988, and seven in FY 1989. These aircraft will have an improved capability to communicate with Air Force AWACS aircraft and will contain the same basic equipment as the EC-130Cs, including 30,000 feet of trailing wire antenna. When replaced, the EC-130Cs will be modified for cargo and other support missions. The first E-6A production aircraft is scheduled for delivery in May 1989. The main base of operations for these aircraft will be Tinker Air Force Base starting in May 1992. Transition bases are Barbers Pt., HI and Patuxent River, MD.

E-2C HAWKEYE

WING SPAN: 81 feet.
LENGTH: 58 feet.
HEIGHT: 18 feet.
WEIGHT: empty, 37,678 pounds; maximum take-off, 51,569 pounds.
SPEED: maximum, 374 mph; cruise, 311 mph.
CEILING: 30,800 feet.
RANGE: 200 nautical-mile radius with six hours on station; ferry range, 1,525 nautical miles.
POWER PLANT: two Allison T56-A-422 turboprop engines.
CREW: five, including personnel assigned primarily to monitor various electronic systems.
CONTRACTOR: Grumman Aerospace.

BRIEFING: This durable carrier-based early warning aircraft has been improved upon constantly since the first E-2A flew in 1961. The E-2C, which made its first flight 10 years later, is equipped with radar capable of detecting targets anywhere within a three-million-cubic-mile surveillance envelope while simultaneously monitoring maritime traffic. Each E-2C also can maintain all-weather patrols; track, automatically and simultaneously, more than 600 targets; and control more than 40 airborne intercepts. An upgrading of its electronic suite and its engine, the latter to the T56-A-427 engine, began in 1986, with these actions aimed at ensuring its airborne-early-warning advantage through the 1990s. In mid-1988 there were widespread reports of cracks in the aircraft's wings; however, this condition had first been encountered in 1980, and an orderly program of repair subsequently developed, with damage being repaired on one E-2C per month. The E-2C dramatically demonstrated its capabilities in international incidents in 1985 and 1986, and has been used most effectively in the greatly expanded U.S. drug-interdiction program. The Customs Service and the Coast Guard each have been provided two Navy E-2Cs for use in that program. Six E-2Cs were funded for the Navy in FY 1989.

TACAMO

HAWKEYE

ORION

P-3C ORION

WING SPAN: 100 feet.
LENGTH: 117 feet.
HEIGHT: 34 feet.
WEIGHT: maximum take-off, 139,760 pounds.
SPEED: maximum, 473 mph; cruise, 377 mph.
CEILING: 28,300 feet.
RANGE: maximum mission radius, 2,380 nautical miles; 3 hours on station at 1,500 feet, 1,346 nautical miles.
POWER PLANT: four Allison T56-A-14 turboprop engines, 4,900 ehp each.
CREW: 10.
CONTRACTOR: Lockheed.

BRIEFING: The prototype of this propeller-driven aircraft, which still is playing a major ASW role for the Navy, first flew in 1958. Since the Orion's basic airframe first was flown, more than half a dozen different improvement programs have been incorporated into it; the most recent major equipment update significantly improves its ability to detect, track, and attack quieter new-generation submarines. Update III modernization is being incorporated into 133 older P-3s; 21 had been modernized by the end of FY 1988. Several P-3s have been converted to electronic-intelligence aircraft and now are in service, with more to come. Modifying a number of P-3C aircraft with lookdown, shoot-down radar also has increased the ability of the Customs Service to track drug smugglers flying low-flying aircraft. Concern about the steadily increasing submarine threat has resulted in Navy plans to incorporate a vastly improved avionics suite (Update IV) to be produced by Boeing into 80 P-3Cs and 125 new Long Range Air ASW-Capable Aircraft (LRAACA). The P-3C Update IV retrofit program will begin production procurement in FY 1991 and delivery in FY 1993. Procurement of the new aircraft is expected to commence in 1990; 25 a year are to be procured. They will be built by Lockheed, which was awarded the development contract fall of 1988.

S-3A VIKING

WING SPAN: 69 feet.
LENGTH: 53 feet.
HEIGHT: 23 feet.
WEIGHT: empty, 26,650 pounds; maximum takeoff, 52,539 pounds.
SPEED: 518 mph.
CEILING: 40,000 feet.
RANGE: more than 2,300 nautical miles.
POWER PLANT: two General Electric TF34-GE-2 turbofan engines.
ARMAMENT: various combinations of torpedoes, depth charges, missiles, rockets, and special weapons.
CREW: four.
CONTRACTOR: Lockheed.

VIKING

BRIEFING: A total of 187 of these carrier-based ASW aircraft were built for the Navy, the last being delivered in 1978. The Navy currently is modernizing 146 of them to S-3B configuration at a rate of two per month; 21 had been modernized by the end of 1988. The resultant S-3Bs incorporate much improved technology for increased radar detection range and classification, advanced acoustic processing, and support measures, and will have a Harpoon missile capability. An additional 16 fleet S-3As are being converted to ES-3A carrier-based electronic reconnaissance aircraft to replace EA-3Bs. Although the current modernization program, which is to be completed in FY 1993, is aimed at enabling the S-3B to counter the submarine threat of the 1990s, it tentatively is scheduled to be replaced by either V-22s or Advanced Tactical Surveillance Aircraft by the late 1990s.

C-130 HERCULES

WING SPAN: 133 feet.
LENGTH: 98-106 feet.
HEIGHT: 38 feet.
WEIGHT: empty, 75,331 pounds; maximum normal take-off, 155,000 pounds; maximum overload takeoff, 175,000 pounds.
SPEED: maximum cruise, 374 mph; economical cruise, 345 mph.
CEILING: 33,000 feet.
RANGE: with maximum payload and allowance for 30 minutes at sea level, 2,046 nautical miles; with maximum fuel and 20,000-pound payload, 4,460 nautical miles.
POWER PLANT: four Allison T56-A-15 turboprop engines. Eight JATO (Jet-Assisted Takeoff) units can also be carried.
CREW: four.
CONTRACTOR: Lockheed.

HERCULES

BRIEFING: The Hercules probably is the most versatile tactical transport aircraft ever built. Its uses appear almost limitless: transport, electronic surveillance, search and rescue, space-capsule recovery, helicopter refueling, landing (with skis) on snow and ice, gun ship, and special cargo delivery. It has even landed and taken off from a carrier deck without benefit of arresting gear or catapults. Its capabilities are appreciated worldwide; more than 50 countries use at least one version of it. It still is serving as a VLF strategic communications aircraft, communicating with ballistic-missile submarines, under the TACAMO program. The Navy is in the process of modernizing its existing fleet of 77 C-130s; an extensive avionics system improvement program is providing modern avionics equipment to the older aircraft to improve system reliability, maintainability, and supportability. Included in the present inventory are 10 new-production KC-130T models in use by the Marine Corps Reserve. Six more KC-130Ts are scheduled for delivery by year's end.

GREYHOUND

C-2A GREYHOUND

WING SPAN: 81 feet.
LENGTH: 57 feet.
HEIGHT: 16 feet.
WEIGHT: maximum take-off, 54,354 pounds.
SPEED: maximum, 352 mph; cruise, 296 mph.
CEILING: 28,800 feet.
RANGE: 1,440 nautical miles.
POWER PLANT: two Allison T56-A-8B turboprop engines; 4,050 shaft horsepower each.
CONTRACTOR: Grumman Aerospace.

BRIEFING: COD (Carrier On-board Delivery) aircraft transport personnel, key logistics items, mail, etc., between shore facilities and carrier task forces at sea. For years the C-1A was the Navy's only COD aircraft; now the Greyhound is the principal aircraft being used for that purpose. Since its basic airframe is that of the E-2C, also built by Grumman, production of the C-2A is not a problem. Nine C-2As were funded in FY 1987 and represent the last buy of these versatile aircraft.

C-9B SKYTRAIN II

WING SPAN: 93 feet.
LENGTH: 119 feet.
HEIGHT: 28 feet.
WEIGHT: empty, 65,283 pounds in passenger configuration, 59,706 pounds in cargo configuration; maximum takeoff, 110,000 pounds.
SPEED: maximum cruising speed, 576 mph; long-range cruising speed, 504 mph.
CEILING: 37,000 feet.
RANGE: at long-range cruising speed, 2,538 nautical miles.
POWER PLANT: two Pratt and Whitney JT8D-9A turbofan engines.
PAYLOAD: 32,444 pounds of cargo or passengers.
CREW: two, plus cabin attendants.
CONTRACTOR: McDonnell Douglas.

BRIEFING: Although the Defense Department at one time sought to require all military airlift to come under the Military Airlift Command, and therefore to reduce the airlift capabilities of the individual services other than the Air Force almost to zero, it quickly became apparent that MAC could not possibly fulfill all individual service requirements. Among major Navy logistics requirements that could not be fulfilled was the airlifting of Naval Reservists to and from training sites. Ultimately, the Navy won approval for the acquisition of C-9 aircraft, the commercial version of which is the DC-9, to meet the airlift needs as the ancient C-118s being used for that purpose finally were being retired, the last in 1985. The Navy completed its buy of C-9Bs in FY 1985 and now has 27 in its transport fleet. "Used" aircraft procured are undergoing a modernization program to allow their operational use beyond the year 2000. All are flown by Naval Reserve squadrons.

SKYTRAIN

GOSHAWK

T-45A GOSHAWK

WING SPAN: 31 feet.
LENGTH: 39 feet.
HEIGHT: 13.5 feet.
WEIGHT: empty, 9,394 pounds; maximum takeoff, 12,758 pounds.
SPEED: maximum, .85 Mach at level flight.
RANGE: maximum with internal fuel, 995 nautical miles.
CEILING: 42,500 feet.
POWER PLANT: one Rolls Royce F405-RR-400L turbofan engine.
CONTRACTOR: British Aerospace, Douglas Aircraft Company.

BRIEFING: The T-45A Goshawk will be a carrier-capable derivative of the existing British Aerospace Hawk trainer aircraft. In 1981 the Navy selected the Douglas division of McDonnell Douglas as its prime contractor for the T-45 Training System, which will feature aircraft, academics, simulators, an integration system, and logistic support. The Goshawk is a two-seat jet aircraft, with redesigned landing gear and fuselage carry-through structure to provide the necessary strength for carrier qualification training requirements. The Navy will have an ultimate production requirement of over 300. The Goshawk, which will be assembled in the United States, will have approximately 50 percent commonality with the British Hawk. Twenty-four Goshawks are being funded in FY 1989. Initial operating capability for the aircraft is 1991.

NAVY AIRSHIP

BRIEFING: In June 1987, the Navy awarded a contract for $118.2 million to Westinghouse-Airship Industries, the latter a British company, for development of one airship. The contract award reflected the growing requirement for the Navy to acquire additional means of waging anti-submarine and anti-air warfare and stems from the 1983 Patrol Airship Concept Evaluation (PACE) program, which highlighted the advantage an airship would have over fixed-wing aircraft, including more time on station and greater endurance. The contract included full maintenance and support for the airship; in addition, another $50.7 million was included for the avionics suite, which was to include either APS-125 or APS-139 radar. There was to be an option for five additional airships. The first flight of the operational development model (ODM) was scheduled for late 1990, with operational suitability trials to commence six months later and to continue for six months. The airship was to be designed in the United Kingdom, and assembly of it carried out at Weeksville, NC, with logistics support to be provided there and at NAS, Lakehurst, NJ. The Naval Air Test Center at Patuxent River, MD, would be the prime ODM evaluation base. The airship would have a maximum flight speed, at stable equilibrium, of 82 knots, be able to attain an altitude of 14,000 feet, and have unrefueled endurance at 40 knots at 5,000 feet of 60.2 hours. It would be able to climb at a rate of 630 feet per minute, be propelled by two 1625-horsepower diesel cruise engines and one 1750-horsepower turboprop sprint engine, and manned by a crew of 12-15. The operational airship, which would be more than twice the size of the Goodyear airship seen on TV screens so often during major athletic events, would have a 30-day mission duration. The Navy had spent $26.9 on its development but, because of budget constraints, decided not to go further with the program, and no funding for it was included in the proposed FY 1989 Navy budget. It also had been suggested that responsibility for ultimate development of the airship be given to the Defense Advanced Research Projects Agency (DARPA), and a Memorandum of Understanding transferring the program to DARPA still is under consideration. Meanwhile, Congress authorized the expenditure of another $30 million toward its development. Whether or not, or how, the program would go forward had not been definitely decided by year's end.

HELICOPTERS/NAVY

SUPER STALLION

CH/MH-53E SUPER STALLION

FUSELAGE LENGTH: 73.3 feet.
OVERALL LENGTH: 99 feet.
HEIGHT: 28 feet.
WEIGHT: empty, CH-53E, 33,226 pounds; MH-53E, 36,745 pounds; maximum allowable gross for both, 73,500 pounds.
SPEED: CH-53E, maximum 150 knots indicated; MH-53E, maximum, 161 knots indicated.
CEILING: 27,900 feet horizontal flight, 16,600 feet hovering.
RANGE: 1,120 nautical miles.
POWER PLANT: three General Electric T64-GE-416 turboshaft engines; 4,380 shp. each.
CREW: three.
CONTRACTOR: Sikorsky.

BRIEFING: The Super Stallion, the largest and most powerful helicopter yet put into production outside the Soviet Union, is designed to serve the Navy and Marine Corps in several roles. It can carry a 16-ton payload 50 nautical miles or a 10-ton payload 500 nautical miles. It can be used for vertical on-board delivery of personnel, supplies, and equipment; support of mobile construction battalions, and removal of damaged aircraft from carrier decks. It can carry 55 troops in an amphibious assault role for the Marines, as well as providing lift and movement of cargo. The first of these helicopters was delivered in 1981; the Navy operates three squadrons. The MH-53E minesweeping version, which is heavier and has a greater fuel capacity than the CH-53E, as well as sophisticated mine-countermeasures equipment, first flew in 1983. Deliveries began in FY 1986; the Navy now operates two squadrons. Seven CH-53Es for the Marine Corps and seven MH-53Es were funded in FY 1989. The Navy advised Congress that Persian Gulf minesweeping operations in 1987 and 1988 confirmed "the valid requirement for organic, rapidly deployable, airborne mine countermeasures systems for fleet protection" and that a planned engine upgrade program will provide the MH-53E with significantly improved time on station, range, and hot-weather capability.

SH-60B/F SEAHAWK

FUSELAGE LENGTH: 50 feet.
OVERALL LENGTH: 64.8 feet.
HEIGHT: 17 feet.
WEIGHT: 21,884 pounds maximum gross.
SPEED: maximum cruise at 5,000 feet, 150 mph.
RANGE: SH-60F, ASW configured, four hours endurance, three hours on station; SH-60B, ASW, two hours, assistance, 3.5 hours.
POWER PLANT: two 1,690 shp T700-GE-401 turboshaft engines.
CREW: SH-60B, three; SH-60F, four.
CONTRACTORS: Sikorsky, SH-60F system, SH-60B aircraft; IBM, SH-60B avionics.

BRIEFING: The SH-60B Seahawk, better known as the LAMPS (Light Airborne Multipurpose System) Mk III helicopter, is a modified version of the Army's Black Hawk. It will be deployed on Ticonderoga-class cruisers, Burke-, Spruance-, and Kidd-class destroyers, and Perry-class frigates, and will provide all-weather capability for detection, classification, localization, and interdiction of ships and submarines. Its secondary missions include search and rescue, medical evacuation, vertical replenishment, fleet support, and communications relay. Since the first Seahawk squadron was formed in 1984, it has enjoyed remarkable success. Initial procurement of the SH-60B was set at 204 aircraft; that number was based on one aircraft per ship. Now, however, the Navy is modifying its Spruance- and Kidd-class destroyers to a dual RAST/LAMPS capability, and as a consequence the SH-60 overall procurement objective is expected to rise. SH-60Bs aboard ships operating in the Persian Gulf in 1987 were armed to make possible more effective defense against possible attacks on tankers being escorted by Navy ships and on Navy ships themselves. The Navy also is acquiring a modified version of the Seahawk as its CV ASW helicopter as a replacement for the SH-3H Sea King. The SH-60F will operate from carriers to protect the inner zone of a carrier battle group from submarine attack. The first production model was delivered in late 1986. The Navy's procurement goal for the SH-60F is 175.

SEAHAWK

RH-53D SEA STALLION

FUSELAGE LENGTH: 67.42 feet.
OVERALL LENGTH: 88.58 feet.
WEIGHT: basic, 25,583 pounds; maximum gross, 42,000 pounds.
SPEED: maximum, 130 knots indicated.
CEILING: 21,000 feet in horizontal flight, 13,400 feet while hovering.
RANGE: perform a 25-nautical-mile radius of action Mark 103 minesweep mission, including 45 minutes for streaming gear, 131 minutes for towing, 45 minutes for retrieving gear, and return with a 20-minute power reserve.
POWER PLANT: two General Electric T-64-GE-415 turboshaft engines.
CREW: three, minimum.
PRIME CONTRACTOR: Sikorsky.

BRIEFING: The RH-53D Sea Stallion is a single main rotor head helicopter designed for both land and ship-based operations. It is equipped with automatic-flight-control and engine-de-icing systems that provide an all-weather capability. Its primary mission is airborne mine countermeasures, which includes mine sweeping, spotting, and neutralization, destruction of floating mines, channel marking, and surface towing. Its secondary utility mission involves the movement of cargo and equipment and the transportation of passengers. The RH-53D has been used extensively in mine-countermeasures

SEA STALLION

SEA KNIGHT

operations throughout the world and most recently in 1987-88 in the Persian Gulf. The Navy operates two active-duty and one reserve squadrons.

HH/CH-46 SEA KNIGHT

FUSELAGE LENGTH: 45.6 feet.
LENGTH: 84.3 feet.
HEIGHT: 17 feet.
WEIGHT: basic, 12,100 pounds; maximum allowable gross, 23,300 pounds.
SPEED: 130 knots indicated.
POWER PLANT: two General Electric T58-GE-10 turboshaft engines.
CREW: three.
CONTRACTOR: Boeing Vertol.

BRIEFING: The Sea Knight is another example of a durable and versatile aircraft that still is providing valuable services more than two decades after it was first flown. Various versions of it have been flown by both the Navy and the Marine Corps. The HH/CH-46D is a tandem-rotor configured transport helicopter that is designed for both land and ship-based operations. It can accommodate 25 passengers or 15 litters, with two medical attendants, or 10,000 pounds of cargo externally in a sling below the fuselage. The Navy uses the CH-46D primarily for delivery of cargo to ships at sea, and the Marines the HH-46D primarily for search and rescue. Since the first flight of the Sea Knight in 1962, it also has served the U.S. Army and the air forces of Canada and Sweden. It has long been out of production.

SH-3H SEA KING

FUSELAGE LENGTH: 54 feet, 9 inches.
OVERALL LENGTH: 73 feet.
HEIGHT: 17 feet.
WEIGHT: empty, 11,865 pounds; maximum take-off, 21,000 pounds.
SPEED: maximum, 166 mph; cruise, 136 mph.
CEILING: 14,700 feet.
RANGE: 542 nautical miles.
POWER PLANT: two General Electric T58-GE-10 turboshaft engines.
CREW: four (including two sonar operators).
CONTRACTOR: Sikorsky.

BRIEFING: The first version of this workhorse ASW helicopter was flown more than 20 years ago. The current model is equipped with sonar, active and passive sonar buoys, magnetic anomaly detection equipment, and electronic surveillance measures equipment, the latter adding an extra measure of missile-defense capability to the

SEA KING

fleet. A basic version of the Sea King was hurriedly converted for use by the British in the Falkland Islands operation and served as an early-warning and ASW helicopter for the Royal Navy's carrier task force. SH-60Fs began replacing SH-3Hs in 1987, and the Navy expects to have all of them replaced by 1999. Roughly 200 remained in the inventory as 1989 began.

SH-2F SEASPRITE

FUSELAGE LENGTH: 38 feet.
OVERALL LENGTH: 53 feet.
HEIGHT: 15 feet, 6 inches.
WEIGHT: empty, 7,040 pounds; normal takeoff, 13,300 pounds.
SPEED: maximum, 164 mph; cruise, 150 mph.
CEILING: 25,500 feet.
RANGE: 367 nautical miles with maximum fuel.
POWER PLANT: two T58-GE-8F turboshaft engines.
CREW: three.
CONTRACTOR: Kaman.

BRIEFING: The prototype Seasprite flew for the first time in 1959. Since then, there have been many versions produced for the Navy under its LAMPS program to provide helicopters for ASW and anti-ship-missile defense operations. Almost every aspect of the helicopter and its equipment have been improved in one way or another over the years as the Navy gained more experience in its utilization. Avionics and equipment systems now installed include: surveillance radar, magnetic anomaly detectors, passive radiation detection receivers, active and passive sonobuoys, smoke markers, computerized tactical navigation system, cargo hook for external loads, and

SEA RANGER

a rescue hoist. Armament includes homing torpedoes; there also is a capability of carrying air-to-air missiles. In both FY 1986 and 1987, funding was included for six aircraft, but no further production is envisioned. Eight aircraft also will be modified between 1987 and 1990. The SH-2F, which operates from FF-1052, FF-1040, FFG-1, CG-25, and FFG-7 class ships, is expected to remain in service as an ASW helicopter until approximately 2010.

TH-57 SEA RANGER

FUSELAGE LENGTH: 31 feet.
OVERALL LENGTH: 39 feet.
HEIGHT: 10 feet.
WEIGHT: empty, 1,595 pounds; maximum takeoff, 3,200 pounds.
SPEED: maximum, 130 KIAS.
CEILING: 20,000 feet, pressure altitude.
RANGE: maximum, 368 nautical miles.
POWER PLANT: one Allison 250-C20B/J turboshaft engine.
CONTRACTOR: Bell Helicopter Textron.

BRIEFING: These popular aircraft, used by the air forces and the navies of several countries, also are a mainstay of the U.S. Army and first saw service in Vietnam in 1969. The TH-57 is a derivative of the Bell Jet Ranger 206. The Navy operates TH-57A, TH-57B, and TH-57C versions, with the first being used for photo, chase, and utility missions, the second primary training, and the third advanced training. Their procurement ended with the 36 included in the FY 1985 budget.

SEASPRITE

WEAPONS/NAVY

AMRAAM

LENGTH: 11 feet, 9 inches.
DIAMETER: 7 inches.
WING SPAN: 1 foot, 9 inches.
WEIGHT: 300 pounds.
SPEED: more than 760 mph.
RANGE: 39 nautical miles.
POWER PLANT: directed rocket motor.
WARHEAD: blast high explosive.
CONTRACTOR: Hughes Aircraft

BRIEFING: Development of this advanced medium-range, air-to-air missile stems from a lengthy study of the likely air threat for the next 25-30 years, and the kind of beyond-visual-range weapon that could best meet such a threat. AMRAAM is the replacement for the venerable Sparrow missile and is to be deployed on F-14 and F/A-18 aircraft, as well as on Air Force and NATO fighters. It is smaller, faster, and lighter than the Sparrow and better able to attack at low level. The pilot will be able to aim at several targets simultaneously. Production of AMRAAM was scheduled to begin in 1984; however, development problems caused costs to soar, and Congress almost killed it in FY 1986. Subsequently, continued development, under severe restrictions imposed by Congress on expenditures, was authorized. In FY 1987 approval of limited production (180 missiles) of AMRAAM was granted. Funding for 400 more missiles was provided in FY 1988, but these were all for the Air Force. In FY 1989, the Navy hoped to procure 50, but Congress authorized funding for only 30, and stipulated that these were to be used only for further research and development purposes. Raytheon has been certified as a second source.

HARM

LENGTH: 13 feet, 8 inches.
DIAMETER: 10 inches.
WING SPAN: 3 feet, 8 inches.
WEIGHT: 807 pounds.
WARHEAD WEIGHT: 146 pounds.
SPEED: more than 760 mph.
RANGE: 22 nautical miles.
POWER PLANT: two-stage solid propellant rocket motor.
WARHEAD: laser terminal plus guidance-aided.
PRIME CONTRACTOR: Texas Instruments.

BRIEFING: Harm is one of the growing family of sophisticated missiles with which fleet aircraft are being equipped. A high-speed, anti-radiation missile, it succeeds Shrike and Arm as the primary anti-radiation, defense-suppression, air-to-surface missile. It is deployed on A-7E, F/A-18, EA-6B, and A-6E aircraft and has increased speed, greater range, improved sensitivity, and the frequency-band coverage needed to counter the current threat. Harm was used effectively against Libyan targets in the Gulf of Sidra in 1986. Procurement of Harm dropped from 988 missiles in FY 1987 to 766 in FY 1988, but is scheduled to climb to 1,307 in FY 1989. Harm also is being procured by the Air Force and by West Germany.

HARPOON

LENGTH: surface/submarine-launched, 15 feet; air-launched, 12 feet, seven inches.
DIAMETER: missile body, 1 foot, 2 inches.
WING SPAN: 3 feet, with booster fins and wings.
WEIGHT: surface/submarine-launched, 1,450 pounds; air-launched, 1,160 pounds.
SPEED: 646 mph.
RANGE: surface/submarine-launched, 60 nautical miles; air-launched, 120 nautical miles.
POWER PLANT: turbojet and solid propellant booster for surface/submarine launch.
WARHEAD: 500 pounds, high explosive, blast penetrator.
CONTRACTOR: McDonnell Douglas.

BRIEFING: This highly reliable anti-ship missile has been in the fleet since 1977. Day-night and all-weather, it can be launched from most surface combatants, as well as from submarines and aircraft. Improvements to it will add to its range and also result in a decrease in altitude in its sea-skimming mode. The Harpoon was used effectively in attacks on Libyan targets during operations in the Gulf of Sidra in 1986. The Navy has under full-scale development and low-rate concurrent production a new infrared Harpoon called SLAM (Stand-off Land Attack Missile) which should be ready to join the fleet in 1989. Total procurement of these missiles in FY 1989 will be 66 Harpoons and 72 SLAMs.

PHOENIX

PHOENIX

LENGTH: 13 feet.
DIAMETER: 15 inches.
WING SPAN: 3 feet.
WEIGHT: 989 pounds.
SPEED: more than 3,040 mph.
RANGE: more than 104 nautical miles.
POWER PLANT: Mk47, Mod. 0 solid propellant rocket.
WARHEAD: proximity fuse, high explosive; weight, 135 pounds.
CONTRACTOR: Hughes Aircraft, Raytheon.

BRIEFING: This long-range air-to-air missile is the mainstay of the weapons system of the F-14 Tomcat, the only Navy aircraft that can carry it. The initial version, the AIM-54A, was operational in the fleet for 10 years; however, it had been provided to the Iranian Air Force prior to the fall of the Shah of Iran in 1979 and was considered to have been compromised. Now out of production, it had enjoyed a success rate of 84 percent and had knocked down targets 120 miles away. It has been succeeded by the AIM-54C, an improved version which has encountered quality-control problems in its manufacture that have caused the Navy on several occasions to halt production of it. A new delivery schedule was renegotiated in early 1987 with Hughes, the initial production source, and monthly production of the missile was increased during the latter months of 1987. Although Hughes' overall production rates now are considered satisfactory, a lack of government furnished components has caused delays in final missile assembly. For that reason, and because FY 1985 deliveries still were in progress, Congress limited FY 1989 authorization of Phoenix to the FY 1988 production rate of 350 missiles; the Navy had hoped to acquire 560. Six of these missiles can be carried by each F-14. They can be launched simultaneously against separate targets. Raytheon now is the second production source for Phoenix.

SIDEARM

LENGTH: 9 feet, 11 inches.
DIAMETER: 5 inches.
WING SPAN: 2 feet, 1 inch.
WEIGHT: 165 pounds.
SPEED: 1,900 mph.
RANGE: more than 3.5 nautical miles.
POWER PLANT: Rocketdyne/Bermite single-stage, solid propellant motor.
WARHEAD: annular blast fragmentation; weight, 25 pounds.
CONTRACTOR: Motorola.

BRIEFING: Sidearm (AGM-122A) missiles are short-range, air-to-ground antiradiation missiles converted from early AIM-9C Sidewinder missiles. Sidearm missiles will be used to detect, home on, and destroy or disable enemy radars. Sidearm can be carried on most fixed

SIDEARM

and rotary-wing aircraft and is to be deployed on the Marine Corps AH-1W helicopter. Procurement of Sidearm averaged slightly above 244 missiles over the 1986-88 period, but no funding was included for procurement of it in the FY 1989 budget.

SPARROW

LENGTH: 12 feet.
DIAMETER: 8 inches.
WING SPAN: 3 feet, 4 inches.
WEIGHT: 510 pounds.
SPEED: more than 2,660 mph.
RANGE: more than 30 nautical miles.
POWER PLANT: Hercules Mk58, Mod. 4 or 5 solid propellant rocket.
WARHEAD: fragmentation warhead WAU-17.
CONTRACTOR: Raytheon, General Dynamics' Pomona Division.

BRIEFING: Navy procurement of this highly successful air-to-air and surface-to-air missile was to have ended in FY 1987 with the funding of 1,716 missiles. The AIM-7M version, the fifth model in the Sparrow series, has considerably greater invulnerability to ECM, better target-tracking capability, and a new low-altitude active fuse. The Navy also converted the AIM-7M variant to RIM-7Ms; that version, with folding wings and clipped tail fins, is compatible with the NATO Sea-Sparrow launcher. It has a somewhat different rocket motor. Current improvements in it will be backfitted into the RIM-7M inventory. With AMRAAM production for the Navy still being delayed, 600 AIM-RIM-7F/Ms were funded by Congress in FY 1988 and another 300 in FY 1989. Sparrow still remains the primary weapon on aircraft of six foreign nations and on NATO ships.

SPARROW

STANDARD

SM-1 MR, SM-2 MR

LENGTH: 14 feet, 7 inches.
DIAMETER: 13.5 inches.
WING SPAN: 3 feet, 6 inches.
WEIGHT: SM-1, 1,100 pounds; SM-2, 1,380 pounds.
SPEED: about 1,900 mph.
RANGE: SM-1, 15-20 nautical miles; SM-2, up to 90 nautical miles.
POWER PLANT: dual thrust, solid fuel rocket.
WARHEAD: proximity fuse, high explosive.
CONTRACTORS: General Dynamics' Pomona Division, Raytheon.

SM-2 ER

LENGTH: 26.2 inches.
DIAMETER: 13.5 inches.
WING SPAN: 5 feet, 2 inches.
WEIGHT: 2,980 pounds.
SPEED: more than 1,900 mph.
RANGE: approximately 65 nautical miles.
POWER PLANT: two-stage, solid-fuel rocket.
WARHEAD: proximity fuse, high explosive.
CONTRACTORS: General Dynamics' Pomona Division, Raytheon.

STANDARD

BRIEFING: The Standard family of missiles is one of the most reliable in the Navy's inventory. A two-model weapon which can be used against missiles, aircraft, and ships, it first came into the fleet more than a decade ago. It replaces Terrier and Tartar and now is part of the weapons suit of more than 100 U.S. Navy and 30 foreign ships. Standard is a superb example of a well-engineered weapon with excellent growth potential; it has encountered few problems during the development and production cycles of its various versions. Although more complex than the heralded Phoenix missile, it cost but 60 percent as much. Over the years range, speed, stability, maneuverability, fusing, accuracy, and overall performance constantly have been improved upon. SM-2 (MR), Blocks II and III, will be the primary air defense weapon for more than 100 ships, including Ticonderoga-class cruisers, Burke-class destroyers, California- and Virginia-class Tartar nuclear-powered cruisers with the New Threat Upgrade (NTU) conversion, Kidd-class destroyers with NTU, and Perry-class frigates with SM-2 conversion. SM-2 (ER), Blocks II and III, will be the primary air defense weapon for Leahy-, Belknap-, Bainbridge-, Truxtun-, and Long Beach-class Terrier cruisers with NTU. An Aegis Extended Range version of SM-2, Block IV, is under development for deployment on future Ticonderoga-class cruisers and Burke-class destroyers. This vertically launched version will incorporate major guidance, air-frame, and missile-booster improvements to permit using the full capabilities of the Aegis phased-array radar and combat system. Procurement of the various versions of Standard will rise steadily in the years immediately ahead, with $598 million funded for that purpose in FY 1989.

TOMAHAWK

TOMAHAWK

LENGTH: 18 feet, 3 inches; with booster, 20 feet, 6 inches.
DIAMETER: 20.4 inches.
WING SPAN: 8 feet, 9 inches.
WEIGHT: 2,650 pounds; 3,200 pounds with booster.
SPEED: about 760 mph.
RANGE: land attack, nuclear warhead, 1,500 nautical miles; land attack, conventional warhead, 700 nautical miles; anti-ship configuration, over 250 nautical miles.
POWER PLANT: Williams International F107-W-R-400 cruise turbofan; solid-fuel booster.
WARHEAD: conventional, 1,000 pounds high explosive.
CONTRACTORS: General Dynamics Convair Division, McDonnell Douglas.

BRIEFING: Tomahawk is an all-weather, subsonic cruise missile that can be fired as a conventional anti-ship weapon or as a land-attack weapon using both nuclear and conventional warheads. All three versions—the anti-ship (TASM), the nuclear land-attack (TLAM-N), and the conventional land-attack (TLAM-C)—now are operational in the fleet. A fourth version, TLAM-D, utilizes a submunitions dispenser with combined effects bomblets for use against such targets as surface-to-air missile sites and revetted aircraft. It still is undergoing testing. By the end of 1988 there were 26 Tomahawk-capable surface ships and 41 Tomahawk-capable SSN-688- and SSN-637-class submarines. Tomahawk's small cross section, ability to fly at low altitude, and low heat emission make it difficult to detect by infrared devices or by radar. It is scheduled for deployment in over 190 platforms, including the Navy's four battleships, each of which will have 32 Tomahawks aboard, and Ticonderoga-class and five nuclear-powered cruisers, Burke- and Spruance-class destroyers, and Los Angeles- and Sturgeon-class submarines. Testing of both the surface-ship Tomahawk vertical launch system (VLS) and the submarine Tomahawk vertical launch system (CLS) have been highly successful, and overall improvements in the entire Tomahawk system continue to be made. The Navy plans to buy approximately 5,000 Tomahawks through 1993, and has been markedly successful in bringing down costs of the missile through dual-source competition. In a remarkably short time, and after a difficult and costly beginning, Tomahawk has become one of the most feared weapons in the Navy's arsenal.

TRIDENT I

LENGTH: 34 feet.
DIAMETER: 6 feet, 2 inches.
WEIGHT: 70,000 pounds.
SPEED: not applicable.
RANGE: 4,000 nautical miles.
POWER PLANT: three-stage solid-fuel rocket, with inertial guidance.
WARHEADS: thermonuclear MIRV (Multiple Independently targetable Re-entry Vehicle) and MARV (Maneuverable Re-entry Vehicle) heads.
CONTRACTOR: Lockheed.

TRIDENT

TRIDENT II

LENGTH: 44 feet.
DIAMETER: 83 inches.
WEIGHT: approximately 126,000 pounds.
SPEED: not applicable.
RANGE: 6,000 nautical miles.
POWER PLANT: three-stage solid-propellant rocket, with inertial guidance.
WARHEADS: thermonuclear MIRV (Multiple Independently targetable Re-entry Vehicle) and MARV (Maneuverable Re-entry Vehicle) heads.
CONTRACTOR: Lockheed.

POSEIDON

LENGTH: 34 feet.
DIAMETER: 6 feet, 2 inches.
WEIGHT: 65,000 pounds.
SPEED: not applicable.
RANGE: 2,170 nautical miles.
POWER PLANT: two-stage, solid-fuel rocket with inertial guidance.
WARHEAD: thermonuclear MIRV (Multiple Independently targetable Re-entry Vehicle).
CONTRACTOR: Lockheed.

BRIEFING: The Trident system makes possible deployment of an improved missile-carrying submarine, the Ohio class, with a much longer range strategic ballistic missile, offsetting improvements in Soviet ASW capability by vastly increasing the area in which submarines can operate and still have their missiles reach their targets. Trident I has a range almost double that of the Poseidon missile it replaces, and Trident II will have a 6,000-mile range. Trident Is are deployed in the first eight submarines of the Ohio class and in 12 of the remaining Franklin-class SSBNs remaining in the fleet. Trident IIs will be deployed on the ninth and succeeding Ohio-class ships and will be retrofitted into the first eight. Introduction of Trident II, which will weigh almost twice as much as Trident I and possess far greater warhead capability, is scheduled for 1989. Procurement commenced in FY 1987 with 21 missiles; 66 are to be acquired in FY 1989.

MAVERICK

LENGTH: 8 feet, 1 inch.
DIAMETER: 11.8 inches.
WING SPAN: 2 feet, 4 inches.
WEIGHT: 459 pounds, 635 pounds with alternative warhead.
WARHEAD: 299 pounds high explosives.
RANGE: 12 nautical miles.
POWER PLANT: two-stage, solid-fuel rocket.
CONTRACTOR: Hughes Aircraft.

BRIEFING: There are two versions of the Maverick missiles. Laser Maverick is a short-range, air-to-surface weapon which will be used in close-air support and battlefield interdiction within amphibious objective areas and in deep support for destruction of targets outside objective areas. It is a variant of the Air Force's TV Maverick with a much larger warhead. It is planned primarily for Marine Corps use, although it is adaptable to Navy aircraft. The second version, IIR Maverick, is an air-launched, direct-attack weapon for day or night use; it has an imaging infrared seeker and uses the same warhead as Laser Maverick. Funding for 1,300 Laser Mavericks and 425 IIR Mavericks was provided in FY 1988, but fiscal constraints resulted in zero funding for those missiles in FY 1989.

RAM

LENGTH: 9 feet, 2 inches.
DIAMETER: 5 inches.
WING SPAN: 1 foot, 5 inches.
WEIGHT: 154 pounds.
SPEED: Supersonic.
RANGE: 4-plus nautical miles.
POWER PLANT: solid propellant rocket.
WARHEAD: 25 pounds, conventional.
CONTRACTOR: General Dynamics, Pomona.

BRIEFING: The Rolling Airframe Missile (RAM) is a joint development and production program with West Germany of a high-fire-power self-defense system against anti-ship missiles. It uses the infrared seeker of the Stinger missile and the rocket motor, fuse, and warhead from the Sidewinder. It can be fired from Sea Sparrow launchers and from a 21-cell stand-alone launcher, and will be installed aboard combatants, amphibious ships, and auxiliaries to complement other anti-missile systems. It will have an IOC in the Navy of 1990. Limited production of the missile was approved in April 1987, and 260 are being sought in FY 1989.

HELLFIRE

LENGTH: 5 feet, 4 inches.
DIAMETER: 7 inches.
WING SPAN: 13 inches.
WEIGHT: 95 pounds.
POWER PLANT: solid-propellant rocket.
WARHEAD: conventional.
CONTRACTOR: Rockwell International.

BRIEFING: This air-to-surface, laser-guided, anti-armor missile was developed by the Army and has been adapted for use on the Marine Corps' AH-1T/J helicopter. The version to be used by the Marines has a longer range than the TOW missile which it replaces and permits greater aircraft maneuverability. Only 200 missiles were requested by DOD in FY 1989 after 1,393 were funded in FY 1988, but Congress authorized 1,000 because of its concern that the DOD budget did not respond adequately to the threat posed by the armored forces of the Soviet Union and the Warsaw Pact.

STINGER

LENGTH: 5 feet.
DIAMETER: 2.25 inches.
WING SPAN: 8 inches.
WEIGHT: 34.5 pounds (including launch tube).
POWER PLANT: solid-propellant rocket.
WARHEAD: conventional high explosive.
RANGE: 3 miles.
CONTRACTOR: General Dynamics' Pomona Division.

BRIEFING: This shoulder-held surface-to-air missile is the successor to the Army's Redeye Missile. It is an infrared homing weapon that can effectively engage jet or propeller-drive aircraft or helicopters at low altitudes. Used by the Marine Corps as well as the Army, it was placed aboard a number of Navy ships in the Mediterranean in the winter of 1983-84 in reaction to threatened terrorist attacks. It also was used successfully by the Royal Navy in the Falklands operation in 1982. The Navy activated its first Stinger missile-armed detachment in the summer of 1987. Funding for 685 missiles was provided in FY 1987, and the final Navy buy of 425 was made in FY 1988.

MARK 50 TORPEDO

LENGTH: 9.5 feet.
DIAMETER: 12.25 inches.
WEIGHT: 800 pounds (approximate).
SPEED: 40-plus knots.
POWER PLANT: Stored chemical energy propulsion system; pump-jet.
GUIDANCE: Active/passive acoustic homing.
WARHEAD: Approximately 100 pounds conventional (shaped charge).
CONTRACTOR: Honeywell, Westinghouse.

BRIEFING: This successor to the Mark 46 torpedo is being developed and produced for use from submarines, ships, and aircraft against the faster, deeper-diving, and more sophisticated Soviet submarines being developed and operated by the Soviet Union. It also will have the capability for use against slower, shallow-diving submarines and surface ships. Combined technical and operational testing of the Mark 50 program has been underway for some time, with, according to the Navy, "superb results". Only 16 torpedoes were funded in FY 1988, but 140 will be procured in FY 1989. The Mark 50 will provide the payload for the conventional variant of the submarine-launched ASW standoff weapon Sea Lance. Westinghouse has been selected as the Mark 50 second source; full competition is scheduled to begin in 1991.

MARK 48

MARK 48 TORPEDO

LENGTH: 19 feet.
DIAMETER: 21 inches.
WEIGHT: 3,520 pounds.
MAXIMUM SPEED: 55 knots.
POWER PLANT: piston engine; pump jet.
MAXIMUM RANGE: 23 miles.
MAXIMUM DEPTH: 500 fathoms.
WARHEAD: 650 pounds high explosives.
CONTRACTORS: Hughes, Gould Ocean Systems Division, Cleveland.

BRIEFING: A wire-guided torpedo, said to be the most complex torpedo ever developed, the Mark 48 is carried by all Navy attack and ballistic-missile submarines. Production of it, which began in 1972, has ended; however, all in the Navy's inventory but about 200 are to be upgraded. That improvement program is to be completed in 1990. An advanced-capability version, the Mark 48 ADCAP, finally went into full production in August 1988 after having been plagued with problems during development and with cost increases since development commenced in 1979. Procurement of 100 torpedoes was funded in FY 1988, and 261 in FY 1989. Full competition between Gould and Hughes, the two production sources, finally is in place.

MARK 46

MARK 46 TORPEDO

LENGTH: 8.5 feet; 14 feet, 9 inches with ASROC booster.
DIAMETER: 12.8 inches.
WEIGHT: 508 pounds; 1,073 pounds with ASROC booster.
MAXIMUM SPEED: 40 knots.
RANGE: 12,000 yards.
POWER PLANT: piston engine (solid propellant) or cam engine (liquid propellant).
ACQUISITION RANGE: 500 yards.
WARHEAD WEIGHT: 96.8 pounds; high explosive.
CONTRACTOR: Honeywell

BRIEFING: Since this lightweight torpedo first was introduced into the fleet in 1967, it has been acquired for use by the navies of 21 other countries. Twelve nations currently are buying the fifth modification of it. The Mark 46 can be launched from surface ships, fixed-wing aircraft, or helicopters against its primary target, submarines. Although the Mark 46 will be the backbone of the Navy's torpedo inventory well into the 1990s, and production is scheduled to continue until 1990, procurement ended with the 500 torpedoes funded in FY 1987. More than 1,300 are to be upgraded in capability to the fifth-modification level.

CAPTOR

LENGTH: 12.14 feet.
DIAMETER: 21 inches.
WEIGHT: 1,997 pounds, including torpedo and mooring.
CONTRACTOR: Goodyear Aerospace, Akron.

BRIEFING: Captor, whose name is a contraction of "encapsulated torpedo," is an anti-submarine system comprising a Mark 46 torpedo inserted in a mine casing. Normally deployed in deep water in the vicinity of routes traveled by enemy submarines, it has the ability to detect and classify submarine targets while surface ships are able to pass over it without triggering the torpedo. It can be launched by surface ships, submarines, and aircraft, including B-52s. Procurement of these torpedoes ended with the FY 1985 buy, although Congress provided funds in FY 1989 for the purchase of 400 improvement kits.

PENGUIN

LENGTH: 120.48 inches.
DIAMETER: 11.2 inches.
WING SPAN: 22.36 inches folded, 56.8 inches deployed.
WEIGHT: 847 pounds.
SPEED: .7 to .9 Mach
RANGE: 19.2 miles.
POWER PLANT: Boost sustain solid propellant rocket motor.
SEEKER: IR, derivative of the AGM-119A seeker.
WARHEAD: 250-pound, semi-armor-piercing derivative of the Bullpup missile.
CONTRACTORS: Royal Norwegian Navy Material Command has overall responsibility. Components are being produced by firms and government agencies from Norway, France, England, Scotland, Sweden, and the United States.

BRIEFING: Penguin is a helicopter-launched anti-ship missile for use by LAMPS Mark III helicopters and by helicopters of NATO allies. It has been in full-scale engineering development and aircraft integration testing is in progress. Procurement of 64 missiles had been requested in FY 1989; however, for budgetary reasons and because of the program's contracting schedule for 1989, no funding was authorized in FY 1989 by Congress.

VERTICAL LAUNCH ASROC (VLA)

LENGTH: 15 feet.
DIAMETER: 12.75 inches.
WEIGHT: 1,000 pounds.
RANGE: approximately 12 miles.
POWER PLANT: solid-propellant rocket.
WARHEAD: conventional, Mark 46 torpedo; nuclear depth bomb.
GUIDANCE: terminal acoustic homing with Mark 46 torpedo.
CONTRACTOR: Honeywell, Martin-Marietta.

BRIEFING: ASROC is a ship-launched ballistic ASW weapon that can be fitted with a conventional torpedo or a nuclear depth charge. It entered service in 1961. The Vertical Launch ASROC (VLA), under development for some years, and scheduled to be received by all ships equipped with the Vertical Launch System (VLS), in time is to be replaced by Sea Lance as an ASW standoff weapon. There was some consideration given in 1988 to canceling the program; however, Congress, concerned that many ships' magazines might wind up empty of these weapons before Sea Lance was deployed, funded in the FY 1989 budget, and directed the Navy to produce, 300 VLAs. Limited production will commence during FY 1989. Sea Lance now is two years into full-scale development, with the program proceeding satisfactorily. Martin-Marietta was selected in 1987 as the second production source.

PHALANX

PHALANX CLOSE-IN WEAPONS SYSTEM

WEIGHT: 12,500 pounds, complete system.
GUN: M61A1 Vulcan (gatling-type).
AMMUNITION: 20mm with high-density penetrating projectile.
MAGAZINE CAPACITY: 989.
FIRING RATE: 3,000 rounds per minute.
CONTRACTORS: General Dynamics' Pomona Division, General Electric's Pittsfield Division.

BRIEFING: The Phalanx Close-In Weapons System (CIWS) is a last-ditch defense system against anti-ship missiles. It combines on a single mount fire-control radars and a six-barrel Gatling gun firing depleted-uranium projectiles at a theoretical rate of 3,000 rounds per minute. Its projectiles are 2.5 times heavier than those made of steel. A total, fully integrated weapons system, it automatically carries out search, detection, automatic threat evaluation, tracking, and firing. Its reliability has been increasing constantly. The Navy has installed or will install 676 systems aboard 44 classes of ships over the next 15-20 years and also has modified or is modifying over 400 of its CIWS installations to improve their capability with increased magazine capacity and enhanced operability, maintainability, and reliability. Competitive procurement commenced during FY 1988, with General Electric's Pittsfield Division having been certified as the second source. Only five new systems for the Navy are included in the FY 1989 budget, although many others will be constructed under the Foreign Military Sales program.

SEA POWER: MARINES

As FY 1989 began, there were 197,200 Marines serving in the Fleet Marine Forces and at various USMC posts and stations around the world. About 1,470 Marines were assigned to security duty at American embassies, legations, and consulates in more than 100 countries. Other Marines were at sea with the U.S. Navy in shipboard detachments. Thirty-three Marine barracks, which traditionally have provided security forces at certain U.S. naval facilities in this country and overseas, are being reorganized into six barracks and 22 security force companies. Thousands served throughout the country as advisers to Marine Reserve units in inspector-instructor roles or on recruiting duty.

More than 9,720 women Marines serve in a wide range of occupational fields; they do not serve in combat arms.

The majority of Marines serve in the Fleet Marine Forces, which deploy units around the world throughout the year or to areas of crisis in preparation for commitment if required in the national interest. Following are the Corps' major commands and duty locations:

Fleet Marine Force Atlantic (FMFLANT), Norfolk, Va. Second Marine Division, Camp Lejeune, N.C.; 2d Marine Aircraft Wing, Cherry Point, N.C.; 2d Force Service Support Group, Camp Lejeune, N.C.

Fleet Marine Force, Pacific (FMFPAC), Camp Smith, Hawaii. First Marine Division, Camp Pendleton, Calif.; 3d Marine Aircraft Wing, El Toro, Calif.; 1st Force Service Support Group, Camp Pendleton, Calif.; 3d Marine Division, Okinawa; 1st Marine Aircraft Wing, Okinawa and Iwakuni, Japan; 3d Force Service Support Group, Okinawa; 1st Marine Expeditionary Brigade, Hawaii.

Marine Corps Combat Development Command, Quantico, Va.; Marine Corps Logistics Base, Barstow, Calif.; Marine Corps Logistics Base, Albany, Ga.; Marine Corps Recruit Depot, Parris Island, S.C.; Marine Corps Recruit Depot, San Diego, Calif.; Marine Corps Air-Ground Combat Center, Twentynine Palms, Calif.; 4th Marine Division/4th Marine Aircraft Wing (Headquarters), New Orleans, La.; 4th Force Service Support Group (Headquarters), Atlanta, Ga.

LARGEST COMBAT DIVISION

With over 17,000 Marines and sailors, the U.S. Marine division is the largest of the world's combat divisions.

Each of the Marine Corps' three active divisions and the reserve division is structured somewhat differently. But a division with the normal complement of three infantry regiments would typically be manned in this manner.

MARINES: 1,055 officers, 16,903 enlisted personnel.

NAVY: 74 officers, 847 enlisted personnel.

A Marine infantry regiment's complement:

MARINES: 147 officers, 2,446 enlisted personnel.

NAVY: 11 officers, 201 enlisted personnel.

In addition to the weapons organic to each of the regiment's infantry battalions, regimental headquarters maintains a number of crew-served weapons primarily for security of command posts, and an anti-tank platoon. A regiment's three battalions field a total of 24 81mm mortars, 27 60mm mortars, and 91 7.62mm machine guns. Their firepower has been increased with the addition of .50 caliber machine guns, 40mm machine guns, the new squad automatic weapon, shoulder-launched multi-purpose assault weapons, an increased number of M203 grenade launchers, and improvements to the present service rifle and the M60E3 machine gun.

A Marine infantry regiment comprises three infantry battalions and a headquarters company. The heavy anti-tank (TOW) weaponry of a Marine division has been doubled from 72 to 144 with the addition of a TOW platoon in each headquarters company infantry regiment. Through infantry battalions a regiment executes its mission, which is to locate, close with, and destroy enemy forces by fire and maneuver, or repel enemy forces by fire and close combat. Usually commanded by a colonel, a regiment can be completely transported by trucks, helicopters, fixed-wing aircraft, amphibious ships, vehicles, or ships.

With combat support a regiment reinforced becomes the ground combat element for a Marine Expeditionary Brigade (MEB), which may be employed separately or as an advance force of a substantially larger Marine Expeditionary Force (MEF). There are nine U.S. Marine infantry regiments in the active forces and three in the Marine Corps Reserve.

The 27 active Marine infantry battalions are built around the traditional 13-man rifle squad, composed of a squad leader and three four-man rifle teams. The active battalions will be enhanced by the addition of 41 enlisted Marines, and the number of active battalions will be reduced to 24. Battalion firepower has been increased 25% over the past five years.

The weapons used by a Marine infantry battalion range from the pistol and rifle to crew-served weapons, including machine guns, anti-tank weapons, and mortars.

The primary mission of a Marine infantry battalion, comprising three rifle companies, a weapons company, and a headquarters and service company, is the same as the infantry regiment's: to locate, close with, and destroy enemy forces by fire and maneuver, or to repel enemy assaults by fire and close combat. The battalion commander normally is a lieutenant colonel; his company commanders are captains.

A battalion usually moves on foot, but has a limited number of light vehicles assigned for transport of some weapons, communications equipment, ammunition, food, and water. The entire battalion and its weapons and equipment can be transported by helicopters or amphibious assault vehicles.

When reinforced with combat-support the battalion becomes the ground combat element of a Marine Expeditionary Unit (MEU).

Marine Air-Ground Task Forces (MAGTFs) are combined arms teams of air and ground forces controlled by a single commander. They may deploy by sea or air, or by a combination of the two. Task organization is based on the mission assigned and the capabilities of opposing forces.

Under a darkening sky, the "go" signal is given to a Marine CH-46 helicopter during Exercise Valiant Usher.

There are three basic types of Marine air-ground task forces. The structure will vary depending on the mission assigned and other circumstances.

A Marine division usually has three infantry regiments; one of the three current active divisions, however, has only two regiments; what might be its third infantry regiment forms the ground combat element of a separate brigade. In addition to its infantry regiments, a division also fields the following units:

Headquarters battalion. This unit provides command, control, and administrative services. It consists of a headquarters company, a service company, a truck company, a military police company, division headquarters, and a communications company. The headquarters company includes a photo-imagery interpretation unit, sensor control and maintenance platoon, and interrogator-translator teams. In addition to security duties, the military police provide beach and traffic control and guard prisoner-of-war stockades.

Artillery regiment. There are four Marine artillery regiments—one in each division. Each has its own unique structure. The 12th Marine Regiment, for example, is split, with one battalion assigned to support the 1st Marine Expeditionary Brigade in Hawaii, and two direct-support battalions and one general support battalion with the 3d Marine Division on Okinawa. The 10th Marine Regiment—which is assigned to the 2d Marine Division—provides an example of a regiment's typical firepower and structure. Commanded by a colonel, the regiment consists of a headquarters battery, three direct-support battalions, and two general-support battalions.

Direct-support battalions are assigned a total of 72 155mm howitzers (towed). One general-support battalion is equipped with 12 eight-inch howitzers (self-propelled), and 18 155mm howitzers (self-propelled). A second G/S battalion is equipped with 18 155mm howitzers (towed). The artillery regiment is the primary source of fire support for the Marine division.

Reconnaissance battalion. This unit conducts ground reconnaissance and surveillance as part of the division. At full strength of 316 Marines, a battalion fields 36 four-man scout teams for reconnaissance behind enemy lines and along the forward edge of the battle area.

Tank battalion. A typical tank battalion consists of 1,291 Marines who are equipped with: 70 M60A1 105mm gun tanks; 72 Tube-launched, Optically tracked, Wire-command-link (TOW) guided missile systems; M88A1 tracked recovery vehicles, and four M60A1 armored vehicle-launched bridges (AVLB).

Assault amphibian battalion. This battalion transports landing forces from amphibious ships to and across the beach, and provides transport in mobile operations ashore. A battalion usually consists of four assault amphibian companies and a headquarters and service company. A battalion is equippped with 187 assault amphibian vehicles (primarily for personnel transport), 15 assault amphibian vehicles equipped to serve as command and control vehicles, and six assault amphibian vehicles designed to retrieve damaged vehicles.

Combat engineer battalion. Four combat engineer companies, an engineer support company, and a headquarters and service company form this battalion of 800 Marines. They perform demolition missions, clear minefields, supervise booby-trap and mine emplacement, and build obstacles, rafts, bridges, and roads.

Force Service Support Group (FSSG). Marines provide combat service support to a MEF in garrison or while deployed. The FSSG is organized into a headquarters and several battalions: service, supply, maintenance, engineer support, motor transport, medical, dental, and landing support. From these units come elements that provide support for independently deployed battalion landing teams, regimental landing teams, Marine Expeditionary Units, or Marine Expeditionary Brigades.

The Fleet Marine Forces

The Fleet Marine Forces, a balanced blend of combined air and ground arms, are primarily trained, organized, and equipped for offensive amphibious employment. Each Fleet Marine Force normally consists of a headquarters unit, one or more Force Service Support Groups, one or more divisions, and one or more Marine aircraft wings; they also may have one or more brigades assigned.

There are two Fleet Marine Forces: Fleet Marine Force, Atlantic (FMFLANT) headquartered at Norfolk, Va.; and Fleet Marine Force, Pacific (FMFPAC) headquartered at Camp H.M. Smith, Hawaii. The two differ considerably in size. FMFLANT consists of the 2d Marine Division, 2d Marine Aircraft Wing, 2d Force Service Support Group.

The major units of FMFPAC are the 1st Marine Division, the 3d Marine Division, the 1st Marine Expeditionary Brigade, the 1st Marine Aircraft Wing, the 3d Marine Aircraft Wing, the 1st FSSG, the 3d FSSG, the 1st Radio Battalion, the 7th Communications Battalion, the 1st Force Reconnaissance Company, the 1st Anglico Company, and a Headquarters and Service Battalion.

The primary mission of the Fleet Marine Forces is to seize objectives held by highly trained and well-equipped enemy forces. Primarily designed for offensive combat, the forces may also be used to defend advanced naval bases.

The forces are trained and equipped for immediate deployment by ship or by air anywhere in the world.

Marine Aircraft Wing

Capability to conduct tactical air operations is essential to the execution of an amphibious operation. To this end, the Marine Corps has pioneered an effective aviation combat arm capable of meeting all requirements of a landing force. These requirements call for a flexible, responsive Aviation Combat Element (ACE) specifically tailored to meet the anticipated tactical situation.

Current organization of Marine aviation consists of the Marine aircraft wing, which is the highest level tactical aviation command in the Fleet Ma-

Marine Expeditionary Force (MEF)

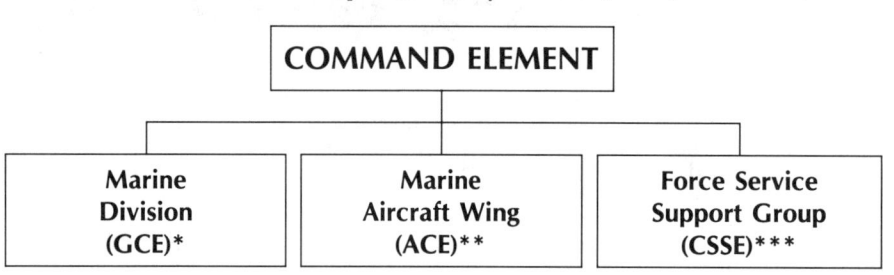

```
                    COMMAND ELEMENT
                    ┌────────┼────────┐
              Marine      Marine     Force Service
             Division   Aircraft Wing Support Group
              (GCE)*      (ACE)**       (CSSE)***
```

The MEF may range in size from less than one full division to several divisions and an aircraft wing or wings. The personnel, weapons, and equipment which illustrate this example of a MEF represent one consisting of one division and one wing; the ground combat element includes nine infantry battalions in three regiments. Normally, a force of this size also would include one artillery regiment, a tank battalion, an assault amphibian battalion, a LAV battalion, a combat engineer battalion, and a reconnaissance battalion. The Force Service Support Group could provide supplies, maintenance, engineering, motor transport, and medical and dental care for 60 days. Commanded by a Marine major general or lieutenant general, the MEF is the largest and most powerful of Marine air-ground task forces.

Personnel:

49,700 Marines; 2,600 U.S. Navy personnel (medical, dental chaplain, etc.); 8,800 Navy support elements (SEALs, beach support, etc.). Total, 55,100.

Aircraft and Missiles:

60 AV-8 V/STOL attack aircraft
48 F-4 or F/A-18 fighter/attack aircraft
20 A-6E all-weather/night attack aircraft
8 EA-6B electronic warfare aircraft
8 RF-4B photo reconnaissance aircraft
12 OV-10 observation aircraft
12 KC-130 refueling aircraft
9 OA-4 tactical control aircraft
60 CH-46 medium-lift assault helicopters
32 Ch-53 (A or D) heavy assault transport helicopters
16 CH-53E heavy-lift assault helicopters
24 AH-1 (W & T) attack helicopters
24 UH-1N utility and command and control helicopters
16 Hawk surface-to-air missile launchers
90 Stinger surface-to-air missile teams

Major Ground Forces Equipment:

70 tanks
80 81mm mortars
216 Dragon missile launchers (anti-armor)
163 TOW missile launchers (anti-armor)
212 assault amphibious vehicles
110 light armored vehicles (LAV)
90 155mm howitzers (towed)
18 155mm howitzers (self-propelled)
12 eight-inch howitzers (self-propelled)
81 60mm mortars
701 .50-caliber machine guns
806 M60 machine guns
189 SMAWS
631 40mm machine guns

*GCE: Ground combat Element
**ACE: Aviation Combat Element
***CSSE: Combat Service Support Element

rine Force. Each wing is task-organized with various groups, squadrons, light anti-aircraft missile battalions, and low-altitude air defense battalions. There are presently four wings, three in the regular forces and one in the reserves, each primarily designed to support one Marine division in an amphibious operation.

The mission of a Marine aircraft wing is to conduct air operations in support of Fleet Marine Forces to include offensive air support, anti-air warfare, assault support, aerial reconnaissance, electronic warfare, and control of aircraft and missiles. As a collateral function, the wing may participate as an integral component of naval aviation in the execution of such other Navy functions as the fleet commander may direct. The following aircraft are found in Marine aircraft groups of a typical Marine aircraft wing. Helicopter Group: CH-53 (heavy lift), CH-46 (medium lift), UH-1 (light lift utility), AH-1 (attack) helicopters as well as OV-10 (aerial reconnaissance/observation). Fixed-Wing Group: A-4, AV-8 (light attack), A-6 (all-weather attack), F/A-18 (all weather fighter/attack), RF-4 (multi-sensor reconnaissance), EA-6 (electronic warfare) and KC-130 (air refueling).

MARITIME PREPOSITIONING FORCES

The advent of maritime prepositioning provides yet another capability to project power ashore or to demonstrate national resolve with naval forces.

In preparing for maritime prepositioning operations, the supplies (30 days' worth) and most of the equipment required for a powerful Marine Expeditionary Brigade are loaded aboard specifically designated and configured merchant ships that are chartered and commanded by the Navy. These Maritime Prepositioning Forces (MPF) then are deployed to what are considered potential areas of conflict in which U.S. forces might become involved. They can reach these anticipated hot spots within seven days. If and when required, the ships proceed to a beach or port in the operating area, one perhaps secured by a 2,000-man forward-deployed Marine Expeditionary Unit. Some 16,500 Marines and naval personnel are airlifted to nearby airfields at the same time. Meanwhile, the tactical aircraft of the MEB's aviation combat element flight-ferry to the area of employment.

Equipment and supplies quickly are offloaded from the MPS and married up with appropriate units. Now combat ready, the brigade moves on to its assigned objectives. It has arrived (anywhere in the world) within five days after the ships are offshore and is heavy enough in terms of firepower and sustainability to permit it to contribute mightily to achieving victory.

The first MPS squadron, consisting of four ships, has been deployed since April 1985 and is currently sailing in the eastern Atlantic. The 6th MEB is the command element for the MPS brigade.

The second squadron, consisting of five ships, deployed in September 1985 and is homeported in Diego Garcia. The 7th MEB is the command element for that MPS brigade.

The third squadron, consisting of four ships, completed loading out in the fall of 1986 and is deployed in the western Pacific. It is homeported at Guam/Tinian. The 1st MEB is the command element for the third squadron's brigade.

Marine Expeditionary Brigade (MEB)

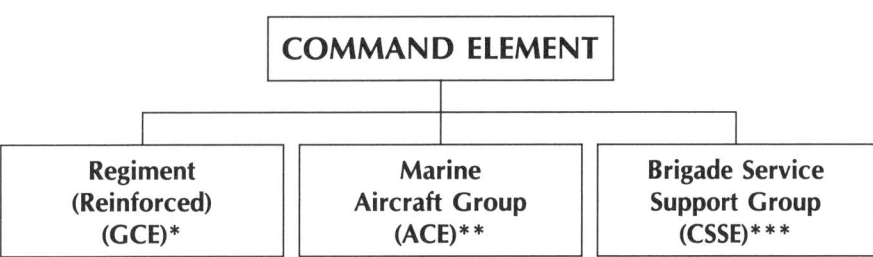

COMMAND ELEMENT
- Regiment (Reinforced) (GCE)*
- Marine Aircraft Group (ACE)**
- Brigade Service Support Group (CSSE)***

The MEB's GCE usually is composed of from two to five infantry battalions, an artillery battalion, a bank company, a combat engineer company, a reconnaissance company, an assault amphibian company, and a TOW platoon. Designed to operate for 30 days without resupply, the MEB quickly can establish procedures for resupply and for substantially longer periods of shore operations. It normally is commanded by a Marine brigadier general and is embarked aboard approximately 26 Navy amphibious ships. The MEB may be deployed forward as a floating ready force or may be airlifted forward rapidly. Three MEB command elements actively prepare for employment with the three maritime prepositioning ship squadrons in the Atlantic and Pacific Oceans. These ships carry substantial proportions of MEB equipment to forward assembly areas for link-up with airlifted personnel and essential equipment.

Personnel:

15,000 Marines; 700 U.S. Navy personnel (medical, dental, chaplain, etc.); 1,250 Navy support elements (UDTs, SEALs, beach support, etc.). Total, 16,950.

Aircraft and Missiles:

- 40 AV-8B V/STOL attack aircraft
- 24 F/A-18 fighter/attack aircraft
- 10 A-6E all-weather/night attack aircraft
- 4 EA-6B electronic warfare aircraft
- 4 RF-4B photo reconnaissance aircraft
- 5 OA-4 tactical control aircraft
- 6 KC-130 refueling aircraft
- 6 OV-10 observation aircraft
- 40 CH-46 medium-lift assault helicopters
- 16 CH-53D heavy assault transport helicopters
- 16 CH-53E heavy-lift, assault helicopters
- 12 AH-1T attack helicopters
- 12 UH-1N utility and command and control helicopters
- 8 Hawk surface-to-air missile launchers
- 45 Stinger surface-to-air missile teams

Major Ground Forces Equipment:

- 17 tanks
- 24 81mm mortars
- 72 Dragon missile launchers (anti-armor)
- 40 TOW missile launchers (anti-armor)
- 27 light armored vehicles (LAV) (Reinforced Company)
- 47 assault amphibian vehicles
- 24 155mm howitzers (towed)
- 6 155mm howitzers (self-propelled)
- 6 eight-inch howitzers (self-propelled)
- 27 60mm mortars
- 138 .50-caliber machine guns
- 255 7.62mm M60 machine guns
- 63 SMAWS
- 114 40mm machine guns

*GCE: Ground Combat Element
**ACE: Aviation Combat Element
***CSSE: Combat Service Support Element

LCACs, which can operate at speeds in excess of 50 knots, speedily bring men and equipment to the beach.

NORWAY PREPOSITIONING PROGRAM

The Norway Prepositioning Program is a strategic mobility enhancement that reduces force closure time to Norway from weeks to days. It provides a creditable deterrent and expands the strategic options available for the rapid reinforcement of NATO's northern flank.

Prepositioning the equipment and supplies for a MEB in Norway facilitates this rapid reinforcement and reduces the MEB airlift requirements by about 4,000 sorties. The Norway Airlanded MEB will provide a credible, self-sustainable, and versatile force capable of executing current plans with minimal reliance on existing strategic airlift. It will be specifically tailored for this contingency and will be comprised of about 13,000 Marines, 150 aircraft, and, when combined with equipment and

Marine Expeditionary Unit (MEU)

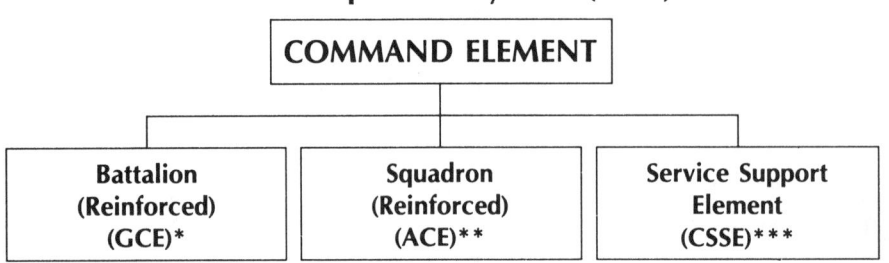

COMMAND ELEMENT
- Battalion (Reinforced) (GCE)*
- Squadron (Reinforced) (ACE)**
- Service Support Element (CSSE)***

Usually sea-based, the MEU is the Marine Corps' most responsive air-ground task force. It normally is prepared to assault with 15 days of ammunition, food, fuel, water, and medical supplies available. It can be reinforced or resupplied rapidly. Usually embarked aboard three to five U.S. Navy amphibious ships, the MEU also may be airlifted. It most often is commanded by a colonel. Two to three MEUs usually are deployed forward or standing ready for immediate movement to forward combat areas or peacetime crisis points.

Personnel:

1,900 Marines; 100 U.S. Navy personnel assigned to Marine units (medical, dental, chaplain, etc.); 490 members of a Navy support element, explosive ordnance demolition teams, Sea-Air-Land teams ([SEALs], and other special-support units). Total: 2,490.

Aircraft and Missiles:

12 CH-46 medium-lift assault helicopters
4 CH-53 (D or E) heavy lift assault transport helicopters
4 UH-1 utility helicopters
4 AH-1 attack helicopters
 The squadron could be reinforced by one VMA Det (6 AV-8) Vertical/Short Takeoff and Landing (V/STOL) attack aircraft and 2 KC-130 aerial refuelers as the tactical situation dictates.
15 Stinger surface-to-air missile teams.

Major Ground Forces Equipment:

5 tanks
8 81mm mortars
32 Dragon missile launchers (anti-armor)
8 TOW missile launchers (tube-launched, optically sighted, wire-guided anti-armor)
14 amphibian assault vehicles
8 155mm howitzers
9 60mm mortars
20 .50-caliber machine guns
60 7.62mm machine guns
21 SMAWS
26 40mm machine guns.

*GCE: Ground Combat Element
**ACE: Aviation Combat Element
***CSSE: Combat Service Support Element

Maritime Prepositioning Forces Brigade

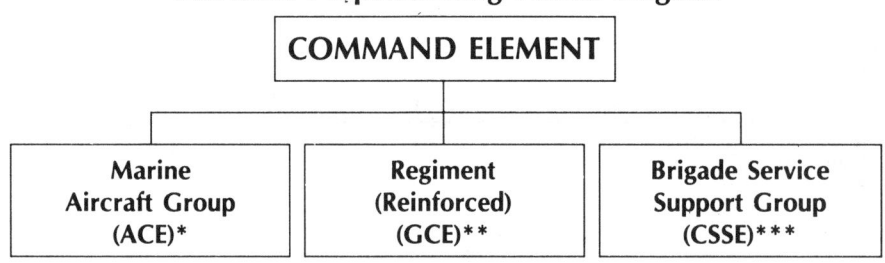

COMMAND ELEMENT
- Marine Aircraft Group (ACE)*
- Regiment (Reinforced) (GCE)**
- Brigade Service Support Group (CSSE)***

Aircraft/Launchers:

40 AV-8s
24 F/A-18 fighter/attack aircraft
10 A-6E all-weather/night-attack aircraft
4 EA-6B electronic-warfare aircraft
4 RF-4B photo reconnaissance aircraft
5 OA-4 tactical control aircraft
6 KC-130 refueling aircraft
6 OV-10 observation aircraft
8 CH-53 heavy-ligt assault helicopters
12 CH-53D heavy-lift assault helicopter transport helicopters
12 UH-1N utility/command and control helicopters
12 AH-1T attack helicopters
12 CH-46 medium-lift assault helicopters

6 Hawk surface-to-air missile launchers
45 Stinger teams

Major Ground & Combat Equipment:

53 tanks
30 light armored vehicles (LAV)
24 81mm mortars
72 TOW missile launchers (anti-armor)
109 assault amphibian vehicles
24 155mm howitzers M198 (towed)
6 155mm howitzers (self-propelled)
27 60mm mortars
303 .50 caliber machine guns
360 M-60 machine guns
6 8" howitzers (self-propelled)
114 MK-19 40mm grenade launchers

*ACE: Aviation Combat Element
**GCE: Ground Combat Element
***CSSE: Combat Service Support Element

Approximate Personnel
USMC = 16,514
USN = 880

supplies carried by strategic airlift in the fly-in echelon, will be able to sustain itself for 30 days. The initial operating capability (IOC) of this program is late 1989.

This MEB is intended for use prior to hostilities and is not a substitute for amphibious assault. Further, it is not a change in traditional roles or missions of the Marine Corps in that it contributes to our maritime strategy designed to keep the vital U.S.-NATO Europe sea lanes of communication open.

COMBAT READINESS

A high level of combat readiness long has been the standard for the Marine Corps. As quality personnel are married up to new and improved equipment, readiness is sharpened to an even finer point. Training and readiness must remain synonymous if the Marine Corps is to continue to be "the force in readiness" and fight "in every clime and place." Marine Corps training demands the demonstration of performance standards at all levels of training, from the fighting skills of the individual Marine required for small unit tactics to those necessary to conduct task-force-level amphibious operations.

Marine Air-Ground Task Forces (MAGTF) participate in a wide variety of exercises in virtually every corner of the globe. Since 1981, the Marine Corps has experienced a modest but steady increase in the number of MAGTF exercises conducted by Marine Expeditionary Brigades (MEB) and Marine Expeditionary Forces (MAF).

Marines and their equipment continue to be rigorously tested by participation in numerous joint-service exercises such as the U.S. Central Command's Gallant Eagle and Bright Star, the Atlantic Command's Solid Shield and Ocean Venture, and the Pacific Command's Team Spirit. These large-scale exercises sponsored by unified commanders include participation by all components, to include those associated with the Maritime Prepositioning Forces (MPF) program, and stress the interoperability among them.

In U.S. European Command exercises such as Northern Wedding and Bold Guard, the Marines have continued to strengthen their position in NATO. MAGTFs, utilizing the prepositioned equipment stationed in Norway, continue to prove that the Marine Corps is a very capable partner in the defense of Norway.

Forward deployed Marine Expeditionary Units (MEU) regularly conduct amphibious landings and raids and noncombatant evacuation exercises to maintain their proficiency.

The Marine Corps provides realistic and challenging training under wartime conditions and allows commanders to exercise all supporting arms on a single range. Combined Arms Exercises (CAX) are conducted through a series of battalion and brigade live-fire exercises at the Marine Corps Air-Ground Combat Center, Twentynine Palms, Calif.

In summary, Marine Air-Ground Task Forces continue to exercise more frequently and more realistically with elements of other services than at any time in the past. With the continued refinement of skills surrounding the utilization of Maritime Prepositioning Forces assets, and those assets prepositioned in Norway, the training readiness of the operational forces continues to reach new heights.

MARINE CORPS RESEARCH, DEVELOPMENT, AND ACQUISITION COMMAND

The final report to the President by the President's Blue Ribbon Commission on Defense Management, the Packard Commission, in June 1986, recommended unambiguous authority for overall acquisition policy, clear accountability for acquisition execution, and plain lines of command for those with program-management responsibilities. The response of the Commandant of the Marine Corps to that charge was the formation in November 1987 of the Marine Corps Research, Development, and Acquisition Command (MCRDAC).

This new command streamlined the Marine Corps' research, development, and acquisition organization and process. The organization integrated various elements of the research, development, and acquisition process that had previously been divided among several Marine Corps activities. This collection and integration of responsibilities in one organization made possible the establishment of Program Managers with clear responsibility for each program, from the establishment of the requirement through the demonstration, validation, development, production, and finally, the deployment phase.

The commanding general of MCRDAC also was designated Deputy Assistant Secretary of the Navy for Research, Engineering, and Systems for Marine Corps programs. This placed the commanding general in the Department of Navy acquisition process and made him responsible for all Marine Corps acquisition programs.

Marine Corps Combat Development Command

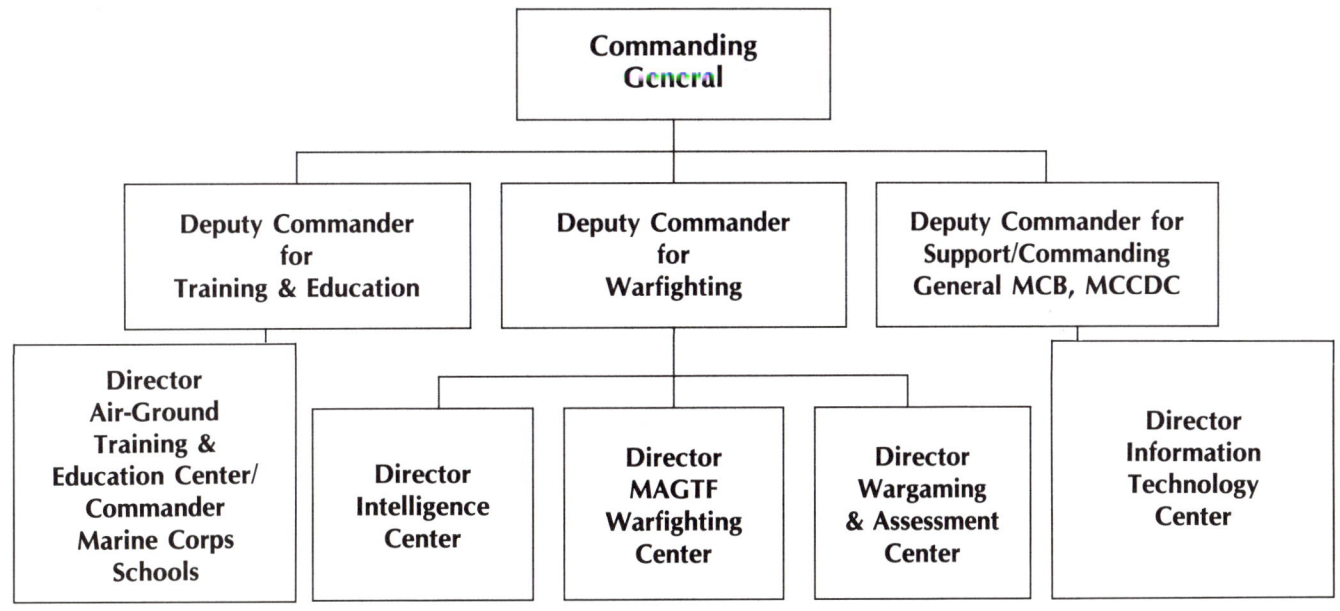

- Commanding General
  - Deputy Commander for Training & Education
    - Director Air-Ground Training & Education Center/Commander Marine Corps Schools
  - Deputy Commander for Warfighting
    - Director Intelligence Center
    - Director MAGTF Warfighting Center
    - Director Wargaming & Assessment Center
  - Deputy Commander for Support/Commanding General MCB, MCCDC
    - Director Information Technology Center

WEAPONS/MARINES

The following weapons and combat vehicles represent those items most common to Marine air-ground task forces or—where noted—which recently have been developed and will be in the hands of Marines in 1989.

RIFLE (M161) and **GRENADE LAUNCHER** (M203)

M16A1 and M16A2 Rifles. A 5.56mm magazine-fed, gas-operated, air-cooled, shoulder-fired rifle, the M16A1 has been the standard rifle for Marines since the late 1960s. It can fire ball, tracer, or blank ammunition on automatic or semi-automatic and weighs 7.9 pounds when loaded with a 30-pound magazine. The M16A2, a substantially improved version of the M16A1, began entering the Marine Corps inventory in FY 1984 and is 100 percent fielded to active and Reserve requirements. The M16A2 has a heavier barrel, improved handguards, a burst-control device (to limit automatic bursts to three rounds), a finger-operated windage and elevation knob, and a muzzle brake (to reduce muzzle rise when firing). The improvements were made by the rifle's original manufacturer, Colt Industries. The M16A2 has a maximum effective range of 800 meters (880 yards). A bayonet-knife, M7, may be mounted on the rifle.

Grenade Launcher, M203. Attached to the M16A1 or M16A2 rifle, the M203 can hurl several kinds of grenades beyond hand grenade range. Types include: high-explosive, white-star parachute illumination, white-star cluster illumination, tactical CS (riot-control gas), high-explosive airburst, high-explosive dual-purpose (for penetrating up to two inches of steel plate), multi-projectile (containing 20 projectiles about the size of No. 4 buckshot), and practice grenades. As Marine fire teams expand in size from four to five members, two grenade launchers per team will be assigned instead of one, as at present.

RIFLE (M16A2)

Personal Defense Weapon. The caliber .45 M1191A1 pistol has served Marines as their primary sidearm for more than 70 years. Carried by officers, staff noncommissioned officers, and other Marines not armed with the rifle, the .45 weighs three pounds and has a maximum effective range of 50 meters (55 yards). A semi-automatic, recoil-operated, magazine-fed, self-loading weapon designed by Colt, it first was manufactured by Colt, then by Ithaca and Remington, for service use. Designed primarily for defense, it also has been used on attack missions on many occasions. Competition to select a replacement was completed in late 1984, with the winner being the Beretta 9mm semi-automatic M9 pistol. A five-year contract for production of the weapon was awarded to Beretta USA Corporation in April 1985. Active and Reserve fielding of the weapon will be completed during FY 1989.

MACHINE GUN (Mk 19, Mod 3)

Machine Gun, .50-Caliber M2. In use for more than 45 years, the .50-caliber machine gun is fired from a tripod as well as from mounts on vehicles and helicopters. It provides heavy automatic fire against personnel, vehicles, aircraft, and fortifications. Air-cooled and weighing 82 pounds, it is fed by metal link belts and has a maximum effective range of 2,000 meters (1.2 miles). The newly structured infantry battalion has eight M2s assigned to each of its weapons companies to give them enhanced coverage against air and ground targets—particularly against the threat of enemy helicopters. The M2 is manufactured by the Saco Defense Systems Division of Maremont Corp.

Machine Gun, M60. The gas-operated, belt-fed M60 provides a heavy volume of controlled fire over a maximum effective range of 1,100 meters (0.7 mile). It weighs 23.2 pounds and fires 7.62mm rounds at a cyclic rate of 550 to 600 rounds per minute. The "sustained" and "rapid"- rates of fire are 100 and 200 rounds per minute, respectively. It uses tracer, ball, blank, armor-piercing, and armor-piercing incendiary ammunition. As infantry battalions are restructured, the six M60 machine guns now in each rifle company's weapons platoon are replaced with newer M60E3s. The M60 is manufactured by the Saco Defense Systems Division of Maremont Corp.

Machine Gun M60E3. A product-improved version of the standard M60 machine gun. Manufactured by the Maremont Corporation, all major components of the M60E3 machine gun, including the barrel, are directly interchangeable with the standard M60 machine gun. Like the M60, the E3 model is an aircooled, link-belt-fed, gas-operated weapon designed to be fired from the shoulder, hip, sitting, or prone position. While the M60E3 retains the performance characteristics of the standard M60, it is 25% lighter, has the bipod mounted on the receiver instead of the barrel, has two pistol grips making it easier to handle during the assault, a swiveling trigger to permit the gun to be fired with heavy gloves or mittens, and a new feed cover to permit the gun to be cocked with the cover closed. These are among other new features which strengthened the weak points while retaining the strong points of the standard M60.

MACHINE GUN (M60)

Machine Gun, Mk19, Mod-3. Entering service in infantry battalions in 1985, the Mk19 fires M430 high-velocity 40mm grenades from linked belts. The grenades are configured in the form of armor-piercing rounds; their use is designed to counter the growing number of infantry fighting vehicles in the armed forces of potential enemies. The Mk19 has a cyclic rate of fire of 325 to 375 rounds per minute with an effective range of 1,600 meters (0.9 mile) and can be ground-or vehicle-mounted on a pedestal. The 75-pound gun also may be mounted on helicopter doors. It can be fired manually or electrically. The Mk19 is a developmental product of the Naval Ordnance Station, Louisville, Ky.

Squad Automatic Weapon (SAW), M249. The SAW began entering Marine rifle battalions in FY 1984. The SAW fires a 5.56mm round at a cycle rate of 850 to 950 rounds per minute. It may be fired from the shoulder, hip, or underarm; its rate of fire can be increased to 1,100 rounds per minute. The weapon's molded plastic magazine holds 200 linked rounds; a 30-round box magazine may be used instead. With one SAW per fire team, the new weapon fills a void in the Marine infantry battalion that has existed since the Browning automatic rifle was phased out 20 years ago. A product of Fabrique Nationale Herstal S.A., the SAW has a firing weight of just over 20 pounds.

Shoulder-launched Multi-purpose Assault Weapon (SMAW). Fielding of the SMAW began in 1984 and now is complete. Designed by McDonnell Douglas Astronautics Co. for breaching masonry structures and earth and timber bunkers, it is accurate up to 250 meters (275 yards). The warhead can differentiate between hard and soft targets—exploding on contact or penetrating before exploding. Fired from a reusable launcher, the 83mm projectile weighs 13.4 pounds and is aimed by use of a telescopic sight alone or by using the sight and a self-contained spotting rifle.

Starlight Scope. Night vision optics for the Marine Corps have been greatly improved. The AN/PVS-5A, individual night vision goggle (NVG) is a two-cell night-device that allows a commander, small-unit leader, and vehicle driver to operate during the hours of darkness. It provides a 40º field of vision and will operate for 12 hours on one disposable 2.7 volt DC battery. The AN/PVS-4 night vision sight is designed for the individual Marine's rifle. It replaces the AN/PVS-2 and is lighter, smaller, provides a better field of view, and has improved performance under more unfavorable environmental extremes.

Hand Grenades and Pyrotechnics. Marines have available for combat use a wide range of hand grenades, which are basically small bombs filled with explosives or chemicals. There are two types of fragmentation hand grenades—one weighing 16 ounces, the other 14 ounces. The 16-ounce M26 has a variety of fuse and safety clip configurations, including: delay fuse, no safety clip; delay fuse, safety clip; and impact fuse, safety clip. The M26 can be thrown 40 meters (44 yards) and has an effective casualty radius of 15 meters (16.5 yards), but some fragments may reach as far as 184 meters (about 200 yards). The M33 fragmentation grenade, two ounces lighter, has the same effective casualty radius. CS or riot-control grenades produce a thick cloud of irritant which causes tears and coughing. White-phosphorous grenades throw phosphorous over an area from 35 to 50 meters (115 to 165 feet) and are used for signaling, screening, incendiary purposes, or inflicting casualties. The AN-M14 incendiary (thermite) grenade weighs 32 ounces and contains a filler which burns for approximately 40 seconds at a temperature of 4,000 degrees. A portion of the filler turns into molten iron that produces intense heat, igniting or fusing whatever it touches. It can ignite combustible materials, destroy weapons and equipment, or burn holes in metal doors. Illumination grenades produce 55,000 candlepower for about 45 seconds and are used to illuminate small sections of the battlefield at night. M18 colored-smoke grenades produce a thick cloud of red, green, or yellow smoke and are used for signaling and screening. They are particularly useful in ground-to-air signaling and are frequently used to mark helicopter landing zones or to aid attack aircraft pilots in identifying friendly positions or lines. Hand-held, rocket-propelled signals are small rockets that are triggered by hand and reach a minimum height of 200 meters (220 yards) before igniting as single-star parachute flares, star-cluster flares, or smoke parachutes. The Marines also have a Bullet Trap Rifle Grenade (BTRG), which is a bullet-launched rifle grenade.

Mines. Explosive devices designed to kill or wound personnel or to destroy or damage equipment, mines may be set to detonate: by a controlled means, such as an electrical switch; by the actions of their victims; or by passage of time. They are considered both weapons and obstacles and may be laid in pattern or without pattern. The typical land mine contains a booster, body, detonator, fuse, and main charge. The M15 anti-tank mine is used against heavy tanks and can be fitted with a variety of fuses; a typical M15 can be initiated by a pressure of 565 pounds (plus or minus 174 pounds). The M16A1 series anti-personnel mine—commonly known as the "Bouncing Betty"—is a bouncing fragmentation mine which, when

SQUAD AUTOMATIC WEAPON (M249)

activated, pops from the ground to a height of about six feet and detonates. Pressure of eight to 20 pounds on three prongs of the fuse, or a pull of between three and 10 pounds on a trip wire, activates the mine. The M18A1 anti-personnel mine—commonly known as the "Claymore"—is a directional fragmentation mine used primarily in protective minefields for defense of outposts and bivouac areas against infiltrators. It is also effective in ambush against personnel and vehicles such as jeeps and trucks. When detonated, by either electrical or non-electrical means, it fires a fan-shaped pattern of spherical steel fragments in a 60-degree horizontal arc at a height of two meters (6.6 feet) and can cause casualties in a radius of 100 meters (110 yards). Among other mines used by the Marines are the M19 and M21, designed for use against tanks and other heavy vehicles. Also being procured now are munitions for the Family of Scatterable Mines (FASCAM). These mines are remotely delivered by artillery or aircraft, have multiple fusing beyond the standard single impulse fuse, contain integral anti-disturbance devices, and have several different self-destruct settings. They can be employed directly on top of an enemy force or used to protect the flanks of an attacking force. The anti-vehicular mines use a directed energy platter charge; the anti-personnel mines are either standing or bounding fragmentation.

DRAGON (M47)

Dragon M47. This surface-attack guided missile system is a recoilless, shoulder-fired, tube-launched, medium anti-tank assault weapon. One man can carry it, and it can be used in all weather conditions, as long as the target is visible. The Dragon M47 system consists of a day or night tracker and a round; the latter has two major components—the launcher and the missile. The day tracker weighs six pounds, the night tracker 22 pounds, and the round 25 pounds. Wartime plans call for 24 trackers to be assigned to the three sections of the Dragon platoon, a unit of the weapons company of the infantry battalion. The Dragon has an effective range of 1,000 meters (0.6 mile); it is manufactured by McDonnell Douglas Astronautics Co. A Dragon night tracker was fielded in FY 1984.

Light Anti-Armor Weapon AT4 (LAW). The AT4 is a self-contained unit consisting of a launcher and a rocket. Carried by a Marine in addition to his own weapon, it is an expendable munition. The 84mm system weighs 14.6 pounds and is 39.4 inches long. The projectile weighs 4.03 pounds and has a muzzle velocity of 951 feet per second. The warhead will penetrate in excess of 350mm of rolled homogeneous armor. The maximum effective range against moving and stationary targets is 300 meters. The weapon is fired from the shoulder, but also can be used for off-route mining. However, its backblast restricts the gunner's choice of firing positions, it is heavy at 14.6 pounds, and it may need more than one hit to kill. Because of the last limitation, the preferred method of engagement is volley fire, where two or more gunners shoot at the same target at the same time.

TOW M22054. The Tube-launched, Optically-tracked, Wire-command-link (TOW) guided missile system was developed as a heavy antitank or assault weapon and can be fired from a tripod, an LAV-AT, or a special truck mount. It can be employed in all weather con-

TOW (M22054)

ditions, as long as the gunner can see the target through the sights. It is the key weapon in the anti-tank company of the Marine tank battalion—three platoons of 24 launchers each. The TOW has a maximum range of 3,750 meters and its high-explosive anti-tank round weighs 47 pounds and travels at a speed of 620 mph. The launcher weighs 205 pounds in the tripod configuration. The missile, designed by Hughes Aircraft Co., has a 20-year shelf life in its container and a 90-day shelf life after the front handling has been removed. The current TOW system was replaced by the TOW 2 in FY 1984. Even with the significant performance advantages the TOW 2 provides, it continues to be considerably less expensive than the other available heavy assault weaons. The TOW 2 system is capable of firing the I-TOW and the TOW-2 missiles.

60mm Mortar. The 60mm mortar is a smooth-bore, muzzle-loaded, high-angle, indirect-fire weapon consisting of a barrel, sight, bipod, and baseplate. Weighing 45.2 pounds, it can be used for direct or indirect fire missions. Maximum rate of fire is 30 rounds per minute, sustained rate of fire 18 rounds per minute. Its range using high-explosive ammunition is 3,600 meters (2.2 miles), 1,500 meters (0.9 mile) using smoke rounds, and 1,000 meters (0.6 mile) using illumination rounds. One round of high-explosive ammunition will neutralize an area 20 meters by 10 meters (66 feet by 33 feet); one mortar firing three rounds will neutralize an area 35 meters by 35 meters (115 feet by 115 feet).

81mm Mortar, M252. The 81mm mortar is a smooth-bore, muzzle-loaded, high angle, indirect fire weapon consisting of a barrel, sight, bipod, and baseplate. Unlike the 60mm mortar, which has a square baseplate, the 81mm mortar has a round base plate and can fire in any direction. The barrel weighs 35 pounds and the M3A1 baseplate 25.5 pounds. Maximum rate of fire is 30 rounds per minute, the sustained rate of fire 15 rounds per minute. The M252 fires high-explosive, smoke, illuminating, practice, and training ammunition. Its maximum range is 5,700 meters.

81mm MORTAR (M29)

ARTILLERY

Marine Corps artillery weapons are generically classified as cannon and are categorized according to caliber and means of transport. The cannon is a piece of fixed or mobile artillery that fires projectiles of various types. Its principal components are a breech, firing mechanism, and tube. The howitzer is a cannon with a barrel length usually between that of a gun and a mortar, capable of high- and low-angle fire, and with a medium muzzle velocity. Each type of Marine howitzer fires a variety of types of rounds, ranging from high-explosive to illumination to chemicals and, in the case of the 155mm and eight-inch howitzer nuclear ammunition.

Like the infantry battalion, the Corps' artillery regiments are in transition. Over the next several years, the M198 155mm howitzer (towed) will replace the 105mm howitzer in the Corps' reserve direct-support artillery battalions. This change will provide the units supported with a much greater degree of fire support over much greater range. The latter howitzer will remain in the inventory for contingency purposes. The table below shows some of the characteristics of each type of artillery in the Corps' inventory.

Weapon	Weight (in pounds)	Range (high-explosive round; in kilometers)[1]	Rate of Fire (sustained; per minute)
M101A1 105mm howitzer (towed)	4,950	11.0	3 rounds
M114A2 155mm howitzer (towed)	12,700	14.6 19.7[2]	1 round
M198 155mm howitzer (towed)	15,740	30.1	2 to 4 rounds[3]
M109A3 155mm howitzer (self-propelled)	53,940	23.7 24.5[2]	1 round
M110A2 eight-inch howitzer (self-propelled)	62,100	20.5	0.5 round

[1] 1km (0.6 mile).
[2] With rocket assist.
[3] Approximate.

COMBAT VEHICLES

Amphibious Assault Vehicles. The Marine Corps' current AAV, the AAV7A1, which was fielded during 1983-1985, is the product of an extensive service life extension program of the LVT7, fielded during 1972-1974. Both the LVT7 and its SLEP were accomplished by FMC Corporation. Of the 1,323 AAV7A1s in the Corps' inventory, 1,153 are AAVP7A1 personnel carriers, 106 AAVC7A1 command-and-control and communications vehicles, and 64 AAVR7A1 recovery vehicles. The AAVP7A1, the troop carrier, can transport 25 Marines and a crew of three, or 10,000 pounds of cargo with the crew of three. The basic AAVP7A1 weighs 38,450 pounds empty, is 26 feet long, and is powered by a turbocharged Cummins Diesel 400-horsepower engine which operates tracked running gear on land; two waterjets (3,025 pounds of force each) propel the vehicle through the water. The AAVC7A1 is a mobile, moderately armored command-and-control center. The AAVR7A1 is a recovery vehicle capable of retrieving vehicles of similar size and weight as well as providing a mobile amphibious intermediate-level repair vehicle to the MAGTF. AAV7A1 improvements include a new power pack, secure communications system, night-vision driving device, nonintegral fuel tank, reinforced suspension, smoke generating system, upgunned weapons station, applique armor, automatic fire sensing and supression system, and improved transmission. The AAV7A1 will extend the Marine Corps' organic amphibious assault capability beyond the year 2000.

MAIN BATTLE TANK (M1A1)

Main Battle Tank, M1A1. Beginning in FY 1989, the Marine Corps will commence procurement of the M1A1 Main Battle Tank, which is scheduled to begin replacing the M60A1 Rise Passive Tank, of which it has acquired 700. The M60A1 has been in the Marine Corps inventory since 1974. It weighs 57.3 tons, has a maximum speed of 30 mph, and a 310-mile cruising range. It mounts a 105mm M68 main gun, a coaxial 7.62mm machine gun, and a dual purpose. 50-caliber machine gun. With gyrostabilization added, it can fire on the move. Powered by a 12-cylinder, 750-horsepower diesel engine, it can carry 63 rounds of 105mm ammunition, 6,000 rounds of 7.62mm machine gun ammunition, and 900 rounds of .50-caliber ammunition. The M1A1 weighs 66.7 tons, has a governed speed of 42 mph and a cross-country speed of 30 mph, and can climb a 60-degree slope at 4.5 mph. It is powered by an AVCO-Textron 1,500-horsepower gas turbine engine. It is armed with a 120mm smoothbore gun, a coaxially mounted M240 7.62mm machine gun, an M240 machine gun loader's weapon, and a .50-caliber M2 machine gun commander's weapon. It has a cruising range of 275 miles, can climb a 42" vertical bank, and traverse a 9' wide trench. The M1A1 is manned by a crew of four. The Marines hope to commence receiving their new tanks early in 1991.

Light Armored Vehicle (LAV). Light armored vehicles manufactured by General Motors of Canada began arriving in 1984. By the end of 1988, all 758 that the Marine Corps was procuring had been fielded. Of this number, 422 were primary assault vehicles (LAV-25s), which are armed with a 25mm chain gun and a 7.62 machine gun as primary and secondary weapons. Other versions of the LAV include LAV-L (Logistics), LAV-M (Mortar), LAV-R (Recovery), LAV-AT (Anti-tank) and LAV-C2 (Command and control). LAVs will be organized into three active and one reserve battalion. Ninety also will be loaded into MPS ships.

LIGHT ARMORED VEHICLE (LAV)

AIRCRAFT/MARINES

SKYHAWK

A-4 SKYHAWK

WING SPAN: 28 feet.
LENGTH: 40 feet.
WEIGHT: empty, 10,465 pounds; full load, 24,500 pounds.
SPEED: maximum at sea level with 4,000-pound bomb load, 645 mph.
CEILING: 49,700 feet.
RANGE: 2,055 nautical miles with external fuel.
POWER PLANT: one Pratt and Whitney 152-P-408A turbojet engine.
ARMAMENT: several hundred variations of loads of more than 10,000 pounds of assorted rockets, bombs, torpedoes, and cannon.
CREW: one.
CONTRACTOR: McDonnell Douglas.

BRIEFING: This aircraft can perform a number of attack missions; it also may escort helicopters during assault operations. Marine A-4s are armed with two internally mounted 20mm cannons and can deliver conventional or nuclear weapons day or night. The last two active A-4 attack squadrons are presently transitioning to the AV-8B and will be complete by 1990. The Marine Corps Reserve has five squadrons of 12 A-4s each. Current plans call for a transition of these squadrons to AV-8Bs and F/A-18s in the 1990s.

A-6E INTRUDER

For specifications for the A-6E, see page 198.

BRIEFING: There are five squadrons of A-6s in the active Marine aircraft wings. The A-6, which can deliver both conventional and nuclear weapons, carries up to 14,000 pounds of armament. It provides ground forces with extremely accurate ordnance support during amphibious assault and extended operations inland during night and all weather conditions.

INTRUDER

HARRIER

AV-8B HARRIER

WING SPAN: 30 feet, 3 inches.
LENGTH: 46 feet, 3 inches.
HEIGHT: 11 feet; 7 inches.
WEIGHT: empty, 13,890 pounds.
MAXIMUM WEIGHT: for short takeoff, 31,000 pounds.
MAXIMUM WEIGHT: for vertical takeoff, 20,700 pounds.
SPEED: 630 mph.
FERRY RANGE: 1,700nm unrefueled.
ARMAMENT: cluster, general purpose and laser-guided bombs, rockets, Maverick, Sidewinder, 25mm cannon.
MAXIMUM ORDNANCE: 16,500-pound bombs.
POWER PLANT: one Rolls-Royce Pegasus II F-402-RR-408 vectored thrust turbofan engine.
CREW: one.
CONTRACTOR: McDonnell Douglas.

BRIEFING: The AV-8B is a V/STOL jet aircraft utilizing a vectored thrust turbofan engine. The normal mode of employment is short takeoff, which requires 300-1,200 feet of ground roll. Landings usually are in the vertical mode to minimize ground roll. The first AV-8B squadron stood up in 1985. The Marine Corps' warfighting requirement is judged to be 13 squadrons of 20 aircraft each. There currently are six squadrons of 20 aircraft, and a training squadron of 24. The Marines' current aviation plan calls for an increase to eight squadrons of 20 aircraft and 33 in the training squadron by 1990. The acquisition objective to support this plan is 328 aircraft.

OSPREY

V-22A OSPREY

BRIEFING: The V-22 Osprey is a joint-services tilt-rotor aircraft being developed by the Navy and the tilt-rotor team of Bell Helicopter Textron, Inc., and Boeing Helicopters. The V-22 was introduced in rollout ceremonies held at Bell's Flight Research Center in Arlington, Texas, 23 May 1988. The Navy awarded a $1.714 billion firm-fixed-price contract to Bell Boeing in 1986 for the V-22's full-scale engineering development. Allison Gas Turbine Division of General Motors is providing T406 6,000-shaft-horsepower engines for the versatile Osprey under a separate Navy $76.4 milliion contract. Six flyable prototype aircraft presently are being built, the first of which made its first flight in late November 1988. The Osprey will be the world's first production tilt-rotor aircraft and is designed to carry 24 combat equipped troops or 10,000 pounds of cargo internally, attain speeds exceeding 300 mph, and achieve altitudes close to 30,000 feet. Presently, at least 657 V-22s will be purchased by the nation's armed forces, with the first Osprey to be delivered to the Marine Corps in early 1992. The Marines require 552 Ospreys to replace its CH-46E Sea Knight and CH-53A/D combat assault helicopters, the Air Force 55 to replace HH-53 helicopters and supplement C-130 aircraft used in long-range special operations, and the Navy 50 to replace its SH-3A and HH-3A helicopters for strike rescue and special warfare. The Army has a requirement for 231 V-22s for medical evacuation, combat assault, and combat resupply, but withdrew from the development program in 1988 because of revised budget priorities. The Navy also is evaluating an ASW variant of the V-22, there is extensive interest in the V-22 by foreign governments, and Bell and Boeing already have signed agreements with British Aerospace, Dornier, and C. Itoh and Mitsui to perform marketing V-22 requirement analyses in England, Germany, and Japan respectively. Other European nations are being approached to perform similar marketing studies. The Osprey also is a prime candidate to help ease the commercial-airport-congestion problem facing travelers around the world. The Federal Aviation Administration already has begun work on the infrastructure required to handle city center-to-center travel and has signed an agreement with the Department of Defense to participate in the more-than-4,000-hour flight test program of the V-22 so it can certify the Osprey for civilian use as early as 1992. The FY 1989 budget includes $335.3 million to purchase long-lead items for construction of 12 aircraft that will make up the initial pilot production lot.

PHANTOM II

F-4 PHANTOM II

WING SPAN: 38 feet.
LENGTH: 63 feet.
HEIGHT: 16 feet.
WEIGHT: empty, 30,328 pounds, combat takeoff, 41,487 pounds; maximum takeoff, 61,795 pounds.
SPEED: maximum at 36,000 feet, 1,630 mph; average, approximately 575 mph.
CEILING: 56,000 feet.
RANGE: area intercept, 683 nautical miles; defensive counter-air, 429 nautical miles; interdiction, 618 nautical miles; maximum, 1,718 nautical miles.
POWER PLANT: two General Electric J79-GE-17A turbojet engines with afterburner.
CREW: two.
CONTRACTOR: McDonnell Douglas.

BRIEFING: This all-weather, multi-purpose fighter/attack aircraft has been in Marine Corps service since the early 1960s. The last two active squadrons currently are transitioning to the F/A-18 Hornet. There are three Marine Reserve F-4 squadrons; these will transition to F/A-18s in the early 1990s. A reconnaissance version, the RF-4B, is operated by the Marine Corps' one photo-reconnaissance squadron; it has 21 aircraft. The carrier-capable, supersonic, all-weather RF-4B is the only fully dedicated reconnaissance aircraft in the Department of the Navy. Plans call for its replacement with the new F/A-18D reconnaissance-capable aircraft in the 1990s.

F/A-18 HORNET

For specifications for the F/A-18, see page 197.

BRIEFING: The F/A-18 is replacing the F-4 Phantom in all 12 of the Marine Corps' fighter squadrons; it has been phasing into Marine Corps operations since 1982. The last three F-4 squadrons will transition to the F/A-18 during 1989.

EA-6B PROWLER

For specifications for the EA-6B, see page 199.

BRIEFING: The EA-6B gives the landing force commander an excellent weapon against enemy air defenses. The earlier EA-6A entered Marine Corps service in 1966. The Corps operates one active EA-6B squadron in the Regular Forces and one EA-6A squadron in the Reserves.

KC-130 HERCULES

WING SPAN: 132 feet, 7 inches.
LENGTH: 99 feet, 10 inches.
HEIGHT: 38 feet, 3 inches.
WEIGHT: empty, 75,368 pounds; loaded, 155,000 pounds.
SPEED: 348 mph at 19,000 feet; cruise, 331 mph.
RANGE: 2,160 nautical miles.
POWER PLANT: four Allison T56-A-15 turboprop engines.
CREW: two pilots, one navigator, one flight engineer, and one radio operator/loadmaster.
CONTRACTOR: Lockheed-Georgia.

BRIEFING: The KC-130 Hercules provides aerial refueling and "assault air" transport of Marines, equipment, and supplies in support of the Fleet Marine Forces. Other missions include air delivery of combat cargo, including resupply by parachute, and long-range delivery of high-priority cargo and personnel. The aircraft, which entered Marine Corps service in 1961, was combat proven in Vietnam. Configured to carry personnel, it can transport 92 Marines or 64 parachutists; configured for cargo, it can transport 26,913 pounds of weapons, equipment, or other supplies. Carrying wounded, it can handle 74 litter patients. The Marine Corps operates three active KC-130 squadrons and one reserve squadron.

OV-10 BRONCO

WING SPAN: 40 feet.
LENGTH: 42 feet.
HEIGHT: 15 feet, 2 inches.
WEIGHT: empty, 6,969 pounds; loaded, 14,466 pounds.
SPEED: 281 mph at sea level.
RANGE: 228 nautical-mile radius.
POWER PLANT: two Garrett T76-G-10/10A/12/12A turboprop engines.
CREW: one pilot, one observer.
CONTRACTOR: Rockwell International.

BRIEFING: The OV-10 is a multi-purpose, observation aircraft used primarily for reconnaissance missions, including control of artillery and naval gunfire spotting. The Bronco also escorts helicopters and is sometimes used for low-level photography. With the second seat removed, the Bronco can transport two litter patients, five parachutists, or 3,200 pounds of cargo. The Bronco is one of the ground force commander's most useful tools for battlefield reconnaissance and special missions. There are two active OV-10 squadrons and one Marine Air Reserve squadron.

HELICOPTERS/MARINES

SEA COBRA

AH-1W SEA COBRA

FUSELAGE LENGTH: 44 feet, 10 inches.
OVERALL LENGTH: 58 feet.
HEIGHT: 14 feet, 2 inches.
WEIGHT: maximum takeoff and landing, 14,750 pounds.
SPEED: maximum, 219 mph.
RANGE: 203 nautical miles.
POWER PLANT: two General Electric T-700-6E-401 engines.
CREW: one pilot, one gunner.
CONTRACTOR: Bell Helicopter Textron.

BRIEFING: The AH-1W provides fire support and fire-support coordination to the landing force during amphibious assaults and subsequent operations ashore. The aircraft is equipped with a 20mm XM197 gun in a nose turret, and can carry 2.75" and 5.0" rockets, Hellfire and TOW anti-armor missiles, and Sidewinder air-to-air missiles. The AH-1W and the older version, the AH-1T, are operated in six composite HMLA squadrons composed of 12 AH 1 and 12 UH 1 aircraft. Warfighting requirements are judged to be 12 squadrons of the same aircraft mix. The current goal is to equip all six HMLA squadrons and a training squadron with the more lethal and high/hot-capable AH-1W by the middle of FY 1991. The acquisition objective to support this goal is 127 aircraft. The Marine Corps Reserve operates two attack helicopter squadrons of 12 AH-1Js each.

UH-1N HUEY

FUSELAGE LENGTH: 45 feet, 10 inches.
OVERALL LENGTH: 57 feet, 3 inches.
WEIGHT: empty, 5,549 pounds; maximum weight loaded, 10,500 pounds.
SPEED: 126 mph.
CEILING: 15,000 feet in horizontal flight; 12,900 feet hovering.
RANGE: 250 nautical miles.
POWER PLANT: two United Aircraft of Canada PT6 turboshaft engines.
CREW: two pilots, one crewman.
CONTRACTOR: Bell Helicopter Textron.

HUEY

BRIEFING: One of the most widely used, versatile, and durable helicopters ever built, the Huey gives Marines support in the ship-to-shore phase of an amphibious assault in shore operations. Early models were used extensively in Vietnam for medical-evacuation and command-and-control missions. The UH-1 entered Marine Corps service in 1964. The UH-1N can carry 8-10 combat-loaded combinations of Marines and/or supplies. As a flying ambulance, it has room for six litter patients and one attendant. It may be armed with a 7.62mm M60 machine gun, a 7.62 GAU-2 B/A mini-gun, a .50 caliber machine gun, and 2.75" rockets. There are six composite UH-1/AH-1 squadrons with 12 UH and 12 AH aircraft each in the active forces, one training squadron, and three UH-1N Reserve units, one with 12 aircraft and two with six aircraft each.

CH-46E SEA KNIGHT

FUSELAGE LENGTH: 45 feet, 3 inches.
OVERALL LENGTH: 84 feet, 4 inches.
WEIGHT: empty 15,835 pounds; loaded, 24,300 pounds.
SPEED: maximum, 166 mph; cruise, 140 mph.
RANGE: 190 nautical miles; ferry range, 578 nautical miles (with three internal tanks).
POWER PLANT: two General Electric T58-GE-16 turboshaft engines.
CREW: two pilots, one crewman.
CONTRACTOR: Boeing Vertol.

102 MARINES

SEA KNIGHT

BRIEFING: The CH-46 transports Marines ashore during an amphibious assault, or from one area of the beachhead to another during shore operations. It also moves equipment, weapons, and supplies, and serves as a search and rescue aircraft. The Marines' main assault helicopter during and since the Vietnam War, the CH-46 has been in USMC service since 1965. The CH-46E—the latest model—is expected to reach the end of its service life during the 1990s.

CH-53A/D SEA STALLION

FUSELAGE LENGTH: 67 feet, 6 inches.
OVERALL LENGTH: 88 feet, 6 inches.
WEIGHT: empty 23,628 pounds; maximum weight loaded, 42,000 pounds.
SPEED: maximum, 196 mph; cruise, 173 mph.
CEILING: 24,200 feet in horizontal flight; 13,400 feet hovering.
RANGE: 250 nautical miles; ferry range, 450 nautical miles.
POWER PLANT: two General Electric T64-GE-413 turboshaft engines.
CREW: two pilots, one crewman.
CONTRACTOR: Sikorsky Aircraft.

BRIEFING: The medium assault CH-53 Sea Stallion helicopter hauls supplies, equipment, and personnel from ship to shore during amphibious assault operations. The aircraft was designed and developed specifically for the Marine Corps by Sikorsky. Loading and unloading, including roll-on and roll-off of some vehicles, is speeded up through the use of a rear ramp. External loads can be carried in slings or nets. It can mount two .50-caliber machine guns. The CH-53, used extensively by the Marines during the Vietnam War, can transport 37 Marines or handle 24 litter patients and four attendants. Capable of lifting 8,000 pounds internally or externally under normal conditions, it can lift an additional 4,000 pounds in certain situations.

The Marine Corps presently operates one Reserve and six active CH-53A/D squadrons. The current Marine aviation plan is to transition two of these squadrons to CH-53Es and three to MV-22s in the 1990s.

CH-53E SUPER STALLION

FUSELAGE LENGTH: 73 feet, 4 inches
OVERALL LENGTH: 99 feet, ½ inch.
WEIGHT: empty, 33,236 pounds; maximum loaded, 73,500 pounds.
SPEED: maximum, 196 mph; cruise, 173 mph.
CEILING: 27,900 feet in horizontal flight; 16,600 feet hovering.
RANGE: 480 nautical miles; ferry range, 990 nautical miles.
POWER PLANT: three General Electric T64-GE-416 turboshaft engines.
CREW: two pilots, one crewman.
CONTRACTOR: Sikorsky Aircraft.

BRIEFING: Able to transport 56 combat-ready Marines or 16 tons of cargo, the Super Stallion is the Marine Corps' most powerful helicopter. It can lift the Light Armored Vehicle (LAV), the 155mm howitzer, and that weapon's prime mover, the MN-923 five-ton truck. The CH-53E also can lift all Navy and Marine Corps fighter, attack, and electronic-warfare aircraft. It can refuel in flight from a KC-130 refueler aircraft. The Marine Corps' warfighting requirements are nine squadrons of 16 aircraft each. Currently there are four squadrons of 16 aircraft each. The Marine aviation plan calls for an increase to six squadrons of 12 aircraft each and a training squadron of 16 aircraft by 1992. The acquisition objective to support this plan is 147 aircraft.

SUPER STALLION

SEA STALLION

SEA POWER: *MARITIME*

The rise or decline in U.S. maritime industries over the years can best be shown through statistics. They effectively and often chronologically chart American shipping and shipbuilding activities and offer a means of comparison to other modes of transportation in U.S. foreign trade. They also show comparative data regarding the size and operation of foreign merchant fleets as well as other competitive factors that reflect upon national commercial and defense considerations. For example:

—Although ships transported more than half the tonnage of American exports and imports, by 1987 only about 4 percent was moved on U.S.-flag ships. And that, of course, produced an adverse impact on the U.S. shipping balance of payments. The cost to the United States in dollar-exchange payments over receipts for such services reached a record high of $2.3 billion.

—In 1950, the U.S.-flag merchant marine ranked second to that of the United Kingdom in number and deadweight tonnage among the merchant fleets of the world. Since then, despite the tremendous rise in the volume and value of American oceanborne foreign trade, the U.S.-flag merchant fleet fell far behind in number and tonnage of ships, relative to other national registries. By 1 January 1987, the U.S.-flag merchant marine ranked in eighth place in number of ships. The merchant fleets registered under the flags of Liberia, Panama, Japan, Greece, the U.S.S.R., the British Colonies and Cyprus outranked the United States.

—By 1987, there were 123 countries with merchant fleets comprising 23,618 merchant-type ships of 1,000 gross tons and over, totaling 593.2 dead-weight tons. Here is a table showing the development of the world merchant fleet since 1939:

Year	Countries	No. of Ships	dwt (millions)
1939	49	12,798	80.6
1950	60	13,282	107.2
1960	74	17,317	171.9
1970	96	19,980	327.0
1980	121	24,867	654.9
1981[1]	122	25,094	662.1
1982[2]	121	25,482	671.0
1983[2]	121	25,579	666.4
1984[2]	121	25,424	656.4
1985[1]	121	25,473	656.3
1986[1]	124	25,238	640.9
1987[2]	123	23,618	593.2

[1] 1 July. [2] 1 January.

(More detailed tables on the merchant fleets of the world will be found on the following pages.)

Table M-1
MAJOR MERCHANT FLEETS OF THE WORLD*
BY NUMBER OF SHIPS
JANUARY 1, 1987

Country	No. of Ships	Rank by No. of Ships	Deadweight Tons (in thousands)	Rank by Deadweight Tonnage
Panama	3,278	1	66,119	2
U.S.S.R.	2,453	2	24,563	5
Liberia	1,550	3	96,406	1
Japan	1,437	4	51,253	3
Greece	1,270	5	45,910	4
China	1,076	6	16,447	9
Cyprus	904	7	21,481	7
British Colonies	543	8	21,908	6
Italy	516	9	11,354	14
Philippines	486	10	12,495	10
United States (Pvt.)	456	11	20,727	8
Korea (South)	455	12	10,715	16
Germany (West)	448	13	4,874	25
Netherlands	437	14	4,217	28
Spain	418	15	7,871	20
Sub Total	15,727		416,340	
All Others	7,891		176,889	
Grand Total	23,618		593,229	

* Data for 1988 will not be available until early 1989.
[1]Oceangoing ships of 1,000 gross tons and over.
[2]Includes United States Government-owned ships.

Statistics show that America depends upon imports for numerous essential materials needed to fuel the nation's domestic economy and its defense industrial base. The lack of only 26 of the 91 materials considered critical and strategic, which the government stockpiles, determines, in large measure, as noted in *The United States Maritime Industry in the National Interest*, by Irwin M. Heine, "... whether the United States can manufacture automobiles and trucks, railroad equipment, commercial and military aircraft, commercial ships and warships of all types, electronic equipment, radar, anti-friction bearings, computers, machine tools, telephones and other communications equipment, every type of arms and ammunition, petroleum refining and petrochemicals, as well as the thousands of civilian goods and military equipment that have become indispensable in the daily lives of the American people and for the security of the nation."

Of the 26 representative essential materials, all must be imported in ships, and most of them in bulk lots.

Yet, since only a small percentage of these cargoes travel on U.S.-flag ships, the United States must depend upon the ships of foreign nations for the transportation of materials essential to the nation's industries and defense. The reliability of foreign ships in times of national emergency cannot always be taken for granted.

The impact of domestic and worldwide economic conditions upon U.S. and foreign shipping operations is reflected in the statistics for ships laid up for lack of business. On 30 June 1988, there were 490 ships of all types, totaling 12,704 tons, laid up throughout the world. This represents a sizable improvement since 30 June 1983, when 1,695 ships were laid up.

Seafaring employment is shown in the table, Seafaring Employment on U.S.-Flag Ships. An important factor in the decline of jobs has been the replacement of many smaller and less efficient ships by fewer, larger, and more productive ships that require small crews.

The impact of domestic and worldwide economic conditions upon U.S. and foreign shipping operations is reflected in the statistics for ships laid up for lack of business. On 30 June 1988, there were 490 ships of all types, totaling 12,704 deadweight tons, laid up throughout the world. This represents a sizable improvement since 30 June 1983, when 1,695 ships were laid up.

Seafaring employment is shown in the table, Seafaring Employment on U.S.-Flag Ships. An important factor in the decline of jobs has been the replacement of many smaller and less efficient ships by fewer, larger, and more productive ships that require smaller crews.

EMPLOYMENT IN THE SHIPYARD MOBILIZATION BASE

In 1982, the Maritime Administration (MARAD) of the Department of Transportation and the Naval Sea Systems Command defined the Shipyard Mobilization Base (SYMBA) in specific terms. Their definition is as follows:

Any facility capable of constructing a vessel over 400 feet in length or having the drydocking capability to repair a vessel over 400 feet in length and any facility capable of performing topside repairs on vessels over 400 feet in length provided that water depth in the channel to the facility is at least 12 feet.

Since October 1982, MARAD has surveyed private United States shipyards which meet the above qualifications to determine production worker employment in the SYMBA. The table below shows results of the surveys. Please note that the total employment is estimated to be 125 percent of production worker employment.

THE U.S. MERCHANT MARINE ACADEMY

The U.S. Merchant Marine Academy, dedicated in 1943, is a tuition-free, four-year accredited college established to prepare young men and women as officers in the American merchant marine and for leadership positions in the maritime industry. Located on Long Island Sound at Kings Point, New York, the Academy is operated by the Maritime Administration of the U.S. Department of Transportation.

Candidates for admission must be nominated by a congressman or senator and must compete for vacancies allocated by state in proportion to its representation in Congress. Enrollment is approximately 850. In 1974 the academy became the first of the federal academies to admit women.

Graduates of the Academy have a variety of options open to them. These include serving as a shipboard merchant marine officer, selecting active military duty as an officer in some branch of the Armed Forces of the United States, or, when shipboard employment is not available, entering the shoreside sector of the maritime industry.

Degrees and Majors: The three basic courses of study, all leading toward a bachelor of science degree, are marine transportation, marine engineering, and the dual license program (which combines the first two curricula). Each graduate receives a merchant marine license certifying qualifications as a third mate, a third assistant engineer, or, in the case of a dual license candidate, both. In addition, each graduate receives a commission as en-

Table M-2

PRIVATE SHIPYARD EMPLOYMENT**
As of October 1, Each Year

	1982 110 Yards	1983 100 Yards	1984 94 Yards	1985 83 Yards	1986 74 Yards	1987 69 Yards
East Coast	82,040	80,981	80,098	77,067	70,412	70,636
West Coast	30,841	23,909	20,411	17,177	15,092	10,666
Gulf Coast	29,752	20,585	21,568	18,550	19,980	20,450
Great Lakes	2,973	1,782	1,964	2,634	4,347	1,824
Non Conus	585	488	273	559	358	364
Totals	146,191	127,745	124,314	115,987	110,189	103,940

**Employment data reflect changes to the original Shipyard Mobilization Base (SYMBA) as identified by the Navy and Maritime Administration. Original 110 private shipyards were deemed essential for mobilization in 1982.

Source: Shipbuilders Council of America

Table M-3

NAVAL SHIPYARD EMPLOYMENT*
As of October 1, Each Year

	1982	1983	1984	1985	1986	1987
East Coast						
Charleston	7,795	8,414	8,329	8,373	8,348	8,557
Norfolk	11,990	13,007	13,388	12,645	12,136	12,502
Philadelphia	9,645	11,535	11,182	10,089	8,708	9,210
Portsmouth	8,062	8,831	8,386	8,422	7,699	8,037
West Coast						
Puget Sound	10,924	12,309	12,404	11,815	11,178	12,201
Mare Island	9,482	10,762	10,013	9,872	9,440	9,763
Long Beach	7,043	7,003	7,083	6,502	5,445	5,875
Pearl Harbor	6,735	7,125	6,854	6,654	6,293	6,218
Totals	71,676	78,986	77,639	74,372	69,247	72,363

*Naval shipyard employment does not include other public sector activities dedicated to Navy ship repair. These other activities include SRFs (Ship Repair Facilities), Trident submarine repair facilities and SIMAs (Shore-based Intermediate Maintenance Activities), among others.

Source: Shipbuilders Council of America

Table M-4

PRODUCTION WORKER EMPLOYMENT IN MAJOR SHIPBUILDING & REPAIR FACILITIES

	Oct. 1982 110 Shipyards	Oct. 1983 100 Shipyards	Oct. 1984 94 Shipyards	Oct.1985 83 Shipyards	Oct.1986 74 Shipyards	Oct 1987 67 Shipyards
East Coast	63,108	62,293	61,614	59,282	54,163	54,300
West Coast	23,724	18,392	15,701	13,213	11,609	8,200
Gulf Coast	22,886	15,835	16,591	14,269	15,369	15,700
Great Lakes	2,287	1,371	1,511	2,026	3,344	1,400
Non Contiguous	450	375	210	430	275	300
Total Production	112,455	98,266	95,627	89,220	84,760	79,900

Source: Shipbuilders Council of America

Table M-5

NEW NAVAL VESSELS UNDER CONSTRUCTION OR ON ORDER IN U.S. PRIVATE SHIPYARDS
(1,000 Light Displacement Tons and Over)

	Jan. 1984		Jan. 1985		Jan. 1986		Jan. 1987		Jan. 1988	
	No.	LDT	No.	LDT	No.	LDT	No.	LDT	No.	LDT
Fast Combat Support Ship (AOE)									1	19,700
Repair Drydock (ARDM)	1	5,300	1	5,300	1	5,300				
Salvage Ship (ARS)	4	10,900	4	10,900	2	5,450				
Guided Missile Cruiser (CG)	12	106,920	14	124,740	12	106,920	13	115,830	13	115,830
Aircraft Carrier (Nuclear) (CVN)	3	213,000	3	213,000	3	213,000	2	142,000	2	142,000
Guided Missile Destroyer (DDG)					1	8,300	1	8,300	3	24,900
Guided Missile Frigate (FFG)	17	46,359	10	27,270	5	13,635	3	8,181	1	2,727
Dock Landing Ship (LSD)	4	44,400	6	66,600	7	77,700	6	66,600	5	55,500
Amphibious Assault Ship (LHD)			1	28,500	1	28,500	2	57,000	3	85,500
Coastal Minehunter Ship (MHC)									1	780
Mine Countermeasures Ship (MCM)	5	5,000	5	5,000	5	5,000	8	8,000	7	7,000
Ballistic Missile Submarine (SSBN)	8	100,000	6	75,000	5	62,500	5	62,500	6	75,000
Attack Submarine (SSN)	19	114,000	18	108,000	15	90,000	17	102,000	19	114,000
Oiler (T-5)	5	45,000	5	45,000	2	18,000				
Ocean Surveillance Ship (T-AGOS) (Monohull)	12	19,200	9	14,400	7	11,200	4	6,400	8	12,800
Ocean Surveillance Ship (T-AGOS) (SWATH)							1	2,486	1	2,486
Oceanographic Survey Ship (T-AGS)					2	17,620	2	17,620	2	17,620
Prepositioning Ship (T-AKX)	5	113,500	5	113,500	2	45,400				
Fleet Oiler (T-AO)	4	38,000	4	38,000	7	66,500	8	76,000	7	66,500
Cable Repair Ship (T-ARC)	1	8,430								
USCG Medium Endurance Cutter (WMEC)	11	13,200	9	10,800	8	9,600	7	8,400	5	6,000
Totals	111	883,209	100	886,010	85	784,625	79	681,317	84	748,343

Source: Shipbuilders Council of America

sign in the U.S. Naval Reserve.

Costs: Upon entrance, each midshipman pays a fee of $663 to cover student activities and personal services.

Financial Aid: The only pay received by a midshipman is $500 a month during two six-month training periods aboard ship.

Application Information: Candidates should contact congressmen and request applications at the end of their junior year in high school. For further information contact:

U.S. Merchant Marine Academy
Admissions Office
Kings Point, NY 11024
Phone: (516) 773-5000

Government Agencies Concerned with Maritime Affairs

U.S. DEPARTMENT OF TRANSPORTATION
400 Seventh St. S.W.
Washington, D.C. 20590
(202) 366-4000

Maritime Administration
Maritime Administrator
(202) 366-5823
Office of Public Affairs
(202) 366-5807
Office of Maritime Labor and Training
(202) 366-5755
Office of Trade Analysis and Insurance
(202) 366-2400

U.S. Coast Guard
2100 Second St. S.W.
Washington, D.C. 20590
(202) 267-2229
Office of Merchant Marine Safety
(202) 267-2200
Office of Merchant Vessel Personnel
(202) 267-0214
Office of Merchant Vessel Inspection Division
(202) 267-2978

FEDERAL MARITIME COMMISSION
1100 L St. N.W.
Washington, D.C. 20573
(202) 523-5707
Chairman
(202) 523-5911
Public Information Office
(202) 523-5707

U.S. DEPARTMENT OF COMMERCE
14th and E Sts. N.W.
Washington, D.C. 20230
(202) 377-2000

Bureau of the Census
Washington, D.C. 20233
(202) 763-4040

National Oceanic & Atmospheric Administration
National Ocean Survey
Office of Marine Operations
6001 Executive Blvd.
Rockville, MD 20852
(301) 443-8910

Division of Foreign Trade
Transportation Branch (Shipping)
(202) 763-7770

U.S. DEPARTMENT OF THE NAVY
Military Sealift Command
Building 210
Washington Navy Yard
Washington, D.C. 20398-5100
(202) 433-0001
Office of Public Affairs
(202) 433-0330

U.S. DEPARTMENT OF LABOR
200 Constitution Ave. N.W.
Washington, D.C. 20210
(202) 523-7316

Bureau of Labor Statistics
441 G St. N.W.
Washington, D.C. 20212
(202) 523-1913

Federal Mediation and Conciliation Service
14th St. and Constitution Ave. N.W.
Washington, D.C. 20427
(202) 653-5290

U.S. DEPARTMENT OF THE TREASURY
15th St. and Pennsylvania Ave. N.W.
Washington, D.C. 20220
(202) 566-2111

U.S. Customs Service
1301 Constitution Ave. N.W.
Washington, D.C. 20229
(202) 566-3962

(Continued on page 244)

Table M-6
MERCHANT FLEETS OF THE WORLD
Oceangoing Steam and Motor Ships[1] of 1,000 Gross Tons and Over as of 1 January 1987
(Tonnage in Thousands)

		Total			Combination Passenger & Cargo			Freighters			Bulk Carriers			Tankers	
	No.	Gross Tons	dwt	No.	Gross Tons	dwt	No.	Gross Tons	dwt	No.	Gross Tons	dwt	No.	Gross Tons	dwt
Total All Countries	23,618	362,179	593,229	352	3,798	1,476	12,786	93,157	118,845	5,481	130,564	227,325	4,999	134,660	245,584
UNITED STATES[2]	720	16,108	24,457	36	493	289	411	6,495	7,446	26	738	1,270	247	8,382	15,452
Privately Owned[3]	456	13,105	20,727	8	139	74	197	4,310	4,571	26	738	1,270	225	7,918	14,812
Government Owned	264	3,003	3,730	28	354	215	214	2,185	2,875	—	—	—	22	464	640
*Albania	10	51	73	—	—	—	10	51	73	—	—	—	—	—	—
Algeria	61	808	966	1	4	3	37	201	288	4	57	93	19	546	582
Angola	13	69	107	—	—	—	12	68	105	—	—	—	1	2	2
Argentina	153	1,908	2,955	—	—	—	86	727	996	18	481	829	49	700	1,130
Aruba	1	127	257	—	—	—	—	—	—	—	—	—	1	127	257
Australia	78	2,237	3,649	—	—	—	23	259	304	33	1,196	2,018	22	783	1,328
Austria	28	129	212	—	—	—	23	56	88	5	73	124	—	—	—
Bahrain	3	17	29	—	—	—	2	5	9	1	12	20	—	—	—
Bangladesh	41	289	413	1	12	6	37	263	384	—	—	—	3	15	23
Barbados	2	3	7	—	—	—	2	3	7	—	—	—	—	—	—
Belgium	76	2,088	3,465	1	13	15	30	347	419	30	1,356	2,490	15	371	541
Benin	1	3	4	—	—	—	1	3	4	—	—	—	—	—	—
Bolivia	2	20	28	—	—	—	2	20	28	—	—	—	—	—	—
Brazil	333	6,047	9,973	3	5	4	154	1,119	1,486	93	2,826	4,806	83	2,097	3,677
*British Colonies	543	13,222	21,908	3	25	7	208	1,656	2,090	240	7,688	13,201	92	3,853	6,610
*Bulgaria	119	1,313	1,942	4	20	22	51	307	372	47	657	1,023	17	329	526
Burma	16	97	128	3	4	13	13	93	125	—	—	—	—	—	—
Cameroon	6	67	82	—	—	—	6	67	82	—	—	—	—	—	—
Canada	85	662	951	3	13	3	28	117	140	14	252	386	40	280	422
Cape Verde	4	8	14	—	—	—	4	8	14	—	—	—	—	—	—
Chile	38	451	754	3	13	3	23	161	226	12	262	488	—	—	—
*China	1,076	10,781	16,447	12	131	69	728	5,226	7,396	196	3,936	6,610	140	1,488	2,373
Colombia	41	421	579	1	11	12	32	285	342	3	92	171	5	33	53
*Cuba	106	800	1,106	2	15	10	82	644	883	9	74	114	13	67	100
Cyprus	904	12,390	21,481	5	36	13	527	2,804	4,286	250	4,891	8,321	122	4,659	8,862
*Czechoslovakia	19	181	270	—	—	—	14	82	112	5	99	159	—	—	—
Denmark	239	4,300	6,561	3	7	3	149	1,698	1,808	11	277	492	76	2,318	4,258
Dominican Republic	10	32	54	2	3	1	9	21	35	—	—	—	—	—	—
Ecuador	52	396	568	2	3	3	31	225	270	1	11	20	18	157	277
Equatorial Guinea	2	6	7	1	3	3	1	3	3	—	—	—	—	—	—
Ethiopia	10	62	77	—	—	—	9	61	75	—	—	—	1	1	2
Fiji	6	17	16	—	—	—	3	11	11	—	—	—	3	5	6
Finland	89	1,001	1,539	2	31	7	48	329	438	12	93	128	27	548	967
France	227	4,912	7,942	7	41	18	125	1,420	1,718	28	925	1,575	67	2,527	4,631
Gabon	3	93	164	—	—	—	2	19	25	—	—	—	1	74	139
Gambia	1	3	3	—	—	—	1	3	3	—	—	—	—	—	—
Germany (East)	158	1,337	1,779	1	19	3	133	907	1,134	20	361	568	4	50	75
Germany (West)	448	3,802	4,874	6	61	33	352	2,736	3,286	16	371	555	74	634	1,000
Ghana	13	91	119	—	—	—	13	91	119	—	—	—	—	—	—
Greece	1,270	25,434	45,910	30	198	92	426	3,584	5,353	594	12,246	21,873	220	9,406	18,591
Greenland	1	1	2	—	—	—	1	1	2	—	—	—	—	—	—
Guatemala	4	9	13	—	—	—	4	9	13	—	—	—	—	—	—
Honduras	119	373	550	—	—	—	89	253	354	11	77	123	19	43	73
*Hungary	20	83	114	—	—	—	20	83	114	—	—	—	—	—	—
Iceland	25	54	89	—	—	—	23	51	84	—	—	—	2	3	5
India	322	6,065	9,985	5	33	26	147	1,407	2,039	111	2,838	4,869	59	1,787	3,051
Indonesia	316	1,439	2,180	6	32	12	214	711	1,038	11	129	192	85	567	939
Iran	118	3,114	5,523	—	—	—	39	395	533	54	1,110	1,847	25	1,608	3,143
Iraq	34	854	1,516	1	7	1	14	82	118	—	—	—	19	765	1,398
Ireland	31	59	90	—	—	—	27	48	72	4	55	90	4	11	18
Israel	40	529	631	—	—	—	36	474	541	—	—	—	—	—	—

Country											
Italy	516	5,947	11,354	9	147	44	204	1,103	1,405	91	2,897	5,040	212	2,800	4,865
Ivory Coast	9	105	136	—	—	—	8	101	130	—	—	—	1	4	6
Jamaica	2	5	5	—	—	—	2	5	8	—	—	—	—	—	—
Japan	1,437	32,818	51,253	6	44	16	605	6,678	6,073	443	13,947	24,397	383	12,149	20,767
Jordan	3	36	57	—	—	—	1	10	14	2	26	43	—	—	—
Kenya	1	1	2	—	—	—	—	1	2	—	—	—	—	—	—
* Korea (North)	52	369	607	1	4	2	43	243	377	5	64	114	3	59	114
Korea (South)	455	5,435	10,715	8	—	—	224	1,307	1,699	161	4,028	6,953	70	1,100	2,062
Kuwait	62	2,128	3,193	—	—	—	33	569	765	—	—	—	29	1,559	2,428
Lebanon	96	420	642	—	—	—	83	283	412	11	123	207	2	14	23
Liberia	1,550	51,154	96,406	10	190	62	318	3,190	4,186	617	17,602	32,983	605	30,171	59,175
Libya	26	777	1,412	—	—	—	14	67	87	—	—	—	12	710	1,325
Malagasy	12	59	82	—	—	—	9	51	69	3	—	—	—	9	13
Malaysia	167	1,577	2,266	1	1	1	105	522	723	21	441	749	40	612	793
Maldives	17	88	142	—	—	—	12	43	68	4	44	73	1	1	2
Malta	151	1,632	2,735	2	19	6	88	414	619	51	910	1,535	10	290	574
Mauritania	1	1	1	—	—	—	—	—	—	—	—	—	—	—	—
Mauritius	8	134	229	1	2	2	3	19	27	4	113	200	—	—	—
Mexico	72	1,189	1,854	1	12	2	18	117	157	12	296	485	42	776	1,213
Morocco	44	301	474	1	—	—	23	70	107	4	92	160	16	128	206
Mozambique	7	11	15	—	—	—	7	11	15	—	—	—	—	—	—
Nassau, Bahamas	222	6,944	12,299	12	175	42	77	516	684	42	1,349	2,389	91	4,903	9,183
Nauru	6	65	92	1	9	8	3	18	25	2	37	58	—	—	—
Netherlands	437	3,009	4,217	4	108	18	345	1,792	2,400	20	446	761	68	662	1,039
New Zealand	24	266	322	—	—	—	12	145	136	7	46	70	5	76	117
Nicaragua	3	19	27	—	—	—	3	19	27	—	—	—	—	—	—
Nigeria	34	396	524	—	—	—	29	317	374	—	—	—	5	79	150
Norway	279	6,856	10,828	22	358	68	100	681	782	56	2,028	3,461	101	3,789	6,517
Omar (Muscat)	4	14	21	1	4	1	2	14	—	—	—	—	—	—	—
Pakistan	36	411	603	3	23	23	31	333	474	1	12	17	1	43	89
Panama	3,278	40,367	66,119	33	487	197	1,770	12,420	16,503	920	17,552	30,372	555	10,088	19,047
Papua	6	12	18	—	—	—	6	12	18	—	—	—	—	—	—
Paraguay	9	20	28	—	—	—	9	20	28	—	—	—	—	—	—
* Peru	52	570	889	—	—	—	31	250	348	11	190	319	10	130	223
Philippines	486	7,377	12,495	13	52	32	200	1,076	1,539	227	5,509	9,514	46	741	1,410
Poland	266	3,122	4,463	2	18	9	163	1,238	1,457	92	1,558	2,468	9	308	529
Portugal	58	959	1,668	1	4	4	30	125	169	13	295	495	14	535	1,001
Qatar	14	293	438	—	—	—	11	182	235	—	—	—	3	112	203
* Romania	282	3,077	4,690	3	9	—	208	1,106	1,431	66	1,590	2,574	8	381	685
Saudi Arabia	134	2,676	4,626	3	12	8	54	541	763	12	356	591	65	1,768	3,264
Senegal	4	14	21	—	—	—	4	14	21	—	—	—	—	—	—
Seychelles	2	2	2	—	—	—	2	2	—	—	—	—	—	—	—
Singapore	416	6,969	11,717	1	2	2	224	1,953	2,678	91	2,654	4,714	100	2,360	4,323
Somalia	5	17	21	—	—	—	5	17	21	—	—	—	—	—	—
South Africa	14	426	515	—	—	—	10	300	286	1	88	167	3	38	62
Spain	418	4,264	7,871	1	33	12	262	833	1,279	67	1,167	2,091	89	2,264	4,501
Sri Lanka	38	549	833	13	336	81	26	211	265	9	242	393	3	96	175
Sudan	11	93	123	—	—	—	11	93	123	—	—	—	—	—	—
Surinam	3	7	9	—	—	—	3	7	—	—	—	—	—	—	—
Sweden	181	1,696	2,114	2	12	3	105	1,056	1,163	16	217	333	58	411	616
Switzerland	29	320	508	—	—	—	12	56	73	10	249	408	7	15	27
Syria	16	46	63	—	—	—	15	43	59	—	—	—	1	3	4
Taiwan	194	4,395	6,791	1	2	1	122	1,594	1,886	54	2,215	3,862	17	584	1,043
Tanzania	4	22	33	—	—	—	4	21	31	—	—	—	—	1	2
Thailand	100	419	624	—	—	—	73	344	508	3	30	48	24	45	69
Togo	6	59	85	—	—	—	6	59	85	—	—	—	—	—	—
Tonga	7	15	22	—	—	—	5	13	19	—	—	—	2	3	3
Tunisia	23	158	224	—	—	—	11	46	53	3	37	58	9	74	114
Turkey	324	2,961	4,967	6	33	12	206	722	1,114	62	1,426	2,462	50	780	1,380
United Arab Emir.	46	613	974	—	—	—	26	230	315	2	17	27	18	365	632
United Kingdom	395	7,926	11,759	13	336	81	151	2,065	2,229	73	2,023	3,537	158	3,503	5,912
Uruguay	10	116	192	—	—	—	6	41	53	—	—	—	4	75	138
U.A.R. (Egypt)	135	905	1,330	9	51	42	100	431	599	16	348	562	10	75	127
* U.S.S.R.	2,453	18,535	24,563	50	445	112	759	9,961	11,978	229	3,606	5,652	415	4,523	6,821
Vanuatu	16	301	543	—	—	—	8	51	83	5	89	147	3	161	313
Venezuela	75	865	1,299	—	—	—	42	262	354	11	105	166	22	498	779
Vietnam	67	300	455	—	—	—	59	252	375	2	14	23	6	34	56
Western Samoa	3	25	34	—	—	—	3	25	34	—	—	—	—	—	—
Yemen	4	200	409	—	—	—	2	6	—	—	—	—	2	195	403
Yugoslavia	264	2,931	4,579	4	16	8	177	1,323	1,878	72	1,290	2,176	11	302	518
Zaire	4	42	60	1	14	15	3	28	44	—	—	—	—	—	—

[1] Tonnage figures may not be additive due to rounding.
[2] Excludes 8 non-merchant type and/or Navy-owned vessels which are currently in the National Defense Reserve Fleet.
[3] Includes 15 Integrated Tug/Barge vessels.
*Source material limited.

Source: U.S. Department of Transportation, Maritime Administration, Office of Trade Studies and Subsidy Contracts

Table M-7

INTERNATIONAL TRANSPORTATION TRANSACTIONS OF THE UNITED STATES, BY TYPE*, 1970-1987
(millions of dollars)

Item	1970	1975	1980	1981	1982	1983	1984	1985	1986	1987
Total Receipts	**3,669**	**6,879**	**14,208**	**15,671**	**15,491**	**16,200**	**17,435**	**18,322**	**19,633**	**22,382**
Ocean transportation	2,256	4,065	7,757	8,028	7,685	8,133	8,849	8,846	9,169	10,040
Export freight earnings	604	1,183	2,641	2,803	2,549	2,881	2,702	2,866	2,610	2,806
Freight earnings on shipments between foreign countries	209	328	588	561	555	575	563	574	576	595
Port expenditures	1,406	2,481	4,435	4,552	4,468	4,562	5,457	5,274	5,843	6,494
Charter hire	37	73	93	112	113	115	127	132	140	145
Air transportation	1,240	2,515	5,946	7,160	7,326	7,596	8,071	8,995	9,595	11,434
Export freight earnings	187	390	742	752	762	576	645	706	783	982
Passenger fares	541	1,039	2,591	3,111	3,174	3,610	3,626	3,648	4,175	5,398
Port expenditures	512	1,086	2,613	3,297	3,390	3,410	3,800	4,641	4,637	5,054
Other transportation	173	299	505	483	480	471	515	481	869	908
Total Payments	**4,058**	**7,971**	**15,397**	**16,961**	**16,482**	**18,225**	**21,876**	**23,528**	**24,189**	**26,945**
Ocean transportation	2,380	4,465	8,447	8,900	8,307	8,624	10,544	11,018	11,619	11,777
Import freight payments	1,444	3,047	5,809	6,073	5,562	5,827	7,755	8,114	8,636	8,852
Passenger fares	245	278	268	287	290	305	305	320	320	328
Port expenditures	316	755	1,905	2,054	1,957	1,980	1,972	2,048	2,125	2,047
Charter hire	375	385	465	486	498	512	512	536	538	550
Air transportation	1,581	3,346	6,705	7,785	7,938	9,361	11,089	12,284	12,281	14,862
Import freight payments	115	246	562	671	725	1,066	1,633	1,666	2,051	2,242
Passenger fares	970	1,985	3,339	4,200	4,482	5,698	6,744	7,565	7,154	8,457
Port expenditures	496	1,115	2,804	2,914	2,731	2,597	2,712	3,053	3,076	4,163
Other transportation	97	160	245	276	237	240	243	226	289	306
Balance	**-389**	**-1,092**	**-1,189**	**-1,290**	**-991**	**-2,025**	**-4,441**	**-5,206**	**-4,556**	**-4,563**

*Source: U.S. Bureau of Economic Analysis, SURVEY OF CURRENT BUSINESS, June issues, and unpublished data. Published in U.S. Bureau of Census STATISTICAL ABSTRACT. June 1988.

U.S. DEPARTMENT OF STATE
2201 C St. N.W.
Washington, D.C. 20520
(202) 647-4000

Office of Citizen Consular Services
(202) 647-3666

Office of Maritime and Land Transport
(202) 647-5840

NATIONAL LABOR RELATIONS BOARD
1717 Pennsylvania Ave. N.W.
Washington, D.C. 20570
(202) 632-4952

U.S. MARITIME TRADE ASSOCIATIONS
American Association of Port Authorities (AAPA)
1010 Duke Street
Alexandria, VA 22314
(703) 684-5700

American Institute of Merchant Shipping (AIMS)
1000 16th St., N.W., Suite 511
Washington, D.C. 20036
(202) 775-4399

Table M-8

NEW NAVAL COMBATANT AND AUXILIARY VESSELS CONTRACTED FOR WITH PRIVATE U.S. SHIPYARDS
(1,000 Light Displacement Tons and Over)

Calendar Year	Total Vessels	Combatant	Auxiliary	Contract Yards	Light Displacement Tons	Initial Shipyard Contract $ Value
1968	15	10	5	4	152,591	638,238,500
1969	6	6	0	3	79,533	453,180,000
1970	6	6	0	2	132,000	758,100,000
1971	15	15	0	3	88,044	1,055,000,000
1972	14	13	1	4	85,522	852,204,347
1973	7	7	0	2	38,727	512,345,000
1974	16	14	2	4	171,100	1,387,375,100
1975	16	13	3	6	106,197	1,677,241,000
1976	20	14	6	8	91,322	1,254,169,000
1977	15	12	3	8	88,616	1,575,271,000
1978	25	20	5	8	119,478	2,506,400,000
1979	13	11	2	6	60,646	1,356,752,936
1980	11	8	3	6	101,072	1,933,654,550
1981	28	13	15	10	97,307	2,842,300,500
1982	28	18	10	11	321,040	7,777,200,000
1983	27	12	15	10	431,760	5,041,400,000
1984	11	11	0	6	104,157	2,848,800,000
1985	11	4	7	7	92,320	1,679,400,000
1986	16	12	4	9	117,816	3,034,868,414
1987	20	12	8	10	127,310	3,521,898,835

Source: Defense '88 Almanac

American Maritime Association
(AMA)
485 Madison Ave., 15th Floor
New York, NY 10022
(212) 319-9217

American Maritime Officers Service
(AMOS)
Suite 3204, 490 L'Enfant Plaza, E,
S.W.
Washington, D.C. 20005
(202) 479-1133

American Waterways Operators, Inc.
(AWO)
1600 Wilson Blvd., Suite 1000
Arlington, VA 22209
(703) 841-9300

Boston Shipping Association
223 Lewis Wharf
Boston, MA 02110
(617) 523-3762

Council of North Atlantic Shipping
Association
600 Lafayette Building
Philadelphia, PA 19106
(215) 922-7510

Federation of American-Controlled
Shipping (FACS)
50 Broadway
New York, NY 10004
(212) 344-1483

Joint Maritime Congress (JMC)
444 N. Capitol St., Suite 801
Washington, D.C. 20001
(202) 638-2405

Labor Management
Maritime Committee, Inc.
100 Indiana Ave. N.W.
Washington, D.C. 20001
(202) 683-2405

Lake Carriers Association (LCA)
915 Rockefeller Building
Cleveland, OH 44113
(216) 621-1107

Marine Towing and Transportation
Employers Association
17 Battery Place, North, Room 1408
New York, NY 10004
(212) 344-9097

Maritime Association of the Port of
New York/New Jersey
17 Battery Place, Suite 1006
New York, NY 10004
(212) 425-5704

Maritime Institute of Research and
Industrial Development (MIRAID)
1133 15th St. N.W., Suite 600
Washington, D.C. 20005
(202) 463-6505

Table M-9

NEW MERCHANT TYPE VESSEL CONTRACTS WITH U.S. PRIVATE SHIPYARDS*
(1,000 Gross Tons and Over)

Year	No.	G.T.	Contracted for Construction Subsidy No.	G.T.	Contracted for Government Account No.	G.T.	For U.S.-Flag No Subsidy No.	G.T.	For Foreign Registry No.	G.T.
1955	18	195,800	2	36,400	7	37,900	6	98,500	3	23,000
1956	57	1,324,600	2	30,000	1	16,500	37	777,800	17	500,300
1957	32	691,700	—	—	2	18,800	26	552,900	4	120,000
1958	22	176,000	19	167,600	—	—	3	8,400	—	—
1959	19	195,600	15	147,600	—	—	4	48,000	—	—
1960	23	269,700	23	269,700	—	—	—	—	—	—
1961	31	431,200	22	239,000	—	—	9	192,200	—	—
1962	15	173,500	14	147,500	—	—	1	26,000	—	—
1963	25	291,300	18	202,800	1	12,000	6	76,500	—	—
1964	18	277,200	17	240,200	—	—	1	37,000	—	—
1965	14	147,900	9	110,100	—	—	5	37,800	—	—
1966	16	244,400	14	202,600	—	—	2	41,800	—	—
1967	29	749,700	11	290,400	—	—	18	459,300	—	—
1968	23	614,400	11	209,800	—	—	12	404,600	—	—
1969	8	309,000	2	36,000	—	—	6	273,000	—	—
1970	13	579,500	8	358,100	—	—	5	221,400	—	—
1971	24	617,000	10	416,100	1	5,000	13	195,900	—	—
1972	47	1,537,900	25	1,218,400	—	—	22	319,500	—	—
1973	41	1,978,000	15	985,200	1	5,000	25	987,800	—	—
1974	15	1,113,300	2	398,000	—	—	13	715,300	—	—
1975	11	507,900	—	—	—	—	11	507,900	—	—
1976	16	339,400	6	120,300	—	—	10	219,100	—	—
1977	12	258,000	9	245,000	—	—	3	13,000	—	—
1978	30	394,000	10	196,500	—	—	20	197,500	—	—
1979	21	487,200	4	140,000	—	—	17	347,200	—	—
1980	7	116,200	—	—	—	—	7	116,200	—	—
1981	8	148,000	2	42,000	—	—	6	106,000	—	—
1982	3	12,200	—	—	—	—	3	12,200	—	—
1983	4	7,200	—	—	—	—	4	7,200	—	—
1984	5	227,400	—	—	—	—	5	227,400	—	—
1885	—	—	—	—	—	—	—	—	—	—
1986	—	—	—	—	—	—	—	—	—	—
1987	—	—	—	—	—	—	—	—	—	—
1988	—	—	—	—	—	—	—	—	—	—

*New contracts that were cancelled are not included in this table.

Source: Shipbuilders Council of America

Maritime Service Committee
Mr. Edward Morgan
P.O. Box 35
Bowling Green Stn.
New York, NY 10274-0035

Mobile Steamship Association
Commerce Building, Suite 600
Mobile, AL 36633
(205) 432-3626

New Orleans Steamship Association
2240 World Trade Center
New Orleans, LA 70130
(504) 522-9392

New York Shipping Association, Inc.
2 World Trade Center
New York, NY 10048
(212) 323-6600

The Tow Boat and Harbor Carriers
Association of NY/NJ
17 Battery Place, Room 1408
New York, NY 10004
(212) 943-8480

Pacific Maritime Association (PMA)
635 Sacramento St.
San Francisco, CA 94111
(415) 362-7973

Pacific Merchant Shipping
Association
635 Sacramento St.
San Francisco, CA 94111
(415) 986-7900

Philadelphia Marine Trade
Association
Lafayette Building
Philadelphia, PA 19106
(215) 922-7510

Table M-10

TWENTY-YEAR ANALYSIS OF THE TOP TEN MERCHANT ORDERBOOKS

	1988 No.	1988 % of World	1988 DWT	1988 % of World	1978 No.	1978 % of World	1978 DWT	1978 % of World	1968 No.	1968 % of World	1968 DWT	1968 % of World
South Korea	121	14.7	10,783,410	32.0	82	4.2	1,502,714	2.8	5	.2	281,000	.4
Japan	159	19.3	8,445,160	25.0	499	26.0	14,018,822	26.2	472	25.6	24,914,010	40.8
Yugoslavia	44	5.3	1,675,668	5.0	43	2.2	1,117,994	2.1	53	2.8	1,284,900	2.1
PRC	57	6.9	1,404,100	4.0	—	—	—	—	—	—	—	—
Brazil	33	4.0	1,379,570	4.1	128	6.6	4,498,240	8.4	44	2.4	434,250	.7
Italy	30	3.6	1,058,760	3.1	56	2.9	1,880,232	3.5	52	2.8	2,040,760	3.3
Spain	30	3.6	993,610	2.9	123	6.4	3,510,974	6.5	83	4.5	1,744,210	2.8
Romania	32	3.9	891,080	2.6	25	1.3	259,520	.5	30	1.6	150,600	.2
Denmark	29	3.5	866,600	2.5	48	2.5	904,435	1.6	34	1.8	2,258,040	3.7
Taiwan	11	1.3	828,410	2.4	32	1.6	932,289	1.7	6	.3	243,420	.4
US	—	—	—	—	60	3.1	3,467,000	6.5	64	3.4	1,221,000	2.0
World	821	—	33,427,982	—	1,918	—	53,493,593	—	1,837	—	61,000,500	—

Source: Shipbuilders Council of America

Shipbuilders Council of America
(SCA)
1110 Vermont Ave. N.W.
Washington, D.C. 20005
(202) 775-9060

Steamship Trade Association of
Baltimore, Inc.
32 South St.
Baltimore, MD 21202
(301) 752-4913

Transportation Institute (TI)
5201 Auth Way, 5th Floor
Camp Springs, MD 20746

United Shipowners of America
1627 K St. N.W., Suite 1200
Washington, D.C. 20006
(202) 466-5388

Source: Department of Transportation, Maritime Administration, Office of Maritime Labor and Training.

AMERICAN MERCHANT MARINE MUSEUM FOUNDATION

American Merchant Marine Museum
U.S. Merchant Marine Academy
Kings Point, New York 11024
(516) 773-5515
Charles M. Resnick, Exec. Director

Calvert Marine Museum
P.O. Box 97
Solomons, Maryland 21688
(301) 326-2042
Ralph E. Eshelman, Director
Paula Johnson, Curator of Maritime
  History

Chesapeake Bay Maritime Museum
P.O. Box 636
St. Michaels, Maryland 21663
(301) 745-2916
John Valliant, Director
Richard J. Dodds, Curator

Columbia River Maritime Museum
1792 Marine Drive
Astoria, Oregon 97103
(503) 325-2323
Stephen L. Recken, Director

East Hampton Town Marine Museum
Bluff Road, P.O. Box 858
Amagansett, New York 11930
(516) 267-6544
Ralph Carpentier, Director

Erie Canal Museum
318 Erie Blvd., East
Syracuse, New York 13202
(315) 471-0593
Vicki B. Quigley, Director

Flagship Niagara
P.O. Box 1026
Harrisburg, Pennsylvania 17108
(717) 787-2891
Michael J. Ripton, Director

The Great Lakes Historical Society
480 Main Street
Vermilion, Ohio 44089
(216) 967-3467
Thomas A. Sykora, Secretary

Hudson River Maritime Museum
One Rondout Landing
Kingston, New York 12401
(914) 338-0021
Marita Lopez-Mena, Director

The Kendall Whaling Museum
P.O. Box 297
Sharon, Massachusetts 02067
(617) 784-5642
Stuart M. Frank, Director
Gare B. Reid, Coll. Manager

Maine Maritime Museum
963 Washington Street
Bath, Maine 14530
(207) 443-1316
John S. Carter, Director Curator

Manitowoc Maritime Museum
75 Maritime Drive
Manitowoc, Wisconsin 54220
(414) 684-0218
Burt Logan, Director

Marine Museum of the Great Lakes
55 Ontario Street
Kingston, Ontario
Canada K7L 2Y2
(613) 542-2261
Maurice Smith, Director

The Mariners' Museum
Newport News, Virginia 23606
(804) 595-0368
William D. Wilkinson, Director
Linda D. Kelsey, Director of Programs
  and Services
Richard Malley

Maritime Museum Association of San
  Diego
1306 North Harbor Drive
San Diego, California 92101
(619) 234-9153
Capt. Peter S. Branson, Director

Table M-11

MERCHANT SHIPS ON ORDER IN WORLD

Year	Europe No.	Europe DWT	Asia No.	Asia DWT	North America* No.	North America* DWT	South America No.	South America DWT
1968	1,193	33,002,950	492	25,549,360	81	1,461,560	52	505,120
1969	1,228	43,380,180	481	29,604,540	78	1,677,570	55	523,990
1970	1,621	58,728,270	523	32,097,930	58	1,484,300	52	516,340
1971	1,758	75,709,310	667	44,548,560	55	1,873,700	60	691,750
1972	1,725	75,186,160	707	58,536,770	82	2,425,900	69	1,555,540
1973	1,368	68,484,300	582	62,727,220	106	3,356,900	56	1,818,540
1974	1,483	102,761,730	970	103,938,970	130	4,762,390	64	2,070,270
1975	1,576	94,121,027	977	99,257,841	134	5,860,240	122	3,883,550
1976	1,234	65,052,073	889	74,813,649	130	5,730,800	206	6,787,265
1977	1,131	40,413,486	772	30,079,866	101	4,907,060	191	6,148,190
1978	997	24,937,407	672	17,445,783	89	4,084,368	154	5,001,100
1979	739	14,226,061	386	9,108,894	81	2,894,600	128	4,122,730
1980	756	15,215,240	470	14,516,096	80	2,035,962	137	4,361,720
1981	868	18,132,876	540	23,934,581	64	1,322,811	126	3,591,570
1982	854	18,759,741	692	29,487,670	49	1,033,185	106	3,281,040
1983	748	17,375,955	568	20,852,876	29	580,650	82	2,786,583
1984	648	13,760,595	898	29,875,490	21	273,282	73	3,016,230
1985	558	10,072,734	780	32,639,896	20	370,150	71	2,896,640
1986	496	8,156,842	514	23,932,122	15	291,060	56	2,511,645
1987	464	8,524,878	472	20,660,216	12	174,766	47	2,445,195
1988	408	9,325,716	367	22,269,290	4	116,600	42	1,719,140
Percent Change	-65.8	-71.7	-25.4	-12.8	-96.3	-92.2	-25.0	+218.0

Sources: *Ships On Order, The Motor Ship*: 1968-1987; *Fairplay*: 1988; Shipbuilders Council of America: U.S. data

Table M-12

NEW MERCHANT TYPE VESSELS 1,000 GROSS TONS AND OVER UNDER CONSTRUCTION OR ON ORDER IN U.S. PRIVATE SHIPYARDS

	Jan. 1982 No.	Jan. 1982 G.T.	Jan. 1983 No.	Jan. 1983 G.T.	Jan. 1984 No.	Jan. 1984 G.T.	Jan. 1985 No.	Jan. 1985 G.T.	Jan. 1986 No.	Jan. 1986 G.T.
Ferry	2	7,930	1	2,930	2	3,215				
Passenger Vessel							1	1,100		
Passenger and Vehicle Ferry							1	2,100		
Tanker	10	258,400	7	176,300	3	75,000	2	179,400	2	179,400
Tug/Barge	9	195,000	4	100,000	2	50,000				
Containership	3	121,470	1	40,490			3	48,000	3	48,000
Container-Ro/Ro Ship	3	55,500	3	55,500						
Dry Bulk Carrier	2	47,000								
Hopper Dredge	3	20,000	1	6,000	1	3,000	1	3,000		
Tuna Purseiner	2	2,000								
Collier	1	23,000	1	23,000						
Incinerator Ship			2	9,700	2	9,700	2	9,700	2	9,700
Oceanographic Research			1	2,500						
Totals	35	730,300	21	416,420	10	140,915	10	243,300	7	237,100

Source: Shipbuilders Council of America

Maritime Museum of the Atlantic
1675 Lower Water Street
Halifax, Nova Scotia
 B3J 1S3 Canada
(902) 429-8210
David B. Flemming, Director
Marven Moore, Curator (A)

The M.I.T. Museum, Hart Nautical
 Collection
265 Massachusetts Avenue
Cambridge, Massachusetts 02139
(617) 253-4444
Warren A. Seamens, Director
John Arrison, Curator

Mystic Seaport Museum
Mystic, Connecticut 06355
(203) 572-0711
J. Revell Carr, Director
Stuart Parnes, Curator of Exh.
Benjamin A.G. Fuller, Curator

Nantucket Historical Association
P.O. Box 1016
Nantucket, Massachusetts 02554
(617) 228-1894
John N. Welch, Administrator
Bruce Courson

National Maritime Museum at San
 Francisco
Golden Gate National Recreation Area
National Park Service
Fort Mason, Bldg. 201
San Francisco, California 94123
(415) 556-3002
Glennie Wall, Manager, Maritime Unit
John Maounis, Maritime Historian

The Navy Museum
Bldg. 76, Washington Navy Yard
Washington, D.C. 20390
(202) 433-4882
Oscar P. Fitzgerald, Director

Table M-13

SHIPS LAID UP THROUGHOUT THE WORLD FOR LACK OF EMPLOYMENT
Comparison: 1973 to 1988

(dry cargo ships and tankers*; in millions of deadweight tons)

Date	Total No.	Total dwt	Dry Cargo No.	Dry Cargo dwt	Tankers No.	Tankers dwt
30 June 1988	490	12,704	382	2,916	108	9,788
31 Dec. 1987	649	16,201	521	5,110	128	11,091
30 June 1987	792	20.58	638	6.38	154	14.2
31 Dec. 1986	953	24.06	786	7.98	167	16.08
30 June 1986	1,021	36.4	795	8.2	226	28.3
31 Dec. 1985	1,212	54.3	913	9.8	299	44.4
30 June 1985	1,257	64.11	924	9.66	333	54.45
31 Dec. 1984	1,302	62.37	968	10.4	344	51.98
30 June 1984	1,471	71.3	1,099	13.1	372	58.2
31 Dec. 1983	1,663	79.8	1,245	16.4	418	63.3
30 June 1983	1,694	97.9	1,247	25.1	447	72.9
31 Dec. 1982	1,549	83.8	1,146	23.6	403	60.1
30 June 1982	861	59.3	511	6.5	350	52.8
31 Dec. 1981	527	27.4	319	2.8	208	24.6
30 June 1981	414	17.3	287	1.9	127	15.4
31 Dec. 1980	402	9.2	325	2.2	77	7.0
30 June 1980	401	14.7	297	2.2	104	12.5
31 Dec. 1979	411	11.1	320	2.7	91	8.4
30 June 1979	507	21.4	363	4.9	144	16.5
31 Dec. 1978	593	30.2	370	7.0	223	23.2
30 June 1978	763	57.0	395	13.5	368	43.5
31 Dec. 1977	657	43.2	335	11.7	322	31.5
30 June 1977	544	37.1	217	6.0	327	31.1
31 Dec. 1976	595	35.7	236	5.3	359	30.4
30 June 1976	704	49.5	234	7.0	470	42.5
31 Dec. 1975	648	46.3	194	7.4	454	38.9
30 June 1975	531	33.4	163	6.0	368	27.4
31 Dec. 1974	154	2.0	108	0.4	46	1.6
30 June 1974	127	0.6	111	0.5	16	0.1
31 Dec. 1973	160	1.0	136	0.5	24	0.5

*Ships of 100 gross tons and over. Ships laid up in the U.S. Reserve Fleet and in the Eastern Bloc are excluded.

Source: "World Merchant Shipping Laid-up For Lack of Employment." Prepared monthly by the General Council of British Shipping, based on "Lloyd's Monthly List of Laid-up Vessels," published by Lloyd's of London Press Ltd.

North Carolina Maritime Museum
315 Front Street
Beaufort, North Carolina 28516
(919) 728-7317
Rodney D. Barfield, Director

Old Dartmouth Historical Society
 Whaling Museum
18 Johnny Cake Hill
New Bedford, Massachusetts 02740
(617) 997-0046
Richard C. Kugler, Director
Virginia Adams, Librarian

Patriots Point Naval and Maritime
 Museum
P.O. Box 986
Mt. Pleasant, South Carolina 29464
(803) 884-2727
J.E. Guerry, Jr., Exec. Director

Peabody Museum of Salem
East India Marine Hall
Salem, Massachusetts 01970
(617) 745-1876
Peter Fetchko, Director
Paul Johnston, Curator of Maritime
 History

Penobscot Marine Museum
Searsport, Maine 04974
(207) 548-2529
Robert D. Farwell, Director
William A. Bayreuther, Curator

Philadelphia Maritime Museum
321 Chestnut Street
Philadelphia, Pennsylvania 19106
(215) 925-5439
Theodore T. Newbold, President
Jane Allen, Curator

The Portsmouth Naval Shipyard Museum
P.O. Box 850
Portsmouth, Virginia 23705
(804) 393-8591
Nancy J. Melton, Director

Radcliffe Maritime Museum
The Maryland Historical Society
201 West Monument Street
Baltimore, Maryland 21201
(301) 685-3750, ext. 40
Mary Ellen Hayward, Curator
L. Byrne Waterman

Sag Harbor Whaling and Historical Museum
P.O. Box 1327
Sag Harbor, New York 11963
(516) 567-1733
George A. Finckenor, Sr., Curator

The Smithsonian Institution
National Museum of American History
Division of Naval History
Washington, D.C. 20560
(202) 357-2249
Dr. Harold Langley, Curator of Naval History

The Smithsonian Institution
National Museum of American History
Division of Transportation
Washington, D.C. 20560
(202) 357-2025
Curator of Maritime History

South Street Seaport Museum
207 Front Street
New York, New York 10038
(212) 669-9400
Peter Neill, President

Suffolk Marine Museum
Montauk Highway
West Sayville, New York 11796
(516) 567-1733
Roger B. Dunkerley, Director

Thousand Islands Shipyard Museum
750 Mary Street
Clayton, New York 13624
(315) 686-4104
Riggs Smith, Director

U.S. Coast Guard Museum
U.S. Coast Guard Academy
New London, Connecticut 06320
(203) 444-8511
Paul H. Johnson, Curator

U.S. Frigate Constellation
Constellation Dock
Baltimore, Maryland 21202
(301) 539-1797
Herbert E. Witz, President

U.S. Naval Academy Museum
Annapolis, Maryland 21402
(301) 267-2108
William W. Jeffries, Director
James W. Cheevers, Senior Curator

U.S.S. Constitution Museum Foundation
Boston Naval Shipyard
Boston, Massachusetts 02129
(617) 242-0543
Richard C. Wheeler, Director
Anne A. Grimes, Curator

Table M-14

SHIP CONSTRUCTION
FOUR-YEAR PLAN—FY88-FY89

($ in millions)

	FY 89	FY 90	FY 91	FY 92
NEW CONSTRUCTION				
TRIDENT	1/1368.1	1/1482.4	1/1546.7	1/1597.0
CVN	—	1/2288.0	696.0	201.5
SSN-688	2/1493.6	2/1503.8	2/1438.3	1/801.2
SSN-21	1/1488.0	583.0	2/2916.6	2/2953.4
CG-47	—	1/951.3	—	—
DDG-5	3/2207.3	3/2394.4	5/3972.6	6/4982.1
LHD-1	1/737.5	41.8	1/1136.5	208.2
LSD-41 (CV)	—	1/294.1	1/304.0	2/595.3
MCM	—	—	—	—
MHC	2/197.2	3/232.6	3/246.4	4/313.7
TAO	2/284.9	2/312.0	1/158.9	—
TAGOS	3/159.6	3/176.5	2/126.7	—
AE	—	—	1/418.0	1/327.2
AOE-6	1/363.9	—	2/903.2	—
ARS	—	1/145.5	—	—
AGOR/TAGS	1/74.0	2/127.4	4/252.1	—
PXM	—	1/114.4	—	4/404.6
LCAC	(9)/192.6	(12)/274.4	(12)/282.3	(12)/289.5
CONVERSIONS				
CV SLEP	135.4	102.8	1/582.4	211.6
AO (JUMBO C)	2/84.9	1/40.3	—	—
TACS (C)	—	—	—	—
OTHER				
SERVICE CRAFT	—	64.5	72.0	151.2
LANDING CRAFT	—	21.9	105.9	107.9
STRAT SEALIFT	—	62.8	13.8	36.9
SEALIFT ENHANCE	—	21.4	21.1	49.4
OUTFITTING	214.7	303.5	273.9	308.6
POST DELIVERY	128.4	220.7	163.6	210.4
TOTAL	9,130.1	11,759.5	15,631.0	13,749.7
SHIP COUNT				
NC/C	17/2	21/1	25/1	21/0

*A new five-year plan is not anticipated until the FY 1990/91 budget is submitted in January 1989.

Source: Shipbuilders Council of America

Chart M-15

Dependency on Navy Work
Private Shipyard Employment

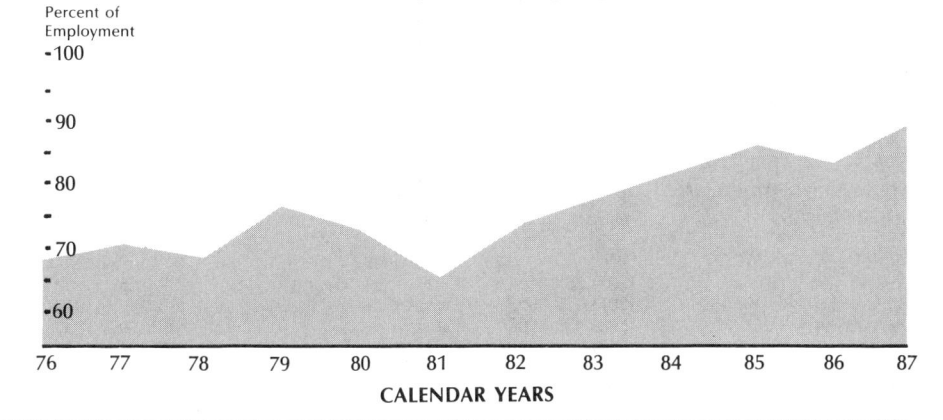

Chart M-16
Private Shipyards with Navy Construction Programs
(1 February 1988)

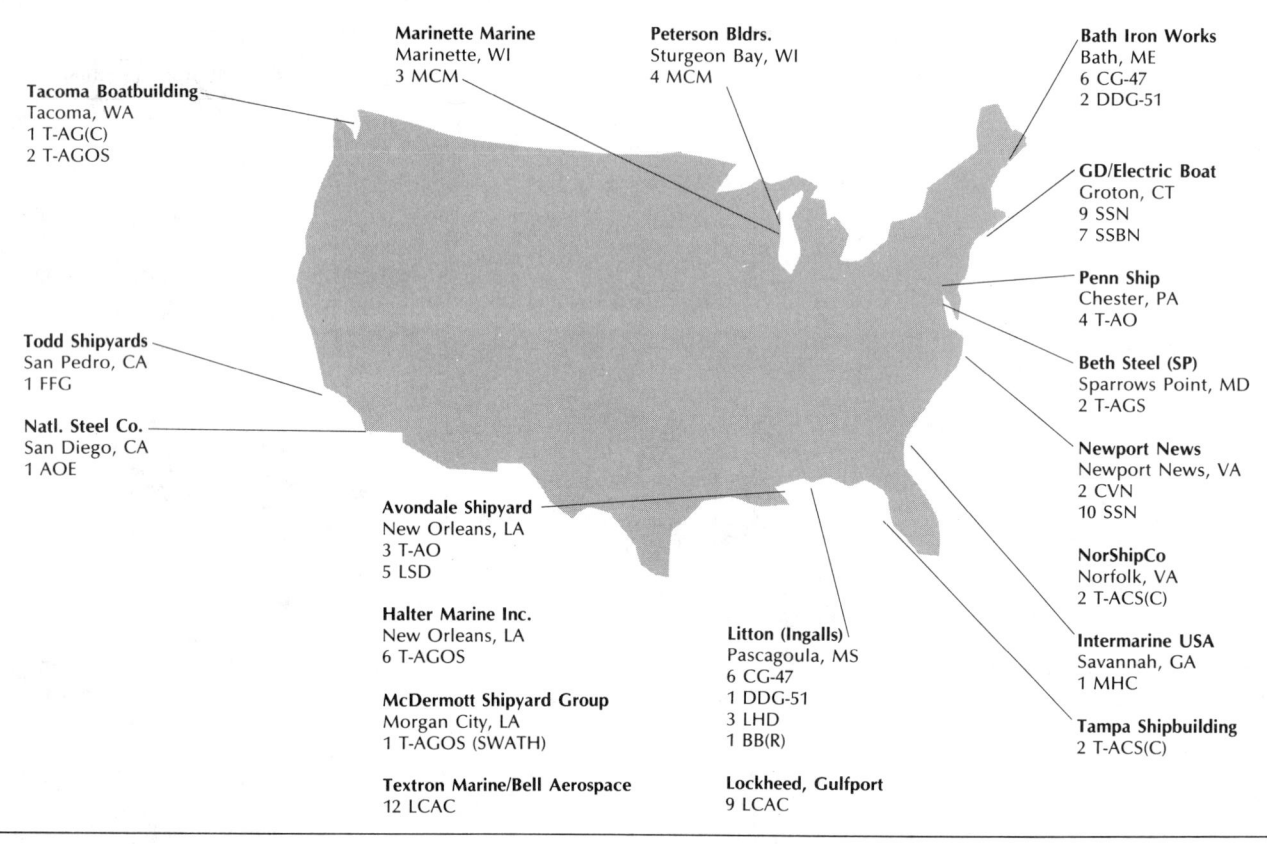

Tacoma Boatbuilding
Tacoma, WA
1 T-AG(C)
2 T-AGOS

Marinette Marine
Marinette, WI
3 MCM

Peterson Bldrs.
Sturgeon Bay, WI
4 MCM

Bath Iron Works
Bath, ME
6 CG-47
2 DDG-51

GD/Electric Boat
Groton, CT
9 SSN
7 SSBN

Penn Ship
Chester, PA
4 T-AO

Todd Shipyards
San Pedro, CA
1 FFG

Natl. Steel Co.
San Diego, CA
1 AOE

Beth Steel (SP)
Sparrows Point, MD
2 T-AGS

Newport News
Newport News, VA
2 CVN
10 SSN

Avondale Shipyard
New Orleans, LA
3 T-AO
5 LSD

NorShipCo
Norfolk, VA
2 T-ACS(C)

Halter Marine Inc.
New Orleans, LA
6 T-AGOS

Litton (Ingalls)
Pascagoula, MS
6 CG-47
1 DDG-51
3 LHD
1 BB(R)

Intermarine USA
Savannah, GA
1 MHC

McDermott Shipyard Group
Morgan City, LA
1 T-AGOS (SWATH)

Tampa Shipbuilding
2 T-ACS(C)

Textron Marine/Bell Aerospace
12 LCAC

Lockheed, Gulfport
9 LCAC

Vancouver Maritime Museum
1905 Ogden Street
Vancouver, British Columbia V6J 3J9
  Canada
(604) 736-4431
Robin R. Inglis, Director

Virginia Beach Maritime Historical
  Museum
P.O. Box 24
Virginia Beach, Virginia 23458
(804) 491-8608
Atsuko I.F. Biernot, Director, Research
  and Education

Whaling Museum Society
P.O. Box 25
Cold Spring Harbor, New York 11724
(516) 367-3418
Ann M. Gill, Director

Port Authorities

Officials at the port authorities listed below will advise on services available. Mention of "American Shipper" will be appreciated.

NORTH ATLANTIC
Eastport	(207) 853-4614
Portland	(207) 772-0690
Portsmouth	(603) 436-8500
Boston	(617) 973-5500
Fall River	(617) 674-5707
Providence	(401) 781-4717
New York/NJ	(212) 466-8337
Albany	(518) 445-2599
Philadelphia	(215) 928-9100
Camden	(609) 541-8500
Wilmington	(302) 571-4600

CHESAPEAKE AREA
Baltimore	(800) 638-7519
Norfolk	(804) 623-8000
Richmond	(804) 743-7678

GREAT LAKES
Buffalo	(716) 855-7411
Cleveland	(216) 241-8004
Toledo	(419) 243-8251
Detroit	(313) 259-8077
Green Bay	(414) 497-3265
Burns Harbor	(219) 787-8636
Chicago	(312) 646-4400
Milwaukee	(414) 278-3511
Duluth	(218) 727-8525
Kenosha	(414) 652-3125

SOUTH ATLANTIC
Morehead City	(919) 726-3158
Wilmington	(919) 763-1621
Georgetown	(803) 527-4476
Charleston	(803) 723-8651
Savannah	(912) 964-3811
Brunswick	(912) 264-7295
Fernandina Beach	(904) 261-0098
Jacksonville	(904) 630-3000
Canaveral	(305) 783-7831
Palm Beach	(305) 842-4201
Port Everglades	(305) 523-3404
Miami	(305) 371-7678

GULF COAST
Manatee	(813) 722-6621
Tampa	(813) 248-1924
Panama City	(904) 763-8471
Pensacola	(904) 435-1870
Mobile	(205) 690-6020
Pascagoula	(601) 762-4041
Gulfport	(601) 865-4300
New Orleans	(504) 522-2551
Baton Rouge	(504) 387-4207
Lake Charles	(318) 439-3661
Beaumont	(409) 835-5367
Port Arthur	(713) 983-2011
Houston	(713) 226-2100
Galveston	(713) 765-9321
Freeport	(409) 233-2667
Corpus Christi	(512) 882-5633
Brownsville	(512) 831-4592

PACIFIC COAST
San Diego	(800) 854-2757
Los Angeles	(213) 519-3840
Long Beach	(213) 437-0041
Hueneme	(805) 488-3677
Richmond	(415) 620-6784
San Francisco	(415) 391-8000
Oakland	(800) 227-2726
Sacramento	(916) 371-8000
Stockton	(209) 946-0246
Coos Bay	(503) 267-7678
Portland	(503) 231-5000
Vancouver	(206) 693-3611
Longview	(206) 425-3305
Tacoma	(206) 383-5841
Seattle	(206) 728-3400
Bellingham	(206) 676-2500

Chart M-17

Private Shipyards with Navy Shipwork During FY 87 (Overhaul and Repair)
(1 March 1988)
(45 SHIPYARDS)

Puget Sound Area
Lake Union DD
Todd Seattle
Marine Pwr & Equip

Portland Area
Lockport
Northwest
Pacific Marine

San Francisco Bay Area
Continental Maritime
Service Engineering

Los Angeles Area
Larson Boat Shop
SW Marine
Todd San Pedro

San Diego Area
Arcwel Corp.
Campbell Ind
Continental Maritime
National Steel & SB
SW Marine

Honolulu, HI
Honolulu Shipyard
Marisco Limited

New Orleans, LA
Avondale Shipyard

Pascagoula, MS
Ingalls

Mobile, AL
Addsco Industries
Bender Shipbuilding

Gulf Coast Area, FL
Runyan Machine

Quincy/Boston Area
GenShip

Bath, ME
Bath Iron Works

Groton, CT
GD-Electric Boat

Brooklyn, NY
G. Marine Diesel

New Jersey Area
Hoboken Shipyards

Chester, PA
Penn Ship

Baltimore, MD
Beth Steel, Sparrows Pt

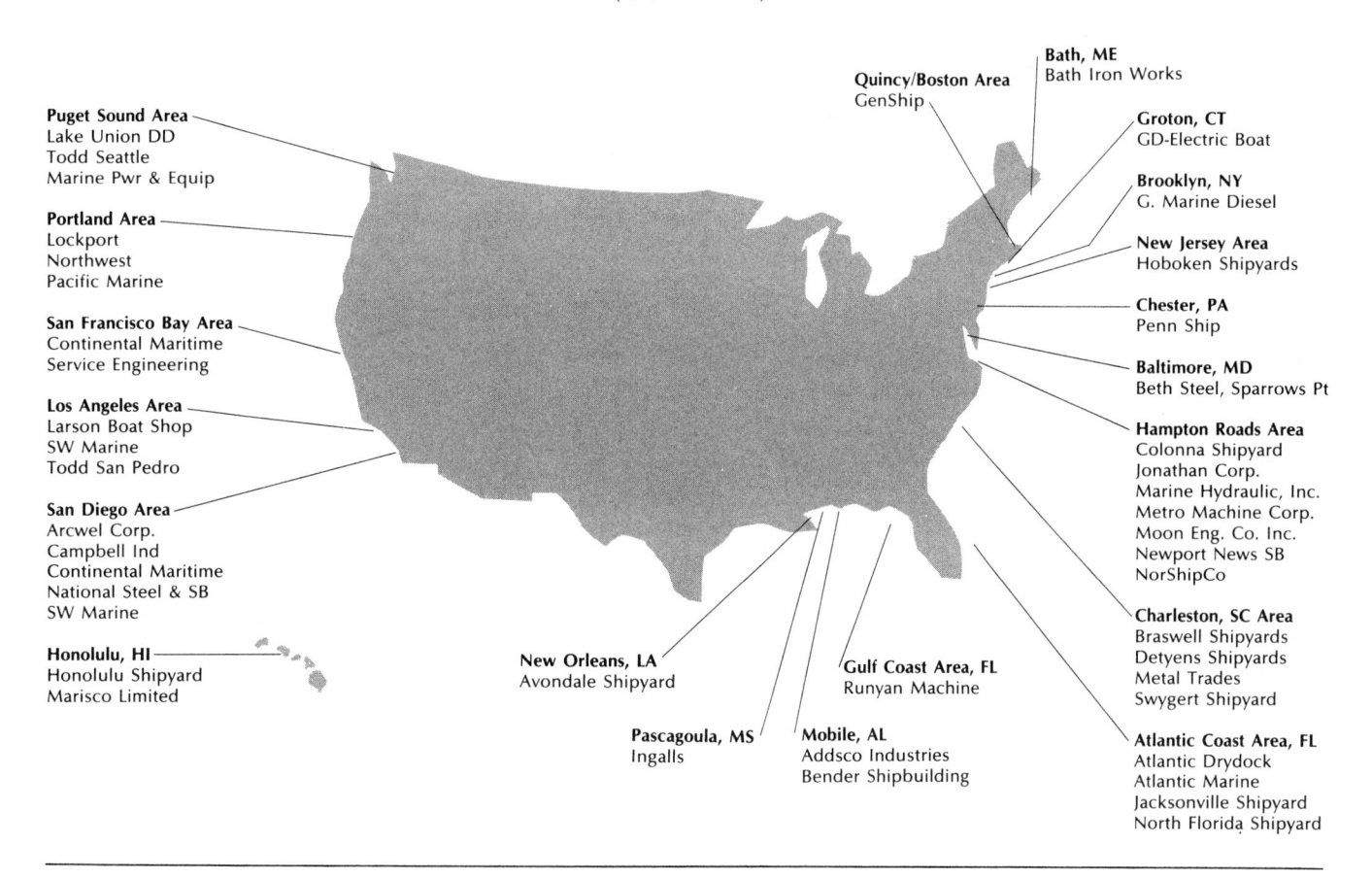

Hampton Roads Area
Colonna Shipyard
Jonathan Corp.
Marine Hydraulic, Inc.
Metro Machine Corp.
Moon Eng. Co. Inc.
Newport News SB
NorShipCo

Charleston, SC Area
Braswell Shipyards
Detyens Shipyards
Metal Trades
Swygert Shipyard

Atlantic Coast Area, FL
Atlantic Drydock
Atlantic Marine
Jacksonville Shipyard
North Florida Shipyard

Chart M-18
Public Shipyards

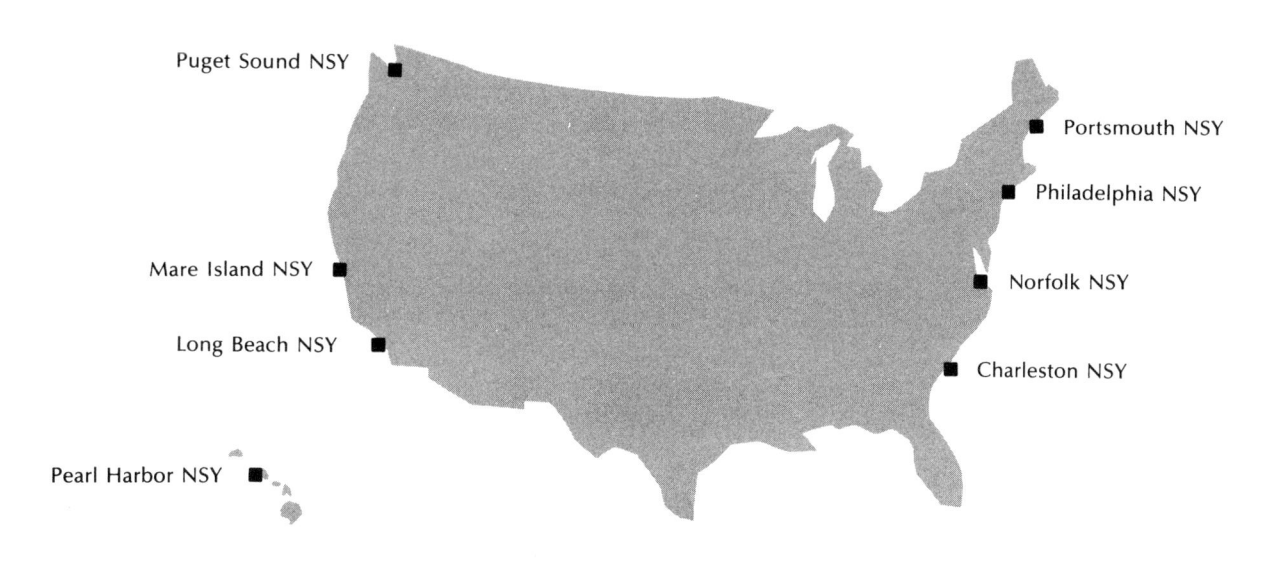

Puget Sound NSY
Portsmouth NSY
Philadelphia NSY
Mare Island NSY
Norfolk NSY
Long Beach NSY
Charleston NSY
Pearl Harbor NSY

SEA POWER: COAST GUARD

The Coast Guard was established on 15 January 1915 as a merger of the Revenue Cutter Service (begun in 1790) and the Life-Saving Service (begun in 1848). It became a part of the newly formed Department of Transportation in 1967.

The strategic objectives of the Coast Guard are:
- To minimize the loss of life, personal injuries, and property damage on, over, and under the seas and waters subject to U.S. jurisdiction.
- To facilitate waterborne activity in support of national economic, scientific, defense, and social needs.
- To maintain an armed force prepared to carry out specific naval or military tasks in time of war or emergency.
- To assure safe and secure ports, waterways, and shoreside facilities.
- To enforce federal laws and international agreements on and under those waters subject to U.S. jurisdiction and on and under the high seas where authorized.
- To maintain or improve the quality of the marine environment.
- To cooperate with other government agencies—federal, state, and local—to assure efficient use of public resources.

The Coast Guard operates the world's largest Search and Rescue (SAR) organization. The search and rescue mission was one of the Coast Guard's earliest functions, and continues to be its most recognized. Ten Rescue Coordination Centers are maintained in the continental United States, Alaska, and Hawaii to coordinate the search and rescue efforts of 26 air stations, over 150 small boat stations, and all cutters assigned a SAR responsibility. About 71% of the Coast Guard's SAR cases involve recreational vessels. Almost 95% of all rescue missions take place within 20 miles of the shore.

A vital role in the SAR program is played by the Coast Guard Auxiliary, whose members participate in about 16% of the distress calls. Also playing a role is the Automated Mutual Assistance Vessel Rescue System, a voluntary movement report system that keeps records of the location of merchant vessels at sea to help mariners give assistance to one another.

ENFORCEMENT OF LAWS AND TREATIES

As the world's largest marine police force, the Coast Guard is charged with the enforcement of all applicable federal laws on the high seas and waters subject to U.S. jurisdiction. The USCG's "police work" ranges from interdiction of narcotics and illegal aliens to combating vessel thefts or hijackings and enforcing marine conservation laws. In order to do this, federal statutes allow Coast Guard personnel to board all U.S. vessels, foreign flag vessels within sovereign jurisdiction of the United States, and foreign vessels on the high seas in accordance with international law or specific special arrangements with the flag states.

In 1973, the Coast Guard seized six vessels loaded with marijuana. By 1987, the number of seizures had jumped to more than 150 annually. The Coast Guard estimates it interdicts between 15% and 20% of all illegal drugs coming into the United States by sea. The Coast Guard was heavily involved with policing the Cuban sealift in 1980, and since 1981 has been conducting a special operation to stop illegal Haitian emigration.

AIDS TO NAVIGATION AND OTHER MISSIONS

To aid navigation, the Coast Guard locates and marks channels and buoys and manages the federal system of 48,072 lighthouses, buoys, daybeacons, fog signals, and radar reflectors. The Coast Guard manages 43,472 privately owned aids to navigation, as well as aids operated for the Department of Defense.

Because buoys are being replaced with less costly land-based or pile structures, the number of Coast Guard buoy tenders has been reduced significantly in recent years. The Coast Guard runs 14 manned and 445 unmanned lighthouses.

The Coast Guard also operates and maintains three types of radio-navigation aids throughout the United States and in other parts of the world:
- About 200 radio-beacons, which are simple and cheap non-directional radio transmitters. They allow vessels

and aircraft to receive direction-finding information from 10 to 175 miles offshore.
- LORAN-C, a low-frequency, long-range navigational radio system that provides mariners with navigation data up to 1,500 miles offshore. The Coast Guard operates 25 domestic LORAN-C stations and 20 overseas (for U.S. military use).
- OMEGA, a worldwide, long-range radio-navigation system with eight transmitting and 50 monitoring stations. It is used for navigation by both sea and air travelers. The Coast Guard operates two OMEGA stations; six more are operated by host countries under international agreements.

Other Coast Guard duties:

Port and environmental safety. Coast Guard officers, serving as Captains of the Port, and other employees at 46 Marine Safety and Inspection offices are charged with enforcing regulations governing waterfront safety and the anchorage of vessels with dangerous cargoes. USCG officers also are charged with ensuring the safe loading and stowage of explosives and other hazardous cargoes aboard ship.

Commercial vessel safety. The Coast Guard enforces safety standards in the design, construction, and equipping of vessels; examines foreign vessels to ensure compliance with U.S. statutes and international agreements; administers standards for licensed and unlicensed maritime personnel; investigates marine accidents; supervises the documentation of U.S. vessels and assignment of their official tonnage; and maintains merchant seamen's records.

The Coast Guard estimates in FY 1989 it will receive reports on 10,000 "marine incidents," inspect 15,000 commercial vessels, make 800 factory visits and inspections, board 30,000 boats, and monitor 2,600 loadings of explosives and other dangerous cargo.

Defense Readiness. The Coast Guard, by statute, always is an armed force of the United States, and shall operate as a service in the Navy in time of war or as the President so directs. In emergencies, Coast Guard vessels and aircraft, as well as specialty-skilled personnel, can be transferred to operational control of Navy commanders for special duties. Coast Guard forces are included in Navy fleet-commander contingency and war plans. In 1984 the new Office of Readiness and Reserve was established at Coast Guard headquarters to place further emphasis on the Coast Guard's commitment to both statutory and military missions in periods of heightened tension.

Building on the unique capabilities and responsibilities of both services, the Navy has established Maritime Defense Zones (MDZ) for the continental United States, Alaska, Aleutians, and Hawaii to provide for integrated coastal and harbor defense. The Maritime Defense Zone concept melds present Coast Guard command and control capabilities, active and Reserve Coast Guard forces and resources providing port security, maritime law enforcement, aids to navigation, surveillance and interdiction, and search and rescue with Navy and Naval Reserve anti-submarine warfare, inshore undersea warfare, mine countermeasures and other specialized units. The MDZ commanders are double-hatted. They currently are the commanders of Coast Guard Atlantic and Pacific areas, Coast Guard vice admirals, who are the senior operational commanders for peacetime Coast Guard operations. The MDZ commands have small Navy and Coast Guard staffs for peacetime planning, training, and exercising. The MDZs will interact with the Army in the land defense of North America, the Air Force for related air defense, and civilian agencies for optimum port utilization in supply/resupply efforts.

Planning, training, and exercising for wartime taskings are and will remain important among the Coast Guard's many peacetime missions. Both active and Reserve Coast Guard forces work together on all aspects of defense readiness. Major cutters participate in Navy fleet exercises. Harbor units routinely conduct mobilization and port breakout exercises. All commands down to port level play in Joint Chiefs of Staff command-post exercises.

Domestic ice operations. Domestic icebreaking is conducted for search-and-rescue missions and for the prevention of flooding caused by ice (an activity coordinated by the U.S. Army Corps of Engineers). These operations are conducted in direct support of the general public. Examples include opening channels to icebound communities which are in immediate need of food, winter fuel, or medical assistance. The Coast Guard will conduct icebreaking operations as needed to facilitate navigation, but it normally will not interfere with private enterprise in conducting icebreaking operations to facilitate navigation. If commercial icebreaking assistance is available and adequate, Coast Guard icebreaking assistance shall not be provided.

Guarding the marine environment. The Coast Guard responds to the accidental or intentional discharge—or substantial threat of discharge—of oil, hazardous substances, pollutants, and contaminants into U.S. waters. In 1987, more than 11,800 pollution incidents were reported to the Coast Guard. The Coast Guard investigated 9,000 oil spills and 400 chemical releases, supervised 250 oil and 26 chemical federally-funded cleanups and monitored 2,400 private-sector cleanups.

Marine science. The Coast Guard operates cutters and aircraft assigned to the International Ice Patrol, funded jointly by 20 signatory nations to detect and predict the drift of icebergs in North Atlantic shipping lanes. The Coast Guard also provides oceanographic services and weather observations and reports in a cooperative program with the National Weather Service of NOAA and the Naval Oceanography Command, and assists other federal agencies in support of national marine science activities.

The Coast Guard has an extensive role in a major new initiative aimed at combating narcotics trafficking across the borders of the United States. In January 1982, the Vice President's Task Force on South Florida Crime was formed to take action against the severe problems faced in the maritime law enforcement efforts of the Southeast U.S. and the Caribbean Basin. Since then, the success of this task force led to the formation of the National Narcotics Border Interdiction Systems (NNBIS), with headquarters at St. Petersburg, FL, and regional centers located at Long Beach, CA; El Paso, TX; New Orleans, LA; Miami, FL; New York, NY; and Chicago, IL. And in October 1985, an NNBIS subregional center was established in Honolulu, HI. In coordinating the efforts of all the federal law enforcement agencies, these centers collate intelligence, assess threats, prioritize targets, maintain statistics, and coordinate special joint operations.

The legislative clarification of the Posse Comitatus Act, which heretofore limited military services from participating in law-enforcement activity, has

Table CG-1

SEARCH AND RESCUE ACTIVITIES

	1982	1983	1984	1985	1986	1987
Search and Rescue Cases	68,552	63,980	57,431	70,062	58,259	55,986
Lives Saved	5,675	5,946	5,645	6,303	7,002	5,788
Persons Otherwise Assisted	157,552	145,662	129,650	136,341	135,404	131,537
Property Loss Prevented (millions $)	524	615.3	801.8	820.3	1,002.2	2,100.0
Program Operating Expense (millions $)	397	410	415	386	319	315

Source: Coast Guard

These fast coastal interceptors are adaptations of the commercial Riviera-class cigarette boats. They operate from Miami on drug interdiction duties.

enabled the other armed services to take an active role in assisting other federal agencies in the performance of the law enforcement mission. Coast Guard Law Enforcement Detachments (LEDETS) and Tactical Law Enforcement Teams (TACLETS) are now able to ride U.S. Navy ships to conduct boardings on suspected narcotics-smuggling-profile vessels at sea. The Navy and Air Force provide surveillance flights for both the Coast Guard and Customs Service, and the Army and Navy have loaned several aircraft to the Customs Service to bolster the air smuggling interdiction effort. As of 1 September 1988, Navy ships and aircraft have been involved in the seizure of 141 drug-smuggling vessels since the beginning of their active participation in the "War on Drugs" in December 1981.

The Coast Guard has primary responsibility for the at-sea enforcement of more than 30 fishery management plans and associated enforcement regulations which regulate domestic and foreign fishing in the U.S. Exclusive Economic Zone (EEZ) pursuant to the Magnuson Fisheries Conservation and Management Act (MFCMA). In addition, the Coast Guard is tasked with monitoring compliance with endangered species and marine sanctuary regulations, as well as certain international fishing agreements in waters beyond the limits of the U.S. EEZ.

Fisheries enforcement activities include surface and aircraft surveillance of major fishing areas and disputed regions as well as thorough boardings of domestic and foreign fishing vessels. A complete inventory of the hold of a foreign fishing vessel may require two or three days for a boarding team to complete.

During 1987, the Coast Guard conducted more than 172 boardings of foreign fishing vessels, issued 29 written warnings and 29 violations, and seized 14 vessels for serious violations of the MFCMA. Some 2,252 boardings of domestic fishing vessels were carried out, resulting in 47 written warnings and 286 violations being issued. No domestic fishing vessels were seized in 1987.

In 1988, the Coast Guard expected to devote 26,000 cutter operating hours to fisheries enforcement and 122,000 cutter operating hours to drug interdiction and general law enforcement.

Waterways management. The Coast Guard's Vessel Traffic Services system coordinates vessel movements in or approaching a waterway to reduce congestion. Vessel Traffic Services are in: San Francisco, CA; Puget Sound, WA; Houston/Galveston, TX; Prince William Sound, AK, and Berwick Bay, LA. Waterways management includes traffic routing, enforcement of speed limits, and limits on the size of vessels in certain waterways and harbors.

Bridge administration. The Coast Guard assumed responsibility for administering bridges over navigable U.S. waters in 1967, shortly after the Department of Transportation was formed. The Coast Guard is charged with ensuring safe and unobstructed navigation through or under bridges, while meeting the needs of other modes of transportation, such as car and truck traffic on the bridges. The Coast Guard determines whether a bridge unreasonably obstructs navigation; if so, federal funds to alter the bridge are requested. The Coast Guard also issues permits for bridge construction or modification and develops drawbridge regulations to ensure non-interference with commerce. It has responsibility for 18,000 bridges in the United States.

Recreational boating safety. The Coast Guard enforces construction and performance standards for recreational boats, educates the public about boat safety, and enforces safety laws. The Coast Guard is the manager of a boating safety program, authorized by Congress, that encourages participation in boating safety by the states, the boating industry, and the boating public. As the states have increased their roles in enforcement and education, the Coast Guard has been able to reduce its direct involvement. The Coast Guard Auxiliary conducts boating education programs and examinations.

Polar ice operations. The Coast Guard supports and promotes national interests in both the Arctic and Antarctic by facilitating travel across ice-covered waters. The "national interests" supported include scientific study by the National Science Foundation, the Department of Defense, and the Coast Guard itself.

U.S. COAST GUARD ACADEMY

The U.S. Coast Guard Academy in New London, CT, has an undergraduate enrollment of 800 men and women. This federal academy, situated along the Thames River, is halfway between New York and Boston.

Degrees and Majors. There are seven majors to choose from: electrical, civil, and marine engineering, government, management, marine science, and mathematics/computer sciences. Each graduate receives a bachelor of science degree and a commission as ensign in the Coast Guard.

Costs. A $1,000 deposit is required upon entrance to defray the cost of uniforms and educational equipment. $300 of this sum is required at the time a candidate accepts a full appointment.

Financial Aid. Each cadet receives about $480 a month for uniforms, equipment, textbooks, and other training expenses.

Admission. Cadets are selected in an annual nationwide competition (no congressional appointments or geographical quotas). Eligibility requirements include satisfactory SAT or ACT scores, good scholastic records, and leadership potential. Each candidate must also pass a medical examination before being accepted.

Application Information. Applications, which are due the December before entrance of a new class in July are available by contacting:

The Director of Admissions
U.S. Coast Guard Academy
New London, CT 06320-4195

or by calling: (203) 444-8500-8503.

COAST GUARD ACTIVE FLEET

Type of Cutter	No.
High Endurance Cutter (WHEC)	
Hamilton Class (378')	12
Secretary Class (327')	1
Casco Class (311')	1
Medium Endurance Cutter (WMEC)	
Famous Class (270')	13
Storis Class (230')	1
Diver Class (213')	3
Reliance Class (210')	16
Cherokee and Achomawi Class (205')	5
Balsam Class (180')	3
Patrol Boats (WPB/WSES)	
Island Class (110')	16
Cape Class (95')	17
Point Class (82')	53
Sea Bird Class (110')	3

High-Endurance Cutters

Hamilton Class

CHASE
 (WHEC-718), New York, N.Y.
BOUTWELL
 (WHEC-719), Seattle, Wash.
GALLATIN
 (WHEC-721), New York, N.Y.
MORGENTHAU
 (WHEC-722), Alameda, Calif.
RUSH
 (WHEC-723), Alameda, Calif.
JARVIS
 (WHEC-725), Honolulu, Hawaii
MIDGETT
 (WHEC-726), Alameda, Calif.

In Modernization

Hamilton Class

HAMILTON
 (WHEC-715), Boston, Mass.
DALLAS
 (WHEC-716), New York, N.Y.
MELLON
 (WHEC-717), Seattle, Wash.
SHERMAN
 (WHEC-720), Alameda, Calif.
MUNRO
 (WHEC-724), Honolulu, Hawaii

Secretary Class

INGHAM
 (WHEC-35), Portsmouth, Va.

Casco Class

UNIMAK
 (WHEC-379), New Bedford, Mass.

Medium Endurance Cutters

Famous Class

BEAR
 (WMEC-901), Portsmouth, Va.
TAMPA
 (WMEC-902), Portsmouth, Va.
HARRIET LANE
 (WMEC-903), Portsmouth, Va.
NORTHLAND
 (WMEC-904), Portsmouth, Va.
SPENCER
 (WMEC-905), Boston, Mass.
SENECA
 (WMEC-906), Boston, Mass.
ESCANABA
 (WMEC-907), Boston, Mass.
TAHOMA
 (WMEC-908), New Bedford, Mass.
CAMPBELL
 (WMEC-909), New Bedford, Mass.
THETIS
 (WMEC-910), Long Beach, Calif.

Under Construction or Approved

FORWARD
 (WMEC-911), Long Beach, Calif.
LEGARE
 (WMEC-912), Long Beach, Calif.
MOHAWK
 (WMEC-913), Long Beach, Calif.

Reliance Class

DILIGENCE
 (WMEC-616), Cape Canaveral, Fla.
VIGILANT
 (WMEC-617), New Bedford, Mass.
ACTIVE
 (WMEC-618), Port Angeles, Wash.
CONFIDENCE
 (WMEC-619), New Bedford, Mass.
RESOLUTE
 (WMEC-620), Astoria, Ore.
VALIANT
 (WMEC-621), Galveston, Texas
STEADFAST
 (WMEC-623), St. Petersburg, Fla.
DAUNTLESS
 (WMEC-624), Miami Beach, Fla.
VENTUROUS
 (WMEC-625), Coast Guard Island, Calif.
DEPENDABLE
 (WMEC-626), Panama City Fla.
VIGOROUS
 (WMEC-627), New London, Conn.
DECISIVE
 (WMEC-629), St. Petersburg, Fla.
ALERT
 (WMEC-630), Cape May, N.J.

In Modernization

RELIANCE
 (WMEC-615), Cape Canaveral, Fla.
COURAGEOUS
 (WMEC-622), Key West, Fla.
DURABLE
 (WMEC-628), Brownsville, Tex.

Cherokee Class

UTE
 (WMEC-76), Key West, Fla.
LIPAN
 (WMEC-85), Ft. George, Fla.
CHILULA
 (WMEC-153), Atlantic Beach, N.C.
CHEROKEE
 (WMEC-165), Norfolk, Va.
TAMAROA
 (WMEC-166), New Castle, N.H.

Balsam Class

CLOVER
 (WMEC-292), Eureka, Calif.
EVERGREEN
 (WMEC-295), New London, Conn.
CITRUS
 (WMEC-300), Coos Bay, Ore.

Storis Class

STORIS
 (WMEC-38), Kodiak, Alaska

Diver Class

ESCAPE
 (WMEC-6), Charleston, S.C.
ACUSHNET
 (WMEC-167), Gulfport, Miss.
YOCONA
 (WMEC-168), Kodiak, Alaska

Icebreakers

Polar Class

POLAR STAR
 (WAGB-10), Seattle, Wash.
POLAR SEA
 (WAGB-11), Seattle, Wash.

Mackinaw Class

MACKINAW
 (WAGB-83), Cheboygan, Mich.

Surface Effect Ships

Sea Bird Class

SHEARWATER
 (WSES-2), Key West, Fla.
SEA HAWK
 (WSES-3), Key West, Fla.
PETREL
 (WSES-4), Key West, Fla.

Icebreaking Tugs

Bay Class

KATMAI BAY
 (WTGB-101), Sault Ste. Marie, Mich.
BRISTOL BAY
 (WTGB-102), Detroit, Mich.
MOBILE BAY
 (WTGB-103), Sturgeon Bay, Wis.
BISCAYNE BAY
 (WTGB-104), St. Ignace, Mich.
NEAH BAY
 (WTGB-105), Cleveland, Ohio
MORRO BAY
 (WTGB-106), Yorktown, Va.
PENOBSCOT BAY
 (WTGB-107), Governors Island, N.Y.
THUNDER BAY
 (WTGB-108), Portland, Maine
STURGEON BAY
 (WTGB-109), Portland, Maine

Patrol Boats

Island Class

FARALLON
 (WPB-1301), Miami Beach, Fla.
MANITOU
 (WPB-1302), Miami Beach, Fla.
MATAGORDA
 (WPB-1303), Miami Beach, Fla.
MAUI
 (WPB-1304), Miami Beach, Fla.
MOHEGAN
 (WPB-1305), Roosevelt Roads, P.R.
NUNIVAK
 (WPB-1306), Roosevelt Roads, P.R.
OCRACOKE
 (WPB-1307), Roosevelt Roads, P.R.

VASHON
 (WPB-1308), Roosevelt Roads, P.R.
ACQUIDNECK
 (WPB-1309), Portsmouth, Va.
MUSTANG
 (WPB-1310), Seward, Alaska
NAUSHON
 (WPB-1311), Ketchikan, Alaska
SANIBEL
 (WPB-1312), Rockland, Maine
EDISTO
 (WPB-1313), Crescent City, Calif.
SAPELO
 (WPB-1314), Eureka, Calif.
MATINICUS
 (WPB-1315), Cape May, N.J.
NANTUCKET
 (WPB-1316), San Juan, P.R.
ATTU
 (WPB-1317), St. Thomas, USVI

BARANOF
 (WPB-1318), Miami Beach, Fla.
CHANDELEUR
 (WPB-1319), Miami Beach, Fla.
CHINCOTEAGUE
 (WPB-1320), Mobile, Ala.
CUSHING
 (WPB-1321), Mobile, Ala.
CUTTYHUNK
 (WPB-1322)
DRUMMOND
 (WPB-1323)

Under Construction

LARGO
 (WPB-1324)
METOMKIN
 (WPB-1325)
MONOMOY
 (WPB-1326)
ORCAS
 (WPB-1327)

PADRE
 (WPB-1328)
SITKINIAK
 (WPB-1329)
TYBEE
 (WPB-1330)
WASHINGTON
 (WPB-1331)
WRANGELL
 (WPB-1332)
ADAK
 (WPB-1333)
LIBERTY
 (WPB-1334)
ANACAPA
 (WPB-1335)
KISKA
 (WPB-1336)
ASSATEAGUE
 (WPB-1337)

PRINCIPAL COAST GUARD OFFICES

Headquarters, U.S. Coast Guard
2100 Second St., S.W.
Washington, D.C. 20593-00001

Atlantic Area District Offices

Commander, Coast Guard Atlantic Area
and Maritime Defense Zone, Atlantic
Governors Island
New York, NY 10004

Maintenance & Logistics Command, Atlantic
Governors Island
New York, NY 10004-5098

First Coast Guard District
408 Atlantic Avenue
Boston, MA 02210-2209

Second Coast Guard District
1430 Olive St.
St. Louis, MO 63101-2378

Fifth Coast Guard District
Federal Building
431 Crawford St.
Portsmouth, VA 23704-5004

Seventh Coast Guard District
1018 Federal Building
51 S.W. First Ave.
Miami Beach, FL 33130-1608

Eighth Coast Guard District
Hale Boggs Federal Building
500 Camp St.
New Orleans, LA 70130-3396

Ninth Coast Guard District
1240 E. Ninth St.
Cleveland, OH 44199-2060

Pacific Area District Offices

Commander, Coast Guard Pacific Area
and Maritime Defense Zone, Pacific
Government Island
Alameda, CA 94501

Maintenance & Logistics Command, Pacific
Government Island
Alameda, CA 94501-5100

11th Coast Guard District
Union Bank Bulding
400 Oceangate Blvd.
Long Beach, CA 90822-5399

13th Coast Guard District
Federal Building
915 Second Ave.
Seattle, WA 98174-1067

14th Coast Guard District
Prince Kalanianaole Federal Building
300 Ala Moana Blvd., Ninth Floor
Honolulu, HI 96850-4982

17th Coast Guard District
P.O. Box 3-5000
Juneau, AK 99802-1217

Regional Maintenance and Logistics Commands (RMLC) have nine (9) Support Centers located at:
 RMLC LANTAREA (Command Headquarters), Governors Island, NY; Boston, MA; Portsmouth, VA; Elizabeth City, NC; New Orleans, LA.
 RMLC PANCAREA (Command Headquarters), Alameda, CA; Kodiak, AK; Seattle, WA; Terminal Island, CA.

SHIPS/COAST GUARD

MORGANTHAU

HIGH-ENDURANCE CUTTERS

Hamilton Class

DISPLACEMENT: 3,050 tons full load.
LENGTH: 378 feet.
BEAM: 42.8 feet.
SPEED: 29 knots.
POWER PLANT: two diesel engines, 7,000 bhp, and two gas turbines, shp. Two controllable pitch propellers.
ARMAMENT: One Mk 75/76 Oto Malera, two 20mm, two triple torpedo tubes.
AIRCRAFT: One HH-52 or LAMPS I helicopter.
COMPLEMENT: 171.
BUILDER: Avondale Shipyards.

BRIEFING: The 12 ships in the Hamilton class, all commissioned in the late 1960s and early 1970s, are the most sophisticated high-endurance cutters. They are used for law enforcement, operational training, military-preparedness exercises, and search-and-rescue missions. Since the early 1980s, a number of the class have been utilized extensively in drug-interdiction and immigrant-interception exercises in the Caribbean. Because of increased national emphasis on drug interdiction, it can be anticipated that operations in support of that goal will continue at an increased rate. In 1977 the Gallatin and the Morganthau became the first Coast Guard ships to have women assigned as permanent members of the crew. Commencing in October 1985, the Hamilton and the Mellon inaugurated an extensive FRAM (fleet rehabilitation and modernization) program which included upgrading these ships' radar, fire-control system, weapons, and flight-deck facilities to make them more compatible operationally with Navy ships. Soon after FRAMs are completed, these cutters will be equipped with Harpoon missiles and Phalanx CIWSs.

MEDIUM ENDURANCE CUTTERS

Famous Class

DISPLACEMENT: 1,780 tons full load.
LENGTH: 270 feet.
BEAM: 38 feet.
SPEED: 19.5 knots.
POWER PLANT: two diesels, two shafts, 7,000 bhp .
ARMAMENT: one 3"/76mm gun; space reserved for Phalanx CIWS and Harpoon missiles..
AIRCRAFT: one HH-52, HH-65A, or LAMPS I helicopter.
COMPLEMENT: 98.
BUILDER: WMEC 901-904, Tacoma Boatbuilding Co.; 905-913, R.E. Derecktor of Rhode Island Inc., Middletown, RI.

BRIEFING: There are eight Famous class cutter currently in commission; the first one, Bear, entered service in 1983. Five others are under construction and will be in service by the end of 1989. Famous class cutters are primarily assigned law-enforcement, defense-operations, and search-and-rescue missions. Their law-enforcement missions have included drug and illegal-immigrant operations and fisheries enforcement activities. These ships are the most modern and advanced medium endurance cutters. They are equipped with a sophisticated command, display, and control (COMDAC) computerized ship-control system which provides for maximum operational effectiveness with reduced crews. They also have a modern weapons and sensor suite and can support and hangar one HH-52A, HH-65A, or LAMPS I helicopter. These ships also can land LAMPS III helicopters. Famous class cutters are replacing aging WHECs and WMECs, all of which are over 40 years old.

HARRIET LANE

Reliance Class

DISPLACEMENT: 907-1,007 tons full load.
LENGTH: 210.5 feet.
BEAM: 34 feet.
SPEED: 18 knots.
POWER PLANT: two diesels, two shafts, 5,000 bhp .
ARMAMENT: one 3"/76.50 cal., two .50 cal. machine guns.
AIRCRAFT: one HH-52 helicopter or one HH-65A.
COMPLEMENT: 70.
BUILDERS: WMEC 615-17, Todd Shipyards; 618 Christy Corp.; 620-24, 626-27, 630, American Shipbuilding; 619, 625; 628-29, Coast Guard Yard, Baltimore.

BRIEFING: The 16 Reliance class cutters are primarily assigned law-enforcement and search-and-rescue missions. These ships originally were classified as patrol craft (WPC), but their classification was changed to medium endurance cutters (WMEC) in 1966. They can support one HH-52 or HH-65A helicopter, but no hangar is provided. One 1 October 1984 Active entered an extensive Major Maintenance Availability (MMA), which now is complete, and the remaining ships of the class will undergo MMA during the next several years. The purpose of the MMA is to correct machinery and equipment problems in order that the class may remain mission capable, supportable, and reliable for the second half of its service life.

POLAR STAR

ICEBREAKERS

Polar Class

DISPLACEMENT: 12,087 tons full load.
LENGTH: 399 feet.
BEAM: 86 feet.
SPEED: 18 knots.
POWER PLANT: three gas turbines, six diesels, three shafts, 60,000 shp.
RANGE: 28,000 miles.
ARMAMENT: two 50 cal. guns.
AIRCRAFT: two HH-52 or HH-65A helicopters.
COMPLEMENT: 163.
BUILDER: Lockheed Shipbuilding, Seattle.

Mackinaw Class

DISPLACEMENT: 5,252 tons full load.
LENGTH: 290 feet.
BEAM: 74 feet.
SPEED: 18.7 knots.
POWER PLANT: two diesels with electric drive, three shafts (one forward, two aft), 10,000 bhp.
AIRCRAFT: one helicopter.
COMPLEMENT: 127.
BUILDER: Toledo Shipbuilding.

BRIEFING: Aside from a small number of icebreaking tugs, four ships represent the nation's entire icebreaking capability. The two Polar Star-class ships are 11 and nine years old, and are the largest ships operated by the Coast Guard. Glacier, the only ship of its class, was 32 years old when decommissioned in 1987; Mackinaw, the only ship of its class, is 43 years old, and designed and configured for use only on the Great Lakes. Congress perceives a need for additional icebreakers but no firm plans for construction have been formalized. There also is some sentiment for having ships built by private firms and then leased by the Coast Guard. The Polar Star ships, capable of breaking ice six feet thick at a speed of three knots, have overcome a series of difficulties encountered in early voyages, including major problems with their controllable-pitch propellers.

PATROL BOATS

Island Class

DISPLACEMENT: 165 tons full load.
LENGTH: 110 feet.
BEAM: 21 feet.
SPEED: 26 plus knots.
POWER PLANT: two Paxman Valento diesel engines, 5,800 shp.
RANGE: 1,900 nautical miles.
ARMAMENT: one 20mm, two M-60 machine guns.
COMPLEMENT: 16.
BUILDER: Bollinger Machine Shop and Shipyard, Inc., New Orleans.

Cape Class

DISPLACEMENT: 106 tons full load.
LENGTH: 95.5 feet.
BEAM: 19 feet.
SPEED: 20 knots.
POWER PLANT: two Detroit diesels, 2,470 shp.
RANGE: 1,900 nautical miles.
ARMAMENT: two .50 cal. machine guns, one M-60 machine gun.
BUILDER: U.S. Coast Guard Yard.

Point Class

LENGTH: 82 feet, 10 inches.
BEAM: 17 feet, 7 inches.
SPEED: 20 knots.
POWER PLANT: two Cummings diesels.
RANGE: 1,580 nautical miles.
ARMAMENT: two .50 cal. machine guns.
COMPLEMENT: 10.
BUILDER: U.S. Coast Guard Yard, except WPB 82345-82349, built by J. Martinac Shipbuilding.

PORT JUDITH

BRIEFING: The primary missions of patrol boats are search and rescue, maritime law enforcement, and port security. The Cape Class WPBs were built between 1953-1959, and the Point class between 1960-1970. These cutters have seen service throughout the world. Several Point class WPBs conducted operations in Viet Nam, and some Cape class WPBs have been transferred to Ethiopia, Haiti, Thailand, and Saudi Arabia. Both classes of WPBs will continue in service through 1996. Sixteen Island class WPBs are providing additional resources to stem the flow of illegal drugs into the United States, and 21 more are on the way. In addition to maritime law enforcement, these cutters will be used for search-and-rescue and defense operations.

NEAH BAY

ICEBREAKING TUGS

Bay Class

DISPLACEMENT: 662 tons full load.
LENGTH: 140 feet.
BEAM: 37 feet, 6 inches.
SPEED: 14.7 knots.
POWER PLANT: diesel-electric, one shaft, 2,500 bhp.
DESIGNED ICEBREAKING CAPABILITY: 22 inches at 3 knots continuous.
RANGE: 1,500 at full speed, 4,000 at 12 knots, 7,000 at 7 knots.
ARMAMENT: two M-60 machine guns.
COMPLEMENT: 17
BUILDERS: WTGB's 101-106, Tacoma Boat Building; 107-109, Bay City Marine.

BRIEFING: These small, multi-mission cutters are especially configured for icebreaking on the Great Lakes, in coastal waters, and in rivers. They incorporate an advanced hull design and engineering plant, along with a hull air lubrication (bubbler) system, for effective icebreaking and winter flood relief operations. The Bay Class cutters embody the Coast Guard's minimally manned cutter concept for personnel economy. In addition to icebreaking, the Bay Class cutters are used for search and rescue, enforcement of laws and treaties, deployment of marine environmental protection equipment, port safety operations, and support for aids-to-navigation.

SEAGOING BUOY TENDERS

Balsam Class

DISPLACEMENT: 1,025 tons full load.
LENGTH: 180 feet.
BEAM: 37 feet.
SPEED: 13 knots.
POWER PLANT: diesel electric, one shaft, 1,000-1,200 bhp.
ARMAMENT: unarmed except for five ships, which have two 20mm guns.
COMPLEMENT: 53.
BUILDER: Various between 1942-45.

BRIEFING: The Coast Guard operates 28 ships of this class. All have been modernized once, and a SLEP program to extend their lives even further commenced in 1981. Despite their age, they have proven to be highly versatile, durable, reliable ships capable of performing a variety of missions at sea. Eleven of these ships have been configured for icebreaking. Also in service are several classes of coastal, inland, and river buoy tenders, most of which are 30 or more years old. All save one of the latter classes are under 500 tons displacement.

SALVIA

CONSTRUCTION TENDERS

BRIEFING: Performing a vital, if unsung, role for the Coast Guard are three classes of construction tenders, totaling 15 ships. Designed for the construction, repair, and maintenance of fixed aids to navigation, all operate in inland waters. One was built in the 1940s, 10 in the 1960s, and four in the mid-1970s. Their equipment includes piledrivers, cranes, and jetting equipment.

HAMMER

124 COAST GUARD

FAST ASSAULT PATROL BOAT

FAST ASSAULT PATROL BOATS

DISPLACEMENT: maximum, 21,270 pounds, including 3,500 pounds of military payload.
LENGTH: 43 feet, six inches.
BEAM: nine feet, six inches.
SPEED: 48 knots at normal displacement, 42 knots at maximum displacement.
POWER PLANT: two 355hp Caterpillar diesels.
RANGE: 400 statute miles at normal displacement, 370 at maximum displacement.
ARMAMENT: no fixed armament; all small arms.
COMPLEMENT: two crew and a 10-man special combat unit.
BUILDER: Tempest Marine, Fort Lauderdale, FL.

BRIEFING: Because it has not had in its inventory a surface craft capable of intercepting "fast boats" (anything faster than 35 knots), the Coast Guard has procured four high-speed power boats that will enable it to better cope with speedy craft being used by drug smugglers. The enormity of the problem faced by the Coast Guard in seeking to intercept "fast boats" was dramatically illustrated in FY 1983-84. During that period, 255 surface craft of the "fast boat" category were encountered by Coast Guard forces, but only 61 seizures were made because of lack of speed by Coast Guard ships and craft. Further, 36 of the seizures resulted from the "fast boat" suffering a casualty. The four new power boats, which are capable of speeds in excess of 35 knots, were delivered in 1987 and now are based in Florida.

SURFACE-EFFECT SHIPS

Sea Bird Class

DISPLACEMENT: 145 tons full load.
LENGTH: 110 feet.
BEAM: 29 feet.
SPEED: 30 knots.
POWER PLANT: two diesels, propulsion; two diesels, two double-inlet, centrifugal fans, lift; two shafts, 3,200 bhp (propulsion), 736 bhp (lift).
ARMAMENT: two .50-caliber machine guns.
COMPLEMENT: 18.
BUILDER: Bell Halter, New Orleans.

BRIEFING: These three craft and a large Navy surface-effect ship are the only vessels of this type in government service, other than the Marines' LCACs, which are not designed for open-water operations. They use a cushion of air trapped between the sidewalls of the ships to lift much of the hull clear of the water, making possible speeds in excess of 30 knots. Used principally for drug interdiction, search and rescue, and missions connected with aids to navigation, they

SEABIRD

operate principally in Caribbean waters out of Key West, FL. Although they have proven to be both versatile and effective, there are no plans for procurement of additional ones.

TRAINING CUTTER

BRIEFING: The Coast Guard's only training cutter, the sailing ship Eagle, is a former German training ship built by Blohm and Voss of Hamburg and launched in 1936. Accepted as reparation after World War II, it arrived at its homeport of New London, Conn., site of the Coast Guard Academy, in 1946. The 1,816-ton, three-masted ship, which recently was extensively overhauled, is 295 feet long, has a sail area of 21,351 feet, and, when the auxiliary diesel engine is used, a range of 5,450 miles at 7.5 knots. It is manned by a complement of 245. In September 1987, Eagle, began a unique cruise to the Caribbean and the Pacific that took it to 17 foreign ports, including four in Australia, before it returned to the Coast Guard Academy in New London in May 1988.

EAGLE

AIRCRAFT/COAST GUARD

Fixed-Wing	Number
HC-130 Hercules	31
HU-25A Guardian	41
VC-11A	1
VC-4A	1
E-2C Hawkeye (on loan from Navy)	3

Helicopter	Number
HH-3F Pelican	42
HH-52A Sea Guard	49
HH-65A Dolphin	65

Source: Public Affairs Division, Office of Boating, Public, and Consumer Affairs, U.S. Coast Guard

HERCULES

HC-130 Hercules

BRIEFING: This extended-range version of the C-130 is a turboprop search aircraft which can transport up to 75 passengers, 50,000 pounds of cargo, or large quantities of rescue-survival and oil-pollution-control equipment. Its range with maximum payload is almost 2,500 miles, and with maximum fuel and light payload it can be extended to more than 5,000 miles. The Coast Guard has replaced all B, E, with H models of the aircraft. Fleet requirements are 41, with 25 ready for operation at any given time. However, budgetary problems may preclude that level being attained for several years.

HU-25A Guardian

BRIEFING: This twin-engine turbofan jet, deliveries of which were completed in 1983, is one of the few aircraft flown by the military services that is built by a foreign company, Dassault-Breguet of France. It is 56.25 feet in length, 17.6 feet in height, and has a crew of five. Its ceiling at Mach .855 is 42,000 feet, and it flies at 350 knots at sea level and 380 knots at 20,000 feet. It has advanced navigation, communications, avionics, and pollution-control equipment, and can deliver pumps, rafts, and rescue gear. Some problems still were encountered with its engines and in logistic support for them; however, corrections have been made. Its performance during its first years of service otherwise has been excellent.

GUARDIAN

126 COAST GUARD

DOLPHIN

HH-65A Dolphin

BRIEFING: These short-range recovery aircraft finally were accepted by the Coast Guard late in 1984 after over two years of coping with a number of problems, including a major one caused by snow ingestion; an exhaust retrofit of the first 17 aircraft has corrected the problem. Meanwhile, they were introduced into full service in warmer operating areas. Manufactured by Aerospatiale of France, and intended as replacements for the HH-52A, they have sophisticated avionics and communications packages, including infrared sensors, to aid rescue operations in bad weather, darkness, or high seas The initial requirement is for 96 aircraft. Sixty-five are presently on board.

HH-3F Pelican

BRIEFING: The Pelican is a Coast Guard version of the helicopter that acquired the familiar title of the Jolly Green Giant from its exploits across a wide spectrum of operations. U.S. production of this twin-turbine, amphibious, medium-range Sikorsky-built aircraft ended years ago. These most efficient workhorses can carry eight rescued persons or bulky cargo, including vehicles, in their search-and-rescue role. To eventually replace them, in 1986 a Navy-administered contract was awarded to Sikorsky for 48 medium-range recovery helicopters (MRR), 32 of which will be for the Coast Guard. They will be designated HH-60J and will be a variant of the Sikorsky basic "Hawk" series. The first of these is scheduled for delivery in 1990, with final delivery by 1993.

SEA GUARD

HH-52A Sea Guard

BRIEFING: The first of these helicopters flew its first mission for the Coast Guard a quarter century ago. Since then, this sturdy Sikorsky-built search-and-rescue aircraft has performed yeoman service indeed. However, its capabilities have been exceeded by those of more modern aircraft, and HH-52As are slowly being replaced in the Coast Guard inventory by HH 65A Dolphins.

PELICAN

SEA POWER: *OCEANOGRAPHY*

Ocean, or what oceanographers call "the world ocean," covers 71 percent of the Earth's surface, making the Earth the only "water planet" in the solar system. The dominant feature of this enormous water mass is the Pacific Ocean, which covers 34 percent of the world—more than all the land masses of the world put together.

Approximately seven percent of the ocean is less than 600 feet deep. The other percentages of depth:

Percent	Depth in feet
14	600 to 6,000
16	6,000 to 12,000
58	12,000 to 18,000
4	over 18,000

OCEAN WATER PRESSURE

Depth (in feet)	Pressure (lbs./sq. in.)
Ocean surface	14.7
600	269
1,200	536
3,000	1,338
7,200	3,208
18,000	8,019
30,000	13,363
36,000	16,124

Some other ocean statistics:

• The average depth of the world ocean is 12,500 feet. The deepest area is 36,000 feet, in the Challenger Deep near Guam. If the world's highest mountain, Mount Everest, were put into Challenger Deep, about a mile of water would cover the mountain.

• About three-fifths of the Northern Hemisphere and four-fifths of the Southern Hemisphere are covered by water.

• About 70 percent of the Earth's population live within 200 miles of a coast and 80 percent of the world's capitals are located within 300 miles of a coast.

• Two dominant features of the watery world, the polar ice caps, contain about 6.5 million cubic miles of fresh water in the form of ice; 90 percent of that total is in the Antarctic, where icebergs containing 300 cubic miles of ice are calved annually.

If both the Greenland and Antarctic icecaps should suddenly melt, the world ocean would rise about 200 feet. New York City would be submerged, with only the tops of the tallest buildings sticking out above the water.

According to *Facts About the Ocean* (the Institute for Marine and Coastal Studies), an iceberg one cubic mile in size contains enough fresh water to supply the needs of a city the size of Los Angeles for 10 years.

• Water pressure in the sea increases 14.7 pounds per square inch for every 33 feet in depth. At 30,000 feet, the pressure is more than six tons per square inch. This could be compared to having pressed against each square inch of your body the weight of an elephant.

THE NAVY AND THE OCEANS

What began in 1830, 16 years after Robert Fulton built the first steam warship, as the Depot of Charts and Instruments, later became the U.S. Navy Hydrographic Office and in 1962, the Naval Oceanographic Office. Here, data are collected from an environment that begins at the sea floor and ends far above the oceans at the earthward edge of outer space. To understand this environment and to operate in it, the Navy studies such phenomena as the propagation of underwater sound, surf and near-shore wave activity (for planning amphibious landings), and the air and sea conditions that affect radar and sonar.

AREAS OF OCEANS AND PRINCIPAL SEAS

Area	Square Miles
Pacific Ocean	63,985,000
Atlantic Ocean	31,529,000
Indian Ocean	28,357,000
Arctic Ocean	5,541,000
Mediterranean Sea	1,145,000
South China Sea	895,000
Bering Sea	878,000
Caribbean Sea	750,000
Gulf of Mexico	700,000
Sea of Okhotsk	582,000
East China Sea	480,000
Yellow Sea	480,000
Hudson Bay	472,000
Sea of Japan	405,000
North Sea	221,000
Red Sea	178,000
Black Sea	168,500
Baltic Sea	158,000

Note: The Caspian Sea is normally classed as a lake rather than a sea, although its margins are claimed as territorial waters. Its area is 152,123 square miles.

Source: U.S. Department of State "Sovereignty of the Sea" Geographic Bulletin No. 3, revised October 1969

The Navy also accumulates information in many forms, and from numerous sources, on storms, wave heights, sea ice, cloud cover, fog, and other weather conditions to produce "optimum track ship routing" for the safe passage of Navy ships and "optimum path aircraft routing" for naval aircraft.

The Navy uses five major geophysical disciplines to collect and process information about the sea.

Hydrography measures the depth of the oceans and coastal areas for the production of charts that serve all warfare areas in terms of safety and accuracy of navigation. Ocean surveys also collect data on gravity and magnetic variations for the targeting of fleet ballistic missiles.

Oceanography is used for the collection of data on ocean chemistry, dynamics, geophysics, marine biology, temperature, salinity, and other physical characteristics of the oceans. The data are used to generate underwater acoustic predictions and for publication of atlases and other documentation of long-term ocean characteristics influencing submarine, anti-submarine, amphibious, surface, and mine warfare operations.

Meteorology investigates atmospheric conditions, collecting global data on winds, clouds, moisture, temperature, pressure systems, air masses, and upper air winds for producing weather forecasts.

Precise Time Operations keeps time by the operation of 22 atomic clocks which compare the resonant frequencies of cesium atoms, measuring time in increments of 1/25th millionth of a second and less.

Astronometry marks the movements of stars as the fundamental reference from which all precise time is established. Precise time and time-transfer services are essential to navigation and particularly to the targeting of long-range missiles and other weapons.

The U.S. Naval Observatory administers programs in precise time operations and astronometry for the production of navigation aids and the measurement of variations in the Earth's rotation.

The Navy's oceanography program provides precise information about the influences of the oceans on weapons design.

Very little can be done to modify natural physical forces, but much can be done to overcome or employ those natural forces, if their effects are known ahead of time. The study of those forces and their effects is one of the principal purposes of the naval oceanography program. The program also focuses on the development of deep-ocean technology for search, rescue, and salvage operations.

A global communications system processes the flow of environmental data into production centers and, by way of oceanography centers, processes the flow of oceanographic products out to fleet operators.

The Navy's oceanography program employs nearly 4,000 military and civilian personnel at production centers in Bay St. Louis, Miss., and Monterey, Calif., and at 70 oceanography centers around the world, at Navy shore stations, and aboard ships at sea. FY 1989 funding is nearly $368 million, with that sum including $1.2 million for shipbuilding. Funding at that level characterizes the Navy's determination to regain the leadership in oceanography.

Toward this end, the Navy has established the position of Oceanographer of the Navy, has increased the number of ships and the number of personnel involved in the at-sea programs and has begun a modernization of the fleet.

Two new deep ocean survey vessels will have entered service by 1989. A contract was awarded in FY 1988 for a multipurpose oceanographic vessel which, while Navy owned, will be bailed to the University of Washington for operation in support of many national programs.

Also, a two-year master's degree program in oceanography, sponsored by the Secretary of the Navy, can enroll about eight students a year. The program is administered jointly by Massachusetts Institute of Technology maritime academy and Woods Hole Oceanographic Institution in Woods Hole, MA.

During 1989 the Navy will award a contract for a new super computer (class VII) to be located in Bay St. Louis, Miss., which will support important ocean modeling development.

The MIT/Woods Hole facility probably is the best known of the nearly 300 sea-grant institutions preparing young people for careers in the ocean sciences. The National Sea Grant College Program was established 20 years ago to meet the growing challenges facing the nation's marine community in the same way that land-grant universities have helped America's agricultural community. The program is administered by the National Science Foundation.

AN AERIAL VIEW of the internationally famous Woods Hole Oceanographic Institution of the Massachusetts Institute of Technology, where a new two-year master's degree program in oceanography is being sponsored by the Secretary of the Navy.

The United States has 14 different federal government departments/agencies with oceanography responsibilities. In order, by size of their oceanography budgets, they are:

Department of Defense (DOD)—Navy and Army (Corps of Engineers).
Department of Commerce (DOC)—National Oceanic and Atmospheric Administration (NOAA).
Department of the Interior (DOI)—U.S. Geological Survey (USGS) and the Minerals Management Service (MMS).
National Science Foundation (NSF).
Department of Transportation (DOT)—U.S. Coast Guard (USCG).
National Aeronautics and Space Administration (NASA).
Department of State (State).
Department of Energy (DOE).
Environmental Protection Agency (EPA).
Smithsonian Institution (SI).
The Department of Agriculture (USDA).

STEADY RISE IN U.S. FISH CONSUMPTION

The fishing vessels that harvest the sea constitute another form of seapower in addition to that of warships and merchant ships. Although rarely numbered with the other fleets, this unglamorous fleet of more than 130,000 vessels brings in the fish Americans are eating in steadily increasing amounts.

According to the Department of Commerce, U.S. per capita consumption of commercially caught fish in 1987 was a record 15.4 pounds, up 0.7 pounds from the previous year and nearly a pound during the last two years.

In 1987, the latest year for which Department of Commerce figures are available, the leading fish landed was menhaden, a marine fish that is a relative of the herring. Of the total menhaden landed, 99% were reduced to meal, oil, and solubles; the rest were used for bait or canned for pet food. The other leading fish species were Alaska pollock (second in quantity, but very low in value), salmon (third in quantity and first in value), crabs (fourth in quantity and third in value), shrimp (fifth in quantity and second in value), lobster (sixth in quantity and fourth in value) and flounder (seventh in quantity and fifth in value).

The U.S. commercial fish catch in 1987 was an estimated 6.9 billion pounds worth $3.1 billion, up 0.9 billion pounds from 1986, and up $352 million in value. Thirteen years ago, the catch was 5 billion pounds, but worth only about $932 million.

More than half of the 1987 catch—3.9 billion pounds—was sold for human consumption. The rest was processed into meal, oil, and fish solubles or used as bait or as animal food.

The leading states in quantity of landings in 1987 were:

Louisiana	1.8 billion
Alaska	1.7 billion
Virginia	710 million
California	452 million
Mississippi	437 million

The United States imported a record $5.7 billion worth of edible fisheries products in 1987, compared with $4.8 billion the year before. U.S. exports of fishery products amounted to $1.6 billion, an increase of $288 million over 1986.

The Soviet Union, with a fishing fleet that includes some 4,300 vessels 100 gross tons or over, consistently has been ahead of the United States in catch, but not in exports. In 1983, the

Table O-1

LEADING FISHING NATIONS
1981-1986

(in millions of metric tons*)

1981

Country	Catch Size
Japan	10.66
U.S.S.R.	9.55
China	4.61
UNITED STATES	3.77
Chile	3.39
Peru	2.75
Norway	2.55
India	2.42
Republic of Korea	2.37
Indonesia	1.86

1982

Country	Catch Size
Japan	10.78
U.S.S.R.	9.96
China	4.93
UNITED STATES	3.99
Chile	3.67
Peru	3.48
Norway	2.50
India	2.34
Republic of Korea	2.28
Indonesia	2.00

1983

Country	Catch Size
Japan	11.25
U.S.S.R.	9.76
China	5.21
UNITED STATES	4.14
Chile	3.98
Norway	2.82
India	2.52
Republic of Korea	2.50
Thailand	2.25
Indonesia	2.11

1984

Country	Catch Size
Japan	12.00
U.S.S.R.	10.59
China	5.92
UNITED STATES	4.81
Chile	4.49
Peru	2.99
India	2.85
Republic of Korea	2.47
Norway	2.45
Thailand	2.25

1985

Country	Catch Size
Japan	11.44
U.S.S.R.	10.52
China	6.78
Chile	4.80
UNITED STATES	4.77
Peru	4.17
India	2.81
Republic of Korea	2.65
Thailand	2.12
Norway	2.11

1986

Country	Catch Size
Japan	11.97
U.S.S.R.	11.26
China	8.00
Peru	5.61
Chile	5.57
UNITED STATES	4.95
Republic of Korea	3.10
India	2.92
Indonesia	2.92
Thailand	2.12

*Weights shown are live weights. Figures do not include marine mammals or aquatic plants. Figures for the United States include the weight of clam, oyster, scallop, and other mollusk shells.

Source: U.S. Department of Commerce

most recent year for which figures are available, the United States ranked second among the leading nations in fishery commodity exports, while the Soviet Union ranked thirteenth.

MINING THE OCEAN'S RICHES

The riches of the ocean come in many forms. In the United States, for example, it is estimated that marine recreational anglers add about $13.3 billion annually to the U.S. economy through direct and indirect expenditures associated with fishing (boats, equipment, fuel, tackle, lodging, etc.). Commerce Department statistics show that an estimated 17 million marine recreational anglers caught about 632 million pounds of finfish on approximately 75.5 million fishing trips in 1987. For some species, such as bluefish and spotted sea trout, the recreational catch greatly exceeded the commercial catch. Other common recreational catches include winter flounder, spot, saltwater catfish, and Atlantic croaker. Excluding catches of industrial species (such as anchovies and menhaden) and freshwater fish, the marine recreational catch comprised an estimated 20 percent of the total U.S. finfish landings used for food in 1987.

Other people fish for oil. One-fifth of the world's proven oil and gas reserves are in offshore fields. In 1984, the sea floor yielded 28 percent of all the oil and approximately 20 percent of all the gas produced in the world. However, by 1987 the yield had been reduced to 26.4 percent of the world's oil and 17.1 percent of the gas.

Veritable fortunes are spent—and earned—by those companies involved in the high-risk ventures to extract "black gold" from the oceanic seabeds. Gasoline shortages in the United States brought both rising fuel prices and a determination to become less dependent on foreign oil. The conditions were ideal for seeking new offshore sources of oil and gas. Between 1975-1980, more than $100 billion was invested worldwide in the exploration and development of offshore oil and gas deposits.

Within the period from 1980-1982, the number of companies that manufacture drilling equipment jumped from 17 to more than 40. Within the same time frame, manufacturers of oil-well pumping units increased from four to an estimated 190 firms. A total of $6.5 billion in capital expansion was invested by publicly owned companies in this industry.

In 1980, there were 548 mobile rigs in existence; by 1984 the number had increased to 806. However, going into 1985, uncertainty over crude oil prices resulted in reduced offshore activity.

Falling oil prices in 1986 led most operators to cut expenses, including capital investment, equipment, staff, and operating expenses, from 35 to 50 percent. Volatile conditions surrounding oil shipping in the Persian Gulf during 1987 and 1988 resulted in increased interest in deep-water oil drilling and exploration in the Gulf of Mexico, and along the coasts of Brazil and Africa. The interest spurred little activity, however, because of another drop in oil prices. And abundant surplus equipment makes it unlikely that any renewed activity will result in many, if any, orders for new drilling equipment during 1989.

Also, the Department of the Interior has adopted a new five-year Outer Continental Shelf (OCS) Oil and Gas Leasing Program for 1987-1991. This will be the third such program and is designed to slow the pace and scope of the OCS program by lengthening the period between sales in most areas from two to three years and reducing the amount of acreage offered for lease.

As we look toward the future, the deep seabed mining of minerals (at depths of three to three and a half miles) could turn out to be equally lucrative—and would have significant political ramifications. Manganese nodules, found in profusion on the sea floor at various locations throughout the world, are a rich source of such metals as copper, nickel, cobalt, and manganese, all of which are essential for the production of steel, alloys, and other industrial products. The world's most valuable known supply of these fist-sized nodules lies deep in the international waters of the Pacific Ocean between Central America and Hawaii. (See map.)

According to *Deep Seabed Mining*, a special report to Congress, "Develop-

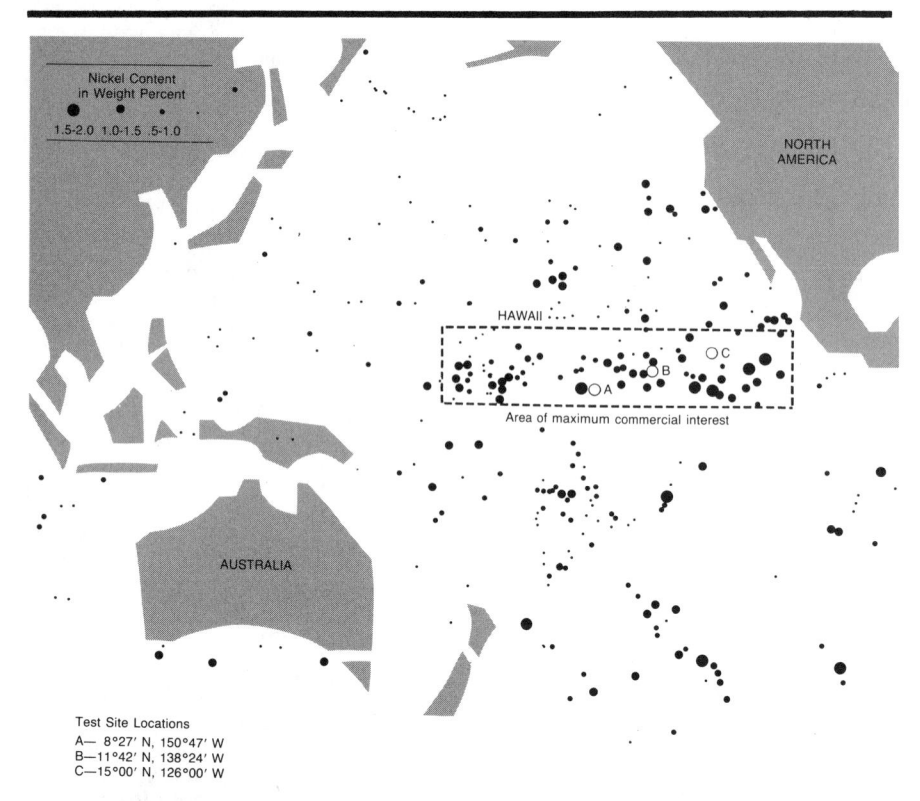

Area of manganese nodule maximum commercial interest and high nickel concentration in nodules with DOMES test site locations (Horn, Horn, and DeLach, 1972*).

*Geological data not subject to rapid changes.

Source: Deep Seabed Mining, U.S. Dept. of Commerce, NOAA—Office of Ocean Minerals and Energy, December 1981

Test Site Locations
A— 8°27′ N, 150°47′ W
B—11°42′ N, 138°24′ W
C—15°00′ N, 126°00′ W

ment of manganese nodule resources by the U.S. private sector would provide the United States with: (1) a stable supply of metals important to the economy at competitive prices; (2) a reduced annual balance of payments deficit; (3) increased investment in a basic industry; and (4) continued leadership in new ocean technologies."

Much also is at stake politically. The United States imports virtually all of its cobalt and manganese. The major sources of these minerals are Zaire and Zambia. By the end of the century, the Soviet Union and South Africa are expected to control virtually all of the world's manganese resources. Thus, access to oceanic mines closer to the United States would assure the United States a virtually uninterrupted supply of these valuable minerals, whatever the political situation in other countries.

Current international law provides no specific uniform regulations governing access to seabed mine sites. In the absence of clear-cut international regulations, Congress enacted the Deep Seabed Hard Minerals Resources Act to provide an interim legal framework. The National Oceanic and Atmospheric Administration (NOAA) has the authority to issue licenses to U.S. citizens for exploration, as well as permits for commercial recovery.

Authorities estimate that each deep seabed mining venture will require an investment of $1 billion to $1.5 billion.

The National Ocean Industries Association (NOIA) is the trade association and lobbying organization which represents ocean-oriented industries. According to NOIA, the range of companies involved in marine work runs the gamut, from the major oil companies and steel corporations to manufacturers of marine products and companies that provide housekeeping and catering services to offshore platforms.

The exploration and mining of oceanic resources require an innovative technology attuned to especially difficult environmental problems. One steel corporation, for instance, fabricated and installed the first all-weather drilling and production platform intended for use in the waters of Cook Inlet off the coast of Alaska. The platform had to be able to withstand the tremendous forces of ice floes and swift tidal currents—problems not encountered on shore.

Solutions for such problems are developed through application of advances in the field of oceanography, the scientific study of the ocean. This young, rapidly growing science is challenging many traditional views about the ocean.

In the summer of 1986, an expedition in the submersible *Alvin*, 1,800 miles east of Miami, discovered black and bluish-white geysers of mineral-rich steam shooting up from the ocean floor. The mineral-laden, 650-degree geysers affect the chemical composition of the ocean, but mining the minerals two miles deep would not be feasible at this time. NOAA scientists who made the find say the deposits found are a natural laboratory to study the process of ore formation in mineral deposits on land, which are similar.

Oceanography is an expensive science, heavily dependent upon the availability of ships and complex observing systems. But if the cost is high, so is the likelihood of important results. The broad applications of the oceanographic sciences are particularly important to the fields of national defense and weather forecasting, but also lead to a better understanding of major oceanic phenomena, improvements in fisheries, the development of aquaculture, and the study and fighting of pollution.

Most academic programs in oceanography are divided into five major areas: biological oceanography, ocean engineering, chemical oceanography, geological oceanography, and physical oceanography. Depending on the institution involved, there may be a sixth area emphasizing the social sciences—the economic and political aspects of problems associated with the use of the sea.

According to the Marine Technology Society, "More than 40% of the people in ocean careers work for the federal government . . . where the bulk of the money for ocean research has come from in the past." Job holders in oceanography include marine microbiologists; phycologists (specialists in algae); coastal, electrical, mechanical, and fisheries engineers; cartographers; meteorologists; and maritime lawyers.

For a complete listing of companies involved in commercial marine endeavors, contact the National Ocean Industries Association, 1050 17th St. N.W., Suite 700, Washington, D.C. 20036, and ask for the NOIA membership directory. (There is a nominal charge for the directory.)

More than 300 colleges, universities, specialized schools, and other institutions offer programs in oceanic and marine studies. Some provide career-training programs, others offer certificates, but most of them grant degrees. Information about the broad spectrum of academic programs available can be obtained from the Marine Technology Society, 2000 Florida Ave., N.W., Suite 500, Washington, D.C. 20009.

Among the international organiza-

Table O-2

SIZE AND AGE OF UNIVERSITY OCEANOGRAPHIC RESEARCH FLEET (SURFACE VESSELS)

Length (in feet)	Name	Operator	"Full Utilization" days at sea per year[1]	Year Built	Desired Retirement[4]
245	MELVILLE[2]	University of California (Scripps Institute)	260	1970	2005
245	KNORR[2]	Woods Hole Oceanographic Institute	260	1969	2004
213	MOANA WAVE[2]	University of Hawaii	260	1973	2003
210	ATLANTIS II[3]	Woods Hole Oceanographic Institute	260	1963	1993
209	CONRAD[2]	Columbia University (Lamont-Doherty)	260	1962	1992
209	T.G. THOMPSON[2]	University of Washington	260	1965	1995
209	T. WASHINGTON[2]	University of California (Scripps Institute)	260	1965	1995
177	ENDEAVOR[3]	University of Rhode Island	240	1976	2006
177	OCEANUS[3]	Woods Hole Oceanographic Institute	240	1975	2005
177	WECOMA[3]	Oregon State University	240	1975	2005
174	GYRE[2]	Texas A&M University	240	1973	2003
170	COLUMBUS ISELIN[3]	University of Miami	240	1972	2002
170	NEW HORIZON	University of California (Scripps Institute)	240	1978	2008
165	FRED H. MOORE	University of Texas	220	1967	1997
135	POINT SUR[3]	California State University (Moss Landing)	220	1981	2011
135	CAPE HATTERAS[3]	Duke University	220	1981	2011
133	ALPHA HELIX[3]	University of Alaska	220	1965	1995
125	R.G. SPROUL	University of California (Scripps Institute)	220	1981	2011
120	RIDGELY WARFIELD[2]	Johns Hopkins University (Chesapeake Bay Institute)	220	1967	2005
80	LAURENTIAN	University of Michigan	200	1974	2004
72	BLUE FIN	University of Georgia (Skidaway Institute)	200	1972	2002
68	CALANUS[2]	University of Miami	200	1970	2000
64	C.A. BARNES[3]	University of Washington	200	1966	1996

[1] As defined by National Science Foundation in 1979.
[2] Ships owned by the U.S. Navy.
[3] Ships owned or constructed by the National Science Foundation.
[4] Based on a 30-year lifetime.

tions dedicated to the study of oceanography are the International Council for the Exploration of the Sea (Copenhagen), the International Hydrographic Bureau (Monaco), the Institute of Oceanology of the Academy of Science and the State Oceanographic Institute (Moscow), the German Hydrographic Institute (Hamburg), the Institut Oceanographique (Paris), the Ocean Research Institute of the University of Tokyo, and the Andhra University at Waltair (India).

Many nations cooperated in the International Decade of the Ocean Exploration (DOE) which began in 1970. The efforts and resources of 52 countries were joined in a massive collaborative program for a full decade in a drive to discover more of the ocean's secrets.

The immense project produced, among other results, a map showing the distribution and composition of manganese nodules, potential sources of copper, nickel, and cobalt; studies revealing that dredging poses the greatest threat to valuable sea-grass resources by directly destroying substrates, the bases on which the grasses grow; a rich lode of basic data which should enhance forecasters' ability to predict large-scale weather or climate changes; and major studies on the effect of pollution on the ocean.

• Geosynchronous satellites provide information about small-scale destructive storms, such as thunderstorms and squall lines. The same satellites provide

Two of NOAA's fleet of oceanographic research ships are the Discoverer (R-102) (top), and the Whiting (S-129). Discoverer, commissioned in 1967, conducts research worldwide. Whiting, commissioned in 1963, conducts hydrographical surveys in connection with nautical charting.

information on a continuing basis about the temperature and mass fields of life-threatening weather phenomena and about the rapidly changing nature of local, regional, and global weather conditions. The ability to forecast potential destructive weather events is greatly enhanced by these satellites.
• Next Generation Weather (NEXRAD), a service planned to be in operation by about 1990, will track and analyze severe storms through the use of information not obtainable by present radars.

Today's seafarers have reliable sources of marine information. Marine Reporting (MAREP), in service for many years, has been expanded. The service relies not only on NOAA weather information, but on continuing reports from people in the marine environment. An increase in the number of recreational sail and fishing boats that need such information and the number of such boats that now have sophisticated radio capability, has brought greater cooperation and more accurate information.

Perhaps the most important development has been new satellite units that can be placed on ships at sea. The International Maritime Satellite Organization (INMARSAT), a private organization of more than 40 countries—including the United States, Canada, and Japan—collects and disseminates both weather and general information.

FORECASTING THE WEATHER

The world's weather, and how it is created, are major concerns of oceanographic scientists because, as a National Science Foundation report says, "The . . . oceans and atmosphere are so closely linked that predicting climate changes requires in-depth knowledge about the dynamic processes affecting the mixing and circulation of heat and other ocean properties."

According to the National Advisory Committee on Oceans and Atmosphere, the federal government spends about $1 billion per year (distributed among several agencies) for weather forecasting, observation, research, and other services.

That figure does not seem exorbitant when balanced against the costs resultant from, and havoc created by, adverse weather conditions. The severe winter cold of 1976-77, for instance, resulted in direct losses to the nation of approximately $26.9 billion. The 1980 heat wave cost the economy between $15 billion and $20 billion. Although no dollar assessment is yet available, the heat wave and drought of 1988 was one of the worst on record and had been compared with that of 1934. Costs are considered certain to surpass those for 1980.

The National Weather Service,

NOAA weather reports help guide fully-laden fishing vessels like this one safely to port with their valuables.

founded in 1870 because of concern over storm losses on the Great Lakes and along the sea coasts, comes under the jurisdiction of the National Oceanic and Atmospheric Administration (NOAA). The cost of *not* having accurate forecasts available to ships was already well recognized when the service was created. In 1868, for example, more than 1,000 ships were sunk or damaged and 321 lives lost on the Great Lakes. The next year nearly 2,000 ships suffered the same fate. Accurate weather prediction and quick dissemination of storm warnings might have prevented some of those losses.

The National Weather Service has come a long way since those days. Communications and technology have greatly improved since the times when "weather kiosks" were set up in some 50 cities to disseminate weather information.

Now, specialized weather services are provided by several federal agencies. The Department of Agriculture provides special forecasts and warnings for farmers, for example. The U.S. Coast Guard marine information broadcasts forecast warnings affecting the operation of oil rigs off the coast of Nova Scotia and fishing off the coast of Alaska. Public television stations carry a daily 15-minute National Weather Service program.

The technology of forecasting also has greatly improved since the days when kites were used to carry weather instruments aloft.

Doppler radars today allow meteorologists to detect the beginning, growth, and intensity of tornadoes whose movements can thus be better predicted.

SEA POWER: *RESERVES*

The steady increase in the capabilities of regular forces and the improvement in their readiness continue to be matched by similar improvements in the nation's sea-service reserve forces. However, whereas the responsibilities of reserve forces continue to increase, the steady rise in their numbers now has leveled off as the result of pressures to reduce defense spending and in turn the size of national budget deficits. At the same time, the utilization of reserve forces in the national drug-interdiction effort and to sweep mines and assist in escorting tankers in the Persian Gulf are indicative of an ever greater reliance upon reserves to augment regular forces in such national endeavors.

The Naval Reserve ended FY 1988 with an authorized end-strength of 130,609 Selected Reservists and 21,991 full-time support personnel. The surge which saw the Naval Reserve Force grow by more than 50 percent in seven years, from a force of 87,000 Selected Reservists to its present strength, has, for now, leveled off and efforts are being directed to refining and improving the quality of manpower resources. In all, Selected Reservists plus full-time support personnel total 152,600 - 20 percent of the Navy's M-Day Force; thus, one of every five sailors and officers on M-Day will be a Reservist.

The basic mission of the Naval Reserve is to train Selected Reservists to be ready to go to war. Numerous training initiatives to improve surface readiness training, better utilize full-time support personnel, reduce span of control problems, and alleviate administrative burdens are being implemented with positive overall results, including more realistic and improved training opportunities.

Currently there are 46 ships in the

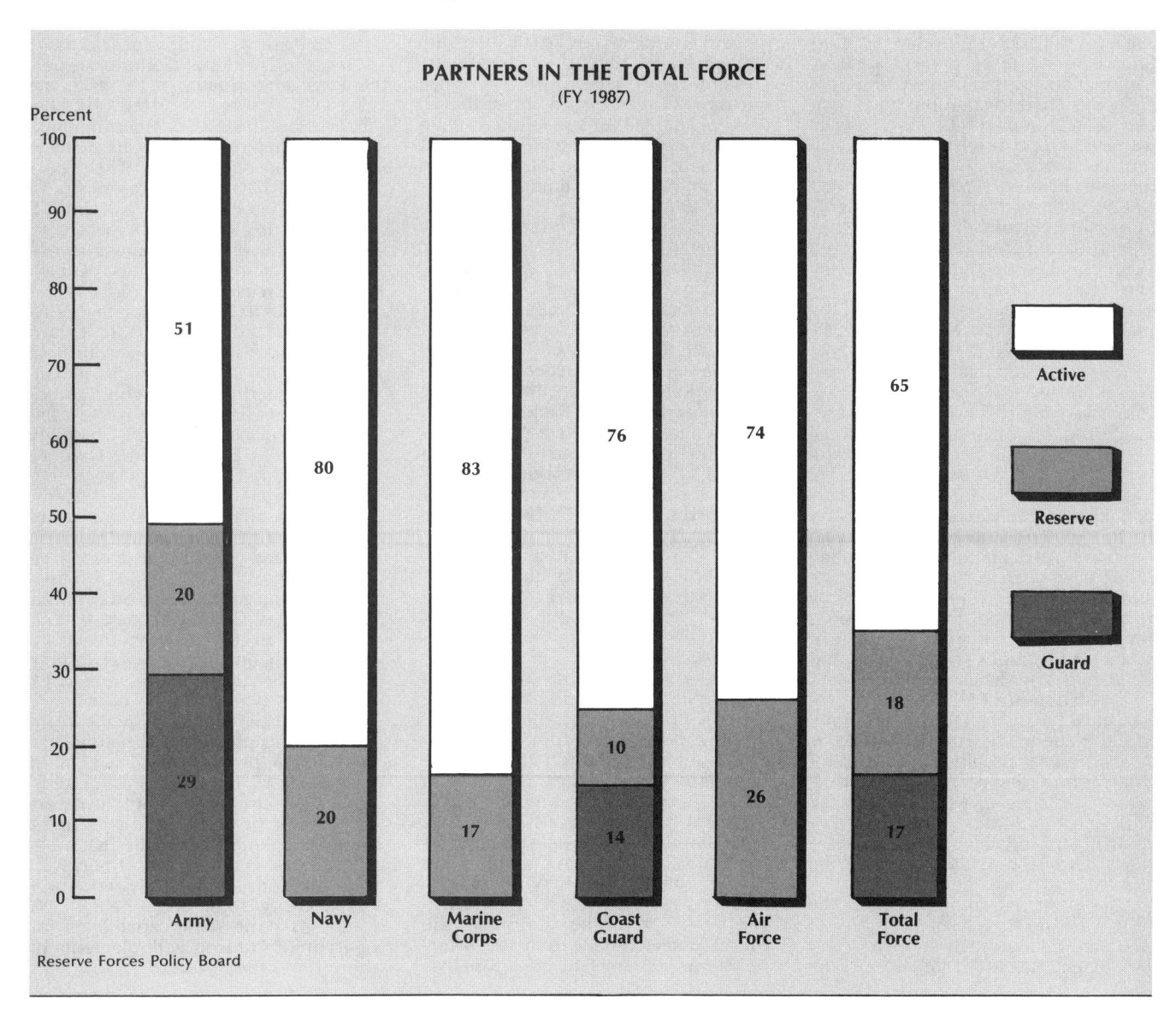

PARTNERS IN THE TOTAL FORCE
(FY 1987)

Branch	Active	Reserve	Guard
Army	51	20	29
Navy	80	20	—
Marine Corps	83	17	—
Coast Guard	76	10	14
Air Force	74	—	26
Total Force	65	18	17

Reserve Forces Policy Board

Naval Reserve Force (NRF) including 22 modern anti-submarine frigates, two amphibious landing ships (LSTs), and 18 ocean minesweepers (MSOs). By 1992, plans call for three more amphibious ships—an LSD, an LPD and another LST; four more frigates; and eight new mine countermeasures ships to replace the aging MSOs.

In the Naval Air Reserve, the addition of more fleet type aircraft has further boosted the Naval Reserve capability. VFA 305, based in Point Mugu, CA, completed its transition to the F/A-18 Hornet; VA-304 at Alameda, CA, began the transition to the A-6E and VP-62 at NAS Jacksonville, FL, is completing transition to the newest P-3C Update III aircraft.

A second Reserve airborne mine countermeasures (HM) squadron, flying the RH-53D helicopter, will be established at Naval Air Station, Alameda, CA in January 1989.

A new helicopter, unique to the Naval Reserve, the Sikorsky HH-60H, is scheduled for initial delivery in July 1989 to Helicopter Combat Support Special Squadron 5 (HCS-5) at Naval Air Station, Point Mugu. This aircraft is specially designed to combine both combat search and rescue and special warfare support missions and will replace two older helicopters in the Reserve inventory, the HH-1K and HH-3A, with substantial improvements in mission performance.

The Naval Reserve medical program continues to grow, most visibly in the Fleet Hospital program. Fourteen of the planned 23 Fleet Hospitals will be manned entirely by Naval Reservists.

1988 was a year that clearly demonstrated the operational readiness of the Naval Reserve Force. Five ocean minesweepers and two Naval Reserve Force frigates were part of the force committed to the Persian Gulf. Manning of these assets was completed in part from active component members and volunteer Selected Reservists. Navy liaison officers, drawn from Reserve Navy Control of Shipping Organization units, have been in the Gulf since the summer of 1987, when the the Navy first was assigned to escort duties there. Reservists in the Special Boat Units also brought specific skills and abilities to the Persian Gulf.

Operating out of 195 training centers in 46 states, the District of Columbia, and Puerto Rico, the Marine Corps Ready Reserve provides 25 percent of the wartime Fleet Marine Force structure. Consisting of two components, the Selected Marine Corps Reserve (SMCR) and Individual Ready Reserve (IRR), it represents 33 percent of the trained manpower pool.

The principal components of the SMCR are the 4th Marine Division (4th MarDiv), 4th Marine Aircraft Wing (4th MAW), and the 4th Force Service Support Group (4th FSSG). The 4th MarDiv is the largest in the Marine Corps and is heavily reinforced to enhance its capability to augment and reinforce the Active component. In addition to its regular complement, the division includes an additional tank battalion, two force reconnaissance companies, two air-naval gunfire liaison companies, two civil affairs groups, and a communications battalion. The 4th MAW, with 18 deployable squadrons, and the 4th FSSG, with additional beach and port and force engineer companies, represent substantial combat and combat service support capabilities. With projected growth to 44,000 by FY 1991 from the current 43,600, the SMCR will continue to represent a sizable portion of the total Marine Corps combat strength.

The IRR is the primary source of trained individuals for active and Reserve units in the event of mobilization. With the increase in the military service obligation of new Marines from six to eight years, the IRR is expected to grow to approximately 74,000 men and women by FY 1991, a 50 percent increase from FY 1986. During FY 1988, one-day IRR recall screening at the 52 mobilization stations resulted in over 78 percent of scheduled IRR personnel processed. This will be followed in FY 1989 with refresher training for volunteering IRR members.

The 4th MAW is undergoing substantial modernization as we approach the 1990s. Activated in FY 1987, the Marine Corps Reserve's aggressor squadron in Yuma, AZ, continues to enhance readiness of the total force. Flying Israeli F-21A Kfir aircraft, VMFT-401 pilots provide valuable instruction to both active and Reserve aviators through simulation of aerial combat tactics employed by potential adversaries. A-4 squadrons continue to be upgraded with the A-4M aircraft, while the transition from F-4S Phantoms to F/A-18 Hornets is programmed to begin in FY 1989. A major milestone was achieved in late FY 1988 with the activation of two new squadrons: VMGR-452, a KC-130T aerial refueling squadron located at Stewart Airport, NY, and HMA-775, an AH-1J attack helicopter squadron at Camp Pendleton, CA.

Modernization of the 4th MarDiv has continued at a rapid pace with the receipt of the M16A2 rifle, 9mm pistol, Squad Automatic Weapon (SAW), Logistics Vehicle Systems (LVS), Multiple Integrated Laser Engagement System (MILES), and the High Mobility Multi-Wheeled Vehicle (HMMWV). Other major items currently being fielded include the Rough Terrain Cargo Handler (RTCH), satellite and HF/VHF communications radios, M198 155mm howitzer, M60E3 machine gun, and the MK-19 40mm Grenade Launcher. Structural enhancements include the activation of a 110-vehicle Light Armored Vehicle (LAV) battalion, and the first of two Tube-Launched, Optically Tracked, Wire-guided (TOW) missile platoons.

The Marine Corps Reserve continued to emphasize integrated training in FY 1988. Exercises and other training involving active-Reserve integration provide a highly trained Reserve manpower pool from which to draw units/individual Marines in the event of mobilization. Approximately 20,000 members of the SMCR had the opportunity to participate in over 20 major exercises in nine foreign countries and the continental United States. Reserve-sponsored exercises were instrumental in providing combined arms, cold-weather, and active force standards training, thus giving reservists the same opportunities as their active duty counterparts to hone skills in command and control, fire-support coordination, amphibious planning, and fire and maneuver.

The Coast Guard Selected Reserve consists of 265 Reserve units organized into 53 Reserve Groups located in 41 states, the District of Columbia, Puerto Rico, and Guam. In FY 1988, the Coast Guard was authorized 14,000 Reservists, but the level of recurring funding provided supported an average strength of only 11,500. The Coast Guard will have 12,000 Reservists on board at the end of the year, and FY 1989 recurring funds are expected to support that level. The most severe problem facing the Coast Guard Reserve Forces Program remains the reduction of its mobilization manpower shortfall. Current Coast Guard Reserve force levels will meet only 44 percent of the additional military manpower needed to perform high priority wartime tasking. This adversely impacts on the Coast Guard's capability to implement U.S. Maritime Defense Zones, secure U.S. strategic ports, and protect water transportation systems and places at risk DOD's strategy to safely and efficiently outload wartime supplies and personnel from U.S. domestic ports. With a goal of reducing its mobilization manpower shortfall, the Coast Guard has embarked on a 10-year plan calling for systematic annual growth, until the Selected Reserve force reaches 26,125 by the end of FY 1998. This will enable the Coast Guard to fulfill 95 percent of its highest priority mobilization requirements. During FY 1988, nearly 3,200 Coast Guard Reservists participated in 32 joint-service exercises throughout the nation and overseas. Participation in these complex exercises tests the readiness of the Coast Guard to perform its wartime missions, particularly its critical port-security role, and enables CG forces to hone their capabilities for operating in unison with elements of the other armed forces.

Defense and Maritime Leaders

Including a Photo Gallery of Flag Officers

Richard B. Cheney

Secretaries of Defense (1947-Present)

James V. Forrestal	September 17, 1947	March 27, 1949
Louis A. Johnson	March 28, 1949	September 19, 1950
George C. Marshall	September 21, 1950	September 12, 1951
Robert A. Lovett	September 17, 1951	January 20, 1953
Charles E. Wilson	January 28, 1953	October 8, 1957
Neil H. McElroy	October 9, 1957	December 1, 1959
Thomas S. Gates Jr.	December 2, 1959	January 20, 1961
Robert S. McNamara	January 21, 1961	February 29, 1968
Clark M. Clifford	March 1, 1968	January 20, 1969
Melvin R. Laird	January 22, 1969	January 29, 1973
Elliot L. Richardson	January 30, 1973	May 24, 1973
James R. Schlesinger	July 2, 1973	November 19, 1975
Donald H. Rumsfeld	November 20, 1975	January 20, 1977
Harold Brown	January 21, 1977	January 20, 1981
Caspar W. Weinberger	January 21, 1981	November 23, 1987
Frank C. Carlucci	November 24, 1987	January 20, 1989

Samuel K. Skinner
Secretary of Transportation

Secretaries of Transportation (1967-Present)

Alan S. Boyd	January 23, 1967	January 20, 1969
John A. Volpe	January 22, 1969	February 1, 1973
Claude S. Brinegar	February 2, 1973	February 1, 1975
William T. Coleman, Jr.	March 7, 1975	January 20, 1977
Brock Adams	January 23, 1977	July 22, 1979
Neil E. Goldschmidt	July 27, 1979	January 20, 1981
Drew Lewis	January 23, 1981	February 1, 1983
Elizabeth Dole	February 7, 1983	September 30, 1987
James H. Burnley, IV	December 3, 1987	January 20, 1989

138 DEFENSE AND MARITIME LEADERS

JOINT CHIEFS OF STAFF

Admiral William J. Crowe, Jr.
Chairman
Joint Chiefs of Staff

Admiral Carlisle A.H. Trost
Chief of Naval Operations

General Larry D. Welch
Chief of Staff
of the Air Force

General Alfred M. Gray, Jr.
Commandant
of the Marine Corps

General Carl E. Vuono
Chief of Staff
of the Army

Chairmen of the Joint Chiefs of Staff (1949-Present)

	From	To
General of the Army Omar N. Bradley, USA	August 16, 1949	August 14, 1953
Admiral Arthur W. Radford, USN	August 15, 1953	August 14, 1957
General Nathan F. Twining, USAF	August 15, 1957	September 30, 1960
General Lyman Lemnitzer, USA	October 1, 1960	September 30, 1962
General Maxwell D. Taylor, USA	October 1, 1962	July 3, 1964
General Earle G. Wheeler, USA	July 3, 1964	July 2, 1970
Admiral Thomas H. Moorer, USN	July 3, 1970	June 30, 1974
General George S. Brown, USAF	July 1, 1974	June 20, 1978
General David C. Jones, USAF	June 21, 1978	June 18, 1982
General John W. Vessey Jr., USA	June 18, 1982	September 30, 1985
Admiral William J. Crowe Jr., USN	October 1, 1985	

Nominations of individuals for other senior positions in the Departments of Defense and Transportation, and for those in the Navy Department and the Maritime Administration, had not been made by President-elect George Bush by the time the Almanac of Seapower was being printed.

NAVY

LINE OFFICERS

William J. Crowe, Jr.
Chairman
Joint Chiefs of Staff

Carlisle A.H. Trost
Chief of Naval Operations

James B. Busey
CINC, Allied Forces
Southern Europe/CINC
U.S. Naval Forces, Europe

Frank B. Kelso, II
CINC, U.S. Atlantic Command/
Supreme Allied Command,
Atlantic

Huntington Hardisty
Commander in Chief
U.S. Pacific Command

Powell F. Carter, Jr.
Commander in Chief
U.S. Atlantic Fleet

David E. Jeremiah
Commander in Chief
U.S. Pacific Fleet

VICE ADMIRALS

Leon A. Edney
Vice Chief
of Naval Operations

James R. Hogg
U.S. Representative
to NATO

Bruce DeMars
Director
Naval Nuclear Propulsion

Edward H. Martin
Deputy Commander in Chief
U.S. Naval Forces, Europe

Robert F. Dunn
Assistant Chief
of Naval Operations
Air Warfare

Paul F. McCarthy, Jr.
Director, Research and
Development Requirements,
Test, and Evaluation

Joseph B. Wilkinson, Jr.
Commander
Naval Air Systems Command

Daniel L. Cooper
Assistant Chief
of Naval Operations
Submarine Warfare

139

140 FLAG PHOTOS—NAVY

VICE ADMIRALS

Jonathan T. Howe
Assistant to the Chairman
Joint Chiefs of Staff

Charles R. Larson
Deputy Chief
of Naval Operations
Plans, Policy, & Operations

Diego E. Hernandez
Deputy Commander
U.S. Space Command

Paul D. Miller
Deputy Chief of
Naval Operations
Naval Warfare

Richard M. Dunleavy
Commander, Naval Air Force
U.S. Atlantic Fleet

Jerry O. Tuttle
Director, J-6
Joint Chiefs of Staff

John T. Parker, Jr.
Director
Defense Nuclear Agency

John H. Fetterman, Jr.
Commander
Naval Air Force
U.S. Pacific Fleet

John A. Baldwin, Jr.
Director, J-5
Joint Chiefs of Staff

Albert J. Herberger
Deputy Commander in Chief
and Chief of Staff
U.S. Transportation Command

William D. Smith
Deputy Chief
of Naval Operations
Navy Program Planning

Joseph S. Donnell, III
Commander
Naval Surface Force
U.S. Atlantic Fleet

John W. Nyquist
Assistant Chief
of Naval Operations
Surface Warfare

Stanley R. Arthur
Deputy Chief
of Naval Operations
Logistics

James D. Williams
Commander
Sixth Fleet
U.S. Atlantic Fleet

Jerome L. Johnson
Commander
Second Fleet
U.S. Atlantic Fleet

VICE ADMIRALS

Roger F. Bacon
Commander
Submarine Force
Atlantic Fleet

Jeremy M. Boorda
Chief of Naval Personnel

Peter M. Hekman, Jr.
Commander
Naval Sea Systems Command

Robert K.U. Kihune
Commander
Naval Surface Force
U.S. Pacific Fleet

John S. Disher
Chief of Naval Education
and Training

James F. Dorsey, Jr.
Commander
Third Fleet
U.S. Pacific Fleet

Henry H. Mauz, Jr.
Commander
Seventh Fleet
U.S. Pacific Fleet

Ronald M. Eytchison
Vice Director
Joint Strategic
Target Planning Staff

REAR ADMIRALS (Upper Half)

Paul D. Butcher
Commander
Military Sealift Command

David G. Ramsey
Chief of Staff
Supreme Allied Commander
Atlantic

Lawrence Layman
Director
Space, Command, & Control
OPNAV

Robert C. Austin
Superintendent
Naval Postgraduate School
Monterey, CA

John F. Addams
Commandant
National War College

Ronald J. Kurth
President
Naval War College

142 FLAG PHOTOS—NAVY

REAR ADMIRALS (Upper Half)

Edwin R. Kohn, Jr.
Deputy & Chief of Staff
Commander in Chief
U.S. Pacific Fleet

Ronald F. Marryott
Deputy Director
Defense Intelligence Agency

Ming E. Chang
Special Assistant
for Inspection Support
OPNAV

Daniel J. Wolkensdorfer
Commander
Operational Test
and Evaluation Force

Richard C. Ustick
Chief of Staff
Commander in Chief
U.S. Southern Command

Dennis M. Brooks
Dir., Warfare Systems
Architecture & Engineering
SPAWARSYSCOM

William M. Fogarty
Director
Plans, Policy, & Operations
U.S. Central Command

James M.G. Seely
Deputy Comptroller
of the Navy, NAVCOMPT

Harry K. Fiske
Vice Director, Strategic
Mobility & Resources
J-4, Joint Chiefs of Staff

Hugh L. Webster
Dep. Dir., Research &
Development Requirements,
Test & Evaluation

John R. Wilson, Jr.
Chief of Naval Research
Office of the Secretary
of the Navy

Dean R. Sackett, Jr.
Commander
U.S. Naval Forces
Japan

Jerry C. Breast
Director for Operations, J-3
U.S. Space Command

William T. Pendley
Director
Plans and Policy
U.S. Pacific Command

Robert J. Kelly
Vice Director, J-3
Joint Chiefs of Staff

John F. Shaw
Deputy Chief of Staff
Plans & Policy, Supreme
Allied Commander, Atlantic

REAR ADMIRALS (Upper Half)

Raymond P. Ilg
Deputy Assistant
Chief of Naval Operations
Air Warfare

James G. Reynolds
Commmander
Submarine Force
U.S. Pacific Fleet

Guy H. Curtis, III
Assistant Deputy
Chief of Naval Operations
Logistics

Theodore E. Lewin
President
Board of Inspection
and Survey

Thomas R.M. Emery
Vice Director
Defense Communications
Agency

Leonard G. Perry
Ordered as
Deputy Commander
Iberian Atlantic Area

D. Bruce Cargill
Deputy Director
Space, Command, & Control
OPNAV

David F. Chandler
Director
Inter-American
Defense College

Robert H. Ailes
Deputy Commander
Weapons and Combat Systems
Naval Sea Systems Command

Thomas R. Fox
Deputy Director
International Negotiations
J-5, Joint Chiefs of Staff

Jeremy D. Taylor
Director, Aviation
Plans & Requirements
Division, OPNAV

Anthony A. Less
Commander, Joint Task
Force, Middle East/
Commander, MIDEASTFOR

Richard C. Gentz
Vice Commander
Naval Air Systems Command

Charles R. McGrail, Jr.
Assistant Deputy
Chief of Naval Operations
Naval Warfare

James D. Cossey
Chief
Naval Technical Training

Richard F. Pittenger
Oceanographer of the Navy

144 FLAG PHOTOS—NAVY

REAR ADMIRALS (Upper Half)

Stephen F. Loftus
Dir., Budget & Reports
NAVCOMPT/Dir., Fiscal
Management Div., OPNAV

Salvatore F. Gallo
Commander
Fleet Air, Mediterranean

Grant A. Sharp
Deputy Assistant
Chief of Naval Operations
Surface Warfare

Michael C. Colley
Deputy Assistant
Chief of Naval Operations
Undersea Warfare

Richard H. Truly
Associate Administrator
for Space Flight, Office
of Space Flight, NASA

Raynor A.K. Taylor
Director, J-3
U.S. Eurpean Command

Stanley E. Bump
Deputy Commander
Iberian Atlantic Area

Roger L. Rich, Jr.
Commander
U.S. Facility
Subic Bay, Philippines

Robert L. Toney
Director, J-4
U.S. Pacific Command

Francis R. Donovan
Assistant Deputy
Chief of Naval Operations
Manpower and Training

Edward W. Clexton, Jr.
Director for Operations
U.S. Atlantic Fleet

William A. Dougherty, Jr.
Commander
Carrier Group FOUR
U.S. Atlantic Fleet

Harold J. Bernsen
Deputy Chief of Staff
Readiness & Resources
U.S. Atlantic Fleet

Thomas W. Evans
Dir., Advanced Submarine
Research & Development,
Naval Sea Systems Command

David N. Rogers
Commander
Carrier Group THREE
U.S. Pacific Fleet

Robert T. Reimann
Deputy Commander
Surface Combatants
Naval Sea Systems Command

REAR ADMIRALS (Upper Half)

Michael P. Kalleres
Director, General Planning
& Program Division, Office
of Navy Program Planning

John F. Calvert
Program Director
Tactical Aircraft
Naval Air Systems Command

Eric A. McVadon, Jr.
Commander
Iceland Defense Force
Keflavik, Iceland

Lyle F. Bull
Commander
Carrier Group FIVE
U.S. Pacific Fleet

Richard D. Milligan
Commander
Cruiser Destroyer Group
TWO, U.S. Atlantic Fleet

Virgil L. Hill, Jr.
Superintendent
U.S. Naval Academy

John K. Ready
Director, Office of
Program Appraisal
Office of SECNAV

Henry G. Chiles, Jr.
Commander
Submarine Group EIGHT
U.S. Atlantic Fleet

REAR ADMIRALS (Lower Half)

Roberta L. Hazard
Director, J-1
(Manpower & Personnel)
Joint Chiefs of Staff

Gerald L. Riendeau
Chief
Military Assistance
Advisory Group, Spain

Willis I. Lewis, Jr.
Commander
Naval Base, San Diego

William J. O'Connor
Deputy Director
Defense Mapping Agency

Wendell N. Johnson
Commander
Naval Base, Charleston

Vernon C. Smith
Deputy Chief
Naval Education
and Training

John J. Higginson
Commander
Naval Surface Group
Long Beach

Thomas J. Johnson
Commander
Naval Base, Guam

146 FLAG PHOTOS—NAVY

REAR ADMIRALS (Lower Half)

Norman D. Campbell
Defense Attache
to France

Harry S. Quast
Director, Department of
the Navy Information
Resources Management

John W. Koenig
Commander
Naval Training Center
Orlando

John W. Adams
Commander
Antisubmarine Warfare Wing
U.S. Pacific Fleet

Ralph W. West, Jr.
Director, Human Resources
Management Division
OPNAV

Gary F. Wheatley
Deputy Dir., Office for
Technology Transfer &
Security Assistance, SECNAV

Raymond G. Zeller
Commander, Cruiser
Destroyer Group THREE
U.S. Pacific Fleet

John M. Kersh
Dep. Dir., U.S. Nuclear
Command & Control Systems
Support Staff, OSD

Henri B. Chase, III
Commander
Amphibious Group ONE
U.S. Pacific Fleet

Dwaine O. Griffith
Director
Deep Submergence Systems
Division, OPNAV

James E. Taylor
Dir., Politico-Military
& Current Plans
Division, OPNAV

Jimmy Pappas
Commander
Naval Base, Norfolk

Robert L. Leuschner, Jr.
Director for Warfare
Systems Architecture
SPAWARSYSCOM

Thomas K. Mattingly, II
Director
Space & Sensor Systems
SPAWARSYSCOM

Daniel C. Richardson
Director
Force Level Plans Division
OPNAV

Gerald E. Gneckov
Commander
U.S. Naval Forces
Southern Command

REAR ADMIRALS (Lower Half)

Roland G. Guilbault
Commander, Cruiser
Destroyer Group TWELVE
U.S. Atlantic Fleet

Larry G. Vogt
Commander
U.S. Naval Forces
Korea

John S. Yow
Commander
Patrol Wings
Atlantic

Cathal L. Flynn, Jr.
Director, J-5
U.S. Special
Operations Command

Wayne E. Rickman
Commander
Training Command
U.S. Atlantic Fleet

Ronald H. Jesberg
Commander
Helicopter Wings
Atlantic

William C. Francis
Director for Operations
U.S. Atlantic Fleet

Phillip D. Smith
Director, Strategy
Plans and Policy
Division, OPNAV

David R. Morris
Commander
Carrier Group EIGHT
U.S. Atlantic Fleet

Frederick J. Metz
Director
CV & Air Station Programs
Divison, OPNAV

Edward B. Baker, Jr.
Commander
Amphibious Group THREE
U.S. Pacific Fleet

Peter G. Chabot
Inspector General
U.S. Atlantic Fleet

Jimmie W. Taylor
Chief of
Naval Air Training

John F. Calhoun
Commander
Naval Training Center
Great Lakes

George H. Strohsahl, Jr.
Commander
Pacific Missile
Test Center

Jesse J. Hernandez
Commander
Patrol Wings
U.S. Pacific Fleet

148 FLAG PHOTOS—NAVY

REAR ADMIRALS (Lower Half)

John W. Bitoff
Commander, Service
Group ONE & Naval
Base, San Francisco

David M. Bennett
Deputy Chief of Staff
for Plans & Operations
U.S. Pacific Fleet

Thomas A. Mercer
Commander
Carrier Group SEVEN
U.S. Pacific Fleet

Leighton W. Smith, Jr.
Commander
Carrier Group SIX
U.S. Atlantic Fleet

Richard C. Macke
Commander
Carrier Group TWO
U.S. Atlantic Fleet

Henry C. McKinney
Commander
Navy Recruiting Command

David R. Oliver, Jr.
Commander
Submarine Group FIVE
U.S. Pacific Fleet

Kenneth L. Carlsen
Commander
Carrier Group ONE
U.S. Pacific Fleet

David B. Robinson
Commander
Cruiser Destroyer Group
EIGHT, U.S. Atlantic Fleet

George W. Davis, VI
Commander, Submarine
Group NINE, PACFLT, &
Naval Base, Seattle

Arlington F. Campbell
Commander
Submarine Group SIX
U.S. Atlantic Fleet

Jerome F. Smith, Jr.
Commander
Cruiser Destroyer Group
FIVE, U.S. Pacific Fleet

Stephen K. Chadwick
Commander, Naval Surface
Group, Mid-Pacific and
Naval Base, Pearl Harbor

Glenn E. Whisler, Jr.
Commander
Amphibious Group TWO
U.S. Atlantic Fleet

Craig E. Dorman
Program Director
ASW Warfare Systems
SPAWARSYSCOM

Geoffrey L. Chesbrough
Commander
Naval Surface Group
Western Pacific

REAR ADMIRALS (Lower Half)

Grady L. Jackson
Cdr., Medium Attack
Tactical Electronic Warfare
Wing, U.S. Pacific Fleet

James B. Greene, Jr.
Program Manager, Aegis
Shipbuilding Project/
DDG-51 Program, NAVSEA

Joseph P. Reason
Commander, Cruiser
Destroyer Group ONE
U.S. Pacific Fleet

Eugene D. Conner
Commander
Military Entrance
Processing Command

Bobby C. Lee
Commander
Fleet Air
Western Pacific

Riley D. Mixon
Command Director
NORAD Combat
Operations Staff

Donald V. Boecker
Commander
Naval Air Test Center

Daniel P. March
Director, Program
Research Appraisal
Division, OPNAV

Douglas Volegnau
Director
Submarine Combat Systems
Naval Sea Systems Command

William P. Houley
Commander
Submarine Group TWO
U.S. Atlantic Fleet

Richard C. Allen
Director for Operations
U.S. Atlantic Fleet

Thomas A. Meinicke
Director, Strategic &
Theater Nuclear Warfare
OPNAV

Raymond G. Jones, Jr.
Director
Military Personnel Policy
Division, OPNAV

Ronald C. Wilgenbusch
Program Director
Information Transfer
Systems, SPAWARSYSCOM

James B. Best
Commander, Fighter Airborne
Early Warning Wing
U.S. Pacific Fleet

Jerry L. Unruh
Chief
Operations/Readiness
Branch, SHAPE

150 FLAG PHOTOS—NAVY

REAR ADMIRALS (Lower Half)

Philip F. Duffy
Commander
U.S. Naval Forces
Central Command

Paul D. Moses
Deputy Director
for Plans and Policy
U.S. European Command

Thomas D. Paulsen
Executive Assistant to the
Chief of Naval Operations

John R. Dalrymple, Jr.
Commander
South Atlantic Force
U.S. Atlantic Fleet

Byron E. Tobin
Commander
Mine Warfare Command

Raymond M. Walsh
Director, Operations
Division, Office of Budget
and Reports, OPNAV

Irve C. LeMoyne
Commander
Naval Special
Warfare Command

W. Lewis Glenn, Jr.
Commander
Training Command
U.S. Pacific Fleet

George H. Gee
Director
Surface Combat Systems
Division, OPNAV

William C. Miller
Director, Undersea &
Strategic Warfare & Nuclear
Development Division, OPNAV

Peter H. Cressy
Director
Aviation Manpower &
Training Division, OPNAV

Frederick L. Lewis
Cdr., Fighter Medium
Attack Airborne Early
Warning Wing, LANTFLT

William A. Owens
Military Assistant to the
Secretary of Defense

Phillip R. Olson
Deputy Director
Strategic Plans & Policy
J-5, Joint Chiefs of Staff

Thomas C. Lynch
Chief of Legislative Affairs

Joseph C. Strasser
Commander
Cruiser Destroyer Group
THREE, U.S. Pacific Fleet

REAR ADMIRALS (Lower Half)

William C. Carlson
Assistant Deputy Commander
ASW & Undersea Systems
Naval Sea Systems Command

Walter J. Davis, Jr.
Commandant
Naval District of Washington

Alvaro R. Gomez
Director
of Naval Communications

Paul W. Parcells
Deputy Assistant SECDEF
Plans and Operations
(Legislative Affairs)

John A. Moriarty
Commander
U.S. Naval Activities
Caribbean

Jon M. Barr
Deputy Director
National Military
Command Center, JCS

James R. Lang
Program Manager, Submarine
Monitoring Maintenance &
Support Office, NAVSEA

Stephen S. Clarey
Comptroller
Naval Sea Systems Command

Luther F. Schriefer
Director, Tactical Air, Surface,
& Electronic WArfare
Development Div., OPNAV

James W. Partington
Commander
Strike Fighter Wing
Atlantic

Thomas D. Ryan
Assistant Inspector General,
Inspections, Office of the
Secretary of Defense

Ralph L. Tindal
Deputy Chief of Staff
logistics, CINCSOUTH

George R. Worthington
Deputy Assistant SECDEF
for Special Operations

Bruce B. Bremner
Command Director
NORAD Combat
Operations Staff

Timothy W. Wright
Deputy Director
National Military
Command Center, JCS

Thomas F. Hall
Deputy Chief of Naval Reserve
OPNAV

152 FLAG PHOTOS—NAVY

REAR ADMIRALS (Lower Half)

David E. Frost
Commander
Naval Space Command

Philip M. Quast
Director, Total Force
Program Division
OPNAV

John B. LaPlante
Commander
Naval Logistics Command
U.S. Pacific Fleet

William L. Vincent
Program Director for ASW
and Assault Programs
Naval Air Systems Command

Ronald J. Zlatoper
Director for Distribution
Naval Military
Personnel Command

Karl L. Kaup
Director
Strategic Submarine
Division, OPNAV

Philip S. Anselmo
Director
Navy Space Systems
OPNAV

William J. Flanagan, Jr.
Director
Surface Warfare Division
OPNAV

James R. Fitzgerald
Director
Anti-Submarine Warfare
Division, OPNAV

Paul E. Tobin, Jr.
Director, Department
of the Navy Information
Resources Management

William A. Earner, Jr.
Comptroller
Naval Air Systems Command

John S. Redd
Commander
Standing Naval Force
Atlantic

Conrad Lautenbacher, Jr.
Inspector General
U.S. Pacific Fleet

John T. Hood
Asst. Deputy Commander for
Combat Systems Engineering
Naval Sea Systems Command

RESTRICTED LINE, SPECIAL DUTY, AND STAFF CORPS FLAG OFFICERS

RESTRICTED LINE ENGINEERING DUTY

REAR ADMIRALS (Upper Half)

David P. Donahue
Fleet Maintenance Officer
U.S. Atlantic Fleet

Myron V. Ricketts
Director
Fleet Support, Atlantic

Malcolm MacKinnon, III
Vice Director
Naval Sea Systems Command

Kenneth C. Malley
Director
Strategic Systems Programs
OPNAV

Lowell J. Holloway
Vice Commander
Space & Naval Warfare
Systems Command

Roger B. Horne, Jr.
Dep. Cdr. for Ship
Design and Engineering
Naval Sea Systems Command

Robert L. Topping
Director
Warfare Systems Engineering
SPAWARSYSCOM

REAR ADMIRALS (Lower Half)

George R. Meinig
Asst. Dep. Cdr. for
Surface Warfare & Antiair
Warfare Systems, NAVSEA

Walter H. Cantrell
Deputy Commander
for Submarines
Naval Sea Sysems Command

John S. Claman
Supervisor of Shipbuilding
Conversion, and Rep;air
Groton

Robert E. Traister
Fleet Maintenance Officer
U.S. Pacific Fleet

Dean H. Hines
Deputy Commander for
Industrial & Facility
Management, NAVSEA

Millard S. Firebaugh
Program Director
Seawolf SSN-21 Submarine
Program, NAVSEA

RESTRICTED LINE (AVIATION ENGINEERING DUTY)

REAR ADMIRALS (Upper Half)

John C. Weaver
Commander
Space & Naval Warfare
Systems Command

154 FLAG PHOTOS—NAVY

REAR ADMIRALS (Upper Half)

Richard D. Friichtenicht
Deputy Commander
for Plans and Programs
Naval Air Systems Command

Thomas C. Betterton
Assistant Commander
for Space Technology
SPAWARSYSCOM

REAR ADMIRALS (Lower Half)

John H. Kirkpatrick
Assistant Commander for
Logistics & Fleet Support
Naval Air Systems Command

Larry E. Blose
Assistant Commander for
Systems and Engineering
Naval Air Systems Command

William C. Bowes
Director, Joint
Cruise Missiles Project
Naval Air Systems Command

Robert G. Harrison
Deputy Assistant
Commander for Fleet/Product
Support, NAVAIR

SPECIAL DUTY (CRYPTOLOGY)

REAR ADMIRAL (Upper Half)

Charles F. Clark
Deputy Director
for Operations
National Security Agency

REAR ADMIRALS (Lower Half)

James S. McFarland
Commander
Naval Security
Group Command

Isaiah C. Cole
Director for Intelligence
U.S. Atlantic Fleet

INTELLIGENCE

VICE ADMIRAL

William O. Studeman
Director
National Security Agency

REAR ADMIRAL (Upper Half)

Thomas A. Brooks
Director of Naval Intelligence

REAR ADMIRAL (Lower Half)

Edward D. Sheafer, Jr.
Deputy Director
for JCS Support
Defense Intelligence Agency

PUBLIC AFFAIRS

REAR ADMIRAL (Lower Half)

Jimmie B. Finkelstein
Chief of Information

OCEANOGRAPHY

REAR ADMIRAL (Lower Half)

James E. Koehr
Commander
Naval Oceanography Command

STAFF CORPS
MEDICAL CORPS

VICE ADMIRAL

James A. Zimble
Surgeon General of
the Navy/Director
of Naval Medicine

REAR ADMIRALS (Upper Half)

William M. Narva
Attending Physician
to Congress

Robert P. Caudill, Jr.
Deputy Director
Naval Medicine
OPNAV

Henry J.T. Sears
Commander
Naval Medical Command

Lewis Mantel
Director
Medical Mobilization
J-4, JCS

REAR ADMIRALS (Lower Half)

Russell L. Marlor
Fleet Surgeon
U.S. Pacific Fleet

Daniel B. Lestage
Fleet Surgeon
U.S. Atlantic Fleet

Donald F. Hagen
Deputy Commander
Health Care Operations
Naval Medical Command

William A. Buckendorf
Deputy Commander
for Fleet Readiness
Naval Medical Command

Donald L. Sturtz
Commander
Naval Medical Command
National Capital Region

Joseph P. Smyth
Commander
Naval Medical Command
European Region

Robert W. Higgins
The Medical Officer
U.S. Marine Corps

David M. Lichtman
Commander
Naval Medical Command
Northwest Region

SUPPLY CORPS

REAR ADMIRALS (Upper Half)

Robert B. Halder
Commander
Naval Medical Command
Southeast Region

Harold M. Koenig
Director
Health Care Operations
OPNAV

Daniel W. McKinnon, Jr.
Commander, Naval Supply
Systems Command and Chief
of the Supply Corps

Robert B. Abele
Vice Commander
Naval Supply
Systems Command

Rodney K. Squibb
Commander
Navy Resale & Services
Support Office

James E. Miller
Asst. Chief of Staff
Logistics/Fleet Supply
Officer, U.S. Atlantic Fleet

James E. Eckelberger
Commanding Officer
Naval Aviation
Supply Office

REAR ADMIRALS (Lower Half)

William E. Powell, Jr.
Commanding Officer
Naval Supply Center
Norfolk

Brady M. Cole
Force Supply Officer
Naval Logistics Command
U.S. Pacific Fleet

Peter DeMayo
Assistant Deputy Commander
for Depot Management
Naval Air Systems Command

Francis L. Filipiak
Assistant Comptroller
Financial Management
NAVCOMPT

William H. Hauenstein
Competition Advocate
General of the Navy

Robert M. Moore
Asst. Commander, Inventory
and Systems Integrity
Naval Supply Systems Command

Harvey D. Weatherson
Commander
Defense Reutilization
& Marketing Service

James A. Morgart
Commanding Officer
Naval Supply Center
Norfolk

Edward M. Straw
Director
Materiel Division
OPNAV

CHAPLAIN CORPS

REAR ADMIRAL (Upper Half)

Alvin B. Koeneman
Chief of Chaplains/
Director of Religious Ministries

REAR ADMIRAL (Lower Half)

David E. White
Deputy Chief of Chaplains/
Deputy Director
of Religious Ministries

CIVIL ENGINEER CORPS

REAR ADMIRALS (Upper Half)

Benjamin F. Montoya
Cdr., Nav. Facilities Eng. Cmd./
Chief of Civil Engineers
of the Navy

David E. Bottorff
Commander, Atlantic Div.
Naval Facilities
Engineering Command

REAR ADMIRALS (Lower Half)

Jon R. Ives
Commander, Pacific Div.
Naval Facilities
Engineering Command

James C. Doebler
Director
Shore Activities
Division, OPNAV

Alan K. Riffey
Vice Commander
Naval Facilities
Engineering Command

JUDGE ADVOCATE GENERAL'S CORPS

REAR ADMIRALS (Upper Half)

Everette D. Stumbaugh
Judge Advocate General
of the Navy

John E. Gordon
Deputy Judge
Advocate General
of the Navy

REAR ADMIRAL (Lower Half)

William L. Schachte
Assistant Judge
Advocate General
of the Navy

DENTAL CORPS

REAR ADMIRAL (Upper Half)

Richard G. Shaffer
Chief of the Dental Corps/
Dir., Dental Care Operations
Division, NAVMEDCOM

158 FLAG PHOTOS—NAVY

REAR ADMIRALS (Lower Half)

Robert W. Koch
Commanding Officer
Naval Dental Clinic
Norfolk

Milton C. Clegg
Commanding Officer
Naval Dental Clinic
San Diego

Ronald P. Morse
Asst. Deputy Chief
of Staff for Dentistry
NAVMEDCOM SW Region

MEDICAL SERVICE CORPS

REAR ADMIRALS (Lower Half)

Donald E. Shuler
Chief, Medical Service
Corps/Vice Commander
Naval Medical Command

Charles R. Loar
Commander
Naval Medical Command
Mid-Atlantic Region

NURSE CORPS

REAR ADMIRAL (Lower Half)

Mary F. Hall
Dep. Cdr., Personnel Mgt.,
Naval Medical Command/
Dir., Navy Nurse Corps

NAVAL RESERVE (TAR)

REAR ADMIRAL (Upper Half)

Albert E. Rieder
Commander
Naval Base, Philadelphia

REAR ADMIRALS (Lower Half)

Richard K. Chambers
Deputy Commander
Naval Reserve Force

Maurice J. Bresnahan, Jr.
Commander
Naval Surface
Reserve Force

NAVAL RESERVE (RECALL)

REAR ADMIRAL (Upper Half)

Francis N. Smith
Director of Naval Reserve

MASTER CHIEF PETTY OFFICER OF THE NAVY

Duane R. Bushey
Master Chief
Petty Officer
of the Navy

NAVAL RESERVE CORPS

Each Naval Reserve flag officer ultimately is given a mobilization assignment. However, since these assignments often change during the years an officer remains active in the Naval Reserve in flag rank, they are not included in the listing which follows.

REAR ADMIRALS (Upper Half)

Tammy H. Etheridge
135 Woodland Circle
Jackson, MS 39216

John E. Love
1002 Spokane Street
Garfield, WA 99130

John D. Summers
3666 Partridge Lane
Roanoke, VA 24017

John L. Sweeney
351 Williams Road
Wynnewood, PA 19096

Kenneth E. Myatt
2841 Cravey Drive
Atlanta, GA 30345

Jack S. Smith
1070 Mountain Creek Trail
Atlanta, GA 30328

Martin W. Leukhardt
3 Crystal Lane
Latham, NY 12110

REAR ADMIRALS (Lower Half)

Samuel E. McWilliams
1859 Vallejo Street
San Francisco, CA 94123

Burton O. Benson
5 Evans Place
Orinda, CA 94563

James M. Strickland
133 Belmont Court
Redlands, CA 92373

Stephen G. Yusem
Township Line Road
Gwynedd Valley, PA 19437

Richard S. Fitzgerald
Route 1, Box 108
Catlett, VA 22019

Richard K. Maughlin
707 Meadow Lake Lane
Great Falls, MD 20634-9728

David A. Janes
1721 La Ramada Avenue
Arcadia, CA 91006

Wallace N. Guthrie, Jr.
1618 Wood Duck Drive
Winter Springs, FL 32708

REAR ADMIRALS (Lower Half)

Larry B. Franklin
2801 Altagate Court
Louisville, KY 40206

Jimmie W. Seeley
2538 Foxwood Road South
Orange Park, FL 32073

William P. O'Donnell, Jr.
113 Countryside Drive
Chagrin Falls, OH 44022

Wilson F. Flagg
63 Scott Ridge Road
Ridgefield, CT 06877

Alexander S. Logan
101 Sedgewick Drive
Scituate, MA 02066

Stanley D. Griggs
204 Lakeshore Drive
Seabrook, TX 77586

James J. Carey
6022 Knights Bridge Way
Alexandria, VA 22310

Robert Smith, III
501 West Rusk
Rockwall, TX 75087

ENGINEERING DUTY

REAR ADMIRAL (Lower Half)

Brian T. Sheehan
387 Mosely Road
Hillsborough, CA 94010

AVIATION ENGINEERING

REAR ADMIRAL (Upper Half)

Clay W.G. Fulcher
18710 Point Lookout
Houston, TX 77058

CRYPTOLOGY

REAR ADMIRAL (Lower Half)

Thomas E. Courneya
1215 East Kirts Street
Troy, MI 48081

INTELLIGENCE

REAR ADMIRAL (Lower Half)

Gene P. Dickey
2214 Scarlet Lane
Grand Prairie, TX 75050

PUBLIC AFFAIRS

REAR ADMIRAL (Lower Half)

Robert A. Ravitz
5 Westview Lane
South Norwalk, CT 06854

MEDICAL CORPS

REAR ADMIRALS (Upper Half)

John D. Tolmie
1543 Abbey Court
Winston-Salem, NC 27103

REAR ADMIRALS (Lower Half)

James G. Roberts
3040 Octavia Street
New Orleans, LA 10125

James J. Cerda
3332 N.W. 133rd Street
Gainesville, FL 32601

Robert L. Summitt
3102 Glenntinnan Road
Memphis, TN 38128

Robert C. Nuss
8151 Blue Jay Lane
Jacksonville, FL 32216

Horace MacVaugh, III
116 Spruce Street
Philadelphia, PA 19106

Paul T. Kayye
Route 1, Box 343C
Angier, NC 27501

Donald E. Roy
8832 North Fuller
Fresno, CA 93710

162 FLAG PHOTOS—NAVY

SUPPLY CORPS

REAR ADMIRALS (Upper Half)

Delbert H. Beumer
452 University Avenue
Los Altos, CA 94022

Donald G. St. Angelo
15126 Williston Lane
Minnetonka, MN 55345

Philip A. Whitacre
1541 Brickell Avenue
Miami, FL 33129

REAR ADMIRALS (Upper Half)

Henry C. Amos, Jr.
6116 Glennox Lane
Dallas, TX 75214

REAR ADMIRALS (Lower Half)

James H. Mayer
6 Mockingbird Court
Movato, CA 94947

J. Ronald Denney
800 Pebble Hill Road
Doyleston, PA 18901

Vance H. Fry
1404 Rowewood Drive
Chattanooga, TN 37421

CHAPLAIN CORPS

Francis W. Keane
22 Vanderbilt Road
Scarsdale, NY 10583

REAR ADMIRAL (Lower Half)

Aaron Landes
8372 Fisher Road
Elkins Park, PA 19117

CIVIL ENGINEER CORPS

REAR ADMIRAL (Upper Half)

David O. Smart
5706 West 98th Street
Overland Park, KS 66204

REAR ADMIRALS (Lower Half)

Paul C. Rosser
64 West Brookhaven Drive
Atlanta, GA 30319

Melvbin H. Chiogioji
15113 Middlegate Road
Silver Spring, MD 20904

JUDGE ADVOCATE GENERAL'S CORPS

REAR ADMIRAL (Upper Half)

Robert E. Wiss
2864 Sheridan Place
Evanston, IL 60201

REAR ADMIRAL (Lower Half)

Gerald E. Gilbert
11113 Cripplegate Road
Potomac, MD 20854

DENTAL CORPS

REAR ADMIRALS (Lower Half)

William B. Finagin
6 Romar Drive
Annapolis, MD 21403

John R. Hubbard
713 South Petty Street
Gaffney, SC 29340

MARINE CORPS

GENERALS

General A.M. Gray
Commandant of the
Marine Corps

Joseph J. Went
Assistant Commandant

LIEUTENANT GENERALS

Stephen G. Olmstead
Deputy Assistant Secretary
of Defense for Drugs,
Policy, and Enforcement

Edwin J. Godfrey
Commanding General
Fleet Marine Forces
Pacific

Ernest T. Cook, Jr.
CG, Fleet Marine Force,
Atlantic/II Marine
Expeditionary Force

John I. Hudson
Deputy Chief of Staff
for Manpower

William G. Carson, Jr.
Deputy Chief of Staff
for Installations
and Logistics

Carl E. Mundy, Jr.
Deputy Chief of Staff
for Plans, Policies
and Operations

William R. Etnyre
Commanding General
Marine Corps Combat
Develpment Command

Charles H. Pitman
Deputy Chief of Staff
for Aviation

MAJOR GENERALS

Norman H. Smith
Commanding General
III Marine Expeditionary
Force/3d Marine Division

Ray "M" Franklin
CG, Marine Corps Research
Development, & Acquisition
Command/DCS for RD&A

John R. Dailey
Commandant
Armed Forces Staff College
Norfolk

James E. Cassity
Commanding General
Marine Corps Logistics Base
Albany, GA

John P. Monahan
Commanding General
I Marine Expeditionary
Force/1st Marine Division

Richard A. Gustafson
Commanding General
2d Marine Aircraft Wing

Edmund M. Looney, Jr.
Director, Logistics Plans,
Policies, & Strategy
Mobility Division, I&L

Orlo K. Steele
CG, 2d Marine Division/
Dep;t. Cdr., II Marine
Expeditionary Force

Hollis E. Davison
Asst. Chief of Staff
C-5, Combined Forces, Korea/
J-5, U.S. Forces, Korea

Robert F. Milligan
Commander
U.S. Forces
Caribbean

Gene A. Deegan
CG, Marine Corps Air
Ground Combat Center
Twentynine Palms, CA

Joseph P. Hoar
Commanding General
Marine Corps Recruit Depot
Parris Island, SC

Royal N. Moore, Jr.
Director, Operations
U.S. Pacific Command

Donald E.P. Miller
Commanding General
3d Marine Aircraft Wing

Robert J. Winglass
Deputy Chief of Staff
for Requirements &
Programs, Headquarters, USMC

166 FLAG PHOTOS—MARINES

MAJOR GENERALS

Michael P. Sullivan
Deputy Commanding General
Marine Corps Combat
Development Command

Jarvis D. Lynch, Jr.
Commanding General
2d Force Service
Support Group

Ronald L. Beckwith
Commanding General
4th Marine Aircraft Wing

Ross S. Plasterer
Commanding General
1st Marine Aircraft Wing

BRIGADIER GENERALS

Matthew T. Cooper
Deputy Commander
& Chief of Staff
U.S. Forces, Japan

Henry C. Stackpole, III
Director, Plans
& Policy Directorate
U.S. Atlantic Fleet

John S. Grinalds
Director, Force Structure
Resource & Assessment
Joint Chiefs of Staff

Robert R. Porter
Director
Naval Council of
Personnel Boards

James D. Beans
Director
Intelligence Division
Headquarters, USMC

John I. Hopkins
Dir., Operations Division
Plans, Policy, & Operations
Headquarters, USMC

Gail M. Reals
Commanding General
Marine Corps Base
Quantico

Matthew P. Caulfield
Director, Inter-American
Region, International
Security Affairs, OASD

Frank J. Breth
Commanding General
Marine Corps Recruit Depot
San Diego

James E. Sniffen
Commander
Marine Corps Logistics Base
Barstow, CA

David V. Shuter
Commander, Marine Corps
Air Bases, West/CG,
MCAS, El Toro, CA

Bobby G. Butcher
Commanding General
6th Marine
Expeditionary Brigade

BRIGADIER GENERALS

George L. Cates
De. CG, Marine Corps
Research, Development,
& Acquisition Command

Richard H. Huckaby
Commanding General
Marine Corps Base
Camp Pendleton, CA

Jeremiah W. Pearson, III
Assistant Deputy
Chief of Staff
for Aviation

Walter E. Boomer
Commanding General
4th Marine Division

Frank A. Huey
Deputy Commander
Fleet Marine Force
Atlantic

John A. Studds
Commanding General
1st Marine
Expeditionary Brigade

William M. Keys
Director, Personnel
Management Division
Headquarters, USMC

William P. Eshelman
CG, 5th Marine Expeditionary
Brigade/Landing Force
Training Command, Pacific

Lloyd G. Pool
Deputy Commander
Fleet Marine Force
Pacific

Donald R. Gardner
Commanding General
Marine Corps Base
Camp LeJeune, NC

Harry W. Jenkins, Jr.
Legislative Assistant to
the Commandant/Director,
Public Affairs Division

Michael P. Mulqueen
Commanding General
3rd Service
Support Group

John P. Brickley
Deputy Director
Training & Education
Center, Quantico

Michael P. Downs
Director, Facilities &
Services Division, I&L
Headquarters, USMC

Duane A. Wills
Director, Plans Div.,
Plans, Policy, & Operations
Headquarters, USMC

Richard L. Phillips
Deputy Director, C4I2,
Director, C4 Division
Headquarters, USMC

BRIGADIER GENERALS

Robert B. Johnston
Commanding General
Marine Corps Base
Camp Butler, Okinawa

Peter J. Rowe
AC/S Joint Operations/Senior
U.S. Naval Officer
Allied Forces North

Clyde L. Vermilyea
CG, Marine Corps Bases,
East/Marine Corps Air
Station, Cherry Hill, NC

Francis X. Hamilton, Jr.
Commanding General
1st Force Service
Support Group

Martin L. Brandtner
Assistant Division Commander
2d Marine Division

Michael E. Rich
Director
Judge Advocate Division
Headquarters, USMC

Robert A. Tiebout
Commander
Defense Electronic Supply
Center, Dayton, OH

Norman E. Ehlert
Cdr., Forward Headquarters
Element/Inspector General
U.S. Central Command

Richard D. Hearney
Deputy Director, J-3
U.S. Eurpean Command

John J. Sheehan
CG, 4th Marine Expeditionary
Force/Landing Force
Training Command, Atlantic

John C. Arick
Assistant Wing Commander
2d Marine Aircraft Wing

James E. Livingston
Deputy Director
National Military Command
Center, JCS

George R. Christmas
Assistant Division Commander
3d Marine Division

Harold W. Blot
V-22 Program Manager
Naval Air Systems Command

James M. Myatt
Director, Manpower
Plans & Policy Division
Headquarters, USMC

Gerald L. McKay
Assistant Division Commander
1st Marine Division

SERGEANT MAJOR OF THE MARINE CORPS

David W. Summers
Sergeant Major
of the Marine Corps

MARINE CORPS RESERVE

Each Marine Corps Reserve general officer is given a mobilization assignment. However, because these assignments are subject to frequent changes, they are not reflected here; only those general officers currently active in the Reserve and their home addresses are listed.

MAJOR GENERALS

Ronald K. Nelson
649 Woodward Drive
Huntingdon Valley, PA
19006-4057

Charles S. Bishop, Jr.
1735B Wildberry Drive
Glenview, IL 60025-1726

William H. Gossell
14303 Juniper Cove, Farmers
Branch, TX 75234-2211

BRIGADIER GENERALS

Jerome G. Cooper
1208 Palmetto Street
Mobile, AL 36604-2645

Richard P. Trotter
2965 307 S. Pharr Court, NW
Atlanta, GA 30305

G. Richard Omrod
100 Gill Road
Haddonfield, NJ 08033-3404

Mitchell J. Waters
347 Shoreline Road
Lake Barrington Shores, IL
60010-1627

John F. Cronin
6333 Silverado
Bend, OR 97702

Joe W. Wilson
635 North Wood Avenue
Florence, AL 35630

COAST GUARD

ADMIRAL

Paul A. Yost, Jr.
Commandant

VICE ADMIRALS

Clyde T. Lusk, Jr.
Vice Commandant

James C. Irwin
Commander, Atlantic Area
and U.S. Maritime Defense
Zone, Atlantic

REAR ADMIRALS

Clyde E. Robbins
Commander, Pacific Area
and U.S. Maritime Defense
Zone, Pacific

Arnold B. Beran
Chief of Staff

William P. Kozlovsky
Commander, Fourteenth
Coast Guard District

Richard P. Cueroni
Superintendent
Coast Guard Academy

Edward Nelson, Jr.
Commander, Seventeeth
Coast Guard District

Howard B. Thorsen
Chief
Office of Law Enforcement
and Defense Operations

Alan D. Breed
Commander, Fifth
Coast Guard District

John W. Kime
Commander, Eleventh
Coast Guard District

Robert L. Johanson
Chief
Office of Engineering

William F. Merlin
Commander, Eighth
Coast Guard District

Thomas T. Matteson
Chief
Office of Personnel
and Training

Richard I. Rybacki
Commander, First
Coast Guard District

REAR ADMIRALS

Martin H. Daniell, Jr.
Commander, Seventh
Coast Guard District

Robert T. Nelson
Chief
Office of Navigation
and Safety

Marshall E. Gilbert
Resource Director/Comptroller

Joseph E. Vorbach
Chief Counsel

George D. Passmore, Jr.
Commander, Maintenance
and Logistics Command
Atlantic

Ernest B. Acklin
Chief
Office of Acquisition

Paul A. Welling
Chief
Office of Readiness
and Reserve

Walter T. Leland
Commander, Maintenance
and Logistics Command
Pacific

Ronald M. Polant
Chief
Office of Command, Control,
and Communications

William P. Leahy, Jr.
Commander, Second
Coast Guard District

Joel D. Sipes
Chief, Office of Marine
Safety, Security,
& Environment Protection

Robert E. Kramek
Commander, Thirteenth
Coast Guard District

Richard A. Applebaum
Commander, Ninth
Coast Guard District

Edward F. Blasser
USPHS Chief
Office of Health Services

MASTER CHIEF PETTY OFFICER OF THE COAST GUARD

Allen W. Thiele
Master Chief Petty Officer
of the Coast Guard

172 FLAG PHOTOS—NOAA

COAST GUARD RESERVE

REAR ADMIRALS

Daniel J. Murphy
90 Sunview Drive
San Francisco, CA 94131

Bennett S. Sparks
3233 Wonder View Drive
Hollywood, CA 90068

NOAA

Francis D. Moran
Director
NOAA Corps

Wesley V. Hull
Director
Ocean & Geodetic Services
National Ocean Service

Sigmund R. Petersen
Director
Pacific Marine Center
National Ocean Service

Ray E. Moses
Director
Atlantic Marine Center
National Ocean Service

J. Austin Yeager
Director
Office of Marine Operations
National Ocean Service

KEY PERSONNEL LOCATOR
DEPARTMENT OF THE NAVY — WASHINGTON AREA ORGANIZATIONS

As of 1 December 1988

SECRETARY OF THE NAVY

HON WILLIAM L BALL III	4E686	695-3131
EXECUTIVE ASSISTANT & NAVAL AIDE		
CAPT P A Dur	4E686	695-4603
SPECIAL ASSISTANT & MARINE CORPS AIDE		
COL D Richwine USMC	4E686	695-5133
ADMINISTRATIVE AIDE		
CDR G Roughead	4E687	695-5410
SPECIAL ASSISTANT PUBLIC AFFAIRS		
CDR J S Zakem	4E686	697-7491
SPEC ASST & SPEECH WRITER TO SECNAV & UNSECNAV		
LT A P Butterfield	4D723	694-4926
SPEC ASST (LEGAL & LEGISLATIVE AFFAIRS)		
CAPT D Williams	4E725	697-6935

UNDER SECRETARY OF THE NAVY

HON H L GARRETT III	4E714	695-3141
EXECUTIVE ASSISTANT & NAVAL AIDE		
CAPT G Emery	4E714	695-2140
SPECIAL ASSISTANT & MARINE CORPS AIDE		
COL T Steele USMC	4E714	695-2002
ASST DEPUTY UNDER SECRETARY (SAFETY & SURVIVABILITY)		
Mr J K Taussig Jr	162	692-3134
DEPUTY UNDER SECRETARY (SPECIAL RESEARCH & ANALYSIS)		
Mr S Cropsey	4E780	697-6684
DEPUTY ASST SECRETARY (TECH TRANSFER & SECURITY AFFAIRS)		
Mr A DiTrapani CP-6	580	692-7260
DIR NAVAL INDUSTRIAL IMPROVEMENT PROGRAM		
Mr W Lindahl	5E689	875-2028
AUDITOR GENERAL		
Mr R L Shaffer NASSIF	501A	756-2117
ASSISTANT FOR ADMINISTRATION		
Mr O R Ashe	4C748	694-5032

OFFICE OF THE SECRETARY OF THE NAVY

OFFICE OF THE GENERAL COUNSEL

MR L L LAMADE	4E724	694-1994
(General Counsel)		
PRINCIPAL DEPUTY COUNSEL		
Vacant	4E724	694-2307
DEPUTY GENERAL COUNSEL (LOGISTICS)		
Mr H J Wilcox CP-5	480	692-7136
ASSOCIATE GENERAL COUNSEL (MANAGEMENT)		
Mr F A Phelps CP-5	480	692-7328
ASSOCIATE GENERAL COUNSEL (LITIGATION)		
Mr C J Turnquist CP-6	1024	746-1000
ASSISTANT GENERAL COUNSEL (ACQUISITION)		
Mr E L Saul CP-5	480	692-7155
ASSISTANT GENERAL COUNSEL (CIVILIAN PERSONNEL LAW)		
Mr J Lynch CP-5	480	692-7186

ASSISTANT SECRETARY OF THE NAVY (FINANCIAL MANAGEMENT)

HON R H CONN	4E768	697-2325
(Comptroller)		
EXECUTIVE ASST & NAVAL AIDE		
CAPT F T Jones	4E768	697-2325
SPECIAL ASST & MARINE AIDE		
LTCOL N M Murray III	4E768	695-7925
DIR DON INFORMATION RESOURCES MGMT		
RADM H S Quast	5B731	695-0103

OFFICE OF THE COMPTROLLER OF THE NAVY

RADM J M SEELY	4E768	695-3377
(Deputy Comptroller)		
SPECIAL ASST		
CDR R J Colucci	4E768	695-3377
COUNSEL		
Mr P M Hitch	4E765	697-5588
ADMIN/FISCAL DIV		
Ms V S Allen	2C317	694-3443
DIRECTOR OF BUDGET & REPORTS		
RADM S F Loftus	4C736	697-7105
ASST COMPTROLLER (FIN MGMT SYSTEMS)		
CAPT W E Daeschner CM-3	425	697-3195

ASSISTANT SECRETARY OF THE NAVY (SHIPBUILDING AND LOGISTICS)
(Crystal Plaza Bldg 5)

HON E PYATT	266	692-2202
EXECUTIVE ASST & NAVAL AIDE		
CAPT P Harrington	266	692-3272
SPECIAL ASST FOR LEGAL AFFAIRS		
CAPT W D Cohen	266	692-3233
SPECIAL ASST & MARINE AIDE		
LTCOL R L Kelly	266	692-2204
PRIN DEP ASST SEC (S&L)		
Mr K Eastin	266	692-3227
ADMINISTRATIVE ASST		
LCDR S Wehmeyer	266	692-3232
DIR SMALL & DISADVANTAGED BUS UTIL		
Mr D L Hathaway	120	692-7122
DIR INSTALLATIONS & FACILITIES		
Mr F Sterns	218	692-7076
DIR SHIPBUILDING		
Mr R Kiss	250	692-7083
DIR AVIATION & ORDNANCE PROGRAMS		
Mr F W Swofford	236	602-4893
DIR INTERNATIONAL PROGRAMS		
Mr F Beer	368	692-2247
DIR MARINE CORPS PROGRAMS		
Mr F Belen	368	692-5962
DIR RESOURCE & POLICY EVALUATION		
Mr R O Thomas	244	692-2355
COMPETITION ADVOCATE GENERAL		
RADM W Havenstein	310	692-3202
DIR SUPPLY SUPPORT		
CDR D A Hempson	236	692-1806
DIR CONTRACTS & BUSINESS MGT		
Mr G Cammack	578	692-3555
SPEC CONTROL ADVOCATE GENERAL		
Mr G Hoffman	334	692-3201
DIR RELIABILITY MAINT & QUAL ASSUR		
Mr W J Willoughby	348	692-9058

ASSISTANT SECRETARY OF THE NAVY (RESEARCH, ENGINEERING & SYSTEMS)

HON T F FAUGHT JR	4E732	695-6315
EXECUTIVE ASST		
CAPT D R Eaton	4E732	695-6315
SPECIAL ASST & MARINE CORPS AIDE		
COL J W Moffitt USMC	4E732	697-2674
PRIN DEP ASST SECY (RE&S)		
Mr R L Rumpf	4E741	697-4928
DEP ASST SECY (ACQ MGT, INTL PGM & CONG SUPP)		
Vacant	5E813	697-1710
DEP ASST SECY (SURF WARF)		
Mr E L Donalson	5E731	694-5090
DEP ASST SECY (C^3IS)		
Vacant	4D745	695-0023
CHIEF OF NAVAL DEVELOPMENT		
RADM J R Wilson Jr BT1	907	696-4258
DEP ASST SECY (AIR)		
Mr W J Schaefer Jr	4E748	694-7793
DIR STRATEGIC PGMS		
Dr W H Smith	5E683	694-4691
DIR ASST SECY (SUB/ASW)		
Mr J Keane	5E777	694-0957
DIR MARINE CORPS PRGS/GROUND		
Vacant	5E779	697-2910

OFFICE OF THE CHIEF OF NAVAL RESEARCH
(Ballston Centre Tower Bldg 1)

RADM J R WILSON JR	907	696-4767
CHIEF OF NAVAL RESEARCH		
ASST CHIEF		
CAPT G F A Wagner	907	696-4261
COUNSEL		
Mr W G Rae	207	696-4271
INTELLIGENCE ADVISOR		
CAPT C D Schneider	1022	696-4275
SPECIAL ASST FOR MARCORPS MATTERS		
COL F J Kirchner USMC	507	696-4274
PUBLIC AFFAIRS OFFICER		
CDR T C Connors	915	696-4917
DIR FINANCIAL MGMT/COMPTROLLER		
Mr G T Maupin	924	696-4277
DIR OPERATIONS, RESOURCES & MGMT		
Dr J J Shepard	315	696-4264

OFFICE OF NAVAL RESEARCH

DIR OFFICE OF NAVAL RESEARCH		
Dr F E Saalfeld	907	696-4517
DEP DIR ONR/PLANNING & ASSESSMENT		
Dr E A Silva	907	696-4484
DIR CONTRACT RESEARCH DEPT		
Dr B B Robinson	811	696-4101
DIR APPLIED RESEARCH & TECH		
CAPT D L Hendrickson	528	696-4224
DIR UNIVERSITY BUSINESS AFFAIRS		
Mr T J Dolan Jr BT3	341	696-4601
DIR ACQUISITION		
Mr J T Bolos	720	696-4607

OFFICE OF NAVAL TECHNOLOGY

DIR OFFICE OF NAVAL TECHNOLOGY		
Dr P A Selwyn	907	696-5115
DEP DIR ONT/PLANNING & ASSESSMENT		
Mr R P Moore	907	696-5117
DIR ANTI-AIR WARFARE ANTI-SURFACE WARFARE SURFACE-AEROSPACE TECH		
Dr F Zimet	507	696-4771
DIR SUPPORT TECH		
Vacant	503	696-4844
DIR ASW UNDERSEA TECH		
Dr A J Faulstich	522	696-5120
DIR LOW OBSERVABLES		
CAPT D Krieger CS # 2	209	696-4251
DIR INDUSTRY RESEARCH & DEVELOPMENT		
Dr R M Culpepper BT3	1212	696-4448

ASSISTANT SECRETARY OF THE NAVY (MANPOWER AND RESERVE AFFAIRS)

HON K P BERGQUIST	4E788	697-2179
EXECUTIVE ASST & NAVAL AIDE		
CAPT L C Wilmot	4E788	695-4537
MIL ASST & MARINE AIDE		
COL M A Rietsch	4E788	697-0975
ADMIN ASST & MARINE AIDE		
LTC M R Cathey	4E794	697-3194
DEPUTY ASST SECY (FORCE SUPP & FAMILIES)		
Mrs A M Stratton	4E777	694-3553
DIR HEALTH AFFAIRS		
CAPT R D Norvell	5D825	694-0855
DEPUTY ASST SECY (RESERVE AFFAIRS)		
Mr S J Routson	4E775	697-7506
STAFF ADVISOR FOR DRUG INTERDICTION		
CAPT R C Cottingham	5D819	697-9326
DEPUTY ASST SECY (MANPOWER)		
Dr K J Coffey (Actg)	4E789	695-4350
DIR MILITARY PERS POLICY		
Mr J R Talbot	5E825	697-1574
DIR PERS AFFAIRS		
CDR C W Tucker	5E825	697-6454
STAFF ASST FOR PERS ACTIONS		
LTC J P Hertel	5E825	697-6454
STAFF ASST FOR PERS ACTIONS		
CDR W H Gay Jr	5E825	697-0981
DEPUTY ASST SECY (CIVPERS POLICY/EEO)		
Ms D M Meletzke (Actg)	4E789	695-2248

BOARDS AND COUNCILS

BOARD FOR CORRECTION OF NAVAL RECORDS

EXECUTIVE DIRECTOR		
Mr W D Pfeiffer	AA2432	694-1402
DEP EXECUTIVE DIRECTOR		
Mr R D Zsalman	AA2432	694-1402

COUNCIL OF PERSONNEL BOARDS

DIRECTOR		
BGEN R R Porter USMC BCT 2	918	696-4365
DEPUTY DIRECTOR		
CAPT L E Hilder BCT 2	918	696-4365

NAVY DEPT BOARD OF DECORATIONS AND MEDALS

SENIOR MEMBER		
RADM M E Chang HOFF 2	8N23	433-2000

OFFICE OF CIVILIAN PERSONNEL MANAGEMENT
(Ballston Centre Tower 1)

MS D M MELETZKE	1104	696-4546
Director		
EXECUTIVE ASST & NAVAL AIDE		
CDR W Howell	1104	696-4546
SPECIAL ASST FOR EEO		
Ms J B Taylor	1105	696-6741
SPECIAL ASST FOR EXEC PERSONNEL		
Mr M Duggins	1106	696-5165
COUNSEL		
Ms J Gnerlich BCT 3	110	696-4717
DIR EMPLOYMENT CLASS & TNG DEPT		
Ms C C Clark	1212	696-4074
DIR WORKFORCE RELATIONS & COMP DEPT		
Mr T J Haycock	1205	696-6597
DIR SYS TECH & FIELD MGMT DEPT		
Mr M Marchesani	1103	696-6272

OFFICE OF PROGRAM APPRAISAL

RADM J K READY	4D730	697-9396
Director		
DEPUTY DIRECTOR		
CAPT C R Saffell	4D730	697-9396
EXECUTIVE ASST		
LCDR J D C Jacob	4D730	697-9396
DEPUTY FOR USMC MATTERS		
COL D B Herbert	4D735	695-7343

(The principal organizational changes that have taken place since the locator was printed 1 October are reflected. However, not all changes could be made prior to publication.)

173

KEY PERSONNEL LOCATOR

OFFICE OF LEGISLATIVE AFFAIRS
RADM T LYNCH	5C760	697-7146
(Chief of Legislative Affairs)		
DEPUTY CHIEF		
CAPT C R Testa	5C760	697-7146
EXECUTIVE ASST		
LCDR M P Campbell	5C760	697-7146
OPS AND LEGIS SUPPORT		
LCDR C D Ruppert	5C765	597-4451
PUBLIC AFFAIRS		
LCDR J Carman	5C768	695-0395
SENATE LIAISON DIV		
CAPT M Bowman	RSOB 182	475-1682
HOUSE LIAISON DIV		
CDR J Kane	RHOB 324	475-1672
NAVY PROGRAMS		
CDR H B Hinkle	5C840	697-3212
LEGISLATION DIV		
CAPT R F Pitkin	5C800	695-5276

OFFICE OF THE JUDGE ADVOCATE GENERAL
(Hoffman Bldg 2)
RADM E D STUMBAUGH (JAGC)	5D838	694-7420
(Judge Advocate General)		
EXECUTIVE ASST		
CDR J Barlett III (JAGC)	5D838	694-7420
DEPUTY		
RADM J E Gordon (JAGC)	9N27	325-9823
EXECUTIVE ASST		
LCDR S J Coyle (JAGC)	9N27	325-9820
ASSISTANT JAG FOR OPS & MGMT		
RADM W L Schachte (JAGC)	9N21	325-9850
PRIN DEP ASST JAG FOR OPS & MGMT		
CAPT H D Bohaboy (JAGC)	9N21	325-9850
ASSISTANT JAG FOR CIVIL LAW		
CAPT J L Hoffman Jr (JAGC)	9N21	325-9850
ASSISTANT JAG FOR MILITARY LAW		
COL C H Mitchell USMC	9N21	325-9850
SPECIAL ASST TO JAG (INSPECTOR GENERAL)		
CAPT M J Gormley III (JAGC)	8N15	325-6117
SPECIAL ASSISTANT TO JAG (COMPTROLLER)		
Mr D J Oppman	8N45	325-0786

OFFICE OF INFORMATION
RADM J B FINKELSTEIN	2E340	697-7391
(Chief of Information)		
DEPUTY CHINFO		
CAPT B Baker	2E340	697-6724
EXECUTIVE ASST		
LCDR S R Pietropaoli	2E340	697-7391
ADMINISTRATIVE FLAG AIDE		
LT K M Wensing	2E340	697-7391
SPECIAL ASST FOR MANPOWER		
CDR W J Rable	2D333	695-6630
ASST CHINFO (ADMIN/RESOURCE MGMT)		
CDR R D Copeland	2D333	694-0937
ASST CHINFO (MEDIA OPERATIONS)		
CDR M C Baker	2E341	697-2904
ASST CHINFO (FIELD OPS/RESERVE PROGS)		
CDR J W Alexander	2E352	695-3161
ASST CHINFO (INTERNAL RELATIONS)		
CDR C L Haney	CWB1046	696-6870
ASST CHINFO (PLANS & POLICY & COMREL)		
CAPT S C Taylor	2E335	697-0250
ASST CHINFO (RADIO & TV)		
Mr H R Hiner	BG168ANA	433-6500

OFFICE OF THE NAVAL INSPECTOR GENERAL
(Washington Navy Yard Bldg 200)
RADM M E CHANG	112	433-2000
FLAG AIDE		
LT J D Hefferman	100	433-2000
DEPUTY NAVAL INSPECTOR GENERAL		
CAPT B W Patton	113	433-2000
DEPUTY NAVAL INSPECTOR GENERAL FOR MARCORPS MTRS		
BGEN J Brickley Arl Annex	2233	694-1533
INVESTIGATIONS OVERSIGHT DIV		
CAPT B Hattan	210	433-4537
INSPECTIONS DIV		
CAPT J D Curry	108	433-2144
AUDIT EVALUATION AND FOLLOW UP DIV		
CAPT T Gill	301	433-3061
PLANS AND ANALYSIS DIV		
CAPT M Hanley	109	433-2268
HEALTH CARE REVIEW DIV		
CAPT D Nelson	300	433-2688

OFFICE OF THE CHIEF NAVAL OPERATIONS

CHIEF OF NAVAL OPERATIONS
ADM C A H TROST	4E660	56007
RADM T D Paulsen	4E672	55664
(Exec Asst)		
CAPT N R Ryan Jr	4E674	53567
(Admin Asst)		
LT D Murphy	4E658	70651
(Naval Aide)		
LT L McCollum	4E658	70651
(Naval Aide)		
MCPON D R Bushey	AA1056	44854
LT F B Fuller	4E674	50532
(Sec Admin)		
LTJG S C Swider	4E674	50532
(Asst Sec Admin)		

VICE CHIEF OF NAVAL OPERATIONS
ADM L A EDNEY	4E644	78347
CAPT T J Lopez	4E636	78347
(Exec Asst)		
CDR P K Landers	4E636	53193
(Admin Asst)		
MAJ M E Clark	4E644	78347
(USMC Aide)		
LT S C Trainor	4E644	78347
(Aide)		
CWO J T Manley	4E632	53193
(Staff Secy)		
LTJG C W Yard	4E632	53193
(Staff Secy)		

DEPUTY CHIEFS OF NAVAL OPERATIONS

DCNO (MANPOWER, PERSONNEL AND TRAINING)/CHNAVPERS
VADM J M BOORDA	AA2072	41101
CAPT H G Sprouse	AA2075	42340
(Exec Asst)		
ADCNO (MPT)		
RADM F R Donovan	AA2068	43051
TOTAL FORCE TRNG & EDUC DIV		
CAPT M A McDevitt (Dir)	AAG831	45216
TOTAL FORCE PROG MPW DIV		
RADM R G Jones (Dir)	AA2821	45571
MIL PERS POL DIV		
RADM R G Jones (Dir)	AA2821	45571
CIVPERS POL PROGRAMS DIV		
Mr R M Felton (Acting)	SKYL-6	756-8480
PRIDE PROF & PERS EXCELLENCE DIV		
RADM R W West (Dir)	AA1070	44259
TOTAL FORCE INFO RES & SYS MGMT DIV		
Mr D Skeen (Dir)	AA1052	41012

ACNO (UNDERSEA WARFARE)
VADM D L COOPER	4E524	50058
DACNO (UNDERSEA WARFARE)		
RADM M C Colley	4E524	50061
STRATEGIC SUBMARINE DIV		
RADM (Sel) K L Kaup (Dir)	4D534	70886
ATTACK SUBMARINE DIV		
RADM T A Meinicke (Dir)	4D482	71981
DEEP SUBMERGENCE SYS DIV		
RADM D G Griffith (Dir)	4D462	72040
UNDERSEA SURVEILLANCE DIV		
CAPT I H Coen (Dir)	5D580	75551
SUB MPWR & TRNG DIV		
CAPT L E Everman (Dir)	4E453	51515

ACNO (SURFACE WARFARE)
VADM J W NYQUIST	4E552	77469
DACNO (SURFACE WARFARE)		
RADM G A Sharp	4E552	54611
SURF WARF PROG & BUDGET DIV		
CAPT M C Foote (Dir)	4D481	74512
NAVAL SPEC WARFARE DIV		
CAPT M Jukoski (Dir)	4D537	77806
SURFACE WARFARE DIV		
CAPT W J Flanagan (Dir)	4D547	71465
SURFACE COMBAT SYS DIV		
CAPT G N Gee (Dir)	4B545	57642
COMBAT LOG, AUX, AMPHIBS & MINE WARF DIV		
CAPT T Triplett (Actg Dir)	4A720	76897
SURF WARF MPWR & TRNG RQMTS DIV		
CAPT J D Pearson (Dir)	4C520	76799

DCNO (LOGISTICS)
VADM S R ARTHUR	4E606	52154
ADCNO (LOGISTICS)		
RADM G H Curtis III	4E606	55183
ASST FOR CIVIL ENGINEERING		
CAPT J M Dougherty Hoff Bldg 2	10N59	325-0556
ASST FOR PLAN/PROG/BUDGET/MNPWR/TRAINING		
CAPT R J Vanni	4C521	54823
NAVAL RESERVE COORD (LOGISTICS)		
CAPT C W Krouch	4C527	54376
JOINT & OPER LOG PLANS & PROG DIV		
Mr J A Bizup (Actg Dir)	4B546	42808
MATERIEL DIV		
RADM E M Straw (Dir)	4B470	54003
STRATEGIC SEALIFT DIV		
Mr J D Kaskin (Dir)	BD766	54001
SHIPS MAINT & MODERNIZATION DIV		
RADM G H Curtis III (Dir)	4B529	79760
SHORE ACTIVITIES DIV		
RADM J C Doebler (Dir)	4B473	52420
ENVIRN PROT SAFETY & OCCUP HLTH DIV		
CAPT R H Rice (Dir) CP-5	654	25577
ILS POLICY, TECH & ASSESSMENTS DIV		
Mr P R Cataldo (Dir)	4B546	43735

ACNO (AIR WARFARE)
VADM R F DUNN	4E394	52374
DACNO (AIR WARFARE)		
RADM R P Ilg	4E394	52629
DACNO (MARINE AVIATION)		
LGEN C H Pitman AA	2335	41023
AVN PLANS & REQS DIV		
RADM J D Taylor (Dir)	4E384	71446
NAVAL AVN MAINT PROG (NAMP) DIV		
CAPT M T Najarian (Dir)	4E360	75507
MARINE AVN PLANS & PROG DIV		
LGEN C H Pitman (Dir) AA	2335	41023
CARRIER & AIR STATION PROGS DIV		
RADM F J Metz (Dir)	4E391	79357
AVN MPWR & TRNG DIV		
RADM P H Cressy (Dir)	4E424	50565

DCNO (PLANS, POLICY AND OPERATIONS)
VADM C R LARSON	4E592	53707
ADCNO (PLANS, POLICY AND OPS)		
RADM J F Dorsey Jr	4E592	55081
STRAT PLANS AND POLICY DIV		
RADM P D Smith	4E566	55620
POLITICO-MILITARY POL & CUR PLAN DIV		
RADM J E Taylor	4E572	52453
TOTAL FORCE & FLT OPS DIV		
CAPT J M Quarterman Jr (Dir)	4D600	76033
STRAT & THEATER NUCLEAR WARF DIV		
RADM W P Houley (Dir)	4E572	54402

DCNO (NAVAL WARFARE)
VADM P D MILLER	4E536	71098
CAPT R D Gumbert	4E536	71098
(Exec Asst)		
RADM C R McGrail, Jr	4E536	73408
(Dep Dir)		
NAVAL WARF ANAL ASSESS & FORCE LEVEL PLANS DIV		
RADM D Richardson (Dir)	4E482	53777
ANTI SUBMARINE WARFARE DIV		
RADM J Fitzgerald (Dir)	5D589	51767
MINE WARFARE DIV		
RADM B E Tobin (Dir)	5E617	71443
TACTICAL READINESS DIV		
CAPT R W Hechtman (Dir)	5D566	75857
STRIKE AND AMPHIB WARFARE DIV		
RADM F L Lewis (Dir)	5E613	71466
ANTI AIR WARFARE DIV		
CAPT E E Killinger (Dir)	2C340	47274
ELECTRONIC WARFARE C³ AND SPACE WARFARE DIV		
RADM M Welch (Dir)	4C652	59590

DCNO (NAVY PROGRAM PLANNING)
VADM W D Smith	4E620	50346
CAPT H C Giffin III	4E620	50347
(Exec Asst)		
GENERAL PLANNING & PROGRAMMING DIV		
RADM M P Kalleres (Dir)	4D662	70517
PROGRAM RESOURCE APPRAISAL DIV		
RADM D P March (Dir)	4A530	70831
FISCAL MANAGEMENT DIV		
RADM S F Loftus (Dir)	4C736	77105

DIRECTORS, MAJOR STAFF OFFICES

ASSISTANT VICE CHIEF OF NAVAL OPERATIONS
CAPT W R McGOWEN	4E623	54337
CAPT G C Wileen	4E623	54336
(Exec Asst)		
ASST FOR CIVPERS AND SES POLICY		
Ms J Eul	4B531	58784
ASST FOR EEO		
Ms S A Lee	2B328	78203
ASST FOR FIELD SUPPORT		
Mr R B Keller Bldg 150 ANA		433-3037
DIR OF NAVAL HISTORY		
Dr R Spector Bldg 57 WNY		433-2210
ASST FOR LEGAL & LEGIS MATTERS		
LCDR P L Fagan	4E629	53480
OPNAV CAREER COUNSELOR		
NCC S J Facsko	4C549	57787
OPNAV COMMAND MASTER CHIEF		
MMCM T L Miller	4C549	57787
NAVAL IMAGING MGMT DIV		
CAPT H H Loving (Dir) Bldg 168 ANA		433-2102
ORG & OPNAV RESOURCE MGMT DIV		
CAPT W T T Hood Jr (Dir)	4D435	70282
OPNAV SERVICES & SECURITY DIV		
Mr H J Loeper III (Dir)	5E595	54253
INTERNAL CONT SYS MGMT DIV		
Mr N J Cook (Dir) Bldg 159 WNY		433-5950

DIRECTOR OF NAVAL INTELLIGENCE
RADM T A BROOKS	5C564	53944
CAPT N H Litsinger	5C564	50124
(Exec Asst)		
DEPUTY DIRECTOR OF NAVAL INTELLIGENCE		
Mr R L Haver	5C600	44408
DEPUTY DIRECTOR FOR CRYPTOLOGY		
RADM J S McFarland	5C564	52988
DEPUTY DIRECTOR FOR INTELLIGENCE PRODUCTION		
CAPT F Levine	5C564	50124
CDR D J Maresh	5C564	50124
(ADMIN ASST)		
ASST FOR CURRENT INTELLIGENCE		
CDR A W Legrow	4D642	72916
ASST FOR LEGAL MATTERS		
LCDR J P Callahan	5C564	70045
ASST FOR INTERAGENCY COORD		
CAPT T E Murphy	5D660	54727
ASST FOR FOREIGN LIAISON		
CAPT N Idleberg	5C565	55333
ASST FOR RESERVE INTEL PROG		
CAPT D R Zickafoose	5B680	56255
ASST FOR RESERVE MATTERS		
CAPT D R Zickafoose	5B680	56255

ASST FOR TECHNOLOGY		
Mr T H Handel	5D660	73299
ASST FOR JNID		
CAPT Oates	Suitland	763-3474
ASST FOR FOREIGN COUNTERINTEL		
RADM J E Gordon	NIC-1	763-3750
ASST FOR SPEC SEC MTRS		
Mr G Philipp	5B660	51754
RESOURCE MGMT DIV		
CAPT C W Maillefert (Dir)	5B681	52907
INTEL & CRYPTO PLANS, POL & RQMTS DIV		
CAPT J C Clark (Dir)	40277	5B688
OPERATIONAL SUPPORT DIV		
CAPT H R Adair (Dir)	5D660	74199
INTEL ANALYSIS DIV		
CAPT J M Eglin (Dir)	5B674	54468
RESEARCH & DEVL REQ DIV		
Mr P M Lowell (Dir)	5D660	72070

DIRECTOR OF NAVAL NUCLEAR PROPULSION PROGRAM
(National Center 2)

ADM B DEMARS		23887

DIRECTOR OF NAVAL MEDICINE/ SURGEON GENERAL OF THE NAVY

VADM J A ZIMBLE (MC)	4E436	70587
CAPT G S Harris (MSC) *(Exec Asst)*	4E436	70587
DEPUTY DIRECTOR OF NAVAL MEDICINE		
RADM R P Caudill Jr (MC)	4E436	76201
DEP DIR OF NAVAL MEDICINE (MARCORPS MEDICAL MTRS)		
RADM R W Higgins (MC) AA	2229	44477
DEP DIR OF NAVAL MEDICINE (RESERVE AFFAIRS)		
RADM J G Roberts (MC)	4C475	72311
RESOURCES DIV		
Mr W G Mattheis (Dir)	4C461	51921
PLANS & POLICY DIV		
CAPT W E Hirschfeld (DC) (Dir)	4C457	71460
HEALTH CARE OPERATIONS DIV		
CAPT H M Koenig (MC) (Dir)	PA#6	653-1727
EDUCATION & TRAINING DIV		
CAPT P M Curran (MSC) (Dir)	PA#6	653-1752

DIRECTOR OF SPACE, COMMAND & CONTROL

RADM L LAYMAN	4C679	53239
RADM D B Cargill *(Dep Dir)*	4C679	53668
C^2 PLANNING AND PROGRAMMING DIV		
CAPT D L Ricketts	5B730	76441
NAVAL COMMUNICATIONS DIV		
CAPT A R Gomez (Dir)	5A718	57284
C^2 SYS DIV		
CAPT R E Kordalski (Dir)	5E569	56667
NAVY SPACE SYS DIV		
CAPT P S Anselmo (Dir)	4C668	70761
INFO MGT SUP DIV		
RADM P E Tobin Jr (Dir)	5B731	50103

DIRECTOR OF NAVAL RESERVE

RADM F N SMITH	4E466	55353
CAPT H L Merritt *(Exec Asst)*	4E466	55353
RADM (Sel) T F Hall *(Dep Dir)*	4E466	44605
RESERVE AIR PROGRAM MGMT DIV		
CAPT T G Palmer (Dir)	4E478	55517
RESERVE SURF PROG MGMT DIV		
CAPT A V Schultz Jr (Dir)	4E427	74551
FINANCIAL MGMT DIV		
CAPT S Simonson (Dir)	4E458	52859
RESERVE PLANNING & PROG DIV		
CAPT M E Arnold (Dir)	4B489	58970
RESERVE MPWR, PERS & TRAINING DIV		
CAPT H E Glad (Dir)	4E433	70075

OCEANOGRAPHER OF THE NAVY
(Naval Observatory, Bldg 1)

RADM R F PITTENGER		653-1299
CAPT J E Chubb *(Dep)*		653-1491
TECHNICAL DIRECTOR		
Mr R Winokur		653-1536

DIRECTOR OF RELIGIOUS MINISTRIES/ CHIEF OF CHAPLAINS OF THE NAVY

RADM A B KOENEMAN	AAG842	44043
CAPT J M Wright *(Exec Asst)*	AAG840	44326
RADM D E White *(Dep Chief of Chaplains of the Navy)*	AAG841	44326

DIRECTOR OF RESEARCH AND DEVELOPMENT REQUIREMENTS, TEST AND EVALUATION

VADM P F McCARTHY	5C686	75533
RADM H L Webster *(Dep Dir)*	5C686	74532
TEST AND EVAL AND FACILITIES DIV		
CAPT R T Fuller (Dir)	5C736	74402
RES AND DEV RQMTS DIV		
CAPT T Williams (Dir)	5C678	45837
SCIENCE AND TECH DIV		
Dr F Shoup (Dir)	5D760	79726

SYSTEMS COMMANDS

NAVAL AIR SYSTEMS COMMAND
(Jefferson Plaza Bldgs 1 & 2)

VADM J B WILKINSON *(Commander NAVAIRSYSCOM)*	JP-1	1200	22280
CAPT J W Heineman *(Exec Asst)*	JP-1	1200	22280
VICE COMMANDER			
RADM R C Gentz	JP-1	1200	22270
DEPUTY COMMANDER			
Mr R V Johnson	JP-1	1200	24156
COUNSEL			
Ms M A Olsen	JP-1	314	27021
SAFETY OFFICER			
CDR C H Yates	JP-2	942	21234
INSPECTOR GENERAL			
CAPT D H Christian	JP-2	124	28582
STAFF JUDGE ADVOCATE			
CAPT E W Hosken	JP-2	140	25555
RESEARCH & TECH DIRECTORATE			
CAPT W D Key	JP-1	412	27439
LEGIS & PUBLIC AFF OFFICE			
Ms D C Prince	JP-1	1242	746-3785
NAVAL AVIATION READINESS OFFICE			
CAPT E E Chelton	JP-1	542	28523
CORP MGMT DIRECTORATE			
Mr M G Akin	JP-1	1276	746-3713
ACQ EX & DEP COM FOR OPS			
RADM R D Friichtenicht	JP-1	1186	22280
DEPUTY ACQUISITION EXEC			
Mr W L Wagner	JP-1	1186	22283
PDA FOR TACTICAL AIRCRAFT PROG			
RADM J F Calvert	JP-1	1186	22282
PDA FOR WEAPONS PROGRAMS			
Mr D P Czelusniak	JP-1	1186	27988
PDA FOR EW & MISSION SUPPORT PROG			
Mr D Distler	JP-1	1186	22283
PDA FOR ASW & ASSAULT PROGRAMS			
CAPT W L Vincent	JP-1	1186	27989
PDA FOR CRUISE MISSILES			
RADM W C Bowes	CG-4	832	27409
ASST COM FOR CONTRACTS			
CAPT W Morris	JP-1	116	20916
ASST COM FOR FLEET SUPPORT & FA MGT			
RADM J H Kirkpatrick	JP-2	480	22690
ASST COM FOR SYS & ENGR			
RADM L E Blose	JP-2	1240	23827
COMPTROLLER			
CAPT W A Earner	JP-1	1114	23924

NAVAL SEA SYSTEMS COMMAND
(National Center Bldgs 2 & 3, Crystal Park Bldg 1)
(Crystal Plaza Bldg 5)

VADM P M HEKMAN JR *(Commander NAVSEASYSCOM)*	NC-3	12E10	23381
CAPT P M Robinson *(Exec Asst)*	NC-3	12E10	23327
LCDR T G Briggs *(Flag Admin Off)*	NC-3	12N16	21455
LCDR J Wilson *(Flag Aide)*	NC-3	12E10	23328
VICE COMMANDER			
RADM M MacKinnon III	NC-3	12E10	23681
DEPUTY COMMANDER			
Mr J N Shrader	NC-3	12E10	26163
CHIEF ENGINEER			
RADM M MacKinnon III	NC-3	4E60	22746
DEP COM COMPTROLLER			
RADM (Sel) S S Clarey	NC-3	12E24	23438
DEP COM CONTRACTS			
CAPT E B Harshbarger	NC-3	5E58	27977
DEP COM FOR SHIP DESIGN & ENG			
RADM R B Horne Jr	NC-3	10E08	22438
DEP COM FOR WPNS & COMBAT SYS			
RADM R H Ailes	NC-2	9W62	20913
ASST DEP COM FOR AAW & SURFACE WARFARE			
RADM G R Meinig Jr	NC-2	9S06	24122
ASST DEP COM FOR COMBAT SYS ENGR			
RADM (Sel) J T Hood	NC-2	7W48	22591
ASST DEP COM FOR ASW & UNDERSEA WARFARE			
RADM (Sel) W C Carlson	NC-2	12N06	28826
ASST DEP COM FOR SUB COMBAT SYSTEMS			
RADM D Valganau	[illegible]	[illegible]	[illegible]
ASST DEP COM FOR ELECTRONIC WARFARE			
RADM G R Meinig Jr	NC-2	9S06	24122
DEP COM FOR INDUSTRIAL & FACILITY MGMT			
RADM D H Hines	CP-5	1174	746-5000
DEP COM FOR NUCLEAR PROP			
ADM B DeMars	NC-2	3N06	23887
DEP COM FOR ACQ, PLANNING & APPRAISAL			
Mr W A Tarbell	CPK-1	1102	746-3000
DEP COM FOR SURFACE COMBATANTS			
RADM R T Reimann	NC-3	9S08	22072
DEP COM FOR SUBMARINES			
RADM W H Cantrell	NC-3	7S18	21564
DEP COM FOR AMPHIB, AUX, MINE & SEALIFT SHIPS			
CAPT J F King	NC-3	8E34	26918
PROG MANAGER, AEGIS PROGRAM			
RADM J B Greene	NC-2	10N18	27395
PROG MANAGER, SEAWOLF CLASS SUBMARINE PROGRAM			
RADM (Sel) M S Firebaugh	NC-3	7N24	27200

SPACE AND NAVAL WARFARE SYSTEMS COMMAND
(National Center Bldg 1)

RADM J C WEAVER *(Commander SPAWARSYSCOM)*	9E44	23006
CAPT D W Cook *(Exec Asst)*	9E44	23007
VICE COMMANDER		
RADM L J Holloway	9E44	28960
DEPUTY COMMANDER		
Mr R E Doak	9E44	23008
COUNSEL		
Mr H J Nathan	11W50	28458
INSPECTOR GENERAL		
CAPT D W Cook	9E44	23007
ASST COM FOR ACQ & TECH MGT		
Mr R P Young	12S18	21006
ASST COM FOR SPACE TECH		
RADM T C Betterton NRL	259	767-9602
DIR OF NAVY LABS		
Mr J L Reed	12E50	22766
COMPTROLLER		
CAPT R A Perron	9N20	23260
DIR OF CONTRACTS		
CAPT J A Schroeder	7E08	27777
MGT & OPERS DIR		
Mr W McCafferty	9S12	746-4000
DIR OF WARF SYS ARCH & ENG		
RADM D M Brooks	9E44	28960
DIR OF SPACE & SENSOR SYS PROG		
RADM T K Mattingly II	2S12	22182
DIR OF INFORMATION TRANS SYS PROG		
RADM L C Wilgenbusch	5E08	28873
INFO MGMT SYS PROG		
CAPT H E Seligson	8N20	28964
MARCORPS SYS PROG		
COL L L Simpleman	5S20	28880
DIR ASW SYS PROG		
RADM C E Dorman	5D616	74735

NAVAL SUPPLY SYSTEMS COMMAND
(Crystal Mall Bldg 3)

RADM D W McKINNON JR *(Commander NAVSUPSYSCOM)*	622	54009
CDR T M McQueen *(Exec Asst)*	622	54922
VICE COMMANDER		
RADM R B Abele (SC)	622	54493
RESALE & SERV SUPP PROG		
CDR W T Kaloupek	606	44034
SMALL/DISADVANTAGED BUSINESS UTIL		
Mr R F Quinn	606	55952
CIVILIAN PERSONNEL PROG OFF		
Mr H Cowles	634	74795
MANAGEMENT INFORMATION CENTER		
Ms D Brown	624	55351
PUBLIC AFFAIRS OFFICE		
Ms N Dimond	638	73795
INSPECTOR GENERAL NAVSUPSYSCOM		
CAPT G W Willis (SC)	520	55391
OFFICE OF COUNSEL		
Mr C J McManus	625	55519
FLEET HOSPITAL PROGRAM OFFICE		
CAPT A W Frost (MC)	221	52136
DEP COM ENG & QUAL ASSURANCE/NAVY SPARES COMPET & LOG TECH PROG MGT OFF		
Mr W H Campbell CSQ 5	Rm 511	22269
SUPPLY CORPS PERSONNEL		
CAPT J T Scudi	2501AA	48765
DEPCOM FIN MGT COMPTROLLER		
CAPT D E Hickman	730	55545
DEPCOM CONTRACTING MGMT		
CAPT J C Cheney (SC)	619	54377
DEPCOM FL SUPP CORP PLANS & LOGS		
CAPT A J Nissalke (SC)	608	73922
ASSTCOM INVENTORY & SYS INTEGRITY		
RADM R M Moore	718	53824
DEPCOM INVENTORY & INFO SYS DEV		
CAPT K E Kittock (SC)	718	56976
DEPCOM TRANSPORTATION		
CAPT C J Nichols (SC) CM 2	Rm112	52954
DEPCOM PHYSICAL DISTRIBUTION		
CAPT W S Draper (SC)	714	53181
DEPCOM SECURITY ASSISTANCE		
CAPT L S Frieberg (SC)	522	50753
DEPCOM ADMIN MGMT		
Mr J Browne	700	746-4300
DEPCOM NAVY PUBS & PRINTING PROG		
Mr J L Cherny Bldg 157-3	WNY	433-2261
DEPCOM NAVY RESALE & SERV SUPP PROG		
RADM R A Squibb (SC) NYC	AV8	456-2444/5
DEPCOM NAVY FOOD SERV SYS OFF		
CAPT J F Anderson (SC) 166-2	WNY	433-3701
DEPCOM NAVY FUEL MGMT SYSTEM		
CAPT J H Carstajen	CAMSTA	274-7467

NAVAL FACILITIES ENGINEERING COMMAND
(Hoffman Bldg 2)

RADM B F MONTOYA (CEC) *(Commander NAVFACENGCOM)*	11N37	325-0400
CDR J P Collins (CEC) *(Exec Asst)*	11N37	325-0403
VICE COMMANDER		
RADM A K Riffey (CEC)	11N37	325-0402
DEP COM FOR FAC ACQ		
CAPT T Tucker	11S59	325-9484
DEP COM FOR PUB WRKS		
CAPT C M Maskell	11N57	325-8541
MILITARY JUDGE STAFF ADVOCATE		
CAPT C Vanderhoef	10N59	325-0056

SPECIAL ASSISTANTS

RADM J B FINKLESTEIN	SPECIAL ASSISTANT FOR PUBLIC AFFAIRS SUPPORT	2E340	77391
RADM F L LEWIS	SPECIAL ASSISTANT FOR SAFETY MATTERS	4A452	57500
RADM M E CHANG	SPECIAL ASSISTANT FOR INSPECTION SUPPORT	WNY BLDG 200	433-2000
RADM E D STUMBAUGH (JAGC)	SPECIAL ASSISTANT FOR LEGAL SERVICES	5D838	47420
RADM T LYNCH	SPECIAL ASSISTANT FOR LEGISLATIVE SUPPORT	5C760	77146
RADM J E GORDON	SPECIAL ASSISTANT FOR NAVAL INVES MTRS & SECURITY	SFC310	763-3750

KEY PERSONNEL LOCATOR

DEP COM FOR MRWR & ORG		
CAPT D Nash	12S25	325-8543
COUNSEL		
Mr M K McElhaney	11N69	325-9067
INSPECTOR GENERAL		
CAPT W Garbe	12N33	325-8548
SMALL BUSINESS ECONOMIC UTILIZATION & CONTRACTOR LIAISON OFF		
Ms R Dubuisson	11N59	325-8549
DIRECTOR OF PROG & COMPT		
CAPT L A Fermo (CEC)	11N19	325-8577
DEP COM FOR CONTRACTS		
Mr P P Buonaccorsi	11S67	325-9121
ASST COM FOR R&D		
Mr A S Bradford	12N45	325-9014
ASST COM FOR ENG & DESIGN		
Mr H H Zimmerman	12S55	325-0032
ASST COM FOR CONSTRUCTION		
CAPT B Runberg	11S59	325-9484
DEP COM FOR MIL READINESS (SEABEES)		
CAPT D J Nash	12S33	325-8555
ASST COM FOR FAMILY HOUSING		
CAPT A Moyle	10N41	325-9246
ASST COM FOR PWCS & DEPTS		
CDR G Everhart (CEC)	10S03	325-8194
ASST COM FOR ENVIRON, SAFETY & HEALTH		
CAPT J Dempsey	10S23	325-0295
ASST COM FOR FAC PLAN & REAL ESTATE		
CAPT J M Dougherty (CEC)	10N59	325-0556
ASST COM FOR MILCON PROGRAMMING		
CAPT B F Folson	10S55	325-8600

NAVY COMMANDS AND ACTIVITIES

MILITARY SEALIFT COMMAND
(Bldg 210 WNY)

VADM P D BUTCHER	404	433-0001
(Commander MSC)		
VICE COMMANDER		
Mr W Sansone	404	433-0007
DEPUTY COMMANDER		
CAPT F M Williamson (Actg)	405	433-0005
LEGISLATIVE & PUBLIC AFF OFF		
Ms M Holtz	243	433-0330
COMMAND DEPUTY EEO OFF		
Mr H Davidson Bldg 172	202D	433-7101
FLAG SECRETARY		
CDR A E Brown	419	433-0004
INSPECTOR GENERAL		
CAPT F M Williamson Bldg 172	202A	433-5099
PERSONNEL, MPWR, & MGMT OFF		
Mrs M L Lewis Bldg 219	324	433-0445
READINESS & PRO INTRODUCTION OFF		
CAPT M A Kubishen	300	433-0497
OPERATIONS OFF		
CAPT J A Peschka	339	433-0075
ENGINEER OFF		
Mr T W Allen	131	433-0170
FORCE MEDICAL OFF		
CAPT J L Hauser (MC) Bldg 219	400	433-0891
SUPPLY OFF		
CAPT A K Paszly	120	433-0116
COMPTROLLER		
Mr W D Savitsky Wolfe Bldg	160	427-5615
STRATEGIC MOBILITY OFF		
COL J A Weiss USA	232	433-0296
COUNSEL		
Mr R S Haynes	425	433-0140
COMMAND INFO SYS OFF		
Mr B Genzlinger	244	433-0320
CONTRACTING OFF		
CAPT W J Pollock	456	433-0315

NAVAL CIVILIAN PERSONNEL CENTER
(6 Skyline Place)

MR R M FELTON	701	756-8447
(Acting Director)		
DEP DIR		
Ms J M Wenger (Actg)	701	756-8450
MGMT & ASSESS		
Ms P Blythe (Actg)	701	756-8450
NCPDS PROJECT MANAGER		
Mr F T Catenaccio BT #3	145	696-5035

NAVAL INTELLIGENCE COMMAND
(Suitland Federal Center)

CAPT F W LEVIN	S200	763-3552
(Commander NAVINTCOM)		
DEPUTY COMNAVINTCOM		
CAPT T L Morgan	S200	763-3553
DEP DIR		
Mr D P Harman	S210	763-3555
INSPECTOR GENERAL		
Mr J Runyon	S207	763-3557
DEPUTY EEO OFFICER		
Mr F L Antoine	S212	763-3540
COMMAND MASTER CHIEF		
ISCM G Zales	S208	763-3551
PJOI/JNIDS		
CAPT J S Oates	S241	763-3462
ASST FOR PROCESSING SYS		
CAPT P B Weller	S235	763-3506
SPEC ASST FOR R&D		
Mr P Lowell	5D675	695-9217
ACNIC MPT & ADMIN		
CAPT L Shelton Jr	S218	763-3544
ACNIC FIN MGMT/COMPT		
Ms B P Swift	S164	763-3410
ACNIC OPERATIONS CTF-168		
CAPT R A Saenz	S246	763-3595
ACNIC SCI SECURITY POLICY		
CAPT M Pelensky	S282	763-3582

NAVAL DATA AUTOMATION COMMAND
(Bldg 166 Washington Navy Yard)

MR R G GARANT		433-4067
(Commander NAVDAC)		
DEPUTY COMMANDER		
CAPT E J BENDAR		433-4067
TECHNICAL DIRECTOR		
Mr L Meador		433-4911
INSPECTOR GENERAL		
CDR B Sharpe		433-4309
COUNSEL		
Mr D Andross		433-4025
COMMAND DEPUTY EEOO		
Ms H A Wilson		433-2041
COMPTROLLER		
Mr C Bolter		433-4299
DIR SYS EVAL & POL		
Mr W O'Brien		433-2872
DIR COMMAND SUPPORT		
CDR D W Palomaki (Actg)		433-4904
DIR DATA COMMUNICATIONS		
CAPT S R Cabik		433-4996
DIR COMPUTER PROG DEVELOP		
CAPT K VanLue		433-2241
DIR COMPUTER SYS OPS		
Mr J N Schauer		433-4917
DIR NAVY DIRECTIVES, POSTAL & RECORDS MGMT		
CDR B Baller		433-2434
DIR ADVANCE TECH, PLAN & MKTING		
Mr J W Gillespie		433-3528

NAVAL MILITARY PERSONNEL COMMAND
(Arlington Annex)

RADM F R DONOVAN	2068	42243
(Commander NMPC)		
CDR J C Biernesser	2068	41477
(Admin Asst)		
CHIEF OF STAFF/EXEC ASST		
CAPT T I Eubanks	2068	48259
DIR CLASSIFICATION SYSTEM		
CAPT E L Naro	ANA	433-5488
DIR ADMIN OFFICE		
CAPT R W Youmans	2705	41100
RESOURCE MGMT OFFICE		
Mr T C Fiocchi	2058	43526
DIR MIL CORRES & CONG LIAISON OFF		
CAPT W P Cooper	2625	41375
NAVY UNIFORM MATTERS OFFICE		
CDR D O Richey	1055	45075
PUBLIC AFFAIRS		
CAPT G I Peterson	1074	42000
OFFICE OF LEGAL COUNSEL		
CAPT R E Coyle	2708	45158
DIR NAVY PASSENGER TRANS OFFICE		
Mr J H Brown	2711	43626
DIR CAREER PROGRESSION DEPT		
CAPT J S Falls	4637	41117
DIR MIL PERS RECORD DATA MGMT DEPT		
CAPT M Yeoman	4074	42767
DIR DISTRIBUTION DEPT		
RADM R J Zlatoper	3072	43454
DIR PRIDE PROFESSIONALISM & PERSONAL EXCEL DEPT		
RADM R W West	1070	44259
DIR MPN FINANCIAL MGMT DEPT		
Mr F Robenhymer	1733	45664
DIR MIL PERS PERFORMANCE & SEC DEPT		
CAPT T W Hutt Jr	1635	43845
DIR NAVRES PERS MGMT DEPT		
CAPT M D Ford CWB	702C	44416
DIR TOTAL FORCE AUTOMATED SYS DEPT		
Mr D Skeen	1050	41012

BOARD OF INSPECTION & SURVEY
(Potomac Annex)

RADM T E LEWIN	6002	653-1133
(President)		
DEPUTY		
CAPT D J Klinkhamer	6003	653-1136

NAVAL SECURITY GROUP COMMAND
(3801 Nebraska Ave NW Wash DC)

RADM J S MCFARLAND	17137	282-0444
(Commander NAVSECGRU)		
DEPUTY COMNAVSECGRU		
CAPT S W Jacobs	17137	282-0444
FORCE MASTER CHIEF		
CTOCM R R Adams	17133	282-0264
INSPECTOR GENERAL		
Vacant	17133	282-0306
ASST COMMANDER (FT MEADE)		
CAPT R A Shriver	8A164	688-6446
ASST FOR ADMIN		
LT W T Matthews	17118	282-0272
ASST FOR PPB & RM/COMPTROLLER		
CAPT C J Malloy	17201	282-0491
ASST FOR MARCORPS MATTERS		
LTCOL P Brown	1118	282-0251
ASST FOR PERS & TRAINING		
CAPT J T Mitchell	1112	282-0459
ASST FOR TELECOM/ADP SYS		
CDR J E Gourley II	17045	282-0758
ASST FOR LOGISTICS & MATERIEL		
CAPT C F Authement	2393	282-0851
ASST FOR SPECIAL OPERATIONS		
CAPT M H Shank	1220	282-0236
ASST FOR TECH DEVELOPMENT		
CAPT J W Moffat	20209	282-0630
ASST FOR RESERVE PLANS & READINESS		
CAPT C H Benjamin	17123	282-0201

NAVAL LEGAL SERVICE COMMAND
(Hoffman Bldg 2)

RADM E D STUMBAUGH (JAGC)	5D838	694-7420
(Commander NAVLEGSVCOM)		
VICE COMMANDER		
RADM J E Gordon (JAGC)	9N27	325-9823
DEPUTY COMMANDER		
RADM W L Schachte (JAGC)	9B21	325-9850
ASSISTANT DEPUTY COMMANDER (OPS & MGMT)		
CAPT H D Bohaboy (JAGC)	9N21	325-9850
DEP ASST TO COMMANDER (INSPECTIONS)		
CAPT M J Gormley III (JAGC)	8N15	325-6117
DEP ASST TO COMMANDER (COMPTROLLER)		
Mr D J Oppman	8N45	325-0786

NAVAL INVESTIGATIVE SERVICE COMMAND
(Suitland Federal Ctr)

RADM J E GORDON		763-3750
(Commander)		
DEPUTY COMMANDER		
COL W Coomes USMC		763-3754
DIR NIS		
Mr J B McKee		763-3751
INSPECTOR GENERAL		
Mr P Reilly		763-3755
DEPUTY EEO OFFICER		
Mrs I Robison		763-3454
DIR INFO SECURITY		
Mr C V Page Wolfe Bldg		427-5900
DIR FOR COUNTERINTELLIGENCE		
Mr W A Worochock		763-3758
DIR FOR CRIMINAL INVEST		
Mr R Powers		763-3759
DIR FOR LAW ENFORCE/PHY SEC		
Mr J O'Hara		763-3390
ASST DIR CAREER SERV		
Mr W K Sumner		763-3768
ASST DIR TECH SERV		
Mr J J D'Avanzo		763-3775
ASST DIR INFO SYS		
Mr J T Oney		763-3777
ASST DIR ADMIN		
Mr R E Childs		763-3783
DIR CAF		
Mr D L Jacobson Wolfe Bldg		427-6026
ASST DIR TRAINING		
Mr D W Dykes		763-3770
DIR TASK FORCE		
Mr L McCullah Half St		475-1057

NAVAL MEDICAL COMMAND
(Potomac Annex)

RADM H J T SEARS (MC)		653-1144
(Commander NAVMEDCOM)		
CAPT H E Phillips (MSC)		653-1146
(Exec Asst)		
VICE COMMANDER		
RADM D E Shuler (MSC)		653-1145
DEP COM FOR FIN MGMT		
Mr J Cuddy		653-1074
DEP COM FOR FLT READINESS & SUPP		
RADM W Buckendorf (MC)		653-1173
DEP COM FOR HEALTH CARE OPS		
RADM D Hagen (MC)		653-1176
DEP COM FOR READINESS & LOGS		
CAPT R J Salmon (MC)		653-1202
DEP COM FOR PERSONNEL MGMT		
RADM M F Hall		653-1168
DEP COM FOR DENTAL CARE		
RADM R G Shaffer (DC)		653-1170

NAVAL TELECOMMUNICATIONS COMMAND
(4401 Mass Ave NW Washington DC)

CAPT T E STONE	19119	282-0550
(Commander NAVTELCOM)		
FLAG AIDE		
Vacant	19127	282-0691
DEPUTY COMNAVTELCOM		
CAPT R Baker	19117B	282-0466
ASST CHIEF OF STAFF MPWR, PERS, TRAINING ADMIN AND RESERVE AFFAIRS		
CAPT R H Pewett	19124B	282-0262
ASST CHIEF OF STAFF OPERATIONS AND READINESS		
CDR W Hill	19235A	282-0821
ASST CHIEF OF STAFF ENGINEERING AND FACILITIES		
CDR S Mohsberg	19351B	282-2500
ASST CHIEF OF STAFF PLANS, INTEG AND MGMT		
CAPT R Baker	19317D	282-0719
ASST CHIEF OF STAFF SUPPLY BUDGET AND PROG		
CDR J M Dykes	19413	282-0545
NAVTELCOM INSPECTOR GENERAL		
CAPT R Michaux	19239	282-0494
DEPUTY EEO OFFICER		
Mr W B Gentry	19110	282-0420
FORCE MASTER CHIEF		
RCMC T E Ward	19117A	282-0468
SPECIAL ASSISTANT FOR FREQUENCY MGMT		
Mr H W Holsopple	19435	282-0581
NAVY COML COMM OFF		
Mr A Dalton	19105	282-0577
DIRECTOR OFC OF NAVY TELCOM CONTRACTING		
CAPT Madroski	19231	282-0864

(Cheltenham, MD)

DIRECTOR NAVAL TELCOM SYSTEM INTEGRATION CENTER		
Mr R J Lynch (Bldg 1)		238-2456
DIRECTOR NAVAL TELCOM AUTOMATION SYS CTR		
Mr W C Bryson (Bldg 31)		238-2170

NAVAL SPACE COMMAND
(Dahlgren)

RADM D E FROST	230	663-7841
(Commander NAVSPACECOM)		
DEPUTY COMMANDER		
COL P D Williams (USMC)		663-7841
TECHNICAL DIRECTOR		
Dr W E Howard III	228	663-7841

STRATEGIC SYSTEMS PROGRAMS
(Crystal Mall Bldg 3)

RADM K C MALLEY	1142	52064
(Director)		
DEPUTY DIR		
CAPT W Taylor	1142	52158
DIR PLANS & PROG		
Mr G Keightley	1140	53013
DIR TECHNICAL DIV		
CAPT J Mitchell	1136	52964

HEADQUARTERS US MARINE CORPS

COMMANDANT OF THE MARINE CORPS

GEN A M GRAY	2000	42500
COL H C Barnum Jr	2004	42500
(Military Secretary)		
SGTMAJ D W Sommers	2106	42475
(SGTMAJ of the Marine Corps)		

ASSISTANT COMMANDANT OF THE MARINE CORPS

GEN J J WENT	2104	41201
LTCOL L M Palm	2104	41201
(Military Assistant)		

CHIEF OF STAFF

VACANT	2010	42541
COL T V Draude	2010	42541
(Secretary of the General Staff)		

SPECIAL PROJECTS DIRECTORATE

COL G S CONVERSE	2108	41515
(Dir)		

(Arlington Annex)

SEPARATE OFFICES

LEGISLATIVE ASSISTANT		
BGEN H W JENKINS JR	1134	41686
COUNSEL FOR THE COMMANDANT		
MR P M MURPHY	2119	42150
THE MEDICAL OFFICER		
RADM R W HIGGINS	2229	44477
THE DENTAL OFFICER		
CAPT R E WILLIAMS	2227	44477
THE CHAPLAIN		
CAPT W A HISKETT (CHC) USN	3026	44491
MARINE CORPS UNIFORM BOARD		
CAPT J A SCARBOROUGH	201 HH	42086

DEPARTMENTS AND DIVISIONS

PLANS, POLICIES & OPERATIONS DEPT

LTGEN C E MUNDY	2018	42503
(DC/S for Plans Pol & Ops)		
BGEN D A Wills	2020	42833
(Dir Plans Div)		
BGEN J I Hopkins	2210	43554
(Dir Ops Div)		

AVIATION DEPARTMENT

LTGEN C H PITMAN	2335	41010
(DC/S for Aviation)		
BGEN J W Pearson	2331	41010
(Dir PPR)		

MANPOWER DEPARTMENT

LTGEN J I HUDSON	4020	48003
(DC/S for Manpower)		
BGEN W M Keys	4000	42533
(Dir Pers Mgmt Div)		
BGEN G Cooper	4104	42508
(Dir Pers Procurement Div)		
BGEN J M Myatt	4026	42518
(Dir Manpower Plans & Pol Div)		
Mr J R Joy	Quantico	640-3808
(Dir Morale Wel & Rec Supt Act)		
COL P F Angle	4304	42890
(Dir Hum Res Div)		

INSTALLATION & LOGISTICS DEPARTMENT

LTGEN W G CARSON JR	562 CWB	42755
(DC/S for Install & Log)		
MGEN E P Looney Jr	574 CWB	56094
(Dir LP Div)		
BGEN M P Downs	744 CWB	42500
(Dir Facilities & Serv Div)		
Mr P E Zanfagna Jr	660 CWB	42403
(Dir Contracts Div)		

REQUIREMENTS & PROGRAMS DIV

MGEN R J WINGLASS	2114	43435
(DC/S for Rqmts and Programs)		

RESERVE DIVISION

LTGEN J.I. HUDSON	1114	41161
(DC/S Reserve Affairs)		

INSPECTION DIVISION

BGEN J P BRICKLEY	2233	41533
(Inspector General)		

FISCAL DIVISION

MR E T COMSTOCK	3000	42590
(Dir)		

COMMAND, CONTROL, COMMUNICATIONS & COMPUTER (C⁴) SYSTEMS DIV

BGEN R L PHILLIPS	3020	48010
(Dir)		

DIVISION OF PUBLIC AFFAIRS

BGEN H W JENKINS	1134	42958
(Dir)		

JUDGE ADVOCATE DIVISION

BGEN M E RICH	1000	42737
(Dir)		

INTELLIGENCE DIVISION

BGEN J D BEANS	3233	42443
(Dir)		

HEADQUARTERS SUPPORT DIVISION

MR L J KELLY	1026	41837
(Dir)		

HISTORY AND MUSEUMS DIVISION

BGEN E H SIMMONS (RET)	Bldg 58 WNY	433-2273

SEAPOWER: Fiction, Fact, and Opinion

SEAPOWER: Fiction, Fact, and Opinion 1988: The Reading Lamp is Lighted

By Brooke Nihart

Again, as in recent years, purely naval books are few and far between as are new books on aviation. The backlist of publishers, including the Naval Institute Press, Nautical and Aviation, Jane's, and Brassey's, as well as others, boast large stocks of past titles still "in print." If one missed any of these in the past they still are available.

We have noted Tom Clancy's novels in past issues. The term "technothriller" was invented to categorize the genre. Now comes Stephen "Flight of the Intruder" Coonts with a new story, *Final Flight*, that some are saying is better than Clancy's *Patriot Games*. The two-striper hero of *Flight of the Intruder*, Jake Grafton, has added a stripe and is air group commander of a supercarrier in the Med where he is opposing terrorists trying to steal nuclear weapons from his special stores magazine. Wow!

More effective and believable yarns are the autobiographical *Flights of Passage* and *Going Downtown* about flying in World War II and Vietnam, respectively. The first, subtitled *Reflections of a World War II Aviator* is the story of an 18-year-old NavCad of 1943 turning into a 21-year-old Marine divebomber veteran three years later. The second, subtitled *The War Against Hanoi and Washington*, is an embittered account by Jack Broughton, Air Force F-105 pilot who gave us *Thud Ridge* some years ago. Broughton critiques the questionable targeting dictated from the secretary of defense's office and the White House. Tom "Right Stuff" Wolfe provides the foreword.

Closer to home is *Forged in Steel: U.S. Marine Corps Aviation*, a great photo-essay in observance of the 75th anniversary of Marine air by ace photographer C.J. Heatley. Marine pilot and astronaut Sen. John Glenn does the foreword.

A British statesman of wisdom once said, "All history is biography." Dr. Ron Spector, Director of Navy History, provides a new biography of Adm. George Dewey in *Admiral of the New Empire*. The victor of Manila Bay had a pervasive influence on the Navy for good and ill into World War I. In the same period, Secretary of the Navy and President Theodore Roosevelt, and naval strategist Adm. Alfred Thayer Mahan were exercising their enduring influence on the Navy which was to last through World War II. Richard Turk tells this story in *The Ambiguous Relationship*.

Stephen Sears' first-class biography of Civil War Gen. George McClellan, *The Young Napoleon*, demonstrates that, despite the intellect and training and organizational abilities of a leader, if he doesn't have a feel for battle and a killer instinct he will fail as a battle leader.

Two other history-as-biography works must be noted for their illumination of the problems and practices of high command. They mostly concern Army leadership, but there was plenty of blue sky and blue water between island objectives in MacArthur's Southwest Pacific theater. *Forged by Fire: Eichelberger and the Pacific War* by J.F. Shortal treats the relations between MacArthur and his little known generals (little known because he saw to it that he got the publicity). William Leary's *We Shall Return! MacArthur's Commanders and the Defeat of Japan* covers some of the same ground, but even more from the joint and combined viewpoint with not only U.S. Army leaders but Navy, Army Air Forces, and Australians getting equal billing.

Many of the Navy books this year come under the heading of history as well, but there are some useful works that focus on current and recent past problems of the Navy. Leading these is *United States Naval Power in a Changing World* by the former Director of Navy History, Vice Adm. Edwin Hooper. Predictably, he applies the historical method and is concerned at our defense policies that ignore lessons of the past.

Interestingly, two new works review the Cuban missile crisis after 26 years to draw political and strategic conclusions. In *Reflections on the Cuban Missile Crisis*, Raymond Garthoff, a Kennedy administration advisor at the time, uses his recently declassified memoranda and other material to trace the history and consequences of our not always incisive actions. *The Cuban Missile Crisis of 1962: Needless or Necessary*, by William Medland, applies historical method to calculate the long-term effect of the incident.

A new edition of *In Peace and War: Interpretations of American Naval History, 1775-1984* provides a textbook survey of where we've been and where we are for midshipmen specifically and questing sailormen in general. George Modelski's and William Thompson's *Seapower in Global Politics: 1494-1993* covers the field from the standpoint of the capital ships. Despite its ever changing form—74 to ironclad to dreadnought to aircraft carrier—the capital ship remains the key to seapower. Special counsel to four secretaries of the Navy during the 1960s, Andy Kerr, in his *A Journey Amongst the Good and the Great* gives the inside scoop of those years and a view of top level naval leadership and bureaucracy.

Popular historian Eric Hammel has put together an exciting and significant account of the crucial carrier battles of August and October 1942, Eastern Solomons and Santa Cruz, which saved the Marines' bacon on Guadalcanal. Look for his *Guadalcanal: The Carrier Battles*. Another distinguished historian, Clayton James, looks at the careers of 18 top American military leaders, seven of them naval, of World War II ... history as biography again.

One of the year's most controversial books, British professor Paul Kennedy's *The Rise and Fall of the Great Powers*, grew out of his earlier *British Naval Mastery*, so is properly included here. The thesis is that great powers overextend themselves and go into decline. In modern times the rise usually has been through the medium of seaborne power projection. Kennedy's application of the theory to the United States has been academically refuted as often as affirmed.

Current or at least recent history is not ignored, and we have the prolific Edgar O'Ballance recounting *The Gulf War* which has caused our "presence" in the Persian Gulf. *Revolution and Rescue in Grenada*, by Reynold Burrowes, is a useful account of the diplomacy and military operations there. The Falklands (or Malvinas if you will) War was entirely naval—amphibious task force, fleet and objective air defense, and landing force seizing the objective. Now Maj. Gen. Nick Vaux, RM, was there commanding 42 Commandos, and gives us his story in *Take That Hill! Royal Marines in the Falklands War*. Former RN officer David Brown has written *The Royal Navy and the Falklands War*, which tells all from assembly of warships and merchantmen, through mountout, passage, advance force ops, air defense, and landings with the attendant problems and successes.

Repeated themes in book publishing have received massive attention from writers, publishers, and readers in the several years that we have been doing this feature for *The Almanac of Seapower*. Books on intelligence and counter-intelligence, strategy and national defense, nuclear weapons, arms control, the strategic defense initiative, and the Russian threat have poured from pens and presses in recent years. As long as the very active threat continues, *glasnost* or not, books on it and the subjects it drives will continue unabated.

So, let's look at the fare on intelligence. Three subsets have continued over recent years. They are the Walker family spy ring, the Cambridge apostle penetration of British and allied intelligence since the late 1920s, and the alleged failures and mishaps of our own intelligence service. Pete Earley gives us *Family of Spies*, in which he interviews the principal Walker spy-ring leader. John Costello's *Mask of Treachery: Spies, Lies, Buggery & Betrayal* is not only the latest word on the apostles Blunt, Burgess, McLean, Philby, et al., but easily wins the prize for the most catchy rhyming and alliterative subtitle. Anthony Cave Brown in his *Spymaster to Winston Churchill* reveals the ups and downs of MI6, Britain's foreign intelligence service. *A Spy's Revenge*, by Richard Hall, tells the inside story of MI5, British counter-intelligence, and the mole searching book, *Spycatcher*, by its agent Peter Wright. *Secrets of the Service*, by Anthony Glees, assesses the problem of Russian penetration of Western intelligence.

CIA gets its annual lumps as well. Gregory Treverton's *Covert Action: The Limits of Intervention in the Postwar World* shows how our initial successes led to later disasters with Vietnam being the biggest. *The Perfect Failure: Kennedy, Eisenhower, and the CIA at the Bay of Pigs* focuses on that disaster while David Wise's *The Spy Who Got Away* examines the FBI's failure to apprehend CIA defector Howard. *Secret Warriors: Inside the Covert Military Operations of the Reagan Era*, by Steven Emerson, recounts our failures from Desert One to the present.

On the high technology front two good accounts of atom bomb development by two top leaders have surfaced: William Lawren's *The General and the Bomb* and Maj. Gen. K.D. Nicols' *The Road to Trinity* give us an authentic military version of the Manhattan Project. The reader is referred to the "Nuclear, Arms Control, and Strategic Defense Initiative" section of the bibliography for titles on these subjects as well as technology competition, a history of military technology, biological and chemical warfare, and weather analysis.

And then there is that perennial and crucial subject, terrorism. Works addressing the terrorist threat are tending to greater sophistication. The psychology of terrorists is receiving increased attention. Maxwell Taylor's *The Terrorist* is one of these, as is Christopher Dobson's and Roland Payne's *Never-Ending War* and Stephen Segaller's *Invisible Armies*. Geoffrey Levitt's *Democracies Against Terror*, Louis Beres' *Terrorism & Global Security*, and Walter Laquer's *The Age of Terrorism* are all useful advanced texts. *Armies in Low-Intensity Conflict* shows what Western armies are doing to counter the unconventional warfare threat.

And we can ask, rhetorically, what is driving the writing and publishing effort of much of the above? The answer, of course, is "the threat." The Russian bear still haunts the world despite the charming Gorbachev, his *glasnost*, and stylish wife, and despite our President dropping "evil empire" from his vocabulary. Academics, diplomats, journalists, and military men continue to write about it with the majority underscoring the seriousness of the threat, or at least urging caution in our dealings and negotiations with the Russians. As we continue to present a soft belly to the Russian bayonet one can but wonder whether anyone in the corridors of power is reading or heeding the available testimony.

The Pentagon's annual *Soviet Military Power* assesses the threat in an authoritative manner and is a readily available point of departure for any consideration of the problem. *Why the Soviet Union Violates Arms Control Treaties* dares to reveal that cheating and deception are an integral ingredient of the Russian character and thus of their negotiating. Hardliner, ambassador, and retired Army Col. William Kintner, in his *Soviet Global Strategy*, surveys the Russian threat and their options through the year 2000. Bittman's *The New Image Makers* shows how the Russians are employing modern PR and advertising techniques to their propaganda and disinformation campaigns. In *The Strategy of Russian Imperialism*, Martin Sicker demonstrates how the Soviet empire is really just a modern version of the old Romanov Russian empire gussied up with Marxist trappings. Agursky's *The Third Rome* asserts a similar theme, citing the double danger of Soviet Leninism and Russian nationalism. And so it goes, book after book. Is anyone out there reading, believing!

So much for my plea for sanity. We must finally mention the annual reference books. For domestic use, Polmar's *The Ships and Aircraft of the U.S. Fleet* in its triennial edition is basic, as is *Jane's Fighting Ships* for the world. For a less pricey tome I suggest *Weyer's Warships of the World* in its 59th edition. *Brassey's Multilingual Military Dictionary* in six languages would appear to be a useful innovation.

THE THREAT

Soviet Military Power: An Assessment of the Threat 1988. By The Department of Defense, GPO, $10.00. Published annually since 1981 by the Pentagon, this issue under a new SecDef inexplicably omits any discussion of the *Spetsnaz* threat.
Why the Soviet Union Violates Arms Control Treaties. By Falcon Associates, Pergamon-Brassey's. An unclassified contract study for the U.S. government shows that cheating and deception were and are integral parts of Russian arms-control negotiation and practice. Obviously not heeded by the administration decisionmakers who engineered the December 1987 summit.
The Sixth Continent: Russia and the Making of Mikhail Gorbachev. By Mark Frankland, Harper & Row, $22.95. A social, cultural, and political overview of the years 1982-1986 with lots of gossip on Kremlin goings on and the Soviet condition by a well-informed British correspondent.
Perestroika and Soviet National Security. By Michael McGwire, Brookings, $8.95 (paperback). Asserts that the Soviet Union is restructuring a shift from WWII strategy to a more realistic limited conflict on its periphery.
The Charm School. By Nelson Demille, Warner Books. A fact-based novel of the KGB's TS training facility. An authentic portrait of Soviet society.
The Soviet Way of Warfare. By William P. Baxter, Presidio Press, $25.00. What the Red Army thinks about itself and how it intends to perform on the battlefield. From Soviet sources.
The Soviet Biochemical Threat to NATO. By John Hemsley, St. Martin's, $45.00. A history of the weapon and how the Soviets plan to use it.
The Soviet Defense Enigma. By Carl G. Jacobsen, Oxford/SIPRI, $47.00. Assesses the Soviet level and sustainability of defense spending.
Soviet Global Strategy. By William R. Kintner, HERO, $24.95. The world threat to democracy and freedom and Soviet options to the year 2000.
The KGB: Police & Politics in the Soviet Union. By Amy W. Knight, Allen & Unwin, $29.95. How the KGB works as a political institution within the Soviet empire.
Uncovering Soviet Disasters: Exploring the Limits of Glasnost. By James E. Oberg, Random House, $19.95. Long before Chernobyl, lack of quality control, common sense, and truthfulness in disclosure caused and concealed Soviet disasters.
The Third Rome: National Bolshevism in the USSR. By Mikhail Agursky, Westview, $48.50. The double danger of Soviet-Leninism and Russian nationalism.
Soviet Succession Struggles: Kremlinology & the Russian Question From Lenin to Gorbachev. By Anthony D'Agostino, Allen & Unwin, $45.00. Russian leadership struggles and how they affect policy.
Reforming the Soviet Economy: Equality Versus Efficiency. By Ed A. Hewett, Brookings, $36.95, $16.95 (paperback). Analyzes Soviet economic performance and reforms of the past quarter century and chances of Gorbachev's success.

BROOKE NIHART, the compiler, describes himself as a Marine who reads and writes (but who uses a hand calculator for arithmetic) and in his dotage runs the Marine Corps museums.

On the Wrong Side: My Life in the KGB. By Stanislav Levchenko, International Defense Publishers/Kampmann, $18.95. The application of M.I.C.E.—money, ideology, compromise, and ego—in the intelligence penetration of Japan.

Soviet Foreign Policy. Edited by Robbin F. Laird, The Academy of Political Science, $12.95. A compendium of scholarly essays on Gorbachev's regime: historical context, domestic changes, policy constraints, policies towards countries and regions, arms control, and more.

The New Image Makers: Soviet Propaganda and Disinformation Today. Edited by Ladislav Bittman, Pergamon-Brassey's, $22.50. Madison Avenue meets Dzezhinsky Square.

The Strategy of Russian Imperialism: Expansion in Eurasia From Mikhail Romanov to Mikhail Gorbachev. By Martin Sicker, Praeger, $37.95. Soviet policies stem from and replicate those of their Russian predecessors.

Soviet Submarine Operations in Swedish Waters: 1980-1986. By Milton Leitenberg, Praeger, $32.95, $9.95 (paperback). A history of the undersea intrusions and the Swedes' faltering response.

Checkisty: A History of the KGB. By John J. Dziak, foreword by Robert Conquest, Lexington Books, $17.95. Dziak, a Georgetown University professor and 25-year veteran of the Defense Intelligence Agency, provides a scholarly and highly readable history of the KGB and its predecessors beginning with the CHECKA. So long as the Soviet Union remains a police state *glasnost* and *perestroika* are impossible. The KGB still reigns and with more power than ever.

Mesmerized by the Bear. Edited by Raymond Sleeper, Dodd, Mead, & Company, $22.95. A panel of distinguished specialists discourse on the Soviet strategy of deception and disinformation toward the West. As one points out, "Lies and deceptions are political weapons of the Soviets ... but it is necessary to realize that they are not just tactics that could be easily changed ... they are an organic consequence of 'real socialism's' very nature."

REFERENCE

The Ships and Aircraft of the U.S. fleet, Fourteenth Edition. Edited by Norman Polmar, Naval Institute Press, $29.95. The guide includes ships, craft, submarines, and aircraft, plus personnel, organization, weapons, and electronics.

RUSI/Brassey's Defense Yearbook 1988, 98th Edition. $61.00, $33.00 (paperback). A classic annual presenting a world strategic view from a British standpoint from the Royal United Service Institute.

Brassey's Multilingual Military Dictionary. $68.00. More than 7,000 key military words and phrases in English-French-Spanish-German-Russian-Arabic based on American English with a British English index.

Strategic Survey 1987-1988. By the International Institute of Strategic Studies, $18.00. A companion piece to *The Military Balance* that examines the significant events of the year, their political contexts, and the trends they signify for international security.

Jane's Warsaw Pact Warships Handbook. By Capt. John Moore, RN, Jane's Information Group, $11.95.

The ACCESS Resource Guide: An International Directory of Information on War, Peace, and Security. Edited by William H. Kincade and Pricilla B. Hayner, Ballinger, $34.95, $14.95 (paperback). The first comprehensive worldwide guide to information sources with details on the type, purpose, and staff size of each organization; its area of specialization; and a list of information it can provide.

Jane's Fighting Ships 1988-1989. Edited by Capt. Richard Sharpe, RN, Jane's Information Group, $150.00. The standard reference for more than 100 years.

Jane's Weapons Systems 1987-1988. By Jane's Information Group, $159.50. All ship and airborne weapons systems covered.

Jane's High Speed Marine Craft and Air Cushion Vehicles 1988. By Jane's Information Group, $165.00. All craft capable of over 20 knots.

Conventional and Nuclear Submarines of the World. By A. Wetterhahn, Jane's Information Systems, $230.00. All types and classes worldwide.

International Defense Directory 1988. By Jane's Information Group, $325.00. Comprehensive guide to government, military, and industrial defense organizations, their personnel, organization, products, and services.

Weyer's Warships of the World 1988/89, 59th edition. Edited by G. Albrecht, foreword by Norman Polmar, Nautical and Aviation Publishing Co., $78.95. In English and German, excellent drawings, and portable size.

The American Defense Annual 1987-1988. By Joseph Kruzel, Lexington, $16.95. Events, policy, and issues of U.S. defense and strategic thinking.

The Language of Nuclear War: An Intelligent Citizen's Dictionary. By Eric Semler, et al, Harper & Row, $9.95 (paperback). A dictionary of more than 1,200 nuclear war terms made understandable to the public.

The Dictionary of SDI. By Harry Waldman, University of Kentucky Press, $35.00, $19.95 (paperback). Complete working vocabulary of Star Wars from ABMs to X-ray lasers with more than 800 entries.

HISTORY

The Ravens: The Men Who Flew in America's Secret War in Laos. By Christopher Robbins, Crown Publishers, $19.95. Air Force pilots in mufti and prop planes flying low in an unknown war.

Guadalcanal: The Carrier Battles. By Eric Hammel, Crown Publishers, $24.95. The battles of August and October 1942, Eastern Solomons and Santa Cruz, respectively, which prevented the main Japanese attack and amphibious forces from reinforcing Guadalcanal, are retold.

The Death of the U-Boats. By Edwin Hoyt, McGraw-Hill, $17.95. Definitive reference to German undersea warfare of World War II and how it affected the political, strategic, and ideological outcome of the conflict.

Marines: Volume One of the Illustrated History of the Vietnam War. By Brig. Gen. Edwin H. Simmons, Bantam Books, $6.95 (paperback). The author completed two tours in Vietnam and has written extensively on Marine Corps participation in that war. This handy book summarizes the 10 years of action from the 1965 landing at Da Nang to the 1975 evacuation of Saigon.

The Ships of John Paul Jones. By William Gilkerson, Naval Institute Press, $32.95 Beautifully illustrated by the author, the work presents the naval hero's craft from the Scottish rowboat of his boyhood, to the brig on which he first went to sea at age 13, to the Russian warships of Catherine the Great which he commanded at the end of his career.

John Paul Jones and the Bonhomme Richard. By Jean Boudroit, translated from the French by David Roberts, Naval Institute Press, $39.95. The author, the world expert on French sailing ships, reconstructs the design of the Bonhomme Richard from contemporary evidence and takes it into battle. Fully illustrated by William Gilkerson.

Great Commanders and Their Battles. By Anthony Livesey, foreword by Gen. Sir John Hackett, introduction by Maj. Gen. Sir Jeremy Moore, RM, Macmillan Publishing Co., $39.95. The tactics and their practitioners that won 20 famous victories spanning 2,000 years.

The Generals: Ulysses S. Grant and Robert E. Lee. By Nancy Scott Anderson and Dwight Anderson, Knopf, $24.95. Two antithetical characters of the American Civil War officer corps: patrician Lee's chivalry and loyalty versus pragmatic Grant's technical competence and managerial expertise.

A Time for Giants: Politics of the American High Command in World War II. By D. Clayton James with Anne Sharp Wells, Franklin Watts, $19.95. The careers of 18 top American military leaders including Ernest King, William Halsey, Chester Nimitz, William Leahy, Raymond Spruance, Holland Smith, and A. Archer Vandegrift.

The Rise and Fall of the Great Powers: Economic Change and Military Conflict From 1500 to 2000. By Paul Kennedy, Random House, $24.95. Failures in economic policies which led to the decline of nations, states, and empires may be a process that is affecting America in the last years of the 20th century. Both praised and attacked.

Behind the Scenes: In Which the Author Talks About Ronald and Nancy Reagan ... and Himself. By Michael K. Deaver with Mickey Herskowitz, William Morrow & Co., $17.95. Among other bits of gossip in this current history are accounts of how Nancy influenced Ronald to take a soft line with the Soviet Union and slow down SDI development.

The Path to Vietnam: Origins of the Ameri-

ca Commitment to Southeast Asia. By Andrew J. Rotter, Cornell University, $29.95. An exhaustive research effort.

Enter the Dragon: China's Undeclared War Against the U.S. in Korea, 1950-51. By Russell Spurr, Newmarket Press, $22.95. The author had the cooperation of Chinese authorities in access to sources.

The Proud Decades: American in War and Peace, 1941-1960. By John Patrick Diggins, W.W. Norton, $19.95. "The 40s and 50s tell Americans more about themselves, and the 60s were an aberration," says the author.

The Key to Failure: Laos and the Vietnam War. By Norman B. Hannah, Madison Books, $19.95. The "key" was not cutting the Ho Chi Minh trail in Laos from the beginning; this failure resulted from incremental decision making, which dealt with symptoms only.

The Art of War in the Western World. By Archer Jones, University of Illinois Press, $34.95. A noted military historian traces the 2,500-year story of the operational aspects of land warfare.

The Forgotten War: America in Korea 1950-1953. By Clay Blair, New York Times Books, $29.95. Good descriptions of battle plans and conflicts between commanders.

The Royal Navy and the Falklands War. By David Brown, Westview, $32.50. Problems and successes of a naval operation.

The Deadly Embrace: Hitler, Stalin, and the Nazi-Soviet Pace, 1939-1941. By Anthony Read and David Fisher, Norton, $25.00. How Stalin's expediency facilitated World War II.

Revolution and Rescue in Grenada: An Account of the U.S.-Caribbean Invasion. By Reynold A. Burrowes, Greenwood Press, $35.00. A chapter in modern diplomacy and warfare that remains an enigma to many observers.

We Shall Return! MacArthur's Commanders and the Defeat of Japan. Edited by William M. Leary, University Press of Kentucky, $25.00. The forgotten commanders of World War II—Krueger, Eichelberger, Blamey, Kenney, Whitehead, Kinkaid, and Barbey—Army, Air Force, Navy, and an Aussie.

The Gulf War. By Edgar O'Ballance, Brassey's, $28.00. An analysis of the seven-year ground war between Iran and Iraq.

Take That Hill! Royal Marines in the Falklands War. By Maj. Gen. N.F. Vaux, RM, Pergamon-Brassey's, $21.95. A first-hand account by the CO of 42 Commando.

NUCLEAR, ARMS CONTROL, AND STRATEGIC DEFENSE INITIATIVE

While Others Build: A Commonsense Approach to the Strategic Defense Inititiative. By Angelo Codevilla, The Free Press, $22.50. How the Reagan administration coopted a growing consensus among defense analysts that America needed a ballistic missile defense, then capitulated to the opponents of such a defense within its own ranks.

The Business of Science: Winning and Losing in the High-Tech Age. By Simon Ramo, Hill & Wang, $19.95. The "R" in TRW addresses the risk of nuclear war and America's flagging ability to compete with Japan and others.

The Dictionary of SDI. By Harry Waldman, Scholarly Resources Inc., $35.00, $19.95 (paperback). Enables the non-specialist to follow the SDI controversy without being put off by high-tech terms.

The Technology War: A Case for Competitiveness. By David H. Brandin and Michael A. Harrison, Wiley Interscience, $24.95. Information may be to the age of technology as oil was to the industrial era. The United States and Japan are the two big players with Third-World Asian countries closing fast, while Europe lags and the Soviet Union is far behind.

Gene Wars: Military Control Over the New Genetic Technologies. By Charles Piller and Keith R. Yamamoto, Morrow, $22.95. Advanced biological warfare? Despite treaties and controls, dangers still exist, such as creating disease organisms for which humans and animals have no defense.

The Road to Trinity: A Personal Account of How America's Nuclear Policies Were Made. By Maj. Gen. K.D. Nichols, William Morrow & Co., $19.95. Nichols, a member of the Manhattan Engineer District that developed the atom bomb, tells how policy decisions were made and the resulting political and security problems.

Making Weapons, Talking Peace: A Physicist's Odyssey From Hiroshima to Geneva. By Herbert F. York, Basic Books, $22.95. One of the designers of the atom bomb, former head of the Lawrence Radiation Laboratory, and test-ban treaty negotiator tells the story of his moral evolution. He dislikes nuclear weapons, respects their authority, acknowledges their danger, and believes the world must disarm—but very slowly.

Technology and War: From 2000 B.C. to the Present. By Martin van Creveld, The Free Press, $22.95. Impact of technology on military organization, weaponry, logistics, intelligence, and command.

Nuclear Fear: A History of Images. By Spencer R. Weart, Harvard University Press, $29.50. How Americans have responded to the new world of nuclear energy and its militarization, by a physicist.

The Other Side of Arms Control: Soviet Objectives in the Gorbachev Era. By Alan B. Sherr, Unwin Hyman, $49.95, $17.95 (paperback). Lightening Russia's defense burden through reduction of nuclear arms.

Calculated Risks: A Century of Arms Control, Why It Has Failed, and How It Can Be Made to Work. By Bruce D. Berkowitz, Simon & Schuster, $18.95. The kinds of agreements that have characterized most of the history of arms control are perverse and unconstructive. Some of the most successful moves toward arms control must be unilateral, such as improving the credibility of U.S. retaliation.

America's Weather Warriors, 1814-1985. By Charles C. Bates and John F. Fuller, Texas A&M Press, $29.95. Our armed forces have led in the development of weather analysis and forecasting but commanders tend to ignore meteorological advice while budgeteers cut funds.

Nuclear Strategizing: Deterrence and Reality. By Stephen J. Cimbala, Praeger, $40.00. Deterrence is shortsighted, as it is dependent on economic analogies and technical fixation which leaves unanswered questions of the relationship between strategy, politics, and long-term defense goals.

New Weapon Technologies & The ABM Treaty. By Herbert Lin, Pergamon-Brassey's, $12.95 (paperback). Continuation of the ABM treaty will remain a precondition to reductions in strategic offensive systems according to this HASC staffer.

SDI: Has America Told Her Story to the World?. By Dean Godson, Pergamon-Brassey's, $9.95 (paperback). We have failed to affect European attitudes towards star wars.

A Fighting Chance: The Moral Use of Nuclear Weapons. By Joseph P. Martino, Ignatius Press, $15.95 (paperback). The just war principle reapplied to nuclear war.

Iron Destinies, Lost Opportunities: The Arms Race Between the U.S.A. and the U.S.S.R., 1945-1987. By Charles R. Morris, Harper & Row, $22.95. A review of the overkill proposition.

ATBMs and Western Security: Missile Defenses for Europe. Edited by Donald L. Hafner and John Roper, Ballinger, $34.95. Defense against tactical missiles.

NATIONAL DEFENSE

1999: Victory Without War. By Richard Nixon, Simon & Schuster, $19.95. A provocative foreign affairs handbook for future presidents on how the United States should position itself for the next millennium—the United States must play a central international role. Designed to dispel Washington's euphoria over the Gorbachev embrace.

Guts and Glory: The Rise and Fall of Oliver North. By Ben Bradlee Jr., Donald I. Fine, $21.95. An error-ridden but moderately fair piece of "New Journalism" which, despite drawbacks, may nevertheless become the standard reference on the subject.

The Geopolitics of Super Power. By Colin S. Gray, University Press of Kentucky, $26.00. A basic explanation of the relation of international political power to geographic setting. It is flawed through lack of consideration of ideology and national culture and psychology.

Military Effectiveness (in three volumes). Edited by Allan R. Millett and Williamson Murray, Allen & Unwin, $150.00. Covers the major powers from 1914 to 1945 in examining varying success in converting resources into fighting power and limiting enemy damage at four levels—political, strategic, operational, and tactical.

Legitimacy and Force: Vol. I: Political and Moral Dimensions, Vol. II: National and International Dimensions. By Jeanne J. Kirkpatrick, Transaction Books, $60.00. The set, $30.00 (paperback). The collected speeches and papers of Kirkpatrick lean towards the pursuit of international human rights over the pursuit of our national interests. Is this her resume aimed at a job in 1989?

The United States and the World. By The Committee for a Free World, $4.95. The authors are among the best and brightest of the anti-communist intellectuals who examine the Middle East, Latin America, and the Pacific.

America Invulnerable: The Quest for Absolute Security From 1812 to Star Wars. By James Chace and Caleb Carr, Summit Books, $19.95. The authors contend that America's foreign and defense policies are an inherited national characteristic but their supporting history often proves them in error.

Secret Warriors: Inside the Covert Military Operations of the Reagan Era. By Steven Emerson, Putnam. Claimed to be a complete and thorough account of the Pentagon's special operations of the 1980s.

National Security Planning: Roosevelt through Reagan. By Michael M. Boll, University Press of Kentucky, $26.00. An illuminating historical account of the crucial assumptions that have motivated the White House since World War II in its effort to maintain a stable world in which American ideals and values can be preserved.

Defending Peace and Freedom: Towards Strategic Stability in the Year 2000. Edited by Brent Scowcroft et al., Atlantic Council, $26.50, $12.95 (paperback). President Bush's National Security Council head and other friends present a policy paper for the new administration.

National Security Strategy of the United States. By Ronald Reagan, Pergamon-Brassey's, $9.95 (paperback). The White House's articulation of America's strategic objectives.

Beyond Military Reform: American Defense Dilemmas. By Jeffrey Record, foreword by Sen. Sam Nunn, Pergamon-Brassey's, $32.00. A Hudson Institute study on the why of alleged military failures despite billions spent.

Defending America's Security. By Frederick H. Hartmann and Robert L. Wendzel, Pergamon-Brassey's, $38.00, $16.95 (paperback). Two war-college professors have written a college textbook that provides the analytical tools to understand U.S. defense policies in the context of national security and international affairs.

Reflections on the Cuban Missile Crisis. By Raymond L. Garthoff, Brookings, $18.95, $8.95 (paperback). A Kennedy administration advisor draws on recently declassified memoranda to review and analyze the origin, action, and consequences of the 1962 confrontation.

BIOGRAPHY

Admiral of the New Empire: The Life and Career of George Dewey. By Ronald Spector, University of South Carolina Press, $24.95, $12.95 (paperback). The Director of Navy History focuses on the public life of the victor of Manila Bay and on his influence on the successes and failures of the Navy in the early 20th century.

Horatio Nelson. By Tom Pocock, Knopf, $22.95. A so-so book about the British naval hero but with new material in the form of previously unpublished letters.

The General and the Bomb: A Biography of General Leslie R. Groves, Director of the Manhattan Project. By William Lawren, Dodd, Mead, $21.95. An SOB of a military engineer drives academic prima donnas until the A-Bomb is a reality.

The Generals: Ulysses S. Grant and Robert E. Lee. By Nancy Scott Anderson and Dwight Anderson, Knopf, $24.95. A contrast of careers and personalities.

George B. McClellan: The Young Napolean. By Stephen W. Sears, Ticknor & Fields, $24.95. The great organizer and theorist who was a battlefield failure, by the author of *Landscape Turned Red*, hailed as the best account of the Battle of Antietam.

Forged by Fire: Robert L. Eichelberger and the Pacific War. By John Francis Shortal, University of South Carolina Press, $24.95. The relations between MacArthur and the little known generals who fought the Southwest Pacific War.

INTELLIGENCE

Family of Spies: Inside the John Walker Spy Ring. By Pete Earley, Bantam. Based on interviews with this most disgusting domestic traitor yet.

"C" The Secret Life of Sir Stewart Graham Menzies, Spymaster to Winston Churchill. By Anthony Cave Brown, Macmillan, $25.00. The rise and fall of Britain's Secret Intelligence Service (SIS), or MI6, under Menzies. "C," considered the model for Ian Fleming's "M" and John le Carre's George Smiley, saw British intelligence's finest hour in the decoding of German ENIGMA and presided over its complete penetration by Russian agents Philby, Burgess, McLean, Blunt, et al.

Covert Action: The Limits of Intervention in the Postwar World. By Gregory F. Treverton, Basic Books, $19.95. The successes in Iran (1953) and Guatemala (1954) spurred us to believe that they could be repeated elsewhere, which in turn led to repeated disasters. The author opines that covert operations may be necessary but they won't remain secret and have unintended results and long-term costs. Now we need such an account of the destabilization efforts against the Philippine, South Korean, and Panamanian governments.

The Perfect Failure: Kennedy, Eisenhower, and the CIA at the Bay of Pigs. By Trumbull Higgins, W.W. Norton & Co., $17.95. A reluctant President Kennedy inherited from the previous administration a dubious CIA plan for toppling Cuba's Castro and then took JCS mere acquiescence as approval when, in reality, the military deemed it insufficient. Well researched and authoritative.

Red Horizons: Chronicles of a Communist Spy Chief. By Lt. Gen. Ion Mihai Pacepa, Regnery Gateway/Kampmann, $19.95. The author, chief of Communist Rumania's foreign intelligence service defected to the United States. He repeats well worn tales of doubtful intelligence coups and describes the decadent activity of the Rumanian Communist nomenaclatura.

The Spy Who Got Away: The Inside Story of Edward Lee Howard, the CIA Agent Who Betrayed His Country's Secrets and Escaped to Moscow. By David Wise, Random House, $18.95. A litany of bumbling counter-espionage by the CIA and FBI.

Secret Warriors: Inside the Covert Military Operations of the Reagan Era. By Steven Emerson, G.P. Putnam's Sons, $17.95. A tale of failures from Desert One to the present. We can only hope that our successes have been kept secret.

A Spy's Revenge. By Richard V. Hall, $8.95 (paperback). The inside story of MI5 Peter Wright's book *Spycatcher*.

The Secrets of the Service: A Story of Soviet Subversion of Western Intelligence. By Anthony Glees, Carroll & Graf, $22.95. MI5 official Roger Hollis was not the mole in British counterintelligence, according to Glees.

Intelligence and Intelligence Policy in a Democratic Society. Edited by Stephen J. Cimbala, Transnational Publishers, $37.50. A collection of essays on the subject intended as a textbook for the growing number of college courses on intelligence.

Camp X, OSS, "Intrepid," and the Allies' North American Training Camp for Secret Agents, 1941-1945. Dodd, Mead & Co., $18.95. The first such school in North America, established in Canada, which trained agents, including early ones of the OSS.

Spy vs. Spy: Stalking Spies in America. By Ronald Kesler, Scribner's, $19.95. The Prague interview of KGB mole in the CIA, Karl F. Koecher, revealing the damage done to our networks in Russia.

Real-World Intelligence: Organized Information for Executives. By Herbert E. Meyer, Weidenfeld & Nicollson, $14.95. Applying the methodology of collection, analysis, and dissemination to the world of business.

Thwarting Enemies At Home And Abroad: How To Be A Counter-intelligence Officer. By William R. Johnson, Stone Trail Press, $8.95 (paperback). This do-it-yourself for the non-professional, if read by all professional naval men, might just be the counter to future Walkers and Pollards.

Captains Without Eyes: Intelligence Failures in World War II. By Lyman B. Kirpatrick, Jr., Westview, $37.50. Reissue of a 1969 classic.

Comparing Foreign Intelligence: The U.S., the U.S.S.R., the UK and the Third World. Edited by Roy Godson, Pergamon-Brassey's, $17.95. A textbook for the new academic discipline of intelligence studies.

The Encyclopedia of American Intelligence & Espionage: From the Revolutionary War to the Present. By G.J.A. O'Toole, Facts on File, $35.00. More than 700 entries from Colonial times to today.

Mask of Treachery: Spies, Lies, Buggery &

INDEX

CONGRESS

Changes in Congress as result of elections 2
Changes in key committees as result of elections 2
Key Senate Committees 2
Key House Committees 2

DEFENSE

Federal Budget Trends 5
Where military dollars are spent 7
Research, development, and evaluation budget 8
Major weapons systems and combat forces 9
Defense shares of economic aggregates 10
Defense budget by appropriation and by component.. 12
Where they serve 13
Strategic forces highlights 14
Minorities in uniform 15
Military and civilian personnel strength 16

NAVY

Naval Academy 17
Where to go for information 18
Base locator 19–20
Changes in ship forces 21
Glossary 22–24
Ship descriptions 25–71
Aircraft descriptions 72–81
Weapons descriptions 82–87

MARINES

Base locator 19–20
Major command and duty locations 88
Division/wing organization 88–89
MEF organization chart 90
MEB organization chart 91
MEU organization chart 92
Maritime Prepositioning Forces Brigade organization
 chart 92
Marine Combat Development Command organization
 chart 93
Weapons descriptions 94–97
Vehicles descriptions 97
Aircraft descriptions 98–102

MARITIME

Major merchant fleets of the world 103
Navy and private shipyard employment 104

Merchant Marine Academy 104–105
Naval vessels under construction or on order 105
Merchant fleets of the world 106–107
International transportation transactions of the United
 States 108
Maritime trade associations 105, 108–109
New merchant-type vessel contracts with U.S. private
 shipyards 109
American Merchant Marine Museum
 Foundation 110–114
Merchant ships on order in the world 111
Ships laid up throughout the world for lack of
 employment 112
Four-year ship construction plan 113
Private shipyards with Navy construction programs .. 114
Port authorities 114
Private shipyards with Navy ship work during
 FY 1987 115

COAST GUARD

Objective and missions 116–117
Search and rescue activities 117
U.S. Coast Guard Academy 118
Active fleet 119
Principal offices 120
Ship descriptions 121–124
Aircraft descriptions 125–126

OCEANOGRAPHY

Facts about the oceans 127
The Navy and the oceans 127–128
Leading fishing nations 129
Mining the ocean's riches 129–131
Size and age of university oceanographic research
 fleet 131
Forecasting the weather 132

RESERVES

Reserve forces strength 133
Partners in the total force 133

Index and photos of defense/maritime leaders .. 135–172
Key personnel locator 173–177
Bibliography 178–183

Betrayal. By John Costello, Morrow, $22.95. The latest, and perhaps the last, word on Russian penetration of the West from the 1920s through the Cambridge apostles. Blunt, Burgess, Philby, et al.

AVIATION

Final Flight. By Stephen Coonts, Doubleday, $18.9i5.

Ghosts: Vintage Aircraft of World War II. By Philip Makanna, Thomasson-Grant, Charlottesville, VA, $36.00. Three-dimensional drawings and modern color photography of 25 types of aircraft still flying today of the 750,000 produced from 1939 to 1945.

Flights of Passage: Reflections of a World War II Aviator. By Samuel Hynes, Naval Institute Press, $16.95. A Marine pilot's experiences from 18-year old aviation cadet in 1943 to a veteran at 21.

Forged in Steel: U.S. Marine Corps Aviation. Photographed by C.J. Heatley III, introduction by Sen. John Glenn, Naval Institute, Press, $37.00. A magnificent visual celebration of 75 years of Marine Corps aviation.

Attack Helicopters. By Cmdr. Howard Wheeler, USN, Nautical & Aviation Publishing, $22.95.

Superfortress: The B-29 and American Air Power. By Gen. Curtis E. LeMay and Bill Yenne, McGraw-Hill, $18.95. Conceived in 1940, it was the largest aircraft ever in full production by 1945 when it bombed Japan into submission and formed the basis of America's first strategic airforce.

The Rise of American Air Power: The Creation of Armageddon. By Michael S. Sherry, Yale University Press, $29.95. A critique of strategic bombing from the moral viewpoint.

Wild Blue Yonder: Money, Politics, and the B-1 Bomber. By Nick Kotz, Pantheon, $18.95. The three-decade search for a replacement for the B-52.

Going Downtown: The War Against Hanoi and Washington. By Jack Broughton, foreword by Tom Wolfe, Orion Books, $18.95. Contempt for those in Washington who sent our pilots on ill-conceived missions in pursuit of an unworkable strategy in the flak and missile-filled skies over Hanoi. A cautionary tale of poor leadership.

NAVY

In Peace and War: Interpretations of American Naval History, 1775-1984. A Second Edition, edited by Kenneth J. Hagan, Greenwood Press, $29.95. A USNA and NROTC textbook surveying American naval history from the Continental Congress' naval act of October 1775 to the present.

Navies, Deterrence, and American Independence: Britain and Sea Power in the 1760s and 1770s. By Nicholas Tracy, University of British Columbia Press, $18.95. The Royal Navy was an instrument of coercive diplomacy to control French action and maintain hegemony over North America. Command failures undid English plans.

Seapower in Global Politics: 1494-1993. By George Modelski and William R. Thompson, University of Washington Press, $35.00. The key to sea power is the capital ship in its ever-changing form.

Brown Water, Black Berets: Coastal and Riverine Warfare in Vietnam. By Lt. Cmdr. Thomas J. Cutler, Naval Institute Press, $21.95. How U.S. Navy elements fought in shoal coastal water and along river mudbanks.

Subchaser to Sicily. By Edward P. Stafford, Naval Institute Press, $17.95. Reserve ensigns and JGs in the Navy's smallest combat ships, and wooden at that.

Vanguard to Trident: British Naval Policy Since World War II. By Eric J. Grove, from Naval Institute Press, $34.95. Cabinet decision, operational realities, naval policies, and problems since the Falklands.

A Journey Amongst the Good & the Great. By Andy Kerr, Naval Institute Press, $14.95. Kerr was special counsel to four SecNavs during the 1960s and gives insider views on the questions of those years.

Modern Amphibious Strategy and Techniques. By James D. Ladd, Brassey's Sea Power Series, $14.95. Comprehensive British view of what has become an American near monopoly.

A Leaf Upon The Sea: A Small Ship in the Mediterranean, 1941-1943. By Gordon W. Stead, University of British Columbia Press, $22.95. RN motor launches in the Mediterranean on clandestine and overt operations.

Naval Engineering and American Sea Power. Edited by Rear Adm. R.W. King, Nautical & Aviation Publishing Co., $25.50. History of maritime technology in the United States.

United States Naval Power in a Changing World. By Vice Adm. Edwin B. Hooper, Praeger, $40.00. Expresses concern over national military policies that ignore lessons of the past.

The Ambiguous Relationship: Theodore Roosevelt and Alfred Thayer Mahan. By Richard W. Turk, Greenwood Press, $32.95. Collaboration to build American naval power in the early 1900s that was to have important consequences in World Wars I and II.

The Cuban Missile Crisis of 1962: Needless or Necessary. By William J. Medland, Praeger, $34.00. A historiographical view of what the crisis meant in the long run.

U.S. Maritime Strategy. By Norman Friedman, Jane's Information Group, $45.00. The subject covered in its national and historical context.

TERRORISM

The Baader-Meinhof Group: The Inside Story of a Phenomenon. By Stefan Aust, The Bodley Head/Salem House, $21.95. About West Germany's Red Army Faction of the 1960s and 1970s and its violence which led to today's destabilizing terrorism.

Counterattack: The West's Battle Against the Terrorists. By Christopher Dobson and Ronald Payne, Facts on File, $6.95 (paperback). Training, armament, tactics, organization of the West's counterterrorist forces by two veteran journalists.

Contemporary Terrorism. Edited by William Gutteridge, Facts on File, $21.95, $9.95 (paperback). A number of the more significant studies on terrorism by the Institute for the Study of Conflict, London.

The Terrorists: Their Weapons, Leaders and Tactics. Revised Edition, by Christopher Dobson and Ronald Payne, Facts on File, $16.95, $9.95 (paperback). Every aspect of terrorism in a completely revised and updated version.

The Terrorist. By Maxwell Taylor, Brassey's, $36.00. This Max Taylor is an Irish professor of psychology who offers a compulsive and illuminating analysis of the terrorist mind.

Nuclear Terrorism: Defining the Threat. Edited by P. Leventhal and Y. Alexander, Pergamon-Brassey's, $29.95. Examines the crisis of nuclear terrorism faced by the West and preventive measures.

Political Murder: From Tyrannicide to Terrorism. By Franklin L. Ford, Harvard University Press, $9.95 (paperback). An anthology of statements about political violence.

The Age of Terrorism. Revised and expanded edition, by Walter Laqueur, Little, Brown and Co., $19.95. Study of national and international political violence.

Never-Ending War: Terrorism in the '80s. By Ronald Payne and Christopher Dobson, Facts on File, $18.95. The mechanics and the minds behind terrorist activity from Beirut to Bolivia and U.S. anti-terror tactics.

Alchemists of Revolution: Terrorism in the Modern World. By Richard E. Rubenstein, Basic Books, $17.95. Explores the relationship between terrorism and social revolution with the conclusion that terrorist action is inherently conservative.

Invisible Armies: Terrorism into the 1990s. By Stephen Segaller, Harcourt Brace Jovanovich, $22.95. An international investigation of the psychology of terrorists.

Anarchist Portraits. By Paul Avrich, Princeton University Press, $27.50. A motley crew of weirdos assembled under the black flag of anarchism are the progenitors of today's terrorists.

Armies in Low-Intensity Conflict. Edited by Drs. David Charters and Maurice Tugwell, Brassey's, $36.00. The adaptation of Western armies to unconventional warfare since 1945.

Democracies against Terror: The Western Response to State-supported Terrorism. By Geoffrey M. Levitt, Praeger. A CSIS Washington paper which examines state support of terrorism which enhances terrorists' striking power, complicates law enforcement and intelligence, and further damages the fragile fabric of international order.

Terrorism & Global Security: The Nuclear Threat. Second edition, by Louis Beres, Westview, $26.50. Detailed treatment of all aspects of the problem.

America the Vulnerable: The Threat of Chemical & Biological Warfare. By Joseph Douglas & Neil Livingstone, Lexington Books, $19.95. The future weapon of choice for terrorists may well be a glass vial or aerosol spray of a deadly chemical or a biological agent.